# The Early Works of John Dewey

## 1882–1898

# John Dewey

## The Early Works, 1882–1898

## *3:* 1889–1892

### *Early Essays*
and
### Outlines of a Critical Theory of Ethics

*Carbondale and Edwardsville*

SOUTHERN ILLINOIS UNIVERSITY PRESS

FEFFER & SIMONS, INC.

*London and Amsterdam*

The Early Works of John Dewey, 1882–1898, *is the result of a co-operative research project at Southern Illinois University. Jo Ann Boydston is the General Editor, Fredson Bowers is Consulting Textual Editor. The Editorial Advisory Board consists of Lewis E. Hahn, Chairman; Joe R. Burnett; S. Morris Eames; William R. McKenzie; and Francis T. Villemain. Polly Dunn Williams is Staff Assistant.*

The text of this reprinting is a photo-offset reproduction of the original cloth edition which contains the full apparatus for the volume awarded the seal of the Center for Editions of American Authors of the Modern Language Association.

This paperbound edition has been made possible by a special subvention from The John Dewey Foundation.

# Contents

## Early Essays

## *Outlines of a Critical Theory of Ethics*

# Introduction

THE CONTENTS of this volume range from an intellectual portrait and memorial appreciation of Dewey's beloved teacher and colleague, George Sylvester Morris, to the technical treatments of theory of knowledge, ethical theory, and psychology. The volume also contains observations on educational theory and practice, including detailed accounts of the teaching of philosophy at the University of Michigan. Along with commentary on men and literature, Dewey wrote reviews of current books, and in some his own philosophy weaves its way into what he writes. During this period he also revised his *Psychology* (1887) in 1889 and 1891. These revisions are not included in this volume because they are incorporated in the definitive edition of *Psychology*, Volume II of *The Early Works of John Dewey, 1882–1898*.

Dewey was brought to the University of Michigan in 1884 by Professor Morris, and the two men enjoyed a rich personal and intellectual friendship. In 1888 Dewey went to the University of Minnesota, but the death of Professor Morris in March 1889 created a crisis in the Michigan department and Dewey was brought back as Professor of Philosophy and Head of the Department. The death of Morris was a deep personal loss to Dewey, and he wrote of Morris that his was a life great "in spirit, and in the quality of its achievements" (p. 3). One of Dewey's first acts as Head of the Department was to employ James H. Tufts, a recent graduate of Yale, to be his assistant. Tufts remained at Michigan for only two years, 1889–1891, leaving to continue his studies toward the doctor of philosophy degree in Germany. Dewey then employed George Herbert Mead to fill the vacancy. Tufts, Mead, and Dewey had important influence on each other. In 1894, when Dewey and Mead joined Tufts at the University of Chicago, the three composed the nucleus of what came to be called the "Chicago School" in philosophy.

During this second period at Michigan, Dewey's thinking underwent significant changes. One of his biographers writes: "During these years Dewey's thinking veered away from traditional Hegelianism and toward the instrumentalism for which he later became famous."[1] The term "instrumentalism" is ambiguous, and toward the end of Dewey's career he abandoned its use. Originally, the term meant that conceptions and theories are instruments which produce future facts. William James applies the theory to the moral aspects of certain concepts and to the sentimental value of various philosophical systems. For Dewey, instrumentalism means a logical theory of concepts, judgments, and inferences, and "it attempts to establish universally recognized distinctions and rules of logic by deriving them from the reconstructive or mediative function ascribed to reason."[2] Dewey was compelled to restate, amplify, and defend this notion of a logical theory of concepts against a host of misinterpretations which developed later, the most notorious being that ideas and concepts are instrumental to the knower or instrumental to what brings emotional and psychological satisfaction to him. If one keeps in mind the logical nature of the theory, then one can see that Dewey's writings contained in this volume on theory of knowledge or logical theory (as he conceived the broad scope of logical theory) reveal definite trends in the direction of an instrumentalist or functional theory of concepts in the context of reflective thinking and decision.

During this period Dewey published six articles and reviews in the field of logical theory,[3] and some of these show the slowly developing, perhaps unconscious, influence of Charles Sanders Peirce, with whom Dewey had studied logic at Johns Hopkins. When Dewey lists the advocates of the new logic, he does not mention Peirce; however, he admitted in later years that the influence of Peirce on his thought was gradual in developing. Ideas put forth in these early articles have affinities with those of Peirce, for Peirce had maintained that logic had made no progress for two hundred years, and that scientific developments during these centuries could be explained by the fact that scientists were motivated by inquiry rather than logical theory. Peirce had argued for the union of logic and science so that this integration could effect a more fruitful method of inquiry. Dewey appears conscious of Peirce's emphasis on experimental inquiry when he writes: "The Newer Logic may be

[1]     George Dykhuizen, "John Dewey and the University of Michigan," *Journal of the History of Ideas*, XXIII (Oct.–Dec. 1962), 513.
[2]     "The Development of American Pragmatism," in *Studies in the History of Ideas*, II (New York: Columbia University Press, 1925), Supplement, 367.
[3]     "Galton's Statistical Methods" (1889); "Is Logic a Dualistic Science?" (1890); "The Logic of Verification" (1890); "The Present Position of Logical Theory" (1891); "How Do Concepts Arise from Percepts?" (1891); "Two Phases of Renan's Life" (1892).

roughly described as an attempt to take account of the methods of thinking employed by science, that is, of the methods the aim of which is truth, and which deal with a material of fact" (p. 75). These early essays set a problem for Dewey on which he worked until the end of his life, the problem of overcoming the dualism which had developed between logic and science. His proposal in these early writings is similar to that of Peirce: Logical forms must be set inside a general pattern of scientific inquiry where a working harmony and unity of all procedures can be effected, and logic must be concerned with the pursuit of truth, which is the goal of all scientific inquiry.

In these essays the themes are current ones, dealing with contemporary writings and contemporary logical theory. They refer to formal logic as if this were traditional Aristotelian logic; they speak of Mill as the defender of empirical logic; and the third alternative is taken to be transcendental logic referred to as that of Wundt, Sigwart, Lotze, Jevons, Bradley, and Bosanquet. They contain a critical review of Venn's *The Principles of Empirical or Inductive Logic* and an essay on Renan's *The Future of Science*. From the topical nature of the themes discussed, from the apparent allegiance of Dewey to the transcendental logic which he refers to as Hegelian (and which, in the case of Lotze, he later criticizes severely[4]), and from the neglect of contemporary early work in modern symbolic logic, one might think that these essays are of little positive value. But there are vital themes developed in these essays which are important later in Dewey's development of a mature logical theory.

The first major theme developed at length in "The Present Position of Logical Theory" is the needed integration of scientific inquiry and logical theory. In this essay Dewey attacks the sterility of formal logic, that is, logic which disclaims any concern with content, with subject-matter, with facts, and insists that a logical theory can be adequate only if it deals with the way inquiry is actually being carried out in its own time. He finds in Mill's kind of logic an appreciation of this necessity, but thinks Mill has accepted the restriction of the old logic as dealing with the form of thought, and this in isolation from the matter of thought. In the "transcendental logic" of the Hegelian tradition he finds a promise of this interrelatedness of logical theory and science, but he thinks that transcendental logic has been rejected by scientists as speculative and metaphysical because

4    Dewey *et al.*, *Studies in Logical Theory* (The Decennial Publications, Second Series, XI [Chicago: University of Chicago Press, 1903]). See Essays II, III, IV for Dewey's criticism of Lotze.

they have not yet appreciated the fact that this logic is not Kantian (metaphysical) but Hegelian, and that it is at least an attempt to analyze the very movement of thought in the real world. He hopes to see a rapprochement of transcendental logic and scientific theory in the future.

The similar theme of the required integration of logic and scientific inquiry recurs in his review of Venn's *Empirical Logic*. He finds Venn is correct in refusing to restrict logic to the formal and in finding that logic is concerned both with ideas and concepts, like psychology, and with the observation of external phenomena, like the observational sciences. His objection is that this dualism should not be made, as in Venn, between an inner, subjective, mentalistic realm of ideas and an outer, objective realm of fact, with logic considered as a third thing intermediate between the two. He shows what he thinks to be the difficulties to which this leads and quotes Venn against himself, as both overtly and tacitly recognizing that there can be no such thing as the bare occurrence of observational facts without the influence of the mind in ordering, selecting, and interpreting them. Dewey interprets the division of ideas and facts as internal to inquiry rather than external.

This theme is further developed in the essay, "The Logic of Verification," in which he considers a possible objection against the position he had taken in the Venn review, that it overlooks the importance to science of verification, that is, the confrontation of the internal concept with the external fact. Dewey's answer is to show the difficulties of interpreting the verification of hypotheses on such dualistic terms, and to reinterpret verification as it occurs in science in terms of his own logical theory.

All of these early essays on logic are concerned with very important themes which recur in Dewey's later writings, the relation of idea to fact, of theory to matter, of concept to percept in inquiry. In these essays all the ideas in his later discussion of this "conjunctive" relation of ideas to facts are foreshadowed. Although the context is what he himself calls "transcendental logic," the way in which these two elements of inquiry are shown to be related is itself pragmatic. In working this out, he refers also to the parallelism of what happens in commonsense knowing with what is done self-consciously in scientific inquiry. He says,

Methods of thought are simply the various active attitudes into which intelligence puts itself in order to detect and grasp the fact. Instead of rigid moulds, they are flexible adaptations. Methods of thought fit fact more closely and responsively than a worn glove fits the hand. They are only the ideal evolution of the fact,—and by "ideal" is here meant simply the evolution of fact into meaning (p. 133).

Dewey says that ordinary perception does unconsciously what science does self-consciously; it follows out a hypothesis by methods of induction and deduction, of analysis and synthesis, and so on, to guide the recognition of facts and the formulation of theories. The difference between ordinary perception and scientific observation is that it is easier for ordinary perception to go astray because its method is unconscious. But "it is one and the same world which offers itself in perception and in scientific treatment" (p. 80), and the method of dealing with it is the same—that of logical method.

The discussion of the relation of method and subject-matter, of idea and fact, is further developed in the discussion of verification. Dewey says that ideas and facts are the same in the innocent experience of the baby, but what happens is that, in developing science, some idea-facts are followed by disappointed expectation, whereas others are supported by new experience and found reliable. The former are distinguished as "ideas" (mere ideas) whereas the latter are accepted as facts. A fact is an idea for which there is no longer tentative status but an accepted one; an idea is a fact about which difficulties are felt. In inquiry, ideas need extension, transformation, and verification; facts need enlargement, alteration, and significance. The process of verification is the "process of transforming the hypothesis, or idea entertained tentatively, into a fact, or idea held definitely" (p. 86). The distinction of universal and particular is set in the same context. The mind "picks out" some one aspect of "facts" and isolates it, and forms a hypothesis or idea which is then set over against the facts from which it has been isolated. The facts are the observed particulars; the isolated idea-hypothesis is the universal. This has a dialectical quality, but it is also in line with the later treatment of the interrelation of concepts and percepts in *Logic: The Theory of Inquiry* (1938). This is especially true of the concluding passage of the essay on verification in which Dewey says that there is no other test of theory than its ability to *work*, to organize facts into itself as specifications of its own nature.

The short essay on Ernest Renan, "Two Phases of Renan's Life,"[5] is important for those looking into the intellectual in-

---

5    Dewey published a later article, "Renan's Loss of Faith in Science," *Open Court*, VII (Jan. 1893), 3512–15. This essay appears in Vol. IV of *The Early Works of John Dewey, 1882–1898.*

fluences on Dewey's life. In 1848 Renan wrote *The Future of
Science*, which Dewey thought was "far from having received
the attention, or exercised the influence, it deserves" (p. 174).
What interests Dewey is the way the old comprehensiveness of
Hegelianism (Absolutism) is transformed by Renan into a
science of philology or language in which the history of man's
development is described as "the law of historic growth, not as
the dialectic unfolding of the absolute" (p. 175). Renan replaces
the category of Being with the category of evolution, and he
proposes that inquiry start with an undifferentiated, homogeneous whole, and through analysis produce the multiplicity,
and through synthesis produce comprehension, a comprehension,
however, which does not destroy the multiplicity. These ideas
alone are enough to merit the attention of scholars interested
in Dewey's development. Renan advocates a genetic approach to the study of the individual and of the human race,
believing that consciousness has *evolved* in man. Furthermore, he believes that the direction of study should be toward
"the psychology of humanity," or what we call today "social
psychology." Dewey also appreciates in Renan his ideas on the
problem of the specialization and the generalization of knowledge; minute studies in monographic form are necessary in the
on-going of science, but Renan thought there was needed an
organizational machinery for the dispersion of the conclusions of
these studies. In 1848 Renan was enthusiastic about the social
and religious significance of science; by 1890 this enthusiasm
had waned, and he had lost faith in science. On the other hand,
it was about 1890 that Dewey was beginning to see the promise
of science as a means of creating in human life a deeper and
richer quality.

During this period Dewey published two very important
articles on T. H. Green, one on his general philosophy and one
on his ethical theory. A third article on Green was published in
1893, and since these three essays are related, they should be
read as a unit.[6] The extent and depth of Dewey's concern with
Green's philosophy reveal both the positive influence which it
had upon him and the difficulties he finds in Green's position. In
the first of these articles, "The Philosophy of Thomas Hill
Green," Dewey assumes the role of expositor more than that of
critic. He claims that "the theoretic difficulties and the practical

---

[6]      "The Philosophy of Thomas Hill Green" (1889); "Green's Theory
of the Moral Motive" (1892); the third article, "Self-Realization as the
Moral Ideal," *Philosophical Review*, II (Nov. 1893), 652–64, appears in
Vol. IV of *The Early Works of John Dewey, 1882–1898*.

aspirations of this last half century are voiced by Green" (p. 16).
Dewey's analysis starts with the speculative side of Green and
explains that Green's philosophy is an attempt to reconcile
science and religion. Green is shown to hold that there is a
principle, spiritual in nature, at the root of ordinary experience
and science which is also the basis of ethics and religion. It
appears that Green was led to this consideration by way of "a
certain conflict between poetry and natural science" (p. 17). The
failure of contemporary philosophers to deal adequately with
poetry sets the problem, for no one seemed to want to relegate
poetry to the realm of feeling or mere illusion, yet poetry could
not be assimilated to the realm of science. Green shows that if
the validity of poetry and religion cannot be shown, then this
applies to ethics as well. Green lays the blame for this conflict
between science and religion upon the empiricists, particularly
those from Locke through Hume, for these philosophers did not
have an adequate view of the role of intelligence. He goes further than this, however, and maintains that "a consistent interpretation of Empiricism sapped the roots of knowledge as well
as of faith" (p. 18).

The crux of the issue as Green sees it is that intelligence is
a spiritual principle uniting science and religion, as well as making possible poetry and ethics. The empiricists, he thinks, had an
inadequate view of the constructive function of intelligence; thus,
if one followed the implications of their contentions, one would
be compelled to deny even that science is possible. This criticism
applies to Herbert Spencer as well, for Green does not find in
Spencer any notion that intelligence has a constructive, synthetic function. There is a connected whole of experience, Green
believes, and the unity of the world implies "a single, permanent,
and all-inclusive system of relations" (p. 22), and this, in turn,
implies "a permanent single consciousness which forms the bond
of relations,—'an eternal intelligence realized in the related facts
of the world' " (p. 22). Divine intelligence is not human intelligence, yet there is a relation between them, for "eternal
intelligence reproduces itself in us, partially and gradually" (p.
22). Scientific order, relations, and laws are grounded in eternal
intelligence, and this spiritual principle of science also reveals
that man is not a mere child of nature, but is capable of a consciousness of a moral ideal and of actions which flow from it.

Green's analysis of human nature shows that sensations
are transformed into theoretic experience and science, a point
with which Dewey is in general agreement. Furthermore, Green
thinks that impulses and wants are "transformed into practical

experience, into moral action" (p. 24). Dewey claims that Green develops the moral ideal in the following way: "The reproduction in man of the consciousness which is an end-in-itself makes man an end in himself, and gives his actions, therefore, both an absolute law and an absolute ideal or good" (p. 24). Green makes much of the point that animals do not have consciousness of an ideal, but man "must know that something ought to be" because "the divine has supervened" (p. 25). Dewey agrees that animals do not seem to have consciousness of ideals, but he does not agree that man's ideals must be lodged in an Absolute. On the contrary, ideals, principles, concepts which direct action are generic; that is, they have developed out of past experience. Ideals are more empirical in their genesis and in their directive functions than Green thinks. Green's ideal is too abstract, too devoid of content, and the unrealized self and the realized self are set in a dualistic opposition to each other. These issues lead to a difference in the meaning which Green and Dewey give to self-realization. For Dewey, self-realization is not a filling-up process of an undetermined self as it is for Green; rather, it is the self acting *as* self and not *for* the self. Dewey agrees with Green up to the point where moral experience involves a process in which the self in becoming conscious of its want, objectifies that want. But the objectified want is not set over against the self; for Dewey this distinguishing process means the method by which the self specifies and defines its own activity, its own satisfaction. Particular desires and ends are simply the systematic content into which the self differentiates itself in its progressive expansion. The ends are not particular and isolated from the self, for each is a member of the self's activity, and each particular becomes universalized in the total activity of the self (p. 161). There is thus a unity of the self, and no opposition of the self to particular and specific desires; in fact, "the unity of the self and the manifold of definite desires" (p. 161) are the synthetic and analytic aspects of one and the same reality. Thus, for Dewey, there is a principle of continuity which runs through his treatment of fact and theory, of form and content, of ideal and real, of ideal self and actual self, and this principle of continuity he later called one of the leading ideas of his view of experience.

One of the ways to characterize the difference between Green and Dewey on their moral theories is to say that Green holds to an *abstract* self-realization theory, whereas Dewey holds to an *empirical* self-realization theory. This becomes more evident when consideration is given to how Dewey develops a functional and empirical view of "capacity" in the article on "Self-Realization as a Moral Ideal" of 1893. Here he takes a suggestion from William James and shows that when we speak of capacity, we are speaking of some activities which can be observed here and now; and because of the connections of these activities with goals achieved in past experience, we can use these observed behaviors as conditions for the formulation of present goals. The moral ideal thus grows out of past experience; it is not a duplication of that experience, to be sure, but its content and its potentiality as an ideal are continuous with the actual experiences which precede it.

There is a further point which should be explored in Dewey's treatment of Green. Both Green and Dewey agree on the constructive and synthesizing role of intelligence in experience; but Green projects this function into an Absolute, whereas Dewey is concerned with human intelligence. Green seeks to find the basis for unity of science, religion, poetry, and ethics in Absolute intelligence, since all these parts of the universe flow from one source and that source has an interrelated character. It is interesting to note that in his later writings, Dewey, like Green, is faced with this problem of the unity of these various activities, and his solution is to ground them in the continuity of an individual life; and since these activities flow from a single source, they are interrelated at least in the manner of their genesis.[7] There remains the difficulty, however, of how an individual human intelligence can relate the various activities of his life to one another; such a harmony requires not only a common source but a functioning interaction of the activities themselves. For instance, the relations of scientific endeavors and moral practices in a single individual life posed a problem on which Dewey worked for many years.

Most of the book reviews written by Dewey during this period are short and descriptive, for example, the reviews of Caird's *The Critical Philosophy of Immanuel Kant* and Erdmann's *A History of Philosophy*. One critical review merits care-

[7]   Dewey writes: "I lay no claim to inventing an environment that is marked by both discreteness and continuity. Nor can I even make the more modest claim that I discovered it. What I have done is to interpret this duality of traits in terms of the identity of experience with life-functions." At the same place, Dewey goes on to say: "There can be no genuine continuity unless an experience, no matter how unique or individualized in its own pervasive quality, contains within itself something that points to other experiences—or, . . . unless experiences '*overlap*' with respect to their subject-matters." "Experience, Knowledge and Value: A Rejoinder," in *The Philosophy of John Dewey*, 2d ed., ed. Paul Arthur Schilpp (The Library of Living Philosophers, I [New York: Tudor Publishing Co., 1951]), 545.

ful study, for it is a treatment of some conceptions of the self, and it ends with a statement of Dewey's analysis of Green's problem, part of which is related to the above discussion on the self. Professor Andrew Seth (also known as A. Seth Pringle-Pattison) published two books, *Scottish Philosophy* (1885) and *Hegelianism and Personality* (1887), and these, along with his "Discussion" comment in *Mind* (IV, 117), afford the stimulus for Dewey's essay, "On Some Current Conceptions of the Term 'Self.'" In this treatment, Dewey limits his analysis to the meanings of the transcendental self, and the language of philosophical idealism in which the discussion is couched is sometimes difficult to follow.[8]

In Seth's treatment of the transcendental self in *Hegelianism and Personality*, Dewey finds essentially three views: (1) "the self is the correlative of the intelligible world" (p. 57); (2) "the transcendental Ego represents *merely* the *formal* unity of the universe" (p. 58); (3) "self is the 'ultimate category of thought'" (p. 59). Dewey finds difficulties with all of Seth's descriptions, and he uses the occasion to make his own analysis of the treatment of "the historical origin of these various meanings, chiefly as found in Kant, incidentally in Hegel as related to Kant" (p. 62). He shows that Kant could not have held any of the three views put forth by Seth, and, in his own reconstruction of Kant, he comes to the following conclusion:

. . . the self cannot be thought of as equivalent, on the one hand, to the world, because this world, as knowable by us, is always subject to certain forms, namely, space and time, which condition sense; nor, on the other hand, as equivalent to the highest category of thought, because the self is more than thought, more than a category, namely, the activity of synthesis of sense through thought. It is, I think, this twofold character of time and space, as at once forms of knowledge conditioned by the self, and yet conditioning self as it works in us, that is the genesis of Green's notion (p. 74).

Dewey thinks that some such reasoning is assumed in Green's adoption of the completely realized self (the Absolute) which makes the animal organism the vehicle of its own reproduction through time. This completely realized self and the unrealized

---

[8]     John Herman Randall, Jr., makes this observation about Dewey's language: "Dewey formed his own instrument of language in the midst of nineteenth-century idealism, in a world eager to talk the new tongue of evolutionary thinking. As our colleague Herbert Schneider has acutely pointed out, Dewey used the language of philosophical idealism to direct evolutionary thought against its conclusions. This proved a most effective technique for undermining and reconstructing idealism." "The Future of John Dewey's Philosophy," *Journal of Philosophy*, LVI (Dec. 1959), 1007.

selves of human beings form the dualism in Green's notion of the self which was the target of Dewey's criticism of Green in the articles discussed above.

The major work in the present volume is *Outlines of a Critical Theory of Ethics*, which grew out of classroom work, but was intended to have a wide circulation. The organization and treatment of subject-matter in this work are an innovation, for ethics texts during this period in American universities were predominantly religious in orientation. Thus some attention should be given to the topics treated and to the sequence of their arrangement. The first part is organized around the concepts of good, obligation, and freedom; the second part treats of the social nature of morality and of moral institutions; the third part deals with the moral life of the individual. It may be noted that Dewey's literary expression in this work is uneven, often ambiguous, and sometimes vague. Some ideas are not thoroughly worked out; some are put forth as mere suggestions. Perhaps Dewey's style can be explained by the fact that he not only is adapting an academic syllabus to a coherent exposition, but is groping his way into a new theory in this field; thus his language is cryptic and his ideas are not always clear. There is little wonder that the reviewers had some rather severe remarks to make about the work, about the ideas put forth, about their organization, and about Dewey's expression. But the work must not be ignored because of these shortcomings. The germinal ideas of much of Dewey's later philosophy are put forth in this work, and this alone gives it significance. Dewey acknowledges Green, Bradley, Caird, and Alexander as men influencing his views, and though he mentions Herbert Spencer and Leslie Stephen, he says that he cannot adopt their standpoint. A student of Dewey's philosophy will detect, however, that he has been influenced by men other than those he mentions.

A significant note appears in the "Preface" which is pertinent to the understanding of the approach to philosophy which persisted throughout Dewey's life work. He says that "comparing opposite one-sided views with the aim of discovering a theory apparently more adequate" (p. 240) is the method he has adopted. Later in his career he called these one-sided views "selective emphases" or "biases" and once said that philosophy is "a critique of prejudices."[9] His effort is to discover a more adequate theory by working through the various one-sided accounts. Dewey's way of philosophizing, whether the field be theory of knowl-

9   *Experience and Nature*, 2d ed. (New York: W. W. Norton and Co., [c1929]), p. 37.

edge or theory of ethics, is to show that all philosophers, from Plato to the present, are of value, for all have laid hold of some important constituent of experience, but each has "failed to place it in the context in which it actually functions."[10] Approaching the history of thought in this manner, Dewey appears to have ambivalent attitudes toward the men whose theories he analyzes. At one time he may lash out with critical severity at one aspect of a philosopher's thought; at another time he may praise the same philosopher for another of his ideas. Furthermore, this philosophic method is vulnerable to a critic who, with a selective bias of his own, can choose a certain passage and interpret it out of context, attributing to Dewey one or another of the positions he is criticizing or treating "dialectically."

The use of the word "critical" in the title of the book obviously means "evaluative." It means that the theories selected are to be compared and analyzed and put into the context of a new theory, in much the same way that Dewey thinks Leibniz critically analyzed and absorbed into his own philosophy the ideas of previous theories. Thus theories as far apart as hedonism and Kant's formalism both have some truth in them, yet each has objectionable parts, and Dewey's "functional" reorganization yields his own theory. Dewey's later writings on ethics, particularly the text he wrote with James H. Tufts in 1908 and revised in 1932, follow this same pattern of analysis and reconstruction. Attention must be given also to the concise "Introduction" to the *Outlines*, for here the definitions and meanings set the stage for the development of the *Outlines*, as well as for Dewey's subsequent ethical thought. The habit of tracing basic terms to their root meanings and early usage pervades much of Dewey's method of thinking; for instance, in this work the term "ethics" is traced to its Greek origin and the term "morals" to the Latin. The distinction between branches of knowledge which describe and those which judge (*de facto* and *de jure*) remains important throughout his career. Dewey did not hold in 1891 or later that it is the business of ethics "to prescribe what man ought to do"; rather, it is the business of ethics "to examine conduct to see what gives it its *worth*" (p. 241). In "Moral Theory and Practice," an article written during the year the *Outlines* was published, Dewey says: "Theory is the cross-section of the given state of action in order to know the conduct that should be; practice is the realization of the idea thus gained: it is theory in action" (p. 109). Thus moral theory is both descriptive and normative.

[10]    Dewey, "Experience, Knowledge and Value," p. 561.

Another important concept put forth in the *Outlines* which figures prominently in later writings is the notion of conduct. For Dewey conduct means the whole of action; conduct is the whole self in activity in contrast to the special social sciences, which deal with partial and segmented aspects of human behavior. Conduct implies more than action in general; it "implies purpose, motive, intention; that the agent knows what he is about, that he has something which he is aiming at" (p. 242). It is the end or ideal "which gives action its moral value" and which gives us "a standard by which we judge particular acts" (p. 243). It should be recalled that the end of conduct for Dewey is not an abstract ideal or an unchanging form as it is for Green; it is an end or ideal which has been constructed out of past experience of an individual's life and the life of men in general. Although the ideal has some stability and persists through time, it is subject to change and modification as experience refines its meaning.

In the first part of the work Dewey takes up four main theories concerning the good: hedonism, utilitarianism, evolutionary utilitarianism, and Kantianism. His detailed criticisms of these theories should not be ignored, especially those of utilitarianism and of Kantianism, for they are pertinent to the careful appraisal of Dewey as borrowing from each theory, although he is neither a full-fledged utilitarian nor a full-fledged Kantian. After critically evaluating their various themes, he selects and rejects certain aspects and uses the selected parts to construct his own theory. An adequate theory is not the "getting of a lot of pleasures through the satisfaction of desires just as they happen to arise," as hedonism claims, and Kantianism fails in the way in which it demands "obedience to law simply because it is law" (p. 300). He says that the satisfied self "is found in *satisfaction of desires according to law*" (p. 300), a law not external to the desires but generic to them. Dewey holds that moral experience results in building up generic universals, rules, and principles which apply to specific kinds of moral situations; it is in this sense that laws are not imposed upon desires from without but are generic.

Some critics claim that over his long life of philosophizing Dewey failed to develop an adequate account of moral duty and obligation.[11] There is little doubt that in his early writings, the

---

[11]     Morton G. White says: "Evidently pragmatism is united on the subject of value but not on obligation or justice. Dewey, in spite of a valiant attempt, has not given us a naturalistic account of obligation." "Value and Obligation in Dewey and Lewis," *Philosophical Review*, LVIII (July 1949), 329.

*Outlines* included, the concern is primarily with the concept of good rather than with those of duty, right, and obligation. Furthermore, Dewey is not clear in the *Outlines* on the relation of duty to the good. When he sets forth his preliminary definitions in the "Introduction," he says: "The end or good decides what should be or *ought* to be. Any act necessary to fulfill the end is a *duty*" (p. 243). Dewey's notion of the end of conduct is linked to desires, the empirical touchstone of his naturalistic theory, and in this sense he can be classified as an axiologist. He criticizes Kant for not taking account of desires and appetites, and claims that the Kantian theory leaves these "untouched or would abolish them—in either case destroying morality" (p. 334).

On the other hand, Dewey cannot accept the views of Bain and Spencer on obligation, although both take desires into account, for their views do not give a clear distinction between the moral control of desires and the coercion of desires by a superior physical force. Dewey holds that the concept of duty limits and transforms a desire, but that the proper context in which to put the relation of duty to desire is one in which a specific desire is related to other desires and interests of the individual, and to the specific needs and demands of the community in which the desire must be fulfilled. Confusion enters Dewey's theory when he seems to say that an act is done from duty if it achieves the end or the good, and when he tries to explain the meaning of the phrase "duty for duty's sake" in a non-Kantian sense. He rejects the notion of doing one's duty in order to conform to an abstract idea, for such an idea leads to a morality which is "at once hard and barren, and weak and sentimental" (p. 339). Then he goes on to say that to be moral an act must be performed for duty's sake, and must not be degraded "into a means for some ulterior end" (p. 339).

It has been mentioned that desires and interests of an individual involve a social context for their fulfillment. The metaphysical dualism of individual and social is avoided by showing that an individual's existence, functioning, and fulfillment cannot be separated from his social environment. The position taken here, reminiscent of Aristotle, is that ethics is concerned with individual conduct, goals, and decisions. It is within this individual-social continuum that Dewey develops his views of individuality and freedom. Freedom of choice depends upon many conditions, such as an individual's emancipation from particular appetites and desires so that he can fashion his conduct in terms of conscious ends, ends many and varied, some of which may even be contrary to one another. Without a plurality of consciously formed ends, there is no freedom of choice. Freedom is not mere random activity, nor is it mere freedom from the restrictions which the social environment places upon it (negative freedom), nor is man endowed with it as a kind of innate gift. Freedom is an achievement of the individual living in society, where the individual-social continuum contains the conditions required for its function.

Dewey's self-realization theory in ethics means that the individual develops within society. He develops by projecting an ideal forged out of his concrete experiences and his particular function in his social setting. Dewey writes: "The exercise of function by an agent serves, then, both to define and to unite him. It makes him a *distinct* social member at the same time that it makes him a *member*" (p. 326). Every individual is marked off from every other individual by his peculiar capacities and the special surroundings in which he functions. The adjustment of individual capacity to environment in the exercise of function effects the realization of individuality, and this accomplishment marks off each individual from others.

One idea in the *Outlines* tends to drop out of the later writings, or to be implicit rather than explicit. This is Dewey's notion of the ethical postulate. It is not an arbitrary postulate, and Dewey qualifies it in many ways. He says: "The basis, in a word, of moral conduct, with respect to the exercise of function, is a faith that moral self-satisfaction . . . means social satisfaction — or the faith that self and others make a true community" (p. 320). The presupposition which Dewey thinks underlies all moral conduct is put again in another way: "In the realization of individuality there is found also the needed realization of some community of persons of which the individual is a member; and, conversely, the agent who duly satisfies the community in which he shares, by that same conduct satisfies himself" (p. 322).

It will be recalled that T. H. Green was led to the consideration of the relation of ethics to science by way of the problem of the relation of poetry to science. The advance of scientific understanding of the world during the nineteenth century was taking place with such rapidity that religious beliefs were being challenged, and it appeared to some thinkers that the whole of man's non-scientific culture would collapse. Most intellectuals outside of science did not want to relegate non-scientific endeavors, such as poetry, to the realm of mere feeling or illusion. Ethics and religion, as well as philosophy, were felt to be threatened by this scientific advance. Some remarks by Matthew Arnold concerning the place of poetry in this intellectual situation were the occasion for Dewey's essay on "Poetry and Philosophy." Arnold gave expression to the intellectual crisis by showing that the old Christian faiths were perishing, and that contemporary man was isolated from nature and from his fellow man. This condition gives man a sense of loss, and a pessimistic view of life ensues. Arnold accepts the authority of science concerning the world, and he contends that "most of what now passes for religion and philosophy will be replaced by poetry" (p. 110). He appears to be a precursor of the positivistic view of science and culture in which the world is denuded of value, and thus value is compelled to take refuge in the realm of art. Dewey was deeply disturbed by Arnold's view, and he sought in this essay to put forth his own views on the relations of science, poetry, and philosophy.

In order to understand the basis for Dewey's views on the roles of these three endeavors in human life, one must first grasp his general theory of meaning. The realm of meanings is wider than that of science. Scientific meanings have relations and implications which go beyond science itself; thus they are not inaccessible to the poet and the philosopher. Furthermore, since meanings are wider in their range than those which science describes, the poet and the philosopher have other meanings at their disposal. Thus, Dewey writes, "As it comes to the poet, life is already a universe of meanings, of interpretations, which indeed the poet may fill out, but not dispense with" (p. 113). Philosophy and poetry have a common root, the meanings found in experience. Dewey then shows that some of these common meanings have been used by both philosophers and poets as their material. Philosophers have written about the pessimistic phases of life, for instance, and so have the poets. At times poets have been exuberant, like Robert Browning with his optimism and faith in life, and so have philosophers. Dewey admits that at some times, including the present period, philosophers lag behind the poets in their sensitivities to the problems of human life, but at other times the poets have built upon the meanings of the philosophers.

If philosophy and poetry have a common source of meanings, what is the difference between them? The difference, according to Dewey, is in their expressions and purposes. Dewey says that the goal of science is knowledge, that the goal of philosophy is wisdom, and that "poetry may deliver truth with a personal and a passionate force which is beyond the reach of theory painting in gray on gray" (p. 112). It appears that Dewey thinks that poetry and art generally make emotional meanings uppermost, while philosophy using the "cold, reflective way of critical system" attempts to justify and organize what poetry "with its quick, naïve contacts, has already felt and reported" (p. 123). Philosophy is concerned with the truths and meanings of experience as they relate to human conduct (morals) and to values generally, or to "the ideals and aspirations of life" (p. 112). Dewey admits that poets may at times be concerned with morals, with the relation of scientific beliefs about the world to beliefs about values, but this is not their chief concern. Both poetry and philosophy are kinds of commentary on life, but their language is different and their functions, although overlapping in some respects, are different also.

Dewey is appreciative of many of the insights of Matthew Arnold, and in later years he turns again and again to ideas he attributed to this poet and critic. Arnold once wrote that "poetry is a criticism of life," and while Dewey thinks that poetry is more than this, he was influenced by Arnold's view in transferring it into philosophy, for he later writes that philosophy "is inherently criticism," and in his own method makes philosophy "a criticism of criticisms."[12]

During this early period Dewey was impressed by another writer, Paul Bourget, who wrote a two-volume work, *Essais de psychologie contemporaine* and *Nouveaux essais de psychologie contemporaine*. This is not a work on psychology, as its title suggests, but a criticism of French literary writers. Dewey's essay on "The Lesson of Contemporary French Literature" reveals that it is the critical method of Bourget, as well as the conclusions which the method produces, which interests him. Dewey thinks that Bourget penetrates into the deeper meanings of French consciousness, tracing "thoughts back to their germ" and indicating how these thoughts are "connected with the contemporary movements of life" (p. 37). This is what criticism should do. It should show the ideas which cause men to feel and to think the way they do; it should reveal how their literary works are expressions of the deeper meanings of their lives. Criticism is thus "the dissection of their thoughts, their emotions, their attitude toward the problems of life" (p. 37). This is what Bourget had done in his work, and the lesson to be learned from him is that "the problem of the nineteenth century reduces itself to a choice between faith and pessimism" (p. 42).

The four years from 1889 through 1892 represented by the writings in this volume were active and fruitful ones for John Dewey; he was directing the department at Michigan; he was

12   *Experience and Nature*, p. 398.

lecturing, teaching, writing, and taking part in community activities. He worked out a syllabus for the introductory philosophy course, wrote numerous comments on educational practice,
and published short philosophical commentaries in *Inlander*. His
philosophical views were taking on definite form, and his mind
was moving toward the more mature statements of many of the
germinal ideas developed during this period. Dewey's two dominant interests at that time were logical theory and ethics, and in
these fields he continued to make notable contributions throughout his life.

*S. Morris Eames*

*15 March 1969*

*EARLY ESSAYS*

# The Late Professor Morris

The story of the outward life of the departed teacher and scholar, George Sylvester Morris, may be briefly told. It was a life great, not in outward circumstance, but in spirit, and in the quality of its achievement.

George S. Morris was born November 15th, 1840, at Norwich, Vermont. After pursuing the courses in the district schools and village academy, usual to the New Englanders of that period, he entered Dartmouth College. He was graduated, with high standing in his class, as Bachelor of Arts in 1861. Three years afterwards, he received the degree of Master of Arts in course from the same institution. The same year he entered Union Theological Seminary in New York City. Here he studied for two years. Doctor H. B. Smith, whose own philosophical ability placed him high among the theologians of our country, discerned the unusual strain of Mr. Morris's mind, and advised him to continue his studies in Germany. This he did, carrying on, as is usual, his studies at more than one University, but chiefly with Trendelenburg in Berlin, and Erdmann and Ulrici in Halle. In 1868, he returned, having acquired a command of the German and French languages, and considerable acquaintance with Italian. He then spent some time teaching in a private family in New York City.

Meantime Doctors Smith and Schaff had projected a "Theological and Philosophical Library." This they desired to open with a history of philosophy. That of Ueberweg was selected, and none was found more fitted to do the work of translating than the scholar fresh from philosophical and

[*First published in the* Palladium, *An Annual Edited by the College Fraternities at the University of Michigan, XXXI* (1889), *110–18. Reprinted in part in* The Life and Work of George Sylvester Morris (*New York: The Macmillan Co.*, 1917), *308–13.*]

language studies in Germany. The translating was performed in such a way that excellent judges, German as well as English, have pronounced the translation superior to the original. All the numerous references to Greek and Latin authorities were verified and translated, ambiguities in style and statement were corrected; the bibliographical references were increased from the ready and ample store of the translator; numerous accounts of the more noted contemporary German philosophers were added. The translation is a monument not only to the breadth and accuracy of Professor Morris's scholarship, but to his entire fidelity and thoroughness in executing whatever was committed to him.

At about this time there was a vacancy in the chair of modern languages at the University of Michigan. Professor Frieze was then acting president, and upon his invitation, an invitation delivered, I believe, in person, Mr. Morris accepted the position. For eleven years the department of modern languages had the benefit of his wide learning, his native love of thoroughness, his culture of mind. During these years, however, he continued to cherish above his other intellectual interests, the study of philosophy, and when in 1878 the opportunity opened for him to give instruction as a lecturer in philosophy in the recently opened Johns Hopkins University, at Baltimore, he gladly responded. For three years he joined this lectureship to his teaching in Ann Arbor. In 1881 the scope of his lectureship in Baltimore was broadened, and he resigned his chair in Michigan University. Only for a year, however, was the University deprived of his inspiring service. Arrangements were made, whereby, as the colleague of Doctor Cocker, he gave one-half of each year to instruction in philosophy in this institution. In 1883, upon the death of Doctor Cocker, Mr. Morris was made professor of philosophy, retaining this position up to the time of his untimely death, upon the 23rd of March, 1889.

Professor Morris was married at Ann Arbor, June 29th, 1876, to Miss Victoria Celle. She, with two children, remain to mourn him who is departed. It would not be possible becomingly to speak of the family-life thus disrupted by death. Its beautiful character is so well known to the students who so often shared in its graceful hospitality, as well as to those to whom this home was a continuation of their own earlier home, that the thought of it is a grateful memory. The tenderness and depth with which Professor Morris, in his lectures upon political philosophy, dwelt upon the institution of the family are more than explained by the natural and close companionships of his own life.

We cannot cease to regret that the entire unconsciousness of Professor Morris that his own experiences could be of interest to others should have deprived us of any more adequate record of his intellectual development, especially in the growth of his philosophic thought. In the opening of his lectures upon *British Thought and Thinkers*, there is an allusion to himself, which is worth quoting, both because of its rarity and because it reveals how early his mind sought the philosophic channel. "I can remember," he says, "how as a mere boy, more than once, in an evening reverie, an experience somewhat in this vein came to me. All my boyish ideas of things seemed, as pure creations of my own fancy, to melt away, and there remained, as the whole sum and substance of the universe, only the empty and inexplicable necessity of being, plus a dull, confused and indescribable sensation as of a chaos of shapeless elements. Then came the return to the world such as it had actually shaped itself in my imagination—the earth, with its green fields and forest-covered mountains, the world-inhabited heavens, the changing seasons, man and his past history and unrevealed earthly destiny, not to mention the myriad little and familiar things which would necessarily crowd the foreground of such a picture in a boy's mind. The view which a moment before had demonstrated so signally its capacity of dissolving again became a slowly changing panorama of a world. It was into such a conception of a world that I, following unwillingly a bent common to the universal mind of man, was more or less blindly seeking to introduce order and permanence. What must be? Why must anything be? Why must all things be? I need not say that the immediate result of my reflections was tolerably negative!" We cannot but wish as we read this that we had more autobiographical fragments to draw upon.

The instruction Professor Morris received in college

does not appear to have appealed to him particularly. Indeed, it seems rather to have impelled him, with a dislike which never left him, from what is often miscalled metaphysics, the partly verbal, partly arbitrary [            ] of various recondite notions. At one period, he was a disciple of the English Empirical School, of the Mills, and of Bain and Spencer. He went so far as to consider himself a materialist. In later years, it was something more than a logical conviction of the purely theoretical short-coming of these forms of philosophy that made him so strong, though so fair and appreciative, an opponent of them. It was also, if we may make use of some remarks of his upon one occasion when materialism was under discussion, the conviction, which personal experience had brought home to him, of their ethical deficiencies, of their failure to support and inspire life. It was in Germany, and immediately under the influence of Trendelenburg, in the main, that his trend of thinking was changed to a manner which he never ceased to regard as more catholic, more profound, more truly experimental. The change seems to have been due to a more adequate acquaintance with the history of philosophy, especially in its classic Greek types. Trendelenburg was among the first of a class of university teachers now numerous in Germany. He based his thinking and teaching mainly upon the history of philosophy, taken in connection with the leading results of modern science. Professor Morris was brought, seemingly, into a position somewhat similar to that of his teacher. At least, he never surrendered the belief that genuine personal philosophic conviction must be based upon a knowledge of philosophy in its historic development. This belief was the basis of his opinion that what American thought needed above all else as a condition of getting out of its somewhat provincial state, was an adequate acquaintance with the great thought of the past. While he held a definite philosophical position of his own, and held it firmly, his instruction was based upon the idea that the main thing after all is to get the individual out of his restricted ways of thinking and in contact with the stream of reflective thought that has been flowing on well nigh twenty-five hundred years. For a time his own philosophic conviction was probably an Aristotelianism modified and developed by the results of science. While Professor Morris never abandoned the positive features of his conviction, later and independent study convinced him that there were wider and deeper truths with which it must be conjoined. Although Trendelenburg had incorporated within his own teaching the substantial achievements of that great philosophical movement which began with Kant and closed with Hegel—the ideas, for example, of the correlation of thought and being, the idea of man as a self-realizing personality, the notion of organized society as the objective reality of man—he had taken a hostile attitude to these positions as stated by Hegel and to the method by which they were taught. While Professor Morris was never simply an adherent of Trendelenburg, he probably followed him also in this respect. At least, he used sometimes in later years to point out pages in his copy of Hegel which were marked "nonsense," etc., remarks made while he was a student in Germany. It thus was not any discipleship which finally led Mr. Morris to find in Hegel (in his own words) "the most profound and comprehensive of modern thinkers." He found in a better and fuller statement of what he had already accepted as true, a more ample and far-reaching method, a goal of his studies in the history of thought.

This is not the place, of course, to attempt any *resumé* of Professor Morris's philosophical thought. That fortunately stands for itself in the writings which he has left; it advances in the "living epistles" which he has written in the hearts and brains of scores of students. But since Professor Morris never held his philosophy by a merely intellectual grasp, since it was fused with his personal character, and gained its color and tone from his own deeper interests, it seems worth while to speak of his thought in relation to his other characteristic qualities,—his love of beauty and his strong religious nature.

All who knew Professor Morris knew how genuine and deep was his appreciation of the beautiful, especially as manifested in poetry and music. In music, indeed, he had not only a theoretical appreciation, but a practical and loving knowledge. This love of the beautiful found an abiding home in the very heart of his philosophy. It gave to his thought a peculiar elevated tone. It brought him into congenial sympathy with some of the greatest spirits of the race, notably Plato. While he did not draw his essential intellectual nutriment from Plato, he did derive from him, in large measure, intellectual inspiration. He never spoke of Plato without a kindling enthusiasm, a warmth of sympathy which no other philosopher ever aroused in quite the same degree. It was this genuine kinship of spirit which led Professor Morris to write in the following words, of Plato: "He is the intelligent poet of philosophy rapt with the moral power and fascination of philosophic truth, and in his wonderful dialogues bringing its resistless spell nearer home to the mind and heart of humanity than any other one whom the earth has been privileged to see. Reason in him is all aflame with feeling, but not mastered by it. He has not simply the acute perception, but the warm impression of eternal and essential being—of truth, beauty, goodness—and he is consequently enabled with the electrical effectiveness of a poetic touch to deliver this impression to mankind." The further tie which bound Professor Morris to the thought of Plato is in the fact that Plato dwells on the ideal character of beauty, not upon its sensuous quality; the ethical factor in beauty is what attracts. It was the beauty of spirit, the beauty of the eternal idea manifesting itself in outward form that drew Mr. Morris. The delight in this factor made his idealism poetic as well as philosophic. There was a prayer of Socrates which Professor Morris was wont to refer to and which he could not quote without his very countenance revealing how much it had been already realized in him: "Beloved Pan and all ye other gods who haunt this spot, give me beauty in the inward soul and may the outward and the inward man be at one."

It was characteristic of Professor Morris that the two writings from which he most often quoted were the *Dialogues* of Plato and the Gospel of St. John. In the fundamental principle of Christianity, he found manifested the truth which he was convinced of as the fundamental truth in philosophy—the unity of God and man so that the spirit which is in man, rather which is man, is the spirit of God.

"The very sense of philosophical idealism," he says in one of his works, "is to put and represent man in direct relation with the Absolute Mind so that its light is his light and its strength is made his." The firmness with which he held this truth is the key to all of his thinking. It is also the key to his attitude towards current religious beliefs. In the ordinary antithesis between the supernatural and the natural, he saw concealed the deeper truth of the antithesis of the spiritual and the natural—an antithesis involving, however, a unity; the natural being only the partial and dependent manifestation of the spiritual. Of such a position, he found all history to be the demonstration, the showing forth. The philosophy of art, of the state, of religion, as well as of knowledge, was to him inexplicable upon any other theory. It was because he found in Hegel not merely the general recognition of this idea, but the attempt to work it out in its bearings upon concrete fact, that he was in later life so attracted to Hegel. The result of this conviction was that his philosophical knowledge gave body and masculine vigor to his religious faith, and his faith stimulated and quickened his theoretical convictions. But we do him wrong to speak of his religious faith and his philosophic knowledge as if they were two separate things capable of reacting upon each other. They were one—vitally and indistinguishably one. In this union, that union of his, his intellectual and moral nature had its roots—a union which made him so complete a man and his life so integral. He was preëminently a man in whom those internal divisions, which eat into the heart of so much of contemporary spiritual life, and which rob the intellect of its faith in truth, and the will of its belief in the value of life, had been overcome. In the philosophical and religious conviction of the unity of man's spirit with the divine he had that rest which is energy. This wholeness of intelligence and will was the source of the power, the inspiring power, of his life. It was the source of the definiteness, the positiveness of his teaching, which, free from all personal dogmatism, yet made the pupil instinctively realize that there was something real called truth, and this truth was not only capable of being known by man but was the very life of man.

The other personal quality which gave color to Profes-

sor Morris's thought was his profound feeling of the organic
relationships of life—of the family and the state. At one with
himself, having no conflicts of his own nature to absorb him,
he found the substance of his being in his vital connections
with others; in the home, in his friendships, in the political
organization of society, in his church relations. It was his
thorough realization in himself of the meaning of these
relationships that gave substance and body to his theory of
the organic unity of man with nature and with God. This
theory, like any theory, may be held in an empty formalism
of thought, but in Professor Morris's teaching, it was quickened and made real by his own practical realization of such
relations in actual life.

Of Professor Morris's writings, nothing can be here
said, excepting to give an incomplete list. Among his earlier
writings are two essays, written for the Victoria Institute of
London, of which he was an associate member, and published by them. The titles of these are: *The Theory of
Unconscious Intelligence as Opposed to Theism* and *The
Final Cause as Principle of Cognition in Nature*. About this
time should be placed an account of the philosophy of Trendelenburg, published in the *New Englander*. Here should be
mentioned also the translation of Ueberweg's *History of
Philosophy*. There was published in the *Journal of Speculative Philosophy*, while Professor Morris was still professor
of modern languages, a lecture, which he had delivered
before a class reading Taine, upon the theory of Art, a
lecture which contains in germ, the ideas later developed in
his lectures upon Æsthetics. Marking his connection with
Johns Hopkins University are *British Thought and Thinkers*, and later the *Exposition of Kant's Critique of Pure
Reason*. The latter was the initial volume of a series of
works, called German Philosophical Classics, and published
by S. C. Griggs & Co. Of this series, Professor Morris was
the proposer and editor, and at the time of his death it
included seven volumes, one of which besides the Kant, that
upon *Hegel's Philosophy of History and State*, was by Professor Morris's own hand. This was his last work. Between
it and the Kant comes an article in the *Princeton Review*
entitled, "Philosophy and its Specific Problems," the book

upon *Philosophy and Christianity*, made up of lectures delivered upon the Ely Foundation before the Union Theological Seminary. He published also, as the first of a series of Philosophical Papers of the University of Michigan, an address which he had delivered before the philosophical society of the University upon *University Education*. About the time when he was seeing through the press his exposition of Hegel, the scheme of a "Library of Philosophy" was under discussion in England. Professor Morris was asked by its editor, Mr. J. H. Muirhead, to write the volume upon the history of logic. Professor Morris was even then thinking of what he should turn to next, and he welcomed with great pleasure the opportunity thus afforded him. Nothing could have been suggested which would have awakened so ready a response. When he spoke of it, he said that for some time back, it had been his desire to give the next years of his work to the study of Real Logic with a view to preparing something that might last. This history of logic gave him in an unexpected way, the chance to make thorough preparation for this treatise upon logic itself. For a year and more before his death he had been busy reading for the history. It is to be feared, however, that nothing was left in shape for publication. Professor Morris's death has brought a loss no less deep, in its way, to the philosophical world at large, than that which has come upon the University, and his circle of personal friends. He was, indeed, in the prime of his work. His own feeling, as expressed in one of those rare moments when he broke through his accustomed reserve in such matters, was that in past work he had been serving an apprenticeship for what he hoped to do.

It remains to speak of Professor Morris as a teacher. There is, indeed, nothing to be said of him as a class-room instructor that is not to be said of him as a man. Nothing could have been more foreign to his character than to assume in any respect an attitude or quality in the class-room different from that which marked him elsewhere. There was the same sincerity, the same simplicity, the same force of enthusiasm in him in one place as in another. No "officialism" such as sometimes gathers about the work of teaching ever touched him. He was everywhere simply and only a man. But Professor Morris had unusual gifts as a philosophic instructor. He was, among other things, a commentator of the first order. That is, he had the selective eye which made at once for the heart of an author under discussion; he had the pregnant phrase that lays bare this heart to the eye of the student. He had the gift of inspiring in his pupils the same disinterested devotion to truth that marked himself. He conveyed in large measure what, in his essay upon *University Education* already alluded to, he himself calls "the power to detect and the will to condemn all essential shams and falsehoods." Scholarship never lost itself in pedantry; culture never masqueraded as mere intellectualism, with ethical inspiration and backing. He was especially successful in arousing pupils with any particular aptitude for philosophy to advanced and independent work. The spirit of his work was that which he declared should be the spirit of all truly University work—a free teacher face to face with a free student. He once defined idealism as faith in the human spirit; this faith he had, and his voice and his influence were always for broadening and freeing the scope and methods of college work, without in any way relaxing the solidity and thoroughness of mental discipline.

Of the place and function of philosophy in University training he had a high conception—not because he in any way would magnify his own office at the expense of others, but because he saw in philosophy the organic bond of all special sciences, "the coördination of all knowledge." The University, to quote again from Professor Morris, "is the institution devoted to the fullest and freest cultivation of the universal condition of human freedom—knowledge of the truth." This end is humane, is ethical; and it is only because philosophy tended to knowledge of the truth, that he made high claims for it. So far was he from desiring any exclusive treatment of philosophy that he writes that "her praises will never be rightfully and effectively sung until they are sung by others than adepts." I can find no better expression of the spirit in which Professor Morris himself taught philosophy than is voiced in one of his own earlier writings. He speaks there of "the noblest common-sense which seeks reform, not simply protest and the demand for change, but by fitly feeding the fountains of intelligence, through which alone a true and authentic reform can be maintained." To feed the fountains of intelligence was precisely, it seems to me, the work of Professor Morris in philosophy. While we cannot estimate the loss to thought in the sudden death of Professor Morris, we cannot be sufficiently grateful that there are so many scattered over the whole land who have felt the quickening touch of his divine love of truth, and who have felt the "fountains of intelligence" within their own breast, called into life and energy by the truth as he bore witness to it.

No attempt can here be made to appreciate the intimate and personal qualities of Mr. Morris. Were I to attempt it, the flood of personal memories and affections would prevent. To those who did not know him, no use of adjectives would convey an idea of the beauty, the sweetness, the wholeness of his character. To those who did know him, it is not necessary to speak of these things. His gentle courtesy in which respect for others and for himself were so exquisitely blended, his delicate chivalry of thought and feeling; his unusual union of intellectual freedom and personal simplicity—who shall speak adequately of these traits? The words of one who knew Mr. Morris only by his outward presence, and through the report of others, comes to my lips: "There was nothing which he held as his own; he had made the great renunciation."

# The Philosophy of Thomas Hill Green

It is no secret that the Professor Grey of Mrs. Ward's *Robert Elsmere* is the *umbra*, if not the *nomen*, of the late Professor Green of Oxford. Professor Green is known in this country, where he is known at all, as the author of certain philosophical treatises and criticisms which the uninitiated, if not the expert, would class as decidedly hard reading. Indeed, it suggests the irony of fate that one whose writings are anything but popular, in the ordinary sense of the term, should become part of the intellectual background —Grey is hardly a living character—of the most popular novel of the day. For Green's writings lack popularity both of style and of aim. Clear they are, but only because they are the adequate expression of thought which is remarkably exact and painstaking, as well as conscientious to a degree that will allow no possible qualification to go unmade, no possible objection to remain unanswered, no possible limitations to be passed over. And they were not written *ad populum*, but for philosophical students, one might say for philosophical specialists. Green's intellectual conscience was so sensitive that he very obviously refrains from any attempt to win assent by any adventitious appeals. He is scrupulous to a fault, it sometimes seems, in refusing any alliance with outside movements or parties that might make for his advantage. In form and in substance he will have his thoughts gain the influence that the truth embodied in them can command, and only that influence.

While Green's influence has been growing year by

[*First published in the* Andover Review, *XI* (*Apr.* 1889), 337–55. *Not previously reprinted.*]

year, and while those whom it has touched, it has touched profoundly, even radically, I do not think that it can be said to have extended beyond the circle of his personal pupils and of philosophical teachers and students. In this country, at least, hundreds must know Professor Grey to whom the "Introductions" to Hume, the *Prolegomena to Ethics*, and the *Lectures on the Principles of Political Obligation* of Professor Green are unknown.

But the remoteness of his philosophy from life is, after all, more apparent than real. There is even a more specific connection of his thought with a novel that pretends to touch life seriously than the general tendency of our times to get the imagination and the understanding upon common ground. The connection is in the character and philosophy of Green; for his character was practical in the highest degree, and it is impossible to hold his philosophy as a mere speculative theory apart from its applications to life. It would be profitless, it might seem impertinent, had not Mrs. Ward set an example, to compare the living Green and the fictitious Grey. But common report, brief sketches by some of his contemporaries, and by some of his pupils, the brief but authoritative biographical account, all speak for the intensely practical bent of his nature, and his philosophy is there to speak for itself. Both theoretically and personally, the deepest interests of his times were the deepest interests of Professor Green. The most abstruse and critical of his writings are, after all, only attempts to solve the problems of his times—the problems which meet us in current magazine discussions, in social and political theory, in poetry, in religion, and in the interpretation of the higher results of science. Professor Caird gives us the clue to the connection of Professor Green's philosophy with the actual life of his times, in saying that one of the main features of Green's character was the distinctness with which he lived by conviction, not by impulse. It was the belief, the profound belief, that all action should spring from conviction, not any love of abstract and abstruse speculations, that made him a philosopher. He saw in what is called philosophy only a systematic search for and justification of the conviction by which man should live. We are not surprised, therefore, when Professor Caird goes on to say that the other main trait of Green's character was the intensity of his intellectual and political interests. His philosophic theory was in the service of these interests, and his political thought and activity was the application of his philosophic conviction. He was (to quote Caird again) "a democrat of the democrats. From a somewhat exclusive interest in the essentials of humanity —in the spiritual experiences in which all men are alike—his sympathies were always with the many rather than with the few."

Upon both sides, the side of philosophic conviction, and the side of political and social life, Green is in closest contact with the deepest interests of his times. In the true sense, his philosophy, however strictly logical and impersonal in form, is vital and concrete. The theoretic difficulties and the practical aspirations of this last half century are voiced by Green. He is in a more real and, I cannot but think, more lasting way the prophet of our times than many hailed as prophets who have addressed themselves to the public in more direct and popular ways. In this article I wish, so far as I may, considering the technical character of the subject-matter and the limits of space, to give an account of the burden of this prophecy. I wish to point out the theoretic conviction by which he met the doubts and questionings of the intellectual life of these times, and the practical conviction in which he articulated the best political desire and conduct of to-day.

Beginning with the speculative side, I may say that Green's object was to reconcile science and religion. But this phrase needs to be carefully interpreted. If it means a forced exegesis of Scripture on the one hand, and a somewhat questionable use of somewhat doubtful facts on the other, nothing was more remote from the intention of Green. Nor did he work in the more legitimate field of showing that the main doctrines of theology find no contradiction in the general theories of science. Indeed, he carefully refrains from the introduction of specifically religious ideas,—almost of the word religion. By the reconciliation of science and religion, I mean the attempt to show that science, as the fundamental, theoretical interest of man, and religion as his fundamental, emotional, and practical interest have a common source and a common guaranty. It was the main work of Green's speculative philosophy to show that there is a spiritual principle at the root of ordinary experience and science, as well as at the basis of ethics and religion; to show, negatively, that whatever weakens the supremacy and primacy of the spiritual principle makes science impossible, and, positively, to show that any fair analysis of the conditions of science will show certain ideas, principles, or categories—call them what you will—that are not physical and sensible, but intellectual and metaphysical.

Professor Green has himself given a statement of his general intention at the beginning of his *Prolegomena to Ethics*. He there points out that there is a certain conflict between poetry and natural science. The ideas contained in the best poetry of our times, the ideas that recommend it to select and serious spirits, are not verifiable by sense. These ideas, if outside the domain of dogmatic theology, are as surely outside the domain of natural science. And yet the most intelligent critics are not willing, says Professor Green, that any justification should be sought for the ideas of poetry. While they cherish these ideas as their own deepest personal convictions, yet they are not willing that their systematic analysis should be attempted. Natural science alone gives certainty and truth; compared with science these ideas are illusions. Yet they are illusions which interest the imagination, and which have power over the heart. Better leave them as they are, these critics say, than attempt a philosophy of them which would be equally an illusion, and which, dull and pretentious, would not touch even the feelings. And yet Professor Green says, in substance, he must insist that fundamental ideas of life and conduct cannot be left to the domain of individual feeling, of poetry, but have an independent justification in the shape of philosophy. This justification he finds to be the more necessary, because, unless the validity of the deeper ideas of poetry and religion can be shown, the conception of a man as a moral being must also vanish. If the underlying ideas of poetry are incompatible with natural science, ethics must also be eliminated. Yet we cannot deny physical science. What shall we do? Analyze the conditions of science, or connected knowledge of matters of fact, and see if it does not presuppose a principle which is not scientific, that is, a principle which is not a matter of fact. If we find embedded in the heart of knowledge of nature a principle not natural, we may then ask whether this same principle is not active in moral experience, if it does not have an expression in the consciousness of a moral ideal and in action in accordance with this ideal.

Professor Green begins accordingly with the complete acceptance of physical science,—not merely of its details, but of its methods and principles. Not in spite of, but through these principles he expects to justify the reality of spiritual and moral ideas. A right examination of science will show it to be not an enemy of poetry and religion, but a most helpful ally. But these phrases should not be misunderstood. It is not science as a body of knowledge of matters of sensible facts, nor science in its characteristic physical methods, that points to an ideal principle which morals may employ. On the contrary, there is an antithesis between the natural and the moral. But a *metaphysical* analysis of science will reveal, as the basis of natural science, a principle which transcends nature, a principle which is spiritual.

If this is true, one may well ask why the belief should be almost universally current that there is something hostile to religion in the principles of science. Green found the reason for this seeming contradiction in the current interpretation of the characteristic empirical philosophy of Great Britain. This interpretation seemed to make spiritual ideas an outlaw, while it amply justified the methods and categories of "experience" and of the science of nature. If this interpretation were correct, if it were possible for a philosophy at once to guarantee a knowledge of the sensible, and render invalid any knowledge of that which lies beyond the sensible, the position that from the fortress of science turns its guns upon religion would be impregnable. Green's first efforts were directed, naturally, to an investigation of this empirical philosophy. He wished to show that it was no more compatible with science than it was with religion; that a consistent interpretation of Empiricism sapped the roots of knowledge as well as of faith. Empiricism cannot be worked in two opposite directions at once. It cannot bless science and curse religion. Green believed that Hume was the historic proof of this statement,—that his skepticism was the legitimate outcome of Locke's empiricism. It was because contemporary thought failed to recognize this that it trusted science as natural and positive, while rejecting philosophy and religion as fanciful and arbitrary. It retained Hume's negation as to theology, but not as to knowledge. It adopted just enough of his skepticism to cling to science and to reject philosophy. Green's first work was, therefore, in a sense, negative and polemic; it was to go over the movement from Locke to Hume, and to show how completely and inevitably it led to a skepticism which meted out to science the same measure that the anachronistic empiricism of to-day would mete out only to religion. This once accomplished, a truly constructive movement might occur. Modern consciousness might be trusted not to deny science, and having once realized that an empirical philosophy made it impossible, would turn to a spiritual philosophy which would justify it. This done, the application of the spiritual principle to ethics and theology would follow as matter of course. This represents fairly, I think, the underlying motive and the general character of Green's first important philosophic work,—the "Introductions" to Hume's *Treatise of Human Nature*.

To give a synopsis of almost four hundred closely printed octavo pages in a magazine article would be neither possible nor edifying. The mode in which the examination is carried on is, however, highly characteristic of Green. The criticism is exhaustive and laborious to the last degree. It contains a minute and thorough analysis of Locke, Berkeley, and Hume, which does not content itself with general views and theories, but takes up every detail of doctrine that in any way bears upon their underlying principles. Nor is it an external criticism. The examination is of Locke himself, and not of Locke as tested by some other thinker. The criticism is directed towards discovering his own self-consistency, and the reasons which made it practically impossible for him to be self-consistent.

The general result may be stated apart from all detail. The contention of Green is that while empiricism must

either make intelligence a mere product or deny to it all
constructive function, as matter of fact it cannot get along
without ascribing certain powers to intelligence. Stated in
another way, empiricism must always base its explanations
upon the reality of certain relations, but these relations,
according to its own theory, must be products. The *basis* of
empiricism is the reality of some relation, whether with
Locke that of substance, or with Hume that of succession.
But the result of empiricism is that every relation is a mere
product of sensations. This contradiction is essential to the
very method of empiricism. It is, to use illustrations of
Professor Green, as if a geologist were to teach that the first
formation of rocks was the product of all layers built upon
it, or as if a physiologist were to teach that a certain digestive act, exercised by some organism, was the cause of that
organism. If the minimum of relation due to intelligence and
not to external causes be allowed, constructive function is
allowed to intelligence, and we have a spiritual principle at
the basis of experience, a principle which may be the source
of morals and of religion as well as of experience and
science. But if all relation is eliminated, then experience as
well as science must be eliminated. "A consistent sensationalism would be speechless."

Three years afterward, in 1877, Green returned to the
charge,—but this time it was the philosophy of Herbert
Spencer and of G. H. Lewes that received his criticism. His
object was the same as in his earlier work: to show the
incompatibility of an empirical philosophy with science, and
to show the necessity for English-speaking people of a new
departure in philosophy. Professor Green had learned, he
tells us in the introductory paragraph of his new work, that
"each generation requires the questions of philosophy to be
put to it in its own language, and, unless they are so put,
will not be at the pains to understand them." As Spencer
and Lewes were the typical representatives of the same kind
of thought as that of Locke and Hume, the philosophy that
separated reality from intelligence, Professor Green thought
he could best justify a philosophy which made reality depend upon intelligence, by an examination of these writers.
It was characteristic of Spencer's philosophy that using the

same empirical method as the earlier empiricists, framing the same theory of knowledge, as built up of impressions forced upon the mind from without, it had tried to unite with this theory of knowledge a positive, constructive philosophy which should rest upon the certainty of particular scientific facts and laws, and upon the certainty of the fundamental conceptions of science, such as the relation of cause and effect, the principle of the persistence of force, etc. Spencer, like Hume, regards knowledge as built up out of sensations; he moves a more extensive, a more cumbrous machinery, but, after all, his encyclopædic marshalling of facts, his broad deploying of scientific forces, comes to the sensational theory of knowledge that possessed the earlier empiricists. And yet Spencer frames a theory of the development of the universe, of life, of mind, and of society. Here, without going into details, is where Green finds the vulnerable point of Spencer. He unites a theory of knowledge which makes science impossible with a theory of the construction of the universe built up at every point upon science. Spencer denies all constructive, all synthetic function to intelligence; he makes intelligence a product of events and forces which are not intelligent. All knowledge is thus a product, an effect of something wholly unrelated to intelligence, hence unknowable. Between knowledge and reality there is thus a great gap fixed. And yet Spencer tells what the laws and forces of the universe are, and how they have produced life and mind. Science, as a body of facts, is to be implicitly relied upon; science, as the process and product of human intelligence, has no objective value. On this contradiction the philosophy of Spencer is based.

Spencer, in a word, only tells us, taking a longer, more roundabout road than the earlier empiricists followed, using the life of the race instead of that of an individual, that experience is the source of knowledge, while he has a theory of experience which would not allow it to be the source of anything. The question, the real question of philosophy, is thus left unanswered: What is experience? How is it constituted? In his *Prolegomena to Ethics* Green takes up this question at first hand. It is impossible even to give the successive steps of the argument, much less the reasonings upon which the conclusions depend. We may, however, summarize some of the leading results. If we ask what is implied in saying that any experience is real instead of illusory, or if we ask how it is that we can distinguish between being and seeming, between fact and fancy, the answer is, because there is a connected whole of experience, "a nature of things." What is mere seeming or unreal is not capable of becoming a member of this unified world. In this unity of the world there is further implied the existence of a single, permanent, and all-inclusive system of relations. But even now we have not found an ultimate fact in which intelligence may rest. We have to ask what is implied in the existence of this system of relations. And the answer is, that its existence has meaning only upon the supposition of a permanent single consciousness which forms the bond of relations,—"an eternal intelligence realized in the related facts of the world."

If it seems to be a far cry from our ability to distinguish fact from fancy to the proof of an eternal self-consciousness, the reader must attribute the gaps to our summary, and not to the argument of Professor Green. The reader must also avoid confusing the argument of Green with the so-called causal proof of the existence of God. The argument does not attempt to show that God is necessary as a cause of the world, but that in the existence of knowable fact, in the existence of that which we call reality, there is necessarily implied an intelligence which is one, self-distinguishing and not subject to conditions of space and time. This intelligence cannot be identified with *our* intelligence, that is, with an intelligence which has a succession of experiences in time, because *our* intelligence is only "a part of the partial world"; it is part of that experience which is to be accounted for. What, then, is the relation of our intelligence to this eternal divine intelligence? Just this, according to Green: the eternal intelligence reproduces itself in us, partially and gradually; it communicates to us piecemeal, but in inseparable correlation, experience, and the world of which we have experience, understanding, and the facts understood.

These are the two fundamental positions of Green's

constructive work: on one side an eternal self-consciousness, as involved in the reality of experience; on the other side, human consciousness as a progressive reproduction of this divine consciousness. Since there is a tendency in some minds to call every philosophic theory pantheistic which does not offer itself as the baldest deism, it may be well to call attention to the two traits which distinguish Green's philosophy from pantheism. One of these traits is found in the relation of God to the world. God may, indeed, be thought as the unity of the world, but only as its *spiritual* unity. God and the world are not facts of the same order, as they must be according to pantheism. God is *self*-consciousness; that is, a consciousness which distinguishes itself from every fact of nature, and from the sum total of such facts, although *apart* from nature this consciousness would not be what it is. In the second place, while pantheism would make the relation of human consciousness to the world and to God one of bare identity and absorption, the relation, according to Green, is one of spiritual, personal unity, and this implies that there be really spirit, personality on *both* sides of the relation.

It may be well to give a statement substantially in Green's own language of what is meant by the human self or man. Our consciousness may mean, he says, either of two things: either a function of the animal organism, which is being made, gradually and with interruptions, a vehicle of the eternal consciousness, or that eternal consciousness itself, as making the animal organism its vehicle. In this process, by which the divine self-consciousness makes the animal operations organic to its own reproduction, it is subject to the limitations and qualifications of the physical conditions to which it subjects itself; and yet, in itself, it retains its essential characteristic, that of being self-consciousness. And so, too, the product, the human consciousness, carries with it under all its limitations and qualifications the characteristic of being an object to itself. Of both the divine and the human consciousness, in other words, it may be said that it is spirit, for each is an object to itself; and of both it may be said that it is person, for each is an end in itself. Of self-consciousness, or spiritual personality, whether in God or in man, it may be said that it is "the only thing that is real in its own right; the only thing of which the reality is not relative and derived."

Experience thus means the continual reproduction in man of an eternal consciousness. This reproduction is limited by physical conditions, by the fact that it takes place in what is otherwise an animal organism, and thus the resulting experience is sensible and not merely rational. Yet this experience, so far as it has any meaning, retains the marks of its spiritual, its rational source; experience comes to us in successive moments, but that which is brought by experience neither comes nor goes,—it is the permanent divine intelligence. Science is simply *orderly* experience. It is the working out of the relations, the laws, implied in experience, but not visible upon its surface. It is a more adequate reproduction of the relations by which the eternal self-consciousness constitutes both nature and our understandings. It is clear how such a doctrine prepares the way for a moral theory,—indeed, in his *Prolegomena*, Green introduces it simply for the sake of getting a philosophical basis for ethics. Having found that in respect to his knowledge man is not a child of nature, but holds from a spiritual source, there is reason to apprehend that this spiritual principle may find expression in action: in consciousness of a moral ideal, and in the determination of action by it.

In truth, we find that man's organism makes him not only a being of sensations, but of impulses and of wants. And just as the sensations, by becoming the organs of a divine spirit, are transformed into theoretic experience and science, so the impulses and wants, as *media* of the same divine spirit, are transformed into practical experience, into moral action. The reproduction in man of the consciousness which is an end-in-itself makes man an end in himself, and gives his actions, therefore, both an absolute law and an absolute ideal or good. As the action of the divine consciousness upon passing sensations makes them into an experience of what *is*, so the same consciousness acting upon transitory impulses creates our practical world, our conception of what is not, but *should* be, *ought* to be. The reproduction of the divine intelligence in us is, therefore, as much a condition of moral as of scientific experience. Indeed, it is more than a condition: the reproduction of the divine intelligence through the organism of our needs and our impulses to satisfy them *constitutes* our moral experience. A purely animal intelligence, one whose life was constituted by sensations and impulses alone, has no conception of any ideal world, of anything that ought to be, of any good, or of any duty. The wholly divine intelligence knows no distinction of real and ideal; the *ought* and the *is* are one to God. But a being like man, in whom the divine has supervened upon the animal, must know that something ought to be, the divine intelligence, the divine will, which for him is not. Hence the constant conflict of the moral life; hence the necessity of living it by faith, not by sight; living, that is, by the conception of something which absolutely ought to be, rather than by the perception of what can be sensibly verified as already in existence.

But this general outline of Green's moral views must be made somewhat more specific. We may, perhaps, best accomplish this by analyzing into four stages our moral experience; that is, the relation of our actions arising from animal wants to the divine practical reason or will. (1) The mere presence of the divine consciousness to our wants constitutes an ideal self, which is both an absolute good and an absolute obligation. And if we ask concerning the nature of this absolute good, *what* it is as distinct from the mere fact *that* it is, the answer is (2), that it can be found only in some development of *persons*, and in that relation of persons to one another which we call *society*; and (3), if this answer is still vague, we may know that the consciousness of an ideal of this nature has been the parent of the institutions and usages and of the social judgments and aspirations through which human life has hitherto been bettered. Hence from these institutions and aspirations we may judge more concretely as to the nature of the ideal. (4) Man's *actual* achievements in morality, his virtue, is decided by the degree in which he is habitually responsive to the demands made upon him by the various institutions and customs in which the ideal good has already embodied itself, and to the spirit which is their source.

The first point is, in substance, that the presence of the permanent self-distinguishing consciousness in man determines man's real good. His good cannot be found in the satisfaction of this and that want, in the enjoyment of this and that pleasure, or in any possible series of pleasures. For the satisfaction of such wants does not satisfy the man, the person. His personality *is*, and is *what* it is only through the activity in him of the divine reason, and only that can really satisfy him which satisfies this reason. This can be found only in its own complete reproduction. What man wants is not satisfaction of any given impulse, but satisfaction of self, and this can be found only in God, because God is man's true self. In other words, by virtue of the supervention of God upon man's animal wants and impulses, man has certain capabilities and aspirations which can be adequately named only by calling them divine. In the realization of these capabilities, human because more than animal, is man's good to be found. This good, the ideal self, is also a law to man. It is absolutely obligatory, that is, obligatory without qualification or exception. It is obligatory because it is man's own real self. Were it a law or a goodness merely external to him, man might be forced or constrained to it, but he could never be obliged to it. But because it is the reality of his own being, man recognizes it as a law binding upon him. It is man's own duty to strive for perfection, because this striving is the expression of his own nature.

The statement that God is the ideal, or even the true self of man, is liable to interpretation from the wrong side, and, indeed, has often been so interpreted. It is taken to mean that God is only a projection of man; that he is an ideal that man forms of what man would be were he perfect, and that, therefore, God has no reality excepting as a conception of man's ideal, and that God becomes real in the degree in which man realizes his ideal. But this is a complete inversion of Green's thought. The reality of God in himself is a condition of our having the notion of Him as our own ideal self, of our attempts, our striving to make this ideal real, and of our measure of success. Human nature is rather the projection of God, that is, the reproduction of Him, through physical conditions, than God the projection of man's ideal. Man forms the conception of what he may possibly be, only because in itself this possibility is more than possible, because it is forever actual. "God *is* all which the human spirit is capable of becoming."

It is hardly a satisfactory explanation of moral experience, however, to say *that* there is an absolute good and an absolute duty constituted by the presence in us of a divine intelligence. We want to know *what* this good is; *what* we shall do in order to do our duty. In part, it must be confessed that this question cannot be answered. We cannot say what in fullness the ideal is until we have realized it. What our capabilities are we shall never know until we have manifested them. Yet every manifestation must conform to the nature of the ideal self which it manifests, and must be a partial revelation of its nature. From these two facts we shall be able to define somewhat more adequately the nature of the ideal.

Secondly, then, since the principle which is reproducing itself in us is a self-conscious personality, we may know that its reproduction must also be a self-conscious personality. Of one thing we may be sure: "Our ultimate standard of worth is an ideal of *personal* worth. All other values are relative to value for, of, or in a person." This ideal cannot be found, then, in impersonal humanity, in some national or world consciousness, in some organization of society, nor in some far-off event, however divine, towards which the world is supposed to be making. "The spiritual progress of mankind is an unmeaning phrase unless it means a progress *of* personal character, and *to* personal character,—a progress of which feeling, thinking, and willing subjects are the agents and substainers." But, on the other hand, this progress can be realized only in society. While its beginning, its process, and its end is in an individual, yet without society, and the conditions afforded by it, there can be no individual, no person. "Society is the condition of development of a personality." "Social life is to personality what language is to thought. Human society presupposes persons in *capacity*, but it is only in the intercourse of men, each recognized by each as an end, not merely a means, and thus as having reciprocal claims, that the capacity is actualized, and that

we really live as persons." And not to speak of society at
large, from a historical point of view, we know that we now
"learn to regard ourselves as persons among other persons,
because we are treated as such. It is through the action of
society that the individual comes practically to conceive his
own personality and to conceive the same personality as
belonging to others; it is society, also, that supplies all the
higher content to this conception, all those objects of a
man's personal interest, in living for which he lives for his
own satisfaction, except such as are derived from the merely
animal nature." This much at least, then, we know of the
end of moral conduct: it is to be found only in the perfection
of persons living together as persons, that is, living in
society.

But, thirdly, the divine consciousness not only presents
itself to man as an ideal in which the capacities of all
persons are realized, but it has communicated itself to some
degree already in man's experience; man's wants and desires and choices have already, to some degree, become the
vehicles or organs of the realization of the divine practical
reason or will. This communication, piecemeal, interrupted,
has constituted the moral experience of the life of the individual and of society in history. History, indeed, cannot be
defined, excepting as the process by which a divine will,
determined by reason, has articulated wants, desires, and
ideas, by making them organic to its own reproduction. The
idea that there is an absolute good, an ideal personality
living in ideal relations to other persons, has been the moving spring, the vital source of all history, while the attempts
to realize it have been the parent of all that makes history
more than a mere succession of events; of its institutions, of
the family, the state, and the church, and of all the customs,
laws, and aspirations of society.

The progress thus made in history in giving the inchoate idea of the good, definite articulation may be considered
under two aspects. One is the extension of the area of the
common good, the practical widening of the range of those
who are considered members of society or interested in the
same good. The other is the fuller determination of the
content of this good. For in either case, it must be

noticed that the good can be conceived only as a *common* good. This was implied when it was said that personality could be realized only in a society of persons. It is implied in the fact that the very idea of a divine consciousness reproducing itself in humanity does away with "all respect of persons." Each being in whom God so communicates himself is a person, an end in himself, and has the rights of personality. An ideal so constituted cannot be exclusive, cannot be other than common. If we put it in a more psychological way, the person who is to realize his capacities has interests in persons; not merely interests in them so far as they are *means* to his own gratification, but interest in them as in himself—interest in their good as in his own. Man cannot be thought as man without this fundamental social interest. This social interest cannot by any possibility be developed or evolved from forms of life which do not already in germ possess it. It is an ultimate fact in human history; a fact without which there would not be human history; a fact not deducible from any other history. A unity of interest, a conception of well-being common to a number of persons, however small the number, the idea of community is the necessary presupposition of all human history. Once given this community, this number of persons who conceive themselves and one another as persons, as ends in themselves, and any conceivable development of morality is possible. Without it, morality has no existence.

Progress in knowledge of and realization of the moral ideal has consisted largely just in the widening of the number of persons among whom there is conceived to be a common good, and between whom there is a common duty. So far as we can discover, in what we call the early periods, the area of those conceived to have common ends was limited to the family, or, at most, to the grouping of families of common birth in the tribe. And even in these limited areas, the grasp of the idea of community of welfare was feeble and incomplete. The woman, the child, were theoretically, and in large manner practically, outside society,—society being defined as the group of persons recognizing themselves and each other as persons. To-day, theoretically at least, it is a belief, almost an axiom, that there is a potential

duty of every man to every other man,—a duty which becomes actual so soon as one has dealings with the other. The
Stoic philosopher, the Roman jurist, the Christian teacher,
have all contributed to the development of the idea of human
equality; the idea that every man and woman is a sharer in
the common good, and hence has the rights and claims of
personality.

If we interrupt the exposition a moment, it is worth
while to notice the extent to which this idea of the value of
personality, of the potentialities contained in the lowest and
the worst of mankind, was a governing motive in the life of
Green. His conscience was developed to a point in which it
became a public and political force as well as a private and
"moral" monitor. His political and historical writings, as
well as his purely philosophical ones, show that he realized
the idea of the personality embodied in every individual, not
merely as a theoretic proposition, but as a claim, even as a
burden upon himself; and his life, as a teacher and as a
citizen, is full of evidence that the "enthusiasm of humanity" was not a vague phrase, an abstract formula, nor an
emotional indulgence with him, but the ruling motive of his
life. To him as to Aristotle the virtues of a good man are
identical with those of the good citizen, and citizenship was
widened from the Greek *polis* to a kingdom "as wide as the
Humanity for which Christ died."

But this extension of the area of the sharers in the
common good is not the only sign of growing correctness in
the moral ideal. Progress is also marked in the fuller content
given to the conception of the common good. In one sense,
indeed, there cannot be said to have been any growth in the
conception. To the Greek philosophers who first articulated
the conception as to the most reflective moralist of to-day,
goodness consisted in "purity of heart," that is, in a character controlled by interest in the good for its own sake, in
conscious direction of the will to human perfection. But as
habits and institutions have arisen in answer to this demand
for perfection, our conception of what this perfection is has
become richer and fuller, and the demands it makes upon us
more comprehensive. "Faculties, dispositions, occupations,
persons, of which a Greek citizen would have taken no

account, or taken account only to despise, are now recognized as having their place in the realization of the powers of the human soul." And "where the Greek saw a supply of possibly serviceable labor, having no end or function but to be made really serviceable to the privileged few, the Christian citizen sees a multitude of persons, who in their actual condition may have no advantage over the slaves of an ancient state, but who, in undeveloped possibility, and in the claims which arise out of that possibility, are all that he himself is. Seeing this, he finds a necessity laid upon him." If we apply this principle to virtues like fortitude and temperance, we find that in idea, in underlying motive, these virtues were the same to the Greek as they are to us. Bravery, then as now meant willingness to do and to bear, to any extreme, in the service of the highest public cause that the agent can conceive, — in one case the cause of the state, in the other, of the kingdom of God, — because it is the more excellent way so to do. But because man has realized his possibilities now so much more than in Greece, because he has revealed so much more his possibilities, the application of bravery is so much wider, so much more exacting, that it hardly seems like the same virtue. Aristotle found it only in the citizen-soldier willing to die for the state. Now the will to endure even unto death finds objects worthy to call forth this will where the Greek saw nothing but ugliness and meanness. It finds expression in the obscure laver of love, as well as in the splendid heroism at which a world wonders. So temperance to the Greek meant only control of the appetites of hunger, thirst, and sex, in the interests of the higher life. That was the sole conception of self-denial open to the Greek. But now interest in the problem of social deliverance, in the development of the "mass of men whom we call brethren, and whom we declare to be meant with us for eternal destinies," forbids a surrender to enjoyments, however innocent, however valuable in themselves, which do not aid in this social deliverance. But we should not allow any self-gratulation over the greater fullness of our moral ideal to hide from us the failures in its realizations. In large degree, the ideal is negative. "It makes itself felt in certain prohibitions, as of slavery, but it has no such effect on the

ordering of life as to secure for those whom we admit not to
be slaves much real opportunity of self-development. So far
as negative rights go,—rights to be let alone,—they are
admitted to membership in civil society, but the good things
to which the pursuits of society are in fact directed turn out
to be no good things for them. Civil society is founded on
the idea of there being a common good, but that idea in
relation to the less favored members of society is unrealized,
and it is unrealized because the good is being sought in
objects which admit of being competed for."

And this brings us to the fourth point under discussion. The first point was, the reader will recall, our consciousness of absolute obligation and good; the second, the
fact that this good consists in the perfections of persons in
society; the third, that the search for this perfection has been
the source of the institutions, habits, and aspirations of
society, and has found expression and got meaning in them;
and the fourth, that the moral character of the individual is
based upon the extent to which he is loyal to the good
embodied in these institutions, in the family, the realm of
social relations, and in the kingdom of God on earth, and
upon the degree in which he endeavors to react upon these
institutions so as to embody in them more fully the freedom
of humanity. It is not enough that man should conform
faithfully to the ideals already articulated in the social relations about him; he must remember the infinite nature of
this ideal; the infinite capacities yet unrealized. And thus the
temper of the individual—so far as he is what he should
be—is a spiritual act which may be described either as
self-abasement or self-exaltation. "Towards an infinite spirit,
which is really the only ideal, the attitude of man, at his
highest and completest, could still be only that of self-
abasement before an ideal of holiness," and yet this attitude must be "one in which the heart is lifted up to God,
in which the whole inner man goes forth after an ideal of
personal holiness." Awe and aspiration, the sources of all
achievements in history, of all advance in individual life,
must be, when all is said and done, the final form of human
endeavor,—awe, marking the individual's sense of the petty
achievements of himself and of humanity before the realities

and requirements of the Infinite Spirit; aspiration, as the realization that this Infinite Spirit is still one in principle with man's spirit, and is, therefore, to be forever aimed at. The most perfect expressions of the moral life may be said to be found in the spirit of the expressions of St. Paul to the Philippians: "I count not myself to have apprehended: but this one thing I do, forgetting those things which are behind and reaching forth unto those things which are before, I press towards the mark for the prize of the high calling of God in Christ Jesus,"—the lowest humility as to self, conjoined with the highest aspiration for self.

This, then, is the sum of the matter. The Spirit of God, of the eternal Reason and Will, which is one with our spirit, because it is one, presents itself to man as the perfect good, and as the source of unconditional duty. As so presenting itself, it has moved man to action, and this action has found expression in history, in the institutions, the laws, the customs, and the expectations, the rights and duties that make our life what it is. The individual introduced into the circle of these complex relations finds this social order, this embodiment of divine Reason, confronting him and demanding of him allegiance and loyalty. This social order is thus the source of obligations to the individual; he is bound to loyal service and self-devotion in courage, temperance, wisdom, self-denial, justice. He is bound, not because this order confronts him externally, but because it is the expression of the Spirit that is in him; because it expresses in reality his own being, which is as yet only in capacity. But in fulfilling these duties man learns of other duties and of other goods. He finds that his highest achievements come short of answering even to the demands which actual institutions and laws make upon him, and he finds that these actual institutions are, after all, but feeble and imperfect expressions of the Spirit which makes him and them what they are in possibility as well as in fact. And thus he finds his highest good in what are sometimes called the "religious virtues," in faith, in humility, in awe, in aspiration, in longing for the union of man's will with God's. But these virtues are one in source and principle with the commonest virtues of everyday life. The attitude of will that finds expression in them finds expression in every recognition of duty, in every attempt by which man sets himself to better himself and others, in every service which the father does in the family, which the citizen performs in the state in the interest of the good of the family and of the state.

What has just been said gives an opportunity for a brief statement of Green's religious views. Religious, it is evident, his whole theory is. Science and the moral life— both are based on the communication to us of a divine, perfect Spirit. Science is inexplicable except upon the supposition of an eternal, all-inclusive Intelligence which reproduces itself in us; the life of duty and of the good is this communication in us of the divine Reason and Will. It would be to be false to the memory of Green to attempt to identify his theories with extraneous creeds, or to attempt to win favor for his philosophy by claiming its agreement with any form of orthodoxy, or by relieving it of any kinship with views that are unpopular. The intellectual sincerity of Green, perfect to human eye, would rebuke any such effort. But since Mrs. Ward so evidently means Grey for Professor Green, and since the two are being popularly identified, it is but historic justice to say that Green's religious teaching goes farther than the position just laid down. Green undoubtedly held that in Jesus Christ this communication of God, which in us, at best, is partial and hindered by seeking of the private self, was perfect and pure. Christ was to Green, in actuality, what every man is in capacity; He was in reality what we are in idea. Undoubtedly he held that Christ was subject to the same physical conditions and possessed of the same physical powers as all men; he would allow neither a miraculous birth nor miraculous, that is, supernatural power; but morally and spiritually, he held Christ to have embodied in his personality perfect union with the Spirit of God. Furthermore, the self-abasement and the self-exaltation which are the highest attainments of the moral life find their adequate expression in language when termed sharing in the death and resurrection of Christ. For it is the death and resurrection of Jesus as eternal facts, as the fundamental expressions of the true life of the Spirit, that are of avail to us. We share in the death of Christ when we share in his spirit of absolute sacrifice of all self-seeking and selfish interest and will; we share in his resurrection when we share in the unity of his Spirit and Will with God's. For the resurrection is the other side of the crucifixion; it is the life of the Spirit, as the crucifixion is the death of the flesh. The desire of St. Paul that he may forget the things that are behind, and reach forth unto the things that are before, also finds expression in his aspiration to know the fellowship of Christ's suffering, to be made comformable unto his death, if by any means he may attain unto the resurrection of the dead. And this is the highest expression of the ethics of Professor Green. We are saved, to use the theological formula, so far as there really is in us interrupted, imperfect, partial though it be, union with that death and resurrection which in Christ was eternal, perfect, and entire.

# The Lesson of Contemporary French Literature

Among the youngest French critics it is Bourget, perhaps, who wears the mantle of Sainte-Beuve. The older writer did not live in the stress of modern science, and his work is more personal and genial, while the abstract and philosophic tendencies often master Bourget. But the latter is yet the inheritor of the spirit of the former. They both understand the word "critic" in the same sense. With each it means putting one's self at the standpoint of the author and seeing what he sees, but with the additional advantage of knowing why he sees as he does. While it is still a rarity to find an English critic who will sympathize enough with a writer to comprehend him, Sainte-Beuve founded a school whose first word is that sympathy is the sole condition of comprehension. And while the English critic who does sympathize and understand usually becomes an enthusiast, a partisan, the French critic remembers that the function of criticism is not exhausted when the meaning of an author is penetrated and exhibited; we must know also the forces which led him, the causes which influenced him in his thought. Criticism, in a word, as understood by the French, is the ability to stand with and outside of an author at the same time. Sympathy and detachment are its mottoes.

Bourget's *Essais de Psychologie Contemporaine* suggests by its very title the characteristics of the essays contained in it. It is not the psychology of the schools; as the word is ordinarily used, it is not psychology at all. But it is criticism of the souls of the writers passed in review. Its aim

[*First published in the* Christian Union, *XL* (*11 July 1889*), 38–39. *Not previously reprinted.*]

is not external description, but internal penetration. It is psychological analysis of the French spirit as revealed in its representative authors; it is the dissection of their thoughts, their emotions, their attitude toward the problems of life. These volumes, then, are something more than endeavors to give various poets and essayists their relative standings. In the thoroughness and subtlety with which they track thoughts back to their germ, in the grasp in which they hold these thoughts connected with the contemporary movements of life, they become intellectual history—a picture of the French consciousness. And it is as such a record that I wish to present them here. Bourget is a critic, not a moralist; and yet there is more textual matter for the moralist in these two small volumes than in many bulky ethical dissertations. They show us the spiritual bankruptcy of the current thinking of a great nation; and they show its origin. Bourget is not a preacher; but his volumes are a comment on one small text: "Without faith ye can do nothing."

But Bourget shall speak for himself. What does he find to be the characteristic note of contemporary French emotion and thought? Hear him. His first volume closes with the words: "I have examined a poet, Baudelaire; a historian, Renan; a novelist, Flaubert; a philosopher, Taine; I have just finished examining one of these composite artists in whom the critic and the creative writer are closely united [Stendhal]; and I have found in all five the same creed of the thoroughgoing emptiness of the universe. These magnificent minds are completely nauseated with the vain strivings of life." His second volume begins: "From all the works passed in review in these ten essays there seems to breathe the same uneasy influence—an influence profoundly and continuously pessimistic." Everywhere, he concludes, is there to be found the gradual enfeebling and paralysis of the will; the decay of hope, courage, and endeavor; the growing belief that the world is a bankrupt, passing paper notes which it cannot redeem.

But the interest does not center in this general conclusion. It gathers about the analysis of the various influences which have shaped this pessimism, and the various forms which it takes. Of the many which Bourget signalizes, we shall select three: dilettanteism, the influence of physical science, and (very briefly) romanticism. It is Renan who affords the occasion for the study of dilettanteism—a term, as Bourget remarks, difficult to define, for it represents rather an attitude of mind than a formulated doctrine. The term, in his use of it, however, means something more than a mere playing at everything. Its significance may be understood when we find that, according to him, Goethe is the great dilettante. It is love of culture for itself. It is capacity for emotional and intellectual metamorphosis, and a capacity which finds constant exercise. It is not far different from the brutal definition by an English writer of liberalism: the feeling that so many things in general are true that nothing in particular is very true. It is, more delicately expressed, a disposition which induces a thinker to lend himself to all points of view without giving himself to any. Its favorite expression is of "shades" of truth. There is no white light; there is an infinite number of shades.

It is not, then, to be confounded with skepticism. It is not inability to discover truth; it is a surfeit of truths. It is not the weariness of mind which says that there is so much to be said on every side of a question that no good comes of investigation; it is the very height of mental agility which plays about all these sides and successively realizes them. It can assert nothing absolutely; there must be the reservation in favor of the contrary also—also, mark you, and not instead. Life, truth, and reality are complex. They cannot be grasped as wholes. Nay, how shall dogmatism go so far as to say that they are wholes? They must be grasped here and there. We get at fragments, and each shift of the kaleidoscope is as true as any other. Hence the true dilettante must refuse to give himself up to any creed, for decisions imply a fixity of mind not consistent with the ability of the soul to vibrate with every note of truth. Every conclusion is an exclusion. Experience is composite, flexile, many-sided. Decisions are hard, fast, and rigorously limited.

If this is not skepticism, it comes to the same result. The part of the wise man is to take no part. His business is to comprehend the dreams of others—nay, more, to let them play through his soul, that he may realize all there is in life, and yet to remember that as one goes another comes which may contradict it. When there are so many values in the world, who shall assert an absolute value? Thus dilettanteism leads to pessimism. It is not the wild pessimism of the nihilist; it is not the soured pessimism of Schopenhauer; it is the mild and tender consciousness that the doom of transitoriness is upon all aspects of life, upon all forms of what we call truth. The sentiment that all shades of belief have their own relative justification, that from its own standpoint each is as true as any other, is, in reality, the sentiment that no belief has justification. Such a feeling is pessimistic, for it finds that the universe takes no sides; it is more than impartial—it is indifferent. The world of the lover of culture has no bias in favor of anything—not even of truth and goodness. It teaches but one thing—the hopelessness of action which is more than playing with various forms of experience in order to obtain from them some self-development. Its imperative is only: Do not give yourself to any; use them only for your own rounded development. And since men have never been able long to persuade themselves that their value is more than that of the universe, the result is pessimism. One cannot but wish that he could follow in detail the application by Bourget of these thoughts to the *credo* of Renan, but we must content ourselves with this impersonal exposition.

This love of many-sided personal development is not the only tendency working for pessimism. Flaubert, De Lisle, Taine, exemplify, if we trust Bourget, a pessimism resulting from the effect of physical science upon the imagination and the emotions. Realism and naturalism are, as he shows, the outcome of the application of scientific methods to human life. The procedure of realism is to start from the exact representation of a group of facts, and then analyze these till we discover their causes. Such a method has no place for personality or character. Such words are only terms which point out a particular set of effects. They are products of antecedent and surrounding forces. Literature becomes a study of heredity and environment. Human nature is simply one part of physical nature. Reason and health are, in Taine's words, happy accidents. Physical nature is a series of ceaseless changes, every change having its cause, and every change having its justification in this cause. From the standpoint of physical science (that is, leaving out purposes or ends), disease is as natural as health, insanity as sanity. Each has its antecedent cause, and what more can you ask for? To quote Taine again: "Moral beings as well as physical are a series of events of which nothing is permanent except the law of change. Nature is one vast aurora borealis." Necessity and change—these are the two conceptions of physical science, and, applied to the treatment of human life in literature, they resolve all human aspirations, loves, and ideals into the insignificant outcome of petty changes. All hope is vain, all effort is fruitless, all aspiration unavailing. Thus there arises from another instrument the swelling tone of the worthlessness of life—the tone of a saddened pessimism. Nature responds to the simulacrum of personality with the ruthless ongoing of blind changes; we can but yield ourselves, and in yielding give up the possibility of moral action and of religious faith. Life is shorn and empty.

Romanticism, again, has proved a tributary to pessimism. Romanticism is the attempt to find the satisfaction of life in the enjoyment of intense emotions; in the constant renewal of feeling; in the production of remote and unwonted forms of sentiment. If the dilettante would put himself in all modes of looking at experience, the romanticist would revel in all moods and ranges of emotion. A varied play of passion is his aim. A succession of vast and ever-changing feelings gives life its value. If the traditions and environment of human life do not admit such a succession, flee to far-away times, to the mediæval age, to lands of chivalry, to fairy countries, or, planting yourself in the present epoch, rebel. As it is law which keeps men in grooves, which forbids them the sought-for stream of emotions, disregard law. As it is especially family life which restricts the display of feeling to the channel, away with family life, and in with the freedom of feeling! In all ways and at hazards, fresh, vivid, and continual emotion! Such was the cry of the romanticists in the instances analyzed by Bourget.

But such a banner could lead its adherents to but one field, that of pessimism. The world is not in harmony with such an ideal. The school staked its belief in the worth of life upon the one point whether life affords the desired abundance and intensity of passions; and it found every passion a pathway to a grave. Lord Byron will serve the English reader as an example both of romanticism and of the pessimism which is its inevitable outcome. Flight and rebellion are both in vain. The every-day world is too much for us, and brings us back to a hard routine. Even escape and rebellion leave us with emotions jaded and with no capacity for renewal.

So much, in substance, we may gather from Bourget as he pursues his studies into the influences which made the style and thought of the representatives of the best French literature of the last fifty years. Hugo is almost the only name of the first rank which does not come within his scope. And everywhere—again in his own words—a nausea of these splendid minds at the emptiness of life. Such a tale tells its own moral without the added index finger of *Hæc fabula docet*. Without faith ye can do nothing, ye are nothing. It is something more than decay of faith in this or that doctrine of Christianity, of this or that dogma of the Church, of this or that school of ecclesiasticism. It is lack of faith in the supremacy of spiritual things; nay, in their reality. It is bankruptcy of idealism; it is apotheosis of the things that can be seen and handled. It tells in modern tones and in strange garb the tale of old, that if hope be confined to the things grasped of the senses, and by the culture of the intellect, and in the play of emotions, then is life indeed most miserable. In the moral determination of the will lie peace, hope, and courage; and the moral determination of the will comes not from the culture of the intellect, from the methods of physical science, nor the abundance of pleasure. It is born of faith in unseen ideals. The intellect may set up a multitude of ideals, and find some value in each. It may set off each against the other. Pure intellectualism is dilettanteism. But choice, moral choice, breaks the equilibrium, and asserts the absolute value of one. Such an act of faith declares that even if the universe seems to the intellect indifferent to all ideals, it at least *will* have an ideal of life by which it will measure all, and for which it will stake all. Leave out faith, and you have in human life level plains of equal richness, each bounded with the horizon of ignorance, and with paths leading everywhere and therefore nowhere. Put in faith, and there is perspective; there is background and foreground; there is goal and way. So, too, the methods of physical science, pure naturalism, lead to pessimism simply because they do not allow that free movement of personality called choice. The sole method of manifesting the reality of personality is for personality to manifest itself in the act which chooses the ideal of absolute value. Back of this choice must lie faith in the supreme reality of such an ideal. Faith involves the determination that personality shall not be the playground of natural forces, but shall itself be a moving force counting for something in the universe. Given faith, the pessimism which results from the conclusions of natural science becomes a buoyant faith that the very natural processes are the tributary mechanisms of an end, a purpose, an ideal which does not manifest itself to the eye of sense. Romanticism, again, is the attempt to state the value of life in terms of that which can be immediately experienced, of feeling. It is denial of a criterion which, though unseen, shall serve to measure all that is seen and felt. Each of these three influences reduces itself, then, to lack of faith, to denial of the power of man to lay hold on spiritual reality. This study of French literature but gives an added testimony to the fact that the problem of the nineteenth century reduces itself to a choice between faith and pessimism. In the things which are seen and temporal lies no permanent satisfaction; in the things which are unseen and eternal lies the value of that which passes away.

# Galton's Statistical Methods

*Natural Inheritance*, by Francis Galton, F.R.S. London
and New York: Macmillan and Co., 1889. ix, 259
pp.

This work is of double interest. Its primary purpose is
biological, being to subject the question of heredity to accurate quantitative and mechanical treatment. As such it is
doubtless the ablest work on the subject extant. But in the
course of his investigation Galton has collected a large mass
of statistical information, and, what is more important, has
developed some new and interesting statistical methods. The
key-note to the statistical side of the work is contained in
Galton's statement that statisticians are apt to be content
with averages, while an average is only an isolated fact.
What is wanted is a method of *calculating distribution*,
and a graphic scheme for reading the distribution. For
example, compared with the knowledge of the average income of an English family, a knowledge of how the total
income of England was distributed would be much more
important. This would tell us the proportion which had
incomes of every grade from the lowest to the highest, and
would enable us to rank any given family at its place in the
scale.

Particularly, in dealing with problems of heredity, is a
scheme of distribution necessary. The knowledge of the
average stature of a kinsfolk conveys little; the knowledge of
how this faculty is distributed among the members of the
kindred would be valuable. Galton's first work was to invent

[*First published in the* Publications of the American Statistical
Association, *N.S. I* (*Sept.* 1889), *331–34. Not previously reprinted.*]

a scheme of distribution. The data to be dealt with, for example, are the strength of pull of 519 males as registered on a Salter's machine. The following are the figures: —

| Strength of pull | Percentage |
|---|---|
| Under 50 pounds,........... | 2 |
| "　60　"　　......... | 10 |
| "　70　"　　......... | 37 |
| "　80　"　　......... | 70 |
| "　90　"　　......... | 91 |
| "　100　"　　......... | 95 |
| Over 100　"　　......... | 100 |

This might be illustrated by a diagram: —

The percentages of strength are marked off on a base line, the number of pounds on the right-hand perpendicular line. Then from each per cent, 2, 10, 37, etc., is erected a perpendicular to a height equal to the corresponding number of pounds,—*i.e.*, from 37 per cent would be erected a perpendicular to a height equal to 70 pounds, since 37 per cent pulled less than 70 pounds. While a line connecting these various perpendiculars will be broken, it is evident that, if the data were numerous enough, and the strengths more closely taken, say to every pound, we would get, approximately, a curved line. The figure, bounded by a curve of this kind is a scheme of distribution. (The perpendiculars, since they serve only for scaffolding, would not apppear in an ordinary scheme.) By taking the measured strength of any individual on the side scale, say 74 pounds, carrying over a horizontal line until it meets the curve, and then dropping a perpendicular to meet the base line, the proportionate rank of the individual may be read off,—in this case 50 degrees. In other words, since 50 per cent exceed and 50 per cent fall short of his strength, he occupies a medium position, and his strength is mediocre. This position Galton always designates by м, and this м is always one of the chief constants in Galton's scheme. He notes that the м has three properties. The chance is an equal one that any previously unknown rank falls short of or exceeds м. The most probable value of any previously unknown measure is м; and, if the curve of the scheme is bilaterally symmetrical as respects M, M is identical with the ordinary average or arithmetical mean. It is evident that we have the start for an application of the theory of probability. Now, if the deviation of any grade from M is considered, that is, the error as respects the mean, we find that every measure in a scheme may be expressed by M + (±D), the + or − signifying up or down from M.

Galton's other constant he designates by Q. It is obtained as follows. Take the perpendicular at 75°, and that at 25°. Subtract the latter from the former and divide by 2, and we get a measure of the general *slope* of the curve of distribution, just as M measures the average height of the curved boundary. What it *really* gives is the deviation from the average, both in excess and in deficiency, of one half the number taken. For example, the Q of the scheme of distribution of stature is 1.7 inches. This means that one half the population differs less than 1.7 inches one way or the other from the average of the whole population.

Now, although this Q stands on its own independent basis, and can be derived from any scheme by dividing the differences of the ranks of 25° and 75° by 2, if the curve is symmetrical, it will be identical with what the mathematicians call the Probable Error. It thus becomes possible to apply the whole calculus of probability to any data capable of being expressed in a normal case of the scheme.

As matter of fact, Galton found a remarkable parallelism between results obtained by observation and those theoretically deduced from the mathematicial calculations. He took, for example, eighteen schemes of distribution, including stature, weight, breathing capacity, strength of blow, keenness of sight, for both sexes, calculated the Q in each, or the measure of deviation that half the deviations exceeded, and half fell short of, and then calculated a mean Q, as it were, for the whole eighteen. The result differs but little from that theoretically obtained by the law of frequency of error. It is evident that Galton might express his scheme in the well-known curve of error, but his curve of distribution contains all that the curve of error contains, and much besides.

For the particular results obtained, I must refer to the

book itself. One is so remarkable that it may be specified. If we call the M of the stature of the whole population P, and the mean stature of the parents P $\pm$ D, the stature of the offspring will be, on the average, P $\pm$ ⅓D. In other words, upon the average, children of parents who are exceptional, or who deviate from the mean, will themselves deviate from the mean only one third of their parents' deviation. Considering the character of his results, it is not wonderful that Galton says: "I know of scarcely anything so apt to impress the imagination as the wonderful form of cosmic order expressed by the 'law of the frequency of error.' The law would have been personified by the Greeks and deified if they had known of it. It is the supreme law of Unreason. Whenever a large sample of chaotic elements are taken in hand, and marshaled in the order of their magnitude, an unsuspected and most beautiful form of regularity proves to have been latent all along."

It is to be hoped that statisticians working in other fields, as the industrial and monetary, will acquaint themselves with Galton's development of new methods, and see how far they can be applied in their own fields. It is, of course, clear that any data dealing with the proportions of distribution of anything whatever can be diagrammatically expressed in Galton's scheme; but if it is to be anything more than a picture for the eye, it must be possible to establish an M and a Q from which the entire scheme of deviations and their relations may be, in turn, deduced, at least approximately. In other words, such a scheme, if its curve were wholly irregular, would not be likely to yield any results. Furthermore, no curve is likely to be regular unless it expresses traits which are the result of accidents, that is, of circumstances which *do* bring about certain results, though they were not intended for that purpose. For example, if we had (what we are not likely to have) accurate data regarding the accumulation of wealth in families from parents to children, there is no great reason for expecting that in two generations we would get results akin to those of Galton regarding natural heredity. The tendency of wealth to breed wealth, as illustrated by any interest table, and the tendency of extreme poverty to induce conditions which plunge children still deeper into poverty, would probably prevent the operation of the law of regression toward mediocrity. It is not likely that children of the poor would be better off, and children of the wealthier poorer in anything like the ratio of ⅔. But if we took generations enough, the operation of "accidents," such as imprudent, extravagant, and dissipated habits among the children of the rich, the growth of new industrial conditions which lessen the value of old forms of wealth, the emergence of money-makers among the poor, the development of social relations which would increase the ambition and chances of the poor, etc., we might find a similar law. That is, these accidents, or circumstances which, although in themselves irrelevant to the distribution of wealth, yet in the long run, largely determine it, would pelt down as it were the swells in the curve, and bulge out its depressions into something like a normal curve of distribution. Whether or not there is any truth in our example, it will serve to illustrate the nature of the data to which Galton's methods may be applied.

# Ethics in the University of Michigan

I suppose I may best supply what is desired if I first say something about the ethical courses to be given in the collegiate year 1889–90, considered as parts of the University curriculum, and then go on to say something of their standpoint and purpose. The only required courses in philosophy in the University are those in logic and psychology, one or other of which must be taken by all candidates for degrees, excepting by the students in the various engineering courses. Psychology is required precedent to the first course in Ethics. This is a lecture course of two hours per week, given in the second semester of the year, and is taken mainly by Juniors. Following this course is a lecture course of two hours per week in Political Philosophy,—taken accordingly mainly by Seniors. In the second semester comes a seminary course in Political Philosophy, which may be taken by candidates for advanced degrees, and by undergraduates, if they are deemed suitably prepared. In recent years special courses in the Ethics of Plato, of Aristotle and of Kant have been given, but it happens that no one of them is upon the programme for this year.

The first course in Ethics is a purely general one; its aim is theoretical rather than historical or practical. The greater number of students in ethics take also the course in the History of Philosophy, three times a week through the year; and this, together with the criticism of various systems in the course in Ethics, is relied upon to give sufficient historical data. Readings and reports by the students are required; the references being to such authors as Aristotle, Plato, Hume, Kant, Mill, Spencer, Stephen, Green, Martineau, etc. For convenience the subject is discussed under three heads. The first is the theory of the Moral Ideal; the second, the objective Moral World; the third, the Concrete

[*First published in the* Ethical Record, *II* (*Oct. 1889*), *145–48. Not previously reprinted.*]

Moral Life of the Individual. The aim of the first part is to discover the ethical ideal,—or answer the question, What is the chief end of man. The question is discussed largely on a basis of comparative criticism; the hedonistic theory, in its simplest form of individualism, and in its development in utilitarianism, and through the theory of evolution, is discussed; then is discussed the so-called theological ethics, as represented by Paley, and the theory of formal obligation, as represented by Kant; and while the attempt is made to recognize the truth in each of the previous forms, it is finally concluded that only the theory that the ideal of conduct is realization of personality answers all the demands of the problem. The same discussions that give conclusions regarding the ideal are shown to answer the problems regarding the basis and nature of obligation, and the nature of goodness. In the second part it is shown that the realization of personality both demands and occasions society, or the community of those having common interests and purposes, regulating themselves by common laws (implicit, conventional, or reflective), and recognizing common rights. This society with its substratum of expectations, institutions, laws and rights is characterized as the objective ethical world, as real in its way as the "external world" is physically. The various forms of this world in the family, the nation, the structure of industrial society, and the church, with their underlying principles, are briefly set forth. In the third part, the individual born into this world, and having to realize the ethical ideal in and through it is considered. In this connection are discussed the way in which the individual becomes aware of moral distinctions, the conditions of his freedom of action, the nature of his concrete duties and rights, and the modes of moral progress in the individual.

The second course, the one in Political Philosophy, begins by stating the various answers which have been given to the questions, first of the nature and origin of the state; secondly, of its functions; and, thirdly, of its constitution and forms. The outline of the subject being brought before the student in this comparative way, the same ground is gone over again from a different stand-point. First is taken up the general theory of society, as a natural (or

biological) organism, and its gradual development into an
ethical organism through the emergence of rational will is
discussed. This ethical organism is shown to involve the
political organization of mankind in the state. The function
of the state is defined as the guaranteeing, defining, and
extending of rights. This necessitates a discussion of the
nature of rights, which really forms the backbone of the
course. The basis of rights, the theory of "natural" and
"positive" rights, the various forms of rights, are taken up.
This gives occasion for consideration of questions relating to
property, punishment, war, etc., which are discussed at
some length. The nature and aim of law is then discussed on
the basis of the results regarding rights. The lectures then
take up questions relating to the actual constitution of the
state, the division of its powers, its various forms as aristocracy, democracy, etc., the tendencies and limits of present
legislation. The latter topic leads up to the questions of
legislation as respects the family, industrial relations, etc.,
and in this connection are considered some of the practical
problems regarding marriage and the labor question. The
course closes with a brief critical discussion of current political ideals, aiming to point out the practical and morally
valid aims of national life. The subject of the seminary
course for 1889–90 is Special Subjects in the History of
Political Philosophy. It is difficult to form the exact line
which a course of this nature will take, but the intention is
to make as exhaustive a study as possible of the various allied theories of the "state of nature," natural rights and the
social contract theory, taking up these topics on the basis of
such authors as Hobbes, Grotius, Locke, and Rousseau.

That these courses are limited in extent as well as in
number is evident; with but two instructors it is impossible
to do much special work in ethics without the neglect of
other departments in philosophy. Another year a course will
probably be offered in the Ethics of Plato, Kant or Hegel.
The limited amount of the work in ethics has been less
noticeable in the past because of the profound ethical spirit
in which the lamented Professor Morris carried on all his
work in philosophy, and which he imparted so successfully
to all his instruction.

# A College Course: What Should I Expect from It?

What should I expect from a college course? is, I believe, the question, my courteous editors of the *Castalian*, which you wish me to answer. It will not be out of the way, I suppose, to take the "I" who is the subject of this expectation as meaning you, me, anybody, what Walt Whitman calls "the common, that is, the divine average." There are certain things which I presume we should all pretty much agree upon. A man ought to expect a body, a physical tool, which is sound, and pliable to his purposes. He ought to have learned the rights of the body, and that these rights cannot be destroyed, nor the body cheated of them. The expectation of so many students in so many generations that the mind can be cultivated along with a systematic and continued neglect, or abuse of the physical system should be abandoned, by one and all, in the year 1890. There are certain intellectual gifts which the average student, and he below the average, should expect, while the very best student may beware lest he fall short. A certain range of information, a certain amount of learning, a mental discipline, that is, a quality of mind at once flexible and concentrated in dealing with new material, a certain attitude of mind, a mental openness and eagerness—these things should be expected almost as a matter of course. And certainly there are some moral results which should come too. One ought—whether one does or not—to expect a training of will, a cultivating and maturing of character, a reverence for truth wherever found, freedom from self-conceit and respect

[*First published in the* Castalian, *Published by the Independents of the Senior Class, University of Michigan*, V (1890), 26–29. *Not previously reprinted.*]

for the opinions of others, sympathy for their purposes, a highness of aim in the affairs of one's life agreeable to the opportunities enjoyed, belief in whatsoever things are true and lovely and of good report. Because such expectations are so normal and so obvious, if I should attempt to enforce them I should probably run either into the Scylla of mere moralisms, or into the Charybdis of a straining for the novel. And yet in attempting to say anything upon this topic, I do not imagine that I shall, after all, do more than repeat these same things—*Nur mit ein bischen andern Worten*. Whether I shall come to my goal with less of the ballast of commonplace or of the top-sail of paradox on account of a roundabout course may perhaps be doubted.

One thing, then, that a University education should do for a man is to rid him of his provincialisms. We all—or almost all—of us come out from a sphere of life somewhat narrower than that into which we come. The question is whether in this emergence we come out of our shells, or bring them with us. Certainly the boy or girl who comes to college judging all things from the standpoint of the way they think and do "in my place," ought to have his horizon of outlook pushed out a little further, and his standard of measurement lengthened. There may be touches of provincialism in manner which nothing but actual contacts will destroy, or which will always remain as the outer tokens of a sturdy, genuine and "home-keeping" spirit. But the voyage one takes in entering college life is a voyage to a far port, and through many countries foreign in space, in time, in manner of speech and thought. If such travelling of the spirit does not remove the narrow and small cast of one's opinion and methods it is failing of its aim. The Germans call the period of youthful culture a period of "self-alienation," because in it the mind gives up its immediate interests and goes on this far journey. Let a man learn on this journey to lay aside the suit, the habit, of mental clothes woven and cut for him in his native village, and to don the foreign costumes. If he be called to wear again his old suit, he will wear it the more easily and naturally for knowing something of the fashion of other men's garments.

And when one gives up his provincialisms let him

make the renunciation complete. Partisanship, of whatever sort, or however disguised, is but provincialism of a larger growth and more imposing mien. The lesson is harder learned; the sacrifice seems greater. It is easy to take boisterousness of thought and expression for earnestness of conviction; the thoughtless assimilation of opinion from an authority already, probably, second-handed, for strength and originality of mind. To be in doubt, to suspend judgment, to await the conviction which can come only from the fact—all this seems weakness. The breadth of sympathy which feels that the world of truth is a sphere which comes into itself again, the fairness of judgment which will know both sides, and the thoroughness which will know even the inside—all this seems like needless painstaking, like unpractical theorizing, in a word, what the newspaper writers call "Mugwumpery." But all this ought a man to expect from his college course. Its name is Freedom.

And finally, a student should expect from his college course a sense of the due proportion and right values of the various interests which may claim his attention. He should find out where their centre of gravity is, and this, not as a matter of theory, but as a practical insight which may serve him instinctively in the affairs of life. He should have ingrained within him the subordination of all learning, of all the sciences and all the arts, to social relationships and sympathies. Cardinal Newman, in one of the few educational books of the world which are neither priggish nor impractical, *The Idea of a University*, says that if he were asked to choose between a university which gave degrees upon examination in all subjects to students without residence and without tutorial supervision, and a university which had no professors or examinations at all, but simply brought a number of young men together for three or four years and then sent them away again, he should "have no hesitation in giving the preference to that university which did nothing, over that which exacted of its members an acquaintance with every science under the sun." And his reason is that an education without the *human* element would produce a generation frivolous, narrow-minded and resourceless, while the contact of "a multitude of young men keen, open-hearted, sympathetic, and observant" would constantly bring out new ideas and views, fresh matter of thought and distinct principles for judging and acting. Above all it would secure a training in the relations and uses of those elements of knowledge necessary for our social being. Free contact of men and women will, at least, produce a "community constituting a whole, it will embody a specific idea, it will represent a doctrine, it will administer a code of conduct, and it will furnish principles of thought and action." In a word, it will develop an ethical atmosphere, and this will secure, as far as it goes, a real intellectual training, for it induces the recognition that "knowledge is something more than a sort of passive reception of scraps and details; it is something, and it does a something."

I have made my quotation somewhat extended, but the idea conveyed seems to me the root of all right ideas about University training. The permanent and fruitful outcome of a college education should be the training of one's *human* nature. This training alone is really practical and preparatory for life, for it alone is ethical. It is the only basis of a genuine intellectual culture, for only as all the studies of a college course find a unity in the human, in the social, do they become more than scraps and fragments. Relationship to man, to his interests and purposes, takes the dust of specialism out of its barren isolation and vitalizes it into germinant principles. With all his getting, then, the college student should require of his college course that it give him that sense of the proportions and right values which can come only of centering all studies in their human relationships.

But all this is rather intangible, you will say, to one who wishes some definite instructions as to what he should expect from his college course. Undoubtedly; but the kingdom of heaven, in learning as in other matters, cometh not with observation. The general effects, the internal results, those which give the set and fix the attitude of the spirit, are the real effects of the college education. The average graduate may have no ready answer to the inquiry five years after his graduation, what use he now makes of all his learning, of his Greek, his Mathematics, his Old High German and his knowledge of Kant's *Critiques*. If he is wise, his thoughts will take somewhat this form: "All this is a matter of no account. The thing of importance is whether I have my interests trained to alert action and ready and wide vibration. Am I avoiding stagnation, both the apparent stagnation of mental idleness, and that stagnation which simulates the form of action but is the mere vacant repetition and imitation of the thoughts of others? Above all, are my sympathies with whatever touches humanity, nearly or remotely, broad and dominant? If so, the Philistine may return to Gath; my college course has fulfilled its purpose, I have the *unum necessarium*—the one thing needful."

# On Some Current Conceptions of the Term "Self"

## I.

It is the aim of this paper to analyze certain conceptions involved in the terms Self and Self-consciousness as currently used. No attempt will be made to judge of the value of the ideas themselves. Indeed, there is such confusion in the use of the conceptions that an independent analysis of them would seem to be a necessary preliminary to any decision upon their validity. Whether or not philosophy is exhausted in the clearing-up of conceptions, it is certain that without an occasional clearing-up philosophy will get so entangled in the *impedimenta* of its own notions as to be hindered in its onward march. Unless this analysis is confined to ideas having or claiming to have some community of meaning, it will include ideas wholly incomparable with one another, and thus end in a mere account of the way in which various writers use the same word. A study of the terminology of philosophy is, no doubt, helpful; but, as that is not intended in this paper, I shall confine my analysis to the conception of the "transcendental self"—to the idea of self which has affiliations with the movement set going by Kant, however divergent its various developments.

For a starting-point, and to a certain extent for a basis, Professor Seth's recent work, *Hegelianism and Personality*, presents itself as convenient, occupied, as it so largely is, with just this notion of the self. In that work, three separate conceptions—used, however, interchangeably—may be dis-

[*First published in* Mind, *XV* (*Jan.* 1890), 58–74. *Not reprinted during the author's lifetime.*]

criminated. In the first place, we have it laid down that "the self *is* the world, and the world is the self. The self and the world are only two sides of the same reality: they are the same intelligible world looked at from two opposite points of view. . . . The mind and the world, subject and object, are convertible terms; we may talk indifferently of the one or the other: the content of our notion remains the same in both cases" (pp. 19–20). This result is based upon an examination of Kant's transcendental inquiry and method which is, so far as quoted above, accepted, to all appearances, by Professor Seth. The meaning of this view of the self may stand out more plainly if we call attention to another feature of it. This is that the "ultimate fact of knowledge is neither pure subject nor pure object" (p. 13). These are both abstractions: to separate them, to make independent existences of them, is to "substantiate abstractions." In truth, the self is a synthetic unity. "It binds together, as related members of one whole, what would otherwise fall apart as unrelated particulars; and, moreover, it is only through this synthesis that the unity of the Self or Ego exists. It is the unity *of* the synthesis, and, apart from its synthetic activity, would no more be real than the particulars of sense would be real without its action." It cannot be identified, in other words, with the mere act of uniting: it includes within itself what is united, just as, on the other hand, what is united has no existence outside of its being united. Because this is so—because, as Professor Seth expresses it (p. 19), "the form is the form *of* the matter, and the matter is, as it were, simply the exhibition of the form"—the self and the world are correlative, and have the same content.

This, then, is the first notion conveyed by the term self —the self is the correlative of the intelligible world. Its content is that of the intelligible world. It even *is* the intelligible world in one of its aspects. And since Professor Seth has expounded with great force the notion that the intelligible world is the only real world, that the unknowable to intelligence is "nonsense" (*Scottish Philosophy*, p. 162), we may say that, according to this notion, the self is one with the real world, when this is considered in its ultimate unity. This view is clear and self-consistent; with its truth we have nothing to do. But we find that the question as to the nature of the transcendental self has not been sufficiently answered. The question is again raised: What is the transcendental self? (*Hegelianism*, top of p. 22). And the question is answered in a way which seems to me the exact opposite of the answer just given. It now turns out that the transcendental Ego represents *merely* the *formal* unity of the universe (p. 27). Although the self was shown to be a single self, its singularity is simply that which belongs to every abstract notion—a logical identity of type (p. 29). It is the "notion of knowledge in general" (p. 30). And, finally, Kant's characterizations of it are quoted. It is "a merely logical qualitative unity of self-consciousness in thought generally." It is a "logical exposition of thought in general" (p. 35). It is, finally, the "mere form of self-consciousness in general" (p. 230).

I confess that, to me, this second position, that the self is merely the formal unity of thought, appears to be the contrary of the first position taken by Professor Seth. There the self was not formal; the form was an abstraction apart from matter. Kant was then rebuked for making the self formal. The necessity of correlating matter and form was the fundamental feature of the transcendental method. So far was the self from being merely formal that it was the world. Instead of being merely logical, the self was the unified universe; it was a synthetic unity which had no existence apart from the particulars unified in the synthesis. But in this second and revised view, Kant is praised for his superior consistency in holding that the self arrived at by his investigation is an abstract condition and not a metaphysical reality or concrete fact (p. 28). The subject which "exists only as the unity of the manifold whose central principle of connexion it is" (p. 17) becomes transformed in ten short pages into a "*focus imaginarius* into which the multiple relations which constitute the intelligible world return"—a "*principle* of unity." To cut short this comparison of contradictory statements, the language first used regarding the self conveys, as clearly as language can convey anything, that the self is objective and real, is ontological; while the second view taken is that the self is merely formal and logical. The first view is that the self and the real cannot be separated without "substantiating abstractions"; the second view is that to unite them is to "hypostatise an abstraction" (p. 30).

But, as we advance further, it appears that the outcome of the transcendental view of the self is not in reality either that the self is the real world, or that the self is a mere logical form or abstract unity of thought. The view which finally emerges is that self is the "ultimate category of thought" (p. 98). So far as the varying expressions permit us to judge, this is Professor Seth's real thought in the matter. It is, at least, the view which is unambiguously reiterated in his "Discussion" in *Mind*, xiv, 117. It is stated once in connection with passages which have been quoted as belonging to the first interpretation: "The transcendental self, as an implicate of all experience, is for a theory of knowledge simply the necessary point of view from which the universe can be unified, that is, from which it becomes a universe" (*Hegelianism*, p. 20). It is elsewhere stated that the transcendental theory of knowledge resolves itself into an immanent criticism of categories, or of the conceptions by which we express and unify our experience. This criticism shows that self-consciousness is the highest category — the most adequate to determine existence. We are thus "justified in using the conception of self-consciousness as our best key to the ultimate nature of existence as a whole" (p. 89). In fine, "self-consciousness is the ultimate category of thought — that through which we think everything else, and through which alone the universe is intelligible to us."

I cannot persuade myself that this third conception of self-consciousness is identical with either of the other two. It means less than the first, which identifies the self with the world; it means more than the second, which makes self-consciousness a merely formal or abstract unity of thought. For it must be remembered that Kant would no more have accepted self-consciousness as the ultimate category of experience, or as a category of experience at all, than he would have accepted it as identical with the real world. In fact, the various expressions which Professor Seth has quoted with approval from Kant are directed as much against making

self-consciousness a category of experience as against making it a real self-existent being. How can the "poorest of all
our ideas" be the richest and most comprehensive principle
of philosophic explanation? The very reason for holding that
the self is merely a logical unity of thought is that the self
cannot be employed to determine experience at all. But
perhaps it may be said that it was just the result of the
Hegelian development of the Kantian method and presuppositions to demonstrate that the self, instead of being the
emptiest of categories, a conception the sole use of which is
to show that all our thoughts are accompanied by consciousness, is the organic system, the reality of all categories. I am
not in the least concerned to deny such a contention. But this
contention only shows the inadequacy of defining the self as
a "merely logical qualitative unity of self-consciousness in
thought generally," and not that it is consistent to unite
such a view with a view that the self is our ultimate principle of verifying and explaining experience. Indeed, the purpose of Kant in calling the self merely logical was to oppose
it to experience; but, when it is said from the point of view
of the Hegelian development of Kant that the self is the
highest logical category, the idea conveyed is that of the
complete correlativity of thought in general, and this
thought in particular, to experience. When Kant speaks of a
logical unity of thought he means that thought is formal, not
real; Hegel in speaking of a logical unity means that
thought is real and not formal. The relation between
thought and knowledge is not at all the same in the two
cases. With Hegel, to say that self is the highest type of
thought is to say that self-consciousness is the ultimate
principle of knowledge. The object of Kant is to show that
the self, since merely a principle of *thought*, is not a principle of *knowledge* at all. While both therefore might call the
self "the logical exposition of thought in general," the
phrase would have absolutely opposed meanings in the case
of the two writers.

No relation of opposition exists between the transcendental self as equal to the real world and as equal to the
ultimate category—between, that is, the first interpretation
and the third which Professor Seth gives. But although not

opposed, they are not the same. To pass directly from the one to the other *would* be to hypostatize an abstraction. The transition may be justifiable, but it cannot, of course, be assumed without justification. The transcendental self may be the highest thought of the world, but it cannot be said to be the correlative of the world, unless the content of the world can be shown to be exhausted in thinking it—or unless the transcendental self is more than a principle of thought. Because thought is objective, it does not follow that it is all there is of objectivity. The world as thought—and thus brought under the principle of self-consciousness—may be real as far as it goes, and yet not be identical with the world as known—with the whole meaning of the real world. The known world may be, for example, a world thought and felt, and not thought alone. Thus while self-consciousness—if it equalled only the ultimate category of thinking—would be an adequate determination of the world as thought, it would, after all, be only a partial determination of the whole as it really exists, and could not thus be called, as Professor Seth at first calls it, a term convertible with the world and having the same content.

These may appear distinctions so notorious that it is trifling to spend so much time upon them; but the fact that so experienced a writer as Professor Seth has presented all three interpretations as explications of the meaning of the "transcendental self" is my excuse for dwelling upon them. There is a certain kinship, indeed, between the three interpretations which would render it easy to pass unwittingly from one to another. The idea of the self as the ultimate category of philosophic explanation stands between the other two. Its content is logical, or thought; and thus when one is arguing against a writer who seems to transform this category into an existence by itself, it is easy to go to the extent of saying that it is *merely* logical, and approve an author who held to the view that it was wholly abstract, even though that author meant by that expression that self was not a category of explanation at all. But, on the other hand, having in mind the fact that self-consciousness is a notion for explaining the world in a sense in which mere "being" or "quantity" or "mechanism" is not,—that it exhausts the meaning of the universe as an object of thought, —it is easy to go to the other extreme, and hold that self-consciousness *is* the intelligible world seen from one of its sides. But none the less the conception of self as merely formal and abstract contradicts the other two conceptions; and these other two, while not mutually incompatible, are so far from being identical with each other that to pass from one to the other without more ado is to "erect an abstraction into a concrete existence."

## II.

As the object of this paper is not to convict Professor Seth of either verbal or real inconsistencies, but to help to clear up certain ambiguities in the current use of the conception of "transcendental self" (these ambiguities finding an unusually clear expression, as it were, in Professor Seth's book), I wish now to pass to the historical origin of these various meanings, chiefly as found in Kant, incidentally in Hegel as related to Kant.

Kant's theory is brought out in his "Transcendental Deduction." This is so familiar that it may be given summarily. Its gist, in the second edition of the *Kritik der reinen Vernunft*, is the proof that the identity of self-consciousness involves the synthesis of the manifold of feelings through rules or principles which render this manifold objective, and that, therefore, the analytic identity of self-consciousness involves an objective synthetic unity of consciousness. That self-consciousness is identical is, in itself, a merely analytic proposition. It means nothing more than that I am I—that what *I* am conscious of is in *my* consciousness, and that what belongs to your consciousness I am not conscious of. It finds its empirical application in the fact that, unless the consciousness which has ideas to-day is identical with that which was conscious yesterday or a year ago, it can no more now be conscious of what it was conscious of then than it can now be conscious of what is in your consciousness. But this does not prove the existence of any real self or substantial mind. It is still an analytic proposition and means that the same consciousness is the same consciousness. But if we ask how we know this sameness or identity of consciousness, the barren principle becomes wonderfully fruitful. For we do not know this sameness through the various successive ideas; they are not the same, but *ex hypothesi* various. And, furthermore, instead of knowledge of the identity of self depending upon them, I should not know them even as various, unless they were already mine. The identity of self-consciousness cannot be derived from knowledge of them, for this knowledge presupposes that identity. But perhaps we may go behind the apparent variety and disparateness of our ideas, and say that one consciousness *accompanies* all these different ideas, and that knowledge of this common element is the knowledge we are in search of. This does not suffice. The mere fact that consciousness accompanies every idea gives no identity unless these ideas are already conceived as *mine*—unless identity is presupposed. Otherwise, I should "have as various and many-coloured a self as I have different ideas." If we say that the *common* element gives us that knowledge of the identity of self which we are in search for, we doubly beg the question. A common element means an identity present in the midst of difference, and thus presupposes the sameness of consciousness through different ideas; and knowledge of this common element could be attained only if it were possible to compare many and various ideas in *one* consciousness, and thus see that they had a common element. These methods of knowing the sameness of consciousness thus presuppose what they would account for.

The sole way of accounting for this analytic identity of consciousness is through the activity of consciousness in connecting or "putting together" the manifold of sense. Since this putting together occurs according to fixed rules and principles, it is an objective synthesis. Knowledge of the identity of self presupposes, therefore, a self which acts synthetically, regularly so, upon sense-material. "The original and necessary consciousness of the identity of one's self is, at the same time, a consciousness of the equally necessary unity of the synthesis of all phenomena according to conceptions. . . . The mind would never conceive the identity of itself in the manifoldness of its ideas, if it did not perceive the *identity of the action by which it subjects this manifoldness to unity.*"

The "Deduction" in the first edition, instead of beginning with the consciousness of self-identity, begins with the consciousness of objects, and asks what is involved in that. The answer is the same. Consciousness of objectivity means unity of self-consciousness, and this not a formal or analytic activity, but one which connects the manifold of sense according to rules or conceptions. Whether, then, we inquire what is involved in mere sameness of consciousness, or what is involved in an objective world, we get the same answer: a consciousness which is not formal or analytic, but which is synthetic of sense, and which acts universally (according to principles) in this synthesis.

Apparently we have here a conception of the transcendental self like the first one laid down by Professor Seth. This self, since its existence is its synthetic activity upon the particular manifold of sense, is thoroughly objective. It has precisely the same content as the real world. And the objective world, since it turns out to be the synthesis of particulars of sense through the action of self according to conceptions, is subjective; it has the same content as the transcendental self. It is the transcendental self looked at as "there," as a product, instead of as an activity or process.

The next step in the analysis is to see why Kant, after having attained to the conception of an objective self, should shift his ground. Kant, in reaching this result, or in his transcendental deduction, has proceeded as if the synthetic action of self and the manifold of sense were wholly constituted through their mutual relations to each other—as if each had no existence excepting as a factor in the self, or in the world, determined by the other. The conceptions exist only as synthetic activity upon the manifold of sense; the manifold of sense exists only as connected by these conceptions. But while Kant has chosen in the "Deduction" to consider them as mutually related to each other, they have a meaning entirely apart from this mutual qualification, which, having been abstracted from in the transcendental deduction, must now be brought in that we may see how it affects the result.

The final meaning of the manifold of sense is found, not in its relation to the synthetic notions of the understanding, but in its relation to a thing-in-itself which produces it. In order to be known by us, this manifold must, indeed, be subjected to synthesis, and enter into relation to the self. But it has its own being entirely apart from such qualification. And, on the other hand, the conceptions of the understanding are not exhaustively determined by their synthetic action upon sense. They have a nature of their own, entirely independent of this synthetic action. The transcendental deduction does not give us, therefore, an analysis of the self, or of knowledge, or of the world as such; but simply of the conditions under which a manifold of sense (having a nature outside its relations to self) is knowable by us, or of the conditions under which conceptions of the understanding become categories of experience, these conceptions having their real and essential meaning, all the while, in a purely logical character which belongs to them apart from knowledge or experience. The transcendental self is thus a name for the incident under which our knowledge occurs, instead of giving the analysis of knowledge itself. It cannot be identified, therefore, as at first it seemed it might be, with either the real object (the thing-in-itself) or with the real subject. Just as the synthetic principles of experience are in themselves logical forms of analytic thought, so the self, in its own nature, is known only as the bare unity of these logical forms, the simple "I think" that must accompany all thought. The introduction of the thing-in-itself, therefore, leads Kant to that view of the self which finally gets expression in the quotations which were made in connection with Professor Seth's second idea of the self. For it must be remembered that the introduction of the thing-in-itself into Kant's philosophy affects all the factors which enter into his account of knowledge—the nature of thought as well as the nature of sensation. It is not an excrescence which can be lopped off without reconstruction of the whole theory of knowledge. Do away with the thing-in-itself, and the conceptions, instead of being *merely* logical, are also real, for their whole existence and meaning will then be found in their synthetic relation to the sense-manifold. And the transcendental self, instead of denoting a "logical exposition of thought in general," marks the synthetic union of the logical with the manifold of sense through regular principles of activity—marks, therefore, the objective character of the self. For if we reconstruct the Kantian theory of knowledge upon its own basis and method of analysis, doing away with the thing-in-itself, the result is to show that the *merely* logical, equally with the *merely* ontological, is an impossible abstraction. The *merely* logical is not at all; the logical *is* only as the thought-factor in the entire determination of experience, requiring another factor in order to constitute the self. That Kant's position of the merely formal abstract character of the self is superior in consistency to that of some Neo-Kantians is, therefore, not so evident as is the inconsistency of the restatement of such a position by one who denies the whole notion of the thing-in-itself.

But even if we correct Kant's analysis by doing away with the thing-in-itself, retaining all features not inconsistent with it, can the result of the transcendental deduction stand without further interpretation? Admitting that the removal of the thing-in-itself would show the transcendental self not as a logical abstraction, but real as experience itself —more real, indeed, in the sense that the reality of experience is shown by analysis to involve the reality of this self, behind which we cannot go—would this removal give a self whose content was the same as the content of the known world? The answer must be in the negative. The known world is constituted by the manifold of sensation, as connected by the self through its principles of synthesis. The content of the world, as known, will not be equivalent to the whole significance of the self, therefore, unless sensation is capable of being connected by principles of synthesis which manifest the entire nature of the self. But the position of Kant (a position entirely independent of any notion of *Ding-an-sich*) is, that sensation is incapable of being so determined as to equal self-consciousness; or, if we put it from the other side, that self-consciousness, even as a real activity of synthesis, can never exhaust all its synthetic capacities upon a material of sense. Sense is, as it were, inadequate to the relations which constitute self-consciousness, and thus there must also remain a surplusage in the self, not entering into the make-up of the known world. The reason for this is, that all the manifold of sense must be determined by certain forms of perception, space and time, before being determinable by the categories of thinking. Perhaps it would be more in accordance with the Kantian spirit to say that sensation, since it is in relation to space and time, must always present itself to the synthetic action of self as a manifold of mutually external particulars. The conceptions are thus not capable of determining sensation independently, but only as sensation is already subject to time- and space-*cadres*. Every category, therefore, must receive its value from its application to sensations already a manifold of external particulars, and the result can be only the system of objects in time and space. No category of experience can be found, accordingly, higher than that which determines most exhaustively the relations of objects and events in time and space, viz., reciprocity. And, correspondingly, no object can be known which is not an object in space and time. Hence the impossibility of making the self an object, since it is the condition of all objects, through its synthetic action upon sense. Stated in more Kantian language, the result would be that self-consciousness is the unconditioned, while experience, owing to the necessary relation of the synthetic activity of self to a material already determined as externally limiting and limited, can never present an unconditioned.[1] There thus remains a distinction between self and experience, due not now to the shadow thrown on knowledge by the thing-in-itself, but by the in-

---

[1] I do not mean to imply that I regard Kant as teaching that objects are first given as objects in space and time, and that the action of thought follows upon the presentation of such ready-made objects; or that there can be perception without conception. On the contrary, I think that Kant teaches very distinctly that space and time (and, of course, with them everything in space and time) do not exist as perceived objects without the action of thought. But he also holds that the manifold of sense which thought synthesizes has already a formal element which determines it to relations of externality. The fact that thought never connects pure sensations as such, but only sensations partially determined by relations of perceptivity, would occupy much the same place now occupied by the notion of schematism in Kant's theory, if this theory were reconstructed merely on the basis of the elimination of the *Ding-an-sich*.

compatibility of sensation, as rendered a manifold of external particulars in space and time, to the unconditioned content of self-consciousness. Experience can never be complete enough to have a content equal to that of self-consciousness, for experience can never escape its limitation through space and time. Self-consciousness is real, and not merely logical; it is the ground of the reality of experience; it is wider than experience, and yet is unknown except so far as it is reflected through its own determinations in experience,—this is the result of our analysis of Kant, the *Ding-an-sich* being eliminated but the Kantian method and all presuppositions not involved in the notion of the *Ding-an-sich* being retained. The resulting conception of the self is, evidently, not equivalent to either of Professor Seth's two first definitions of the self. It is not a mere abstract and formal logical unity, for it involves the action of thought upon sense, and is thus synthetic and objective; and yet it is not one side of the world of experience. The world of experience is constituted by it, but the world of experience does not exhaust it.

We have next to consider the relation of this revised Kantian conception of self to the third notion of self stated in Professor Seth's book—the idea of self-consciousness as the highest category of thought and of explanation. So far we have dealt only with the general idea of thinking as synthesis of sense according to principles. The different forms of synthesis, or the categories, we have not dealt with. Kant, as is well known, had twelve of them, which he derived without further examination from certain notions which he found to be involved in the formally logical theory of judgment. It was the work of Hegel, first, to give an *independent* derivation of them, as contrasted with Kant's taking them for granted; secondly, to give an *organic* derivation of them, in placing them in relation to one another, as contrasted with the simple juxtaposition of them which is found in Kant; and, thirdly, to show the category of self-consciousness as their basis and system, instead of stopping short with reciprocity, and placing the categories in opposition to self-consciousness. Now, accepting Hegel's work so far as it thus relates to the categories, and accepting his criticisms upon the Kantian procedure in reference to them, let us again revise the Kantian results in view of Hegel's position. Will this give us the self as the supreme category of experience? The answer must be in the negative. In one way the Kantian conception will include more than the Hegelian; in another way, less. It includes more, because what Kant offers is not primarily the self as a category of explanation at all, but the self as the real ground (not, however, to be confused with cause) of experience.[2] It includes less, because, however ready Kant might be to admit the Hegelian criticism and derivation of the categories as superior to his own, he could not admit that self-consciousness may be used as a category of experience. Self-consciousness would still have the function of the Idea for Kant. It would be an ideal regulative of experience, not a category constitutive of it.

Considering first this latter point, we may say that, admitting Kant's derivation of the categories from the forms of syllogistic logic to be insufficient and artificial, granting that it is impossible to stop short with the category of reciprocity, it does not follow that the category of self-consciousness is a category of experience. The distinction between conceptions of *thought* and conceptions of *knowledge* still remains. The reason for this we have already seen. It is the peculiar relation of the categories to sense as qualified by the forms of space and time. While, therefore, we might have the thought of self-consciousness, and while as a thought it would not be empty but would be, in another sense from that in which Kant actually uses the term, the vehicle of all notions of thought—their organism, it would be impossible to use this category so as to determine sense by it. For it is impossible as long as we retain Kant's fundamental presupposition—the idea of the partial determination of sensation by relation to perception, apart from its relation to conception—to employ self-consciousness as a principle of explaining any fact of experience. Every fact of experience is capable of adequate explanation without any such category; or, conversely put, experience can never con-

---

[2]     It will be understood that we are now speaking of Kant as revised by the elimination of the *Ding-an-sich*.

vey anything adequate to the notion of self. Self-consciousness would thus be an ideal category—that is to say, it
would suggest the notion of a possible experience, unlike
anything that *we* can possibly experience. It would be a
notion which should regulate the successive organization of
our present experience by pointing to a goal that yet we
never could reach, and which should also point out the
limitation of our present experience.[3]

The reconstruction of the Kantian theory of categories
in the light of the Hegelian logic would give the following
points. First, it would derive the conceptions from a common root and place them in some organic connection with
one another. Secondly, it would place the Notion of the
understanding and the Idea of reason in some connection
with each other. The reason, with its Ideas, would not then
appear, as it does now, an accidental afterthought of Kant,
or an arbitrary derivation from the theory of the syllogism.
The conception included under the Idea would follow by
immanent development and criticism from what are now
called Notions of the understanding, and would follow as
their basis in thought. The distinction between them would
be between conceptions that may be used to connect sensations subject to space- and time-forms and those that may
not be so used. Thirdly, the ideas of organism and teleology,
which also now appear to be unconnected with the rest of
the Kantian philosophy, sprung upon us without intrinsic
necessity, would form part of the content of the Idea as
distinguished from the Notion. And, finally, the distinction
Kant now makes between theoretical and practical reason,
between the fact which is and the ideal which ought to be,
would get an organic connection with the rest of the philosophy. This gives the outline of a reconstruction of his ethics;
for it would appear that it is just the business of moral
experience to overcome that distinction between experience
and self-consciousness which theoretical knowledge cannot

[3]     The distinction would thus be analogous to, perhaps identical with,
the distinction Kant draws between our intelligence, in which the immediate and the mediate element never wholly coincide, and an intelligence which may be described either as Intuitive Reason or a Rational
Intuition.

remove. All this we can get, if we read Kant with the eyes of Hegel; but self-consciousness as an actual category of our scientific experience we cannot get unless we simply substitute Hegel for Kant.

But it is time to turn to the other point: that the transcendental self of Kant is more than self-consciousness as a supreme category of explanation. It is more, because the self of Kant (the self as it would be with the *Ding-an-sich* eliminated) is more than any category: it is a real activity or being. And it cannot be said to be more than a category only because he has hypostatized a category—that if he had understood himself he would have seen that it was just a category. There is a fundamental distinction between the Kantian critique of pure reason and the Hegelian theory of categories which makes their results disparate. Kant's object is not the examination of *thought*, but the examination of *knowledge*; and his method is not a consideration of the significance, placing, relative adequacy and inadequacy of the conceptions or aspects of thought with a view to discovering the entire meaning of thought; his method is an analysis of the *actual* factors which actually constitute knowledge. One of these factors is thought, and, therefore, the complete carrying out of the method would undoubtedly involve an examination of thought as specified into its various conceptions. But because the Hegelian *Logic* is the development of one factor in Kant, it will hardly do to say that the purpose of the Kantian *Critique* is exhausted in the purpose of Hegel's *Logic*. At least, if we do say it, it should be with the distinct consciousness that we are not completing Kant, but are abandoning the characteristic feature of his undertaking and of his method. This is, I repeat, not an immanent "criticism of categories" but an analysis of experience into its aspects and really constituent elements. And in the course of this analysis Kant comes upon a self which through various principles of synthesis puts together the manifold of sense and, thereby, constitutes experience. This, indeed, is not a theory of creation; it is not an attempt to tell how a self set to work, or by necessity would set to work, to make a universe. But because it is not a theory of creation, it does not follow that it is only a criticism of categories. The assumption that there is no middle ground between a theory of creation and a mere analysis of forms of objective thought is, to say the least, a curious one. Kant's method is the analysis of the known universe or of experience; and as a result it discovers a self acting through thought upon sensation. Thought as synthetic is action upon sense, and sense is through the synthetic action of thought. If we call them factors of experience it must be with the recognition of their intrinsic unity with each other. The self constitutes this unity; it is the activity which is the source of the correlative synthesis of thought and sense. That analysis of reality should give anything but reality would be a strange result. And the reality found by the Kantian method through analysis of reality is a self which through thought is synthetic of sense determined to be a manifold of limiting particulars by relation to space and time.

There are two strains in Kant: one is inquiry into the necessary thought or logical conditions of experience; the other is the inquiry into the actual nature of experience. The *Logic* of Hegel undoubtedly works out the former to its consistent results. The latter it does not come in contact with. The former inquiry asks what are the forms or principles by which we must think the world; or, from the other side, what the world must be, as thought. The answer is that to think the world in its completeness is to think it as self-consciousness. Now this proposition is, as I attempted to show in the earlier portion of this article, not convertible with the proposition that the world *is* self-consciousness, unless it is also shown that the world is only and just as it is for thought. But the result of Kant's inquiry into the *actual* nature of experience is to show (to his satisfaction, I mean, the *truth* of the results not being under examination) that it includes another element besides thought, namely, feeling, and that on account of this element—or at least on account of its peculiar relation to forms of perception—the world as experienced can never equal the world as thought. That is, while to *think* the world completely is to think it as self-consciousness, it is the very characteristic of experience or *knowledge* that it cannot be complete—and hence cannot give self-consciousness.

We have thus another conception of self-consciousness to put beside the three obtained from the analysis of Professor Seth. This is the conception which we reach in reconstructing Kant by means of the elimination of the *Ding-an-sich*, and by that more complete working-out of the logical side of his analysis of experience which was made by Hegel. This is the self as the activity of synthesis upon sense. Starting from this notion the other three notions may be at once placed with reference to it. The self as the *merely* logical or abstract unity of thought falls away entirely. Self-consciousness as a category of experience becomes changed into an ideal which serves at once to organize and to reveal the incompleteness of experience. Where (as in ethics) the ideal *is* the reality, self-consciousness is again a real category of experience—but of practical experience, not of theoretical. The self which could use the category of self as a category of both practical and theoretic experience would be a self whose content was the same as that of the world. "The self and the world are only two sides of the same reality" in this case. While from the standpoint of Hegel's *Logic* (I am not speaking of the rest of his philosophy) such a result could be reached only by substantiating a category, from the standpoint of Kant's *Critique* it would be reached as an analysis of the reality of experience—if it were reached at all. But it can be reached only as an ideal which serves by contrast to manifest the incompleteness of experience as it presents itself to us.

It is evident that we are now upon the verge of another difficulty. As long as sensation was regarded as given by a thing-in-itself, it was possible to form a conception of the self which did not identify it with the world. But when sense is regarded as having meaning only because it is "there" as determined by thought, just as thought is "there" only as determining sense, it would seem either that the self is just their synthetic unity (thus equalling the world) or that it must be thrust back of experience, and become a thing-in-itself. The activity of the self can hardly be a third something distinct from thought and from sense, and it cannot be their synthetic union. What, then, is it? This is, I take it, the problem which finally emerges, when Kant is made self-con-

sistent by the elimination of the thing-in-itself, and when the
logical or thought-factor of his philosophy is developed in
the Hegelian manner. It is precisely, as it seems to me, the
difficulty which comes to the front in Green's reconstruction
of Kant. It is to meet this difficulty that he frames the idea
of a completely realized self making an animal organism the
vehicle of its own reproduction in time. The conditions of
the problem are: a denial of the *Ding-an-sich*; the analysis
of knowledge into thought, and feeling which is ἕτερον to
thought; the recognition that this feeling, after all, exists
only as determined by thought; and the belief that feeling
enters into *our* knowledge only under conditions of space
and time, although space and time, in themselves, are feeling determined by thought. No space remains to consider
how far Green's conception of an eternal self communicat-
ing itself gradually through physical conditions, and
thereby constituting a human self, meets the demands of the
problem. But it is evident that, when the problem is conceived as just stated, the self cannot be thought of as equivalent, on the one hand, to the world, because this world, as
knowable by us, is always subject to certain forms, namely,
space and time, which condition sense; nor, on the other
hand, as equivalent to the highest category of thought,
because the self is more than thought, more than a category,
namely, the activity of synthesis of sense through thought.
It is, I think, this twofold character of time and space, as at
once forms of knowledge conditioned by the self, and yet
conditioning self as it works in us, that is the genesis of
Green's notion. The truth of the conditions upon which it
rests—that is, Kant read in the light of Hegel so far as is
necessary to make Kant consistent—is not under examination here; but if we grant it, the theory of Green is a genuine
attempt to meet a genuine problem, and not a mere hypos-
tasis of an abstraction.

# Is Logic a Dualistic Science?

The Newer Logic may be roughly described as an attempt to take account of the methods of thinking employed by science, that is, of the methods the aim of which is truth, and which deal with a material of fact. It thus contrasts with the old scholastic logic, which may be roughly described as an attempt to deal with thinking *in vacuo*, that is with methods which leave out (or abstract from) the material of fact, and which have no aim except non-contradiction of their own premises—self-consistency. We may call the latter the Logic of argument, not of truth; but the former is the Logic of science, *i.e.*, of actual knowledge.

Lotze, Sigwart, Wundt in Germany, Jevons, Bradley, and Bosanquet in England are representative names in this new logic. To it also Venn's *Empirical Logic* is a most noteworthy recent contribution. While written from a philosophical standpoint differing from that of most of the foregoing names, it has an aim common with theirs. It treats thinking as a process having relation to truth. I confess, for my part, that I could have wished Venn had chosen another philosophical standpoint; but without going into matters of ultimate interpretation, Venn raises plenty of questions well worth discussion on their own account as purely logical. Among these, as one of the most important, I would place this: Does logic imply a duality, which for logic is ultimate? Venn answers in the affirmative, calling attention however to the fact, that he means only to assert that dualism is ultimate for *logic*; the metaphysical question is not raised.

Venn's own statement is as follows: We must take for granted a duality. On the one hand, outside of us, there is

[*First published in* Open Court, *III* (16 Jan. 1890), 2040–43. *Not previously reprinted.*]

the world of phenomena pursuing its course; and, on the other hand, within us, there is the observing and thinking mind. Logic is concerned with the judgments of the latter about the former. "The thorough-going retention of this duality is one of the leading characteristics of the whole treatment adopted in this work" (p. 22). He then goes on to show the evils resulting from a purely subjective or a purely objective treatment. The latter "would confine us to a bare statement of those laws which lie at the basis of all inductive inference," while logic must always bring in the attitude of the mind in estimating or appreciating facts. The objective view would thus exclude the whole field of inference. The purely subjective treatment, on the other hand, would reduce logic to the bare logic of self-consistency, without relation to the true or to the false. So Venn concludes (p. 26) that while there are "some sciences, like Psychology, in which the primary reference is throughout to the mental processes, there are others, like the ordinary physical sciences, in which the primary reference is throughout to the external phenomena. But a science like logic, which has to do with the processes of the human mind when judging about phenomena, occupies necessarily an intermediate position."

Now when I say that all that Mr. Venn says about the evils of a purely subjective or purely objective treatment seems to me wholly sound, and that I would agree with him in saying logic deals with the process of thought in judging about phenomena,—when I say this, I may seem to have closed the door to further discussion. But I would call attention to the fact that these phrases may have two meanings. They may mean that the mental process, the "internal thought," and the objective phenomena, the "external thing," are, for logic at least, wholly independent and separate data, and that then the logical process comes in as a third thing and brings one to bear upon the other. This is the sense in which Mr. Venn interprets the dualism and is the sense in which I should reject it. Or, again, the dualism may be interpreted as being *inside*, as it were, the logical process. That is to say, we may hold that the "mental process of the mind in judging about phenomena" is for logic, at least, ultimate and decisive. The duality between the object perceived and the thought conceived is not one with which the logical process begins, but is the result of a logical process; that is, so far as *logic* has anything to do with it.

We may illustrate the difference as follows: *There* is the physical object, the sun moving in the heavens. *Here* is my idea or concept of this object. Does logic begin with this dualism and then go on to consider how the idea may be brought into conformity with the object?

Mr. Venn would answer "Yes." To me it seems as if the judgment of the mind were, for logic, the primary fact, and as if the distinction between the idea and the fact were one which takes place within and on account of the judgment—the logical process. The question involves more than at first appears. Are there, for logic at least, two worlds, of which one has to be brought into conformity with the other, or is there but one world, and that one logical through and through?

If the question concerned a world of objects wholly unrelated to mind, it would be impossible to discuss it without raising all manner of metaphysical difficulties; but, fortunately, Mr. Venn accepts the doctrine of the "relativity of knowledge." He says (p. 16), "we postulate a world or aggregate of objects—not out of relation to human faculties in general, which would be absurd—but conditioned in relation to our representative state of faculties." And on page 28 he expressly says: "We are in no wise concerned with the question which for ages perplexed philosophers, viz., in what sense our ideas 'resemble' or are 'copies of' actual external objects. All that we compare is the impression at first hand and at second hand, the presentation and the representation." And so on page 384 he says, that it is the general aim of logical processes to secure a complete and accurate correspondence between what we think and conceive within us, and what we *observe* and *feel* without us. The question is then: How are perception and observation logically related to thinking, to conception? Does logic take up its task when these are furnished to it ready-made, thus having a dualistic basis, or do logical processes enter equally into both perception and conception, so that, from a certain standpoint, each has a logical character?

I shall attempt to sustain the latter position. In holding that logic is not dualistic, because logical processes enter into presentation as well as into scientific methods, I may, in some sense, rely upon the authority of Mr. Venn himself. One of the striking features of his logic is the way in which he attacks our "habit of regarding what we call 'objects' as being in a way marked out by nature, always and for all beings" (p. 6). This habit is so far from being justified that as he says (p. 5), "Select what object we please—the most apparently simple in itself, and the most definitely parted off from others that we can discover—yet we shall find ourselves constrained to admit that considerable mental process had been passed through before that object could be recognized as being an object, that is as possessing some degree of unity, and as requiring to be distinguished from other such unities." And Mr. Venn shows clearly and decisively, to my mind, that in the most elementary recognition of an object processes of analysis and synthesis of very considerable complexity are involved. In his forcible comparison, to expect a dog who could not exercise quite a complex analysis and synthesis to perceive a rainbow, would be hardly more reasonable than to expect him to "see" the progress of democracy in the place where he lives—although the ultimate constituent sensible events are as accessible to his observation as they are to ours (p. 7; compare pp. 143–44).

In a like manner, Mr. Venn attacks what he well calls the "alphabetic" view of nature; the idea that objects come to us, so sharply discriminated and separated that one may be represented by A, another by B, and so on. "Generally speaking what we mark out by the letters A, B, C, are more or less fictitious entities, that is, they are manifold groups, held together in a mental synthesis with the cohesive assistance of names. . . . The mere reference to individuals as the basis or starting point of our instruction presupposes that something has already been done to recognize and constitute these A, B, C as individuals" (p. 345).

Now it seems to me that as soon as we give up the view that objects are presented to the mind already distinguished from others and united into cohering wholes, we are tacitly admitting that logical processes enter into the recognition, or observation of facts. When we go further and say that the individual object becomes such to us only through a process of mental synthesis and analysis, it seems to me that the admission is more than tacit—it is express. The only ground on which the logical character of recognition of objects could be denied, would be that mental analysis and synthesis are not logical processes. I hardly think Mr. Venn would take this position; still less can I see how he or any one else would uphold it. Mr. Venn when treating more expressly of the nature of analysis and synthesis, remarks (p. 398) that "these processes are best regarded as being merely subdivisions of a much more far reaching process, viz., that of framing hypotheses or suppositions. Set this faculty to work; employ it in separating wholes into their parts and gathering up parts in order to constitute new wholes, and we have what are known as analysis and synthesis." From this view it would certainly follow that our first perceptions of objects, being due to analysis and synthesis, are, in a sense, tentative hypotheses which we form in order to account for our experiences. Of course from the standpoint of ordinary experience it sounds absurd—and is absurd for that matter—to say that "the fire burns" is a hypothesis. But from the logical standpoint, it is far from being absurd. Whence the whole chemical theory of combustion, and what is the need of it, unless the first judgment that "fire burns" is, after all, only a tentative and crude analytic-synthetic process, needing to be carried farther, to be corrected, and, finally, transformed into a hypothesis more nearly agreeing with facts? If this is not evident, substitute the judgment "the sun moves" for the one "the fire burns." The objection most likely to be made to this doctrine that presentation itself has a logical value and basis, is, I imagine, that logical processes begin only when we are aiming at truth—only when we have a definite end in view which controls the process, and that there is no such aim or end in ordinary observation. That we are not *consciously* aiming at truth and that there is no *conscious* criterion or standard which controls the mental process in pre-scientific perception, is, of course, admitted. And this unconscious functioning of logical processes in perception seems to me to be just its *differentia* (logically, I would not say psychologically or metaphysically) from scientific thinking. Ordinary perception and scientific reflection have just the same material, and follow, in the rough, the same methods. There is hypothesis, induction, and deduction, inference, generalization, classification, analysis, synthesis, whatever logical process you please to take, in the perception of the sun as shining. But for the very reason that these processes are unconsciously followed they are uneconomical, imperfect, incorrect; they contain irrelevant material and leave out what is really coherent. In a word, since the logical principles are unconscious, the result is largely illogical, that is, false. Compare such a statement as "the sun shines" with the statement which a modern astronomer would make, when speaking from the standpoint of science, about just the same experience. The latter judgment would be carefully qualified; it would be accurately quantified; the conditions, chemical and physical, of the fact would be developed. The transformation would be so great that an ordinary layman reading the scientific proposition would probably not recognize that it had any kinship to his judgment—"the sun shines." But the real subject-matter would be the same.

We do not have then two things first given—one, the facts of observation, the other the mental concepts, and then, thirdly, a logical process, starting from this dualism, and attempting to make one side of it conform to the other. Knowledge from the first, whether in the form of ordinary observation or of scientific thinking, is logical; in ordinary observation, however, the logical process is unconscious, dormant, and hence goes easily and inevitably astray. In scientific thinking, the mind knows what it is about; the logical functions are consciously used as guides and as standards. But knowledge, experience, the material of the known world are one and the same all the way; it is one and the same world which offers itself in perception and in scientific treatment; and the method of dealing with it is one and the same—logical. The only difference is in the degree of development of the logical functions present in both.

We get the same result, if we consider from a somewhat different point of view the relations of observation and inference. And here, again, Mr. Venn may furnish the starting-point. For he himself admits that we cannot find any material which is "pure" observation—that is observation without any element of inference. "Really ultimate data can no more be reached than can a first point or absolute limit in time or space." "The starting point is a merely conventional one, assumed for convenience. Everywhere, wherever we look or find ourselves, we seem to be in possession of data which are familiar to us and are justified by experience. This is our starting point, and not any really primitive data" (pp. 115 and 116). The ground for this position will occur to anyone familiar with Mill's analysis of the proposition, "I saw my brother at a certain hour this morning," where he points out that everything is inferential excepting some data of color. Venn chooses a somewhat more complex case. Some one proposes to join a walking party and it is said of him: "I can see plainly enough that he will not be fit for our excursion." The least analysis would resolve this into: "I see the man is ill, and therefore conclude he cannot take a long walk." But do we *see* that the man is ill? Obviously, we only see that he is pale, has a lax gait, etc., and hence *infer* he is ill. And each one of these apparent observations may be analyzed into an inference. Even our estimate of paleness, a color pure and simple, psychological analysis shows to be no ultimate datum, but in great part an inference.

Now if it be admitted that observation involves inference indefinitely continued, what becomes of the duality which logic had to assume as its starting-point? If there is no *pure* presentation, no fact of sense-perception not already qualified by logical processes, how can it be said that logic has to do with a comparison of the concept with the datum of presentation? Logic seems somehow to be concerned with the observation itself. Instead of having a dual material supplied to it, it is present wherever there is any known material. There is but one world, the world of knowledge, not two, an inner and outer, a world of observation and a world of conception; and this one world is everywhere logical. As the world of ordinary perception it is logical, but its logical character is undeveloped, is latent, and hence is utilized at random, that is to say, extravagantly and erroneously. As the world of scientific reflection, it is more completely logical, because its logical character is brought to consciousness, is rendered explicit, and is thus used as a criterion, or a standard, in a word, as the truth by which the false and the irrelevant may be excluded. The result is that logic has no dualistic basis.

# The Logic of Verification

In a recent article in the *Open Court* having the title "Is Logic a Dualistic Science?" I attempted to show as against Mr. Venn's recent work that logical processes do not deal with the comparison of ideas, on the one hand, with perceptions on the other; the reason, in general, being that logical processes enter into the structure of perceptions as well as of ideas, and that, therefore, such processes could not be considered as beginning with the comparison of ready-made perceptions and conceptions. The opinion was then advanced that there is but one world of knowledge, whether in the form of perceptions or of ideas, and that this world is logical all the way through.

To this doctrine an objection somewhat after this fashion might be raised: Such a conception makes the process of verification impossible. If there is but one realm of knowledge, what is the standard of truth? with what shall we compare our *ideas* in order to verify them? If logic has a dualistic basis, the question is easily answered; on one hand, there is the world of conceptions, of ideas, on the other, the world of perceptions, of facts. And we test our ideas by comparing them with facts. But upon the theory of a single realm of knowledge, logical throughout, no such comparison and testing is possible. It seems upon this theory that the only criterion of truth is the consistency of ideas with themselves, and every one knows that ideas may be self-consistent, and yet untrue, or even highly absurd.

Undoubtedly the objection points to a serious difficulty, one which must be reckoned with. I shall not attempt to evade it by denying that there is a relative distinction at

[*First published in the* Open Court, *IV* (*24 Apr. 1890*), 2225–28. *Not previously reprinted.*]

least, between idea and fact. I shall rather ask what does this distinction of idea and fact (speaking always from the logical point of view) mean and how does it arise? If an objection lies against the unitary theory advanced, a still stronger objection lies against the dualistic theory. This objection I may state as follows: What is this world of facts by comparison with which we test our ideas? Is it the real, the true world? This supposes that this real world, the actual facts, are known. But if they are known, so that they can afford the standard of verification, why do we go to the trouble of forming a theory, of making a hypothesis? If we already know the facts, it certainly seems a waste of energy and of time to frame guesses, to elaborate ideas simply for the sake of going through the meaningless process of seeing whether or not they agree with a truth already perfectly known. It is evident that we only form a theory, or entertain ideas, as distinguished from facts, when we are not in possession of the truth, when we are in search of it. *Per contra*, if the facts by which we are to test our theory are not the real facts but the facts as they *seem* to be, the facts as *previously* known, there is another difficulty. It is just because we suspected these apparent facts of not being real, that we framed a theory which should get nearer to the reality of the case. It would certainly be a curious operation to test our theory by a standard whose discrediting had led to the formation of the theory. This then is the dilemma with which I would confront the dualistic notion. If the standard by which we are to test our ideas is the real fact, the actual truth, then, by the necessity of the case, the standard is unknown; if the standard is facts as they seem to be, as already apprehended, it is worthless. The only standard of value is out of reach; the attainable standard is no standard at all. In either case, verification would seem to be an impossible process.

I hope this result may at least induce us to consider the other point of view; the notion that we do not have ideas separate from facts, which we proceed to compare one with the other, but that the (undoubted) distinction between idea and fact is itself logical, brought about by and within logical processes.

Let me begin with a well-known psychological fact— that which Bain calls "primitive credulity." So far as we can judge, early childhood makes no difference between ideas and facts. It does not recognize its ideas *as* ideas, but it at once projects them into the outer realm. Suggest an idea to a baby, by saying some word which he recognizes, the name of a known object or person, and the baby looks around him to see that object. A child's mind is like an animal's; it is intensely practical. Ideas, as such, do not appeal to it. The thing, the action, is what the child is after. A baby's inability to entertain a question, or even after it can answer questions relating directly to fact, its inability to consider questions involving a "whether this or that," testify to its incapacity to hold an idea in its ideal aspect. What is it that breaks up this primitive intellectual innocency; this immediate transformation of idea into fact? Apparently, it is the disappointment of expectation, at first, and then as a further development of this, the dim perception of contradictions. The baby, when he hears the word "Papa," looks about him and does not see his father; probably, at first, the new idea, what he actually sees, simply expels the other idea. The idea of father is not retained before the mind long enough for the contradiction to be perceived. But there is at least the shock of unrealized expectation, and the feeling of the necessary adjustment to the new idea. As the mind's power of holding its ideas fixed becomes greater, the new idea will not simply drive out the other, substituting itself for it, but will struggle with it for possession of the mind. Now the actual idea contradicts the idea which the mind is endeavoring to project into actuality; it prevents this projection. It is, as it seems to me, this two-fold process: on one hand, the retaining of an idea before the mind, on the other, its repulsion from actual fact through a stronger contradictory idea, which leads the mind to the hitherto unentertained recognition of an idea as only ideal, as a *mere* idea.

This analysis seems to me to be verified by the phenomena of illiterate and savage life, of dreams, and of hypnotism, so far as we can appeal to that unsettled sphere. The difficulty savages have of discriminating ideas from facts is a commonplace of ethnology. The absence of contradictory facts retained in the mind leads us to take everything we dream as real, while we dream it. The savage continues to think of it as real when he awakes; it is only something that happened in another region of experience, when the soul sallied forth from the body. And while I would not speak dogmatically regarding hypnotism, Janet and others seem to have made it probable that its essential phenomenon is *dissociation*, the severing of the connections between groups of ideas united in ordinary sense-perception and thought. These connections being broken down, the mind experiences no contradiction on being told while in a room of a house that it is in a boat upon the ocean. The idea, having no other body of ideas over against which it is set, is taken, as in childhood, for a fact.

But to return to the argument. The mind learns through the contradictions existing between its ideas that not all can be projected as facts; some must be dismissed as false, or, at least, retained only tentatively as *possible* facts. It is this tentative holding of an idea which constitutes the logical distinction of idea and fact. The fact is the idea which nothing contradicts, which harmonizes with other ideas, which allows the mind free play and economical movement. The idea is at first the fact about which difficulties are felt, which opposes a barrier to the mind's movement, and which, if not in opposition to other facts, is, at least, in opposition to *apparent* facts. In a word, the distinction between "idea" and "fact" arises along with the distinction between real and apparent fact.

Let us test this result by considering scientific hypothesis. The mind frames a hypothesis or theory, because it is dissatisfied with its present (or rather former) judgments. The ideas which it has formerly taken to be facts, it has come to look upon with suspicion. The hypothesis is an idea which is supposed to be fact, or at least, to be nearer fact than previous ideas. But, till it can be verified, it is held only tentatively, and this holding may be of all degrees of comparative assurance, from a mere suggestion or question to a well-defined theory. The process of transforming the hypothesis, or idea entertained tentatively, into a fact, or idea held definitely, is verification. We saw at the outset the difficulties which beset the ordinary crude notion of verification, that which considers it as a process of comparing ready-made ideas with ready-made facts; let us see how our present notion meets these difficulties.

In the first place, what are the facts in contrast with which the hypothesis is regarded as merely an idea? They are not a *fixed* something; fixed either in amount, or in quality. If the idea, the hypothesis needs extension, transformation and verification, the "facts" in their turn, are in need of enlargement, alteration and significance. Take, for example, the hypothesis of evolution. The facts by which this theory is to be verified or disproved are not a fixed, unchangeable body; if the theory gets its verification through the facts, the facts get a transformed and enlarged meaning through the theory. I do not mean simply that the theory leads to the discovery of new facts, though this is noteworthy, and, I think, inexplicable on the dualistic assumption. But suppose there is some animal of which absolutely no new observation has been made since the formation of the theory of evolution; our knowledge of that animal, the *facts* of the animal have been, none the less, transformed, even revolutionized. Let this instance illustrate the relation of the facts to the idea; if the idea, the theory, is tentative, if it is pliable and must be bent to fit the facts, it should not be forgotten that the "facts" are not rigid, but are elastic to the touch of the theory.

In other words, the distinction between the idea and the facts is not between a mere mental state, on one side, and a hard and rigid body on the other. Both idea and "facts" are flexible, and verification is the process of mutual adjustment, of organic interaction. It is just because the "facts" are not final, settled facts that the mind frames its hypothesis or idea; the idea is the tentative transformation of these seeming facts into more real facts.

More in detail, we may consider the process as follows: The mind attacks the mass of facts which it suspects not to be facts piece-meal. It picks out some one aspect or relation of these "facts," isolates it (technically the process of abstraction), and of this isolated relation it forms a hypothesis, which it then sets over against the facts from which this relation has been isolated. The isolated relation constitutes, technically, the universal; the background of mass of facts is the particular. The verification is the bringing together of this universal and particular: if the universal confronted with the particulars succeeds in filling out its own abstract or empty character by absorbing the particulars into itself as its own details, it is verified. And there is no other test of a theory than this, its ability to *work*, to organize "facts" into itself as specifications of its own nature. But on the other side, the particulars attacked by the universal do not remain indifferent; through it they are placed in a new light, and as facts gain a new quality. Organized into the theory, they become more significant; what had previously been oppositions and even contradictions among them is removed, and we get a harmonious system. The important point then is to see that verification is a two-edged sword. It does not test and transform the "idea," the theory, any more than it tries and moulds the "facts." In other words, if the idea is tentative, needing to be brought before the court of the facts, so also the "facts" are inadequate and more or less contradictory—that is, they are only apparently facts. They need therefore to be harmonized and rendered significant through the idea, the hypothesis. We may indifferently describe the process as a movement of the theory upon the facts whereby the latter are rendered more rational, *i.e.*, more significant and harmonious, or as a confronting of the theory by the facts, whereby it is verified. The actual result is the same in either case: we simply describe it from two points of view.

To recapitulate the whole matter: the distinction between idea and fact is a relative one, not an absolute separation; it is made for the sake of what we may term either a more real and more complete fact, or a more adequate and certain idea. There is a period, not only in childhood, but in every science, and as to every subject-matter in every science, when idea and fact are at one. But contradictions arise; the mind therefore holds idea and fact apart, regarding the idea as tentative and the fact as apparent. To this stage, there supervenes a period in which the mind attempts to get a definitive idea—or, from the other side, a real fact. It therefore by observation, experiment, and all other means at its disposal, makes its idea as definite and coherent as possible, and thus frames a hypothesis or theory. This theory it brings to the apparent facts, in order to organize them, to give them new and additional significance. So far as this is accomplished, idea and fact again become one, to remain one until further contradictions are discovered when the process must again be gone through with. And this is the description of the actual process of knowledge, of science. We have first an unconscious identification of idea and fact, and on this basis the universe, the realm of experience, is built up. But this universe lays itself open somewhere to suspicion; this suspected aspect is held apart from the rest, as an idea, the remainder being left undisturbed as "fact." The idea is wrought over as an idea into a scientific hypothesis, and is then projected again into the facts. As verified it becomes an essential part of the facts, changing to some degree or other the character of these facts. But this new universe again behaves suspiciously: the suspicious "fact" is again arrested and condemned as a *mere* idea, but passing through the reformatory of thought issues as an hypothesis, and is turned out again into the free world of fact.

This continued process of breaking up and recombination by which knowledge detects, condemns, and transforms itself is verification. Thus the analysis of this process confirms the former contention that the logical sphere is integral and unitary.

# Philosophy in American Universities: The University of Michigan

The Philosophical Courses of the University of Michigan may be conveniently classified under three heads: —

## I. Beginning

1. ELEMENTARY LOGIC, in which there are two courses, one general covering the rudiments of syllogistic and deductive logic in which Jevons is used as the basis, the other in inductive logic, intended especially for scientific students, in which Fowler is used.

2. ELEMENTARY PSYCHOLOGY. The main facts regarding modern scientific researches and methods, and the various attempts at their philosophic interpretation. Dewey's *Psychology* is the book used in connection with this course.

3. INTRODUCTION TO PHILOSOPHY. A course of lectures on the main problems and principles of the theory of knowledge and reality. Each of the foregoing courses is for one semester.

## II. Intermediate Courses

1. HISTORY OF PHILOSOPHY. Ancient and Modern. Lectures and readings designed to give information regarding both the historical development of thought, and the main problems developed in its course. The department of philosophy owns a large number of copies of the chief thinkers in

[*First published in the* Monist, *I (Oct. 1890), 150–51. Not previously reprinted.*]

modern philosophy, Locke, Descartes, etc., etc., and these are assigned to members of the class for readings and reports. Each student thus becomes acquainted with at least half-a-dozen of the leading writers at first-hand.

The course runs through the year.

2. ETHICS, THEORETICAL (one-half year) AND SOCIAL (Political Philosophy, one-half year also). The theoretical course attempts to arrive at an account of the ethical ideal by means of a critical consideration of the principal modern ethical theories, especial attention being paid to Utilitarianism, Evolutionary Ethics, and Kantianism. The second division of the course discusses the ethical basis and value of society and the state, law and rights, in connection with an account of the political theories of Plato, Aristotle, Grotius, Hobbes, Locke, Kant, Rousseau, Hegel, etc.

3. ÆSTHETICS. This course, like the previous one, unites the historical and theoretical treatment of æsthetic doctrines and results. It is designed largely to aid students in the interpretation and criticism of literature. It is a half-year course, and is followed by a half-year course (given in the English Department) on the Principles and Methods of Literary Criticism.

4. PHYSIOLOGICAL PSYCHOLOGY. Lectures, assigned readings and elementary experiments, and demonstrations. There is established, as yet, no separate psycho-physical laboratory, but the new-equipped physiological laboratory of the University is, through the courtesy of the Professor of Physiology, at the disposal of students in this line. Half-year course.

5. SCIENCE AND PHILOSOPHY OF RELIGION. Lectures, readings, etc., designed to give an account of the chief methods employed and results achieved in the modern historical and comparative study of religions. And also an account of the principal theoretical interpretations of religion. Half-year course.

## III. Advanced Courses

1. KANT'S *Critique of Pure Reason.* A study of Kant's masterpiece at first-hand. This is accompanied by a shorter subsidiary course, treating of the development of the Kantian system, and criticisms upon it. Caird's *Critical Philosophy of Kant*, is read and discussed in connection with the latter course. Half-year course.

2. HEGEL'S *Logic.* A study of Wallace's translation of the lesser *Logic* of Hegel. Half-year course.

3. THE LOGIC OF SCIENTIFIC METHODS. A lecture course taking up the study of the Logic of Science, and intended to make the hearers acquainted with the standpoint and spirit of such authors as Lotze, Sigwart, Wundt, Mill, Jevons, Bradley, Bosanquet, and the modern movement in logic generally. Half-year course.

4. PROBLEMS IN HIGHER ÆSTHETICS. A brief course for graduate students in Æsthetics.

5. SEMINARY IN ETHICS. Discussion of the treatment of some main ethical problems by the chief modern ethical writers.

The Elementary courses are conducted mainly by text-books and recitations; the Intermediate courses by lectures and assigned readings, reports and essay-writings. The Advanced courses are pursued by class discussions, conversations, etc., on basis of work done independently by the student.

The teaching is carried on by John Dewey, J. H. Tufts, and F. N. Scott.

# Moral Theory and Practice

In the first number of this journal four writers touch upon the same question,—the relation of moral theory to moral practice.* Professor Sidgwick touches it incidentally in raising the query whether what is wanted is not moral insight as much as reinforcement of moral motives; Mr. Adler touches it in discussing the relation of the organization and work of ethical societies to ethical theory; Mr. Bosanquet has one of its aspects for his subject in discussing the functions of such societies in promulgating moral ideas; and, finally, Mr. Salter is led to conceive that a great service to moral philosophy has been the fact that it has separated the "ought" from judgment as to what is, and thus kept open a region beyond science.

If any one of these writers had happened to find it within his scope directly to discuss the question of the relation of moral theory and practice, it is not likely that this article would ever have been written, but finding the subject touched upon, without direct analysis, in so many ways, I was led to attempt to clear up my own ideas. The very presence of four such articles seems to indicate that the question is in the air, and that, therefore, any moderately rational effort to clear it up for one's self may not be without interest. If Mr. Adler and Mr. Salter seem to be made the objects of my remarks in this clearing-up process, I hope it will not be attributed to a polemic spirit. Rather than seek some more impersonal, and therefore more remote, form of statement, it seems good to let the tensions discharge as they

* [Felix Adler, "The Freedom of Ethical Fellowship"; Bernard Bosanquet, "The Communication of Moral Ideas as a Function of an Ethical Society"; William M. Salter, "A Service of Ethics to Philosophy"; Henry Sidgwick, "The Morality of Strife."]

[*First published in the* International Journal of Ethics, *I (Jan. 1891), 186–203. Not previously reprinted.*]

first arose; and it is through these articles of my friends that they arose.

It seems to me that I can detect in much of current ethical discussion a lurking idea that moral conduct is something other than, or over and above, conduct itself,—understanding by conduct distinctively human action, that based upon and realizing ideas. Because the notion lurks it is difficult to dislodge,—all the more when the lurking is so evanescent that one feels, in attacking it, as if the holder of its fortress might himself disown its presence. But there is an ally of this idea which is not indeed marshalled in open array upon the battle-field, but about whose presence there can be no doubt,—the idea that moral theory is something other than, or something beyond, an analysis of conduct,— the idea that it is not simply and wholly "the theory of practice." Moral theory, for example, is often regarded as an attempt to find a philosophic "basis" or foundation for moral activity in something beyond that activity itself. Now, then, when the question comes up as to the relation of moral theory and moral conduct, the man who denies any intrinsic connection is without doubt in possession. One will hardly have the hardihood to stand and assert that until the Platonic, or the Kantian, or the Spencerian system of philosophy has been "proved," moral activity is impossible. Again, moral theory is not seldom conceived as, in Mill's phrase, a nautical almanac, or an ethical prescription or cook-book,—a collection of "rules" for conduct. When this view of moral theory is held, I, for one, shall not say nay to the man who states that there is no intrinsic connection between theory and practice. The hortatory pulpit and its modern congener and heir-apparent, the editorial page of the newspaper, may be left to uphold the idea that precepts are the great moral force of the world. But yet it does not go assured that there is no intrinsic relation between theory and practice. The trouble may be, after all, in an aborted conception of theory.

What, then, is moral theory? It is all one with moral *insight*, and moral insight is the recognition of the relationships in hand. This is a very tame and prosaic conception. It makes moral insight, and therefore moral theory, consist simply in the every-day workings of the same ordinary intelligence that measures dry-goods, drives nails, sells wheat, and invents the telephone. There is no more halo about the insight that determines what I should do in this catastrophe of life when the foundations are upheaving and my bent for eternity lies waiting to be fixed, than in that which determines whether commercial conditions favor heavy or light purchases. There is nothing more divine or transcendental in resolving how to save my degraded neighbor than in the resolving of a problem in algebra, or in the mastery of Mill's theory of induction. It may be well to bow with bated breath before every working of intelligence, but to baptize moral insight with any peculiar sacredness is to find a changeling in our hands,—sentimentalism.

Moral theory, then, is the analytic perception of the conditions and relations in hand in a given act,—it is the action *in idea*. It is the construction of the act in thought against its outward construction. *It is, therefore, the doing, —the act itself, in its emerging*. So far are we from any divorce of moral theory and practice that theory is the ideal act, and conduct is the executed insight. This is our thesis.

It is true a man can walk without a certain kind of knowledge of the process of locomotion; that he can eat without a certain kind of knowledge of foods and of digestive processes.[1] But if this is to prove that conduct is other than an expression of "theory," of the conceptions of intelligence, the basis of this analogy must be looked after. A man can plough without a knowledge of aeronautics, but this hardly proves that ploughing comes before a knowledge of how to plough, and that the knowledge of how to plough is gleaned from reflecting upon the various acts of ploughing already performed. A man may talk through a telephone without understanding the theory of its construction, but it would hardly be a safe inference that therefore he could talk through it without knowing what he was going to say, much less without knowing how to talk. The child who walks may not "understand the mechanism of locomotion," but he had once painfully and slowly to form a theory of walking none the less. I should hardly know where to find a better exam-

---

[1]    See in Mr. Adler's article, Vol. I, No. 1, pp. 20, 21.

ple of the dependence of conduct upon theory than the toil of learning to interpret and connect those signs upon which the mastery of the act of locomotion rests. And if Mr. Adler thinks the dependence of practice upon theory in locomotion has ceased with adult life, the observation of some patient suffering with complete cutaneous anæsthesia will serve to test the hypothesis. What the well-worn illustrations of walking without knowledge of the theory of locomotion, of reasoning without knowledge of the syllogism, etc., prove is that a man may know some things without knowing others, —others which, in ultimate analysis, are related. Where, however, there is anything which deserves the name of conduct, there is an idea, a "theory," at least as large as the action. Because the theory is narrow in scope it is not lacking; and it is narrow only so far as the corresponding act is abstract and partial. The average man can walk without *much* theory, because walking is not an act of *great* content. The specialist in locomotor diseases, and the painter of men and animals in motion, finds in his larger activity a knowledge of the mechanism not out of place.

And I hope the reader will not miss the point in the illustrations. For any *act* (as distinct from mere impulse) there must be "theory," and the wider the act, the greater its import, the more exigent the demand for theory. It is not likely that the wheels of moral movement are to be reversed after two thousand and more years. It was Socrates who initiated the movement, when he said that "an unexamined life is not one to be led by man." Whatever may be the case with savages and babes, the beginning of every ethical advance, under conditions of civilized existence, must be in a further "examination of life." Not even customary morality, that of respectability and of convention, is freed from dependence upon theory; it simply lives off the funded results of some once-moving examination of life.[2]

---

[2]     As Mr. Adler never expressly defines what he means by moral theory, his stand-point is, of course, difficult to deal with. But it seems to be taken for granted throughout that moral theory is something apart from the practice of which it is the theory. We are told of "borrowing from the realm of ideas a sufficient reason for accepted rules of action." We are told of motives which are different from professed doctrines, and finally of ethical theory as dealing with ideas *imported* from the region of speculation and of science, etc. (pp. 21, 22). What is this "rule" of

Perhaps, however, I shall be told that I am somewhat disingenuous in identifying an idea of action with moral theory; that theory perforce means a reflective and systematic account of things, while an idea means simply a mental conception of what should be done. I hope there is some such objector, for it gives me occasion to say that I think that such a separation of theory from idea is at the root of the confusion which I am trying to clear up. My claim is precisely that an idea of what is to be done and moral theory are identical; that the sole difference between the idea of a child, that he ought to learn the multiplication-table, or be kind to his baby-sister, and the widest moral theory—the one recognized as theory by every one—is simply one of degree of analysis of what practice is, and not a difference of kind. Action to the child is narrow and partial, and his theory is limited.

To come to close quarters with what seems to me a radically false notion of moral theory, let us take the council of pundits, called into being by Mr. Bosanquet. The question is regarding the morality of breaking down the responsibility of the parent for the sake of a good to the child. Now the reason that the answer of these pundits, as recorded by Mr. Bosanquet (p. 83 of No. 1), is of no special use is not because it is theory, but because it is *not ethical* theory. It seems a truism to remark that every theory is of its own subject-matter, and must be wholly relevant to its subject-matter. And yet this truism is all we need in order to see that the pundits have not given a conclusion in terms of moral theory at all. Conduct is absolutely individualized. Abstract action, action which is not categorical through and

---

action? If it is not an idea, a theory, 1 should like to know why it is allowed longer to cumber the earth. The morality of external command is no morality at all. Again, men indeed *profess* doctrines which do not touch their characters, but neither do the professions touch their intellects, —*i.e.*, they are not doctrines at all, but dogmas. For a doctrine, a theory, is, I take it, a mode of intellectual activity; a dogma, a burden or load upon intellectual activity. To identify moral theory with ideas imported from outside moral practice without any attempt to justify such a conception of theory is, I submit, a most startling performance. I should have supposed antecedently that theory is theory of practice. Is it not time that, before an attempt is made to divorce practice from theory, we should have a little effort to define what is meant by theory?

through, is the one last contradiction of logic and of life. There is no such thing as conduct in general; conduct is what and where and when and how to the last inch. The pundit, then, who begins his sentence with "If" is engaged in an analysis to reach a conclusion, and not with the conclusion as such at all. If he deserves a place on the council, he will surely decline to consider an abstract case when brought before him. Or, rather, so far as he does consider the abstraction, it will be simply for the sake of the sure-footedness gained in going on to consider the concrete,—to make certain that no important condition has missed due regard in the analysis. He will say, "Let me know your specific case in all its concreteness and we will spell it out together, not in order to find some abstract rule under which it may be brought, but in order that we may see what *this* case really is." And the resulting moral "theory" is the theory of the case,—a thorough-going analysis of it. The need for such analysis is simply that the needed action may be truly moral (that is, intelligent practice); that it may meet all the demands of the relationships involved, instead of being one-sided, that is, more or less sentimental.

What I am getting at, in a word, is that the ordinary idea of moral theory shears off the very factors which make it *moral* theory at all and reduces it to the plane of physical theory. Physical science does deal with abstractions, with hypothesis. It says, "If this, then that." It deals with the relations of conditions and not with facts, or individuals, at all. It says, "I have nothing to do with your concrete falling stone, but I can tell you this, that it is a law of falling bodies that, etc. You must make your own allowances in applying this universal formula to the special case, according to the peculiar circumstances of the special case." Now, the pundit who should allow his final deliverances to go out in the form of "If this, then that," (excepting as a way of saying "I do not know enough of this concrete case to have any theory about it"), would be denying the sole condition of *moral* theory; he would be mutilating the moral fact, the individualized act, till it was a mere bundle of abstractions.

Shall I be told, then, that there can be no such thing as moral theory at all? That it is impossible to get a theory which shall be concrete and individualized as the act is concrete and individualized? Ah, but my objector, there *is* such a thing. Every man, before he acts, always has such a theory unless his act is one of mere impulse. It is true enough that he may not exhaust, that he may never exhaust, all the real concreteness of the act; but none the less his idea of the act is individualized as far as it goes; it may be a smaller individual than the real act, but this does not make it an abstract universal. What he sees, in a word, is *this* act, although the "this" he sees may not be the true complete "this."

What we come to is: Moral theory cannot exist in a book. It is, I believe, a popular superstition to identify science with a lot of formulæ and statements in a book. I have my doubts whether even the physical sciences exist as a lot of general statements held apart from facts; I suspect that our physical sciences have their existence only in our neutral attitude toward the world of fact, that they get real existence only as they become part and parcel of the meaning of the world that we daily perceive. But I am very certain that moral science is *not* a collection of abstract laws, and that it is only in the mind of an agent as an agent. It is his perception of the acts that need doing,—that is, his perception of the existing world of practice in all its concrete relationships.

In last analysis, then, the value of our council of pundits will depend upon this: not whether theory helps practice, but whether the council is capable of the kind of theory demanded. Moral theory, so far as it can exist outside of the particular agent concerned with a special act, exists in the mind of him who can reproduce the condition of that agent. Just because moral practice is so individual or concrete, you can theorize for another only as you "put yourself in his place." Browning's "Martin Relph" or "Clive" is then the model for our band of pundits rather than Kant's *Critique of Practical Reason*.[3] Put in logical terms, the question is whether our judges can use, in their judgments, the "category" of self, or only that of abstract law.

---

[3]    You meet persons who want to argue about such a poem. They are parallel with those who reduce moral theory to a lot of ifs and ands.

"This is all aside from the point," I think I shall hear. The question is not whether theory must be back of action, but whether a given theory of ethics, the Kantian, the Hedonistic, the Hegelian, must be behind it. Well, if this is the point, I would it were clearly stated. It is a dangerous procedure which concludes that because moral practice can occur without this or that ethical analysis, therefore there is no intrinsic and absolutely indispensable connection of theory and conduct.

But let us take the point so raised. What shall we say of the relation of an ethical "system," that of Mill or Spencer, to moral conduct? Or, adopting the phraseology of Mr. Bosanquet, let us admit that so far we have been speaking of "moral ideas," and now go on to raise the question of the value of "ideas about morality" for action.

I must revert again to the position already taken. Moral conduct is precisely that which realizes an idea, a conception. The breadth of action (so far as moral value is concerned and not historical outcome) is measured by the insight of the agent. What are the conditions which require action, and what is the action which they demand? Just so far as this question is raised and answered, action is moral and not *merely* instinctive, or sentimental. This is evidently a work of analysis. Like every analysis, it requires that the one making it be in possession of certain working tools. I cannot resolve this practical situation which faces me by merely looking at it. I must attack it with such instruments of analysis as I have at hand. *What we call moral rules are precisely such tools of analysis.* "I ought not to lie." Very well, then, would doing so and so be telling the truth? What *is* telling the truth in this instance? "I should do as I would be done by." Very well; what would I have done to me in this case? that is to say, what are the personal relations involved here? Some, who would be the first to repudiate the practical consequences in the way of casuistry logically involved, entertain the idea that a moral law is a command: that it actually tells us what we should or should not do! The Golden Rule gives me absolutely no knowledge, of itself, of what I should do. The question of what in this case I should do in order to do as I would be done by has still to be resolved, though the Golden Rule be a thousand times my maxim. The rule is a counsel of perfection; it is a warning that in my analysis of the moral situation (that is, of the conditions of practice) I be impartial as to the effects on me and thee. Or, it is the statement of a principle,—the principle of individuality, that the activity of every man concerned has an equal claim for consideration; that though I be a great Pharisee or the high-priest himself, I am bound to consider the welfare of that miserable sinner of a publican as I would my own. About the specific act to be done it tells, I repeat, not a jot. But it is a most marvellous tool of analysis; it helps me hew straight and fine in clearing out this jungle of relations of practice.

What this rule is, that every rule is which has any use at all. This is the grain of truth in Mill's idea of a nautical almanac. The almanac, after all, does not tell the sailor where he is nor how to navigate. It is an aid in his analysis of the required conditions of right navigation. In the supreme art of life the tools must be less mechanical; more depends upon the skill of the artist in their manipulation, but they are none the less useful. Our mastery of a required case of action would be slow and wavering if we had to forge anew our weapons of attack in each instance. The temptation to fall back on the impulse or accident of the moment would be well-nigh irresistible. And so it is well we have our rules at hand, but well only if we have them for *use*.

What is the connection of this, however, with special philosophic systems? Just this: the rule as a tool of analysis is an idea. The Golden Rule is, as suggested, the idea of the value of individuality; the rule of truthfulness is the idea of the transparence of media in all human exchanges, etc. A philosophic theory of ethics is a similar idea, but one of deeper grasp, and therefore wider hold. It bears much the same relation to the particular rule as this to the special case. It is a tool for the analysis of its meaning, and thereby a tool for giving it greater affect. It is hardly necessary, I suppose, to profess the deepest respect for the Golden Rule, but this is not inconsistent with recognizing that if it were not held open to reflective criticism, to analysis of meaning and bearing, it would surely degenerate into a mere external command. That it, or any other rule, may be a workable tool, that it may really give aid in a specific case, it must have life and spirit. What can give it the life and spirit necessary to make it other than a cramped and cramping petrification except the continued free play of intelligence upon it?

The Golden Rule itself, in other words, except as an idea among ideas, would speedily become either an external command, a merely speculative abstraction (an ideal with a big I, and no r for reality at all), or that deadest of all dead things, a preacher's mere exhortation. What would this particular rule have amounted to practically if there had not been ideas back of it, which vivified it by taking it out of its isolation, and by making it one element in a vast picture of the world,—the Pauline idea, for example, of a divine spirit incarnate in all mankind, and the Stoic idea of a republic of humanity? And if the Golden Rule now seems to stand and do its work by itself, it is because these other larger ideas, and such as they, have so realized themselves; have died as mere ideas, and been buried in the common consciousness of men, now arising thence as in effect a normal part of the outlook upon life. They have become so integrated with the content of the Golden Rule that the latter itself has become a vast idea, or working tool, of practice.

Now it will be found, upon examination, that every philosophic theory of ethics performs in its degree this same service. It serves, at its time, to preserve the minor rule, the instrument of the ordinary man, from fossilizing. Let rules be conceived as formal prescripts of some outside law-giver, human or divine, and utilitarianism responds with its new criticism,—its insistence upon their relation to human welfare. Let rules slip away into sickly sentimentalism, or harden into rude militarism, and a Kant responds with his equal assertion of law and freedom.[4] And in time these ideas filter into the average consciousness, and their truth becomes, wholly unawares to the average consciousness, a part

---

[4]     I hope I shall not be understood as endeavoring to account for the genesis of these ethical systems. I am simply illustrating the part they may play in keeping alive and active moral "rules."

of the ordinary insight into life,—a part of the meaning of the world of practice in which we live. Life looks different to-day to the man to whom Bentham and Kant are not even names, because of the formulæ of the greatest good, the autonomy of will, and the categorical imperative. In conclusion, it is a piece of scholasticism to suppose that a moral rule has its own self-defining and self-applying content. What truth-telling, what honesty, what patience, what self-respect are change with every change of intelligence, with every added insight into the relations of men and things. It is only the breath of intelligence blowing through such rules that keeps them from the putrefaction which awaits all barren idealities.

There is and can be, then, no rigid line between "ideas about morals" (if only they be really ideas,—movements of intelligence) and "moral ideas." The former are the latter in the making. It is only as our moral ideas, our conceptions of this and that thing which needs doing, are reinforced and reconstructed by larger inquiries into the reality of human relationships that they are preserved. And it is only as our ideas about morals realize themselves, only as they become part of the working behavior of the mind towards its concrete duties, that they are other than curiosities for the collector of the bric-a-brac of thought. That they are other, that the history of ethical thought is a record of profound interest to him who has the eyes to read, is because this history is a history of enlarging action; because moral theories are man's first reconstruction of the moral world into a larger and freer one.

And while it lies somewhat beyond my topic, I cannot refrain from saying that no undertaking is more tedious, because more fruitless, than the attempt to pump up moral motive forces. Set as low an estimate as we please upon the place of knowledge in action, and as high a value as we can upon the emotions, how are we to get the interest, the emotion? People are somewhat tired of hearing, "You ought to do thus and so"; they are somewhat tired of hearing, "If you would only do this and somebody else would do that, and so on, how much better everything would be." This condition of fatigue may be due to the depravity of human nature; but I think it is rather due to its goodness; human nature refuses to be moved except in the one truly human way,—through intelligence. Get the fresher, more open outlook, the refined and clarified intelligence, and the emotions will take care of themselves. They *are* there, and all they need is freeing. And it is, in power and not in word, the truth that makes free. Besides intelligence, I see but two means of moral emergence: that of hortatory preaching and that of some scheme as panacea. And both of these, it seems to me, are but attempts to replace intelligence by argument. And what, after all, is argument but halved—or quartered —intelligence?[5]

But I have another and perhaps a larger wave to face. What is the relation of knowledge, of theory, to that Ought which seems to be the very essence of moral conduct? This is the question raised by Mr. Salter, and, as I understand him, he contends that no amount of science, of knowledge, can establish obligation, either in general or in a particular case. For science is of the "is," duty of the "ought," and the "ought" is separate from the "is."

I hardly know where to begin in dealing with this conception. It opens immense fields of philosophy, both historically (compare, for instance, the movement of German ethics from Kant to Hegel) and theoretically. Besides, I seem to find two minds in Mr. Salter, with one of which I am in most hearty agreement. After contrasting in the blankest manner the world of fact and of morals, he goes on to suggest that moral forces are not only rightfully supreme over the actual forces in the world at any time, but "are so interwoven with the order of things that nothing out of harmony with them can long stand" (p. 117). This would imply that moral forces *are*, and that they do not exist nobody knows where outside the actual world, but are themselves supremely actual. With this view I find myself, as I

[5]     As Mr. Adler discusses the relations of theory and practice, not *per se*, but in connection with the wisdom of founding an ethical society upon a philosophic system, I may avoid misunderstanding if I say that I am not discussing the latter question even by implication. It is one thing to believe that moral theory is in so chaotic and fractional a state that consciously to build an organization upon some one part of it would lead to formalism and inefficiency. It is surely another to hold that moral practice and moral theory have no essential and intrinsic unity.

remarked, in large sympathy; but (aside from the fact that I can see no way of reconciling it with Mr. Salter's other mind) it needs much analysis. If this view means that "justice" and "love" (the moral forces specified by Mr. Salter) are something in themselves, a superfine addendum to the rest of things, or a sort of tempering of the otherwise hard physical forces, I can only confess my incapacity to frame any corresponding conception. If it means that "justice" and "love" are not something in themselves which somehow rule over and sanctify the rest of reality,—morally lawless and unsanctified in itself,—but are the actual forces of reality, taken at a certain angle and scope of working, it conveys intelligibly to me.

But limiting the question as best I can, I should say (first) that the "ought" always rises from and falls back into the "is," and (secondly) that the "ought" is itself an "is,"—the "is" of action.

The "ought" is never its own justification. We ought to do so and so simply because of the existing practical situation; because of the relationships in which we find ourselves. We may, by an abstraction, which is justifiable enough as a means of analysis, distinguish between what is and what should be; but this is far from meaning that there is any such separation in reality. Let us take, then, a specific case: Here is a street-car conductor, and the question is whether he should (ought to) join in a strike which his Union has declared. I do not intend to make and resolve some hypothetical case, but simply, in order to get out of that undoubtedly adorable, yet somewhat vague, realm to which we so naturally incline when we discuss obligation, call up the kind of fact which constitutes obligation. The man thinks of his special work, with its hardships, indeed, and yet a work, an activity, and thus a form of freedom or satisfaction; he thinks of his wage, of what it buys; of his needs, his clothing, his food, his beer and pipe. He thinks of his family, and of his relations to them; his need of protecting and helping them on; his children, that he would educate, and give an evener start in the world than he had himself; he thinks of the families of his fellows; of the need that they should live decently and advance somewhat; he thinks of his bonds to his Union; he calls up the way in which the families of the corporation which employs him live; he tries to realize the actual state of business, and imagines a possible failure and its consequences, and so on. Now where in this case do we get beyond concrete facts, and what is the "ought" but the outcome of these facts, varying as the facts vary, and expressing simply and only the situation which the facts form, so far as our man has the intelligence to get at it? And how does this case differ from any case of moral action?

What has become of moral rules and laws in this case? I cannot go over the ground already gone over (pp. 100, 101 of this article), but I must repeat that a man's duty is never to obey certain rules; his duty is always to respond to the nature of the actual demands which he finds made upon him,—demands which do not proceed from abstract rules, nor from ideals, however awe-inspiring and exalted, but from the concrete relations to men and things in which he finds himself. The rule, at worst and at best, is but an aid towards discriminating what the nature of these relations and demands is. It may be true, as Mr. Salter says, that the Golden Rule does not indicate anything that happens; in the same sense, however, it is true that the law of gravitation does not indicate anything that is. Both laws, as *mere* laws, are abstractions or hypotheses; and to keep them abstractions, to keep them away from the facts, is to keep them from indicating, or pointing to, anything. Taken in any full meaning, the law of gravitation indicates an order of physical fact in which matter behaves thus and so; the Golden Rule indicates an order of social fact, in which it is true that persons act thus and so, and not simply desirable that they should act thus and so. The Golden Rule has no more meaning apart from the real constitution of a social order than the law of gravitation has apart from the real constitution of matter and force.

In a word, a man has not to do Justice and Love and Truth; he has to do justly and truly and lovingly. And this means that he has to respond to the actual relations in which he finds himself. To do truly is to regard the whole situation as far as one sees it, and to see it as far as one can; to do justly is to give a fit and impartial regard to each member of this situation, according to its place in the system; to do lovingly is to make the whole situation one's own, not dividing into parts of which one is a warm *meum* and the other a cold *tuum*.

The correctness of the exact definitions given is a matter, of course, of no importance. The point is that all definitions given must be given in the same terms, — terms, that is, not of mere "oughts," but of concrete ways of acting in reference to a situation, not unearthly, but of facts. Let, for example, our conductor be fixed upon justice. Now, just so far as he is able to resolve "justice" into specific relations between men and men, so far he will have a definite end in view, and such emotions as are aroused within him will simply quicken him in his effort to realize these relations. But just so far as he cannot translate "justice" into such actual relations, so far it becomes a sentiment, — it is justice in general, at large. And this sentiment is almost sure to turn into a bitterness of feeling which leads astray, — to a blind feeling that things should be overturned because they are not what they should be.

And every duty, every ought, so far as it is not the outcome of analysis of the situation demanding action, must come to some such mere feeling. The logical consequences of the separation of the "ought" from the "is" is worshipping blind impulses, labelled love of justice, of truth, of humanity. Its final term is the apotheosis of sentiment, of the pious sigh, "Oh, would that things were otherwise!" If the "ought" escapes this mire, it is only to run upon a rock, — the bare, brute fact of "oughtness" with no essential meaning. It stiffens into a rigid external must, imposed no one knows why or how. The attempt to keep the "ought" unrationalized undoubtedly springs from a desire to keep it pure; to free it from dependence upon some ulterior reason, in the sense of a reason behind the act itself. But to deny that the moral act, the "ought," has a meaning behind the act itself is not incompatible with recognizing that the "ought" itself has a reason, that it is a perfect nest of meanings. To evacuate the "ought" of this intrinsic rationale is to drive out all moral quality and render it the compulsion of a superior force. It is only because the "ought" rests upon and expresses the "is" that it is something more than vague, ill-directed sentiment or rigid external command.

If the "ought" and the "is" are so close to each other, where is the relative distinction? Here: the "ought" is the "is" of *action*. There seems to be an opinion that obligation, the "oughtness," is something superadded to the analysis of the act itself; that we may have examined never so thoroughly the content of a proposed act, of some suggested end, without the idea of obligation ever presenting itself, the result being some intellectual judgment regarding bare fact. Some machinery, the exact nature of which I have never found stated, is then called in to clap on the "ought," and thus give a moral aspect to a hitherto coldly intellectual matter.

The creaking, lumbering *Deus ex machina* which in nick of time projects its proper entity upon the stage of human knowledge has, however, so often been replaced by the smooth, swift workings of a single intelligence, that we may gather courage for the hope that the "ought" too is from intelligence rather than a somewhat let down from supernal flies or sprung from an unearthly trap.

It must be remembered that the material of judgment here is practical, not theoretical. The question is not concerning the given state of things, but concerning an end to be adopted; or, rather, it is concerning the bare actual fact only so far as that points to some active outcome, to some end. The difference between a practical and a theoretical consciousness is that the former is consciousness of *something to be done*. And this consciousness of something to be done is the consciousness of duty. Suppose, once more, our conductor. He has thought out, as best he may, the existing situation, and has come to the conclusion that the only act which meets the situation, as he understands it, is to join the strike. Now, does he require some new power of mind to bring in the "ought," and to tell him that this is the act that should be done? The very question he has been considering is a question of action, of practice; what is the especial line of conduct to be followed here? The outcome of his reflections has been just: *This* step is the one to be taken. The difference between saying, "This act is the one to be done, this act will meet the situation," and saying, "The act *ought* to be done," is merely verbal. The analysis of action is from the first an analysis of what is to be done; how, then, should it come out excepting with a "this should be done"? Just as the consciousness of truth is not adventitious to a judgment of fact but constitutes its content, so the consciousness of obligation is not an annex to the judgment of action. Any being who is capable of acting from ideas—that is, whose conduct is the attempted realization of proposed ends—must conceive of these ends in terms of something to be done—of obligation. And that is what is meant by saying not only that the "ought" rests upon and expresses the "is," but that it is itself the "is" of action. What we ordinarily call an "is" is simply the "is" of fact at rest. If action, or the following out of ideas, is not a fact, with just the same claims to be considered a part of the real world as a stick or a stone, a planet, or an earthworm, then, and then only, have Mr. Salter's remarks about the separation of the "is" and the "ought," the unverifiableness of moral ideas, the attractiveness and authority of moral ideas apart from facts, and the existence of a domain beyond science, any shred of meaning.

Imagine a scene of ceaseless movement; needs, relations, institutions ever moving on. In the midst of this scene appears an intelligence who identifies himself with the wonderful spectacle of action. He finds that its law is his law, because he *is* only as a member sharing in its needs, constituted by its relations and formed by its institutions. This intelligence would know this scene that he may know himself. He puts forth his grasp, his *Begriff*, and arrests the movement. Taking the movement at a certain point and holding it there, intelligence cuts a cross-section through it to see what it is like. It has now mastered the situation, the case "is" thus and so. Then intelligence removes its brake, its abstracting hold, and the scene moves on. That to which intelligence sees it moving is the "ought to be." The "ought to be" is the larger and fuller activity into which it is the destiny and glory of the present fact to pass.

This, then, is the relation of moral theory and practice. Theory is the cross-section of the given state of action in order to know the conduct that should be; practice is the realization of the idea thus gained: it is theory in action.

# Poetry and Philosophy

> The future of poetry is immense, because in poetry our race, as time goes on, will find an ever surer and surer stay. There is not a creed which is not shaken; not an accredited dogma which is not shown to be questionable; not a received tradition which does not threaten to dissolve. Our religion has materialized itself in the fact, in the supposed fact; it has attached its emotion to the fact, and now the fact is failing it. But for poetry the idea is everything. . . . Poetry attaches its emotion to the idea, the idea *is* the fact. . . . More and more mankind will discover that we have to turn to poetry to interpret life for us, to console us, to sustain us. Without poetry our science will appear incomplete; and most of what now passes for religion and philosophy will be replaced by poetry.—*Matthew Arnold*

"Not a creed unshaken," "not a dogma unquestioned, every tradition threatening to dissolve,"—this is Matthew Arnold's counterphrase to Carlyle's "Our relations all an inquiry and a doubt." In a world of disintegrated intelligence and a broken authority, Arnold sees men more and more turning to poetry for consolation, for stay, for interpretation. There is absence of any coherent social faith and order; there is doubt whether any theory of life at once valuable and verifiable, true to intelligence and worthy to the emotion, is any longer possible, and yet there is also demand for authority and for instruction. We may say science is verifiable, but it lacks sympathy, consolation, humanity; it does not afford instruction where instruction is most wanted,—in the ordering of life. What once afforded all this, says Mr. Arnold, has lost its hold as truth; it no

[*Commencement address at Smith College, 18 June 1890. First published in* Andover Review, *XVI, 105–16. Reprinted in* Characters and Events, *ed. Joseph Ratner (New York: Henry Holt and Co., [c1929]), I, 3–17, with the title "Matthew Arnold and Robert Browning."*]

longer appeals verifiably to us. This is the difficulty of the situation: the true does not inspire, does not aid; that which once gave stay and interpretation is no longer true. In poetry men find a wide interpretation of life, noble ideas about life, and also a kind sympathy with all its colored moods, with all phases of its movement. Keen feeling, wide sympathy, noble ideas, serious emotion, are found there. What more do we want? What more natural than, in the difficulty of our times, men turning to poetry for guidance? We may well believe that poetry is more and more becoming our religion and our philosophy. Here, let us also add, there is no need to ask if this or that be scientifically true. "For poetry the idea is everything; all else is illusion. For poetry the idea is the fact."

We have the thought of Matthew Arnold before us. What shall we say of it? Shall we make bold to criticise the position? Spite of the clear insight of this great critic, shall we venture to say that his insight was essentially limited in range? that he saw but a small part of the forces really at work in modern thought?

We need not be detained by what our critic says regarding the existing disintegration of intellectual authority in matters of belief. Making allowance for overstatement, all will admit readily that there is enough of unrest, enough of doubt in modern thought, to make it worth while to raise this question, Where shall we find authority, the instruction which our natures demand? Shall we cease to find it in philosophy, or in science, and shall we find it in poetry?

I think none desire that poetry shall not be more and more the vehicle of serious thought and ennobling emotion, that it shall not more and more convey genuine and helpful interpretation of life. *Absit omen.* We have fallen too much on days of trivial subjects, ornate treatment, cheap sentiment, and artificial imagery not to sympathize with all that Mr. Arnold says about the high calling of poetry. We cannot too often return to the idea that its purpose is to deepen the sense of what is worthy, of what is permanent in life. The question only presses the more earnestly: How is poetry to interpret valuable meanings of life, how to animate to the execution of them; how is it to be kept from the evils that threaten it, from the frivolous, the sensual, the artificial? Can it do all this, if it is not backed and sustained by something which commends itself to the intelligence? Call this something what you will, theology, philosophy, or theory of life, how can poetry preserve its genuineness and its sustaining force, if it cut loose from all verifiable account of the universe? Who shall keep the keeper? I know of but one answer. Truth, and truth alone, can do this. And I confess I do not understand how that can be true for the imagination, for the emotions, which is not also true for intelligence.

It is easy to disparage science, it is easy to laugh at philosophy, with its "reasoning about causation and finite and infinite being." Both are remote enough from our immediate spiritual and ethical interests. Face to face with the supreme question concerning the right ordering of life they seem ludicrously insufficient. But, after all, science means only knowledge,—philosophy, only love of wisdom, only the essay at reaching the meaning of this experience of ours. I cannot believe that the attempt to know truth, to grasp the meaning of experience, is remote from conduct, from the ideals and aspirations of life. In the words of Carlyle, I verify my own conviction: "Belief, indeed, is the beginning and first condition of all spiritual force whatsoever; only so far as imagination is *believed* can there be any use or even any enjoyment of it." The imagination rests upon belief; it is from belief that it gets its cue to stay, to interpret, its consolation. If there is belief in the high and serious values of the universe, with what glory shall not the imagination portray and inspire life, what consolations shall not issue from it! But let intelligence lose this belief in the meaning and worthiness of experience, and poetry is but the tricking out of illusions, the devising of artifices. I can well comprehend that poetry may deliver truth with a personal and a passionate force which is beyond the reach of theory painting in gray on gray. Indeed, it is the emotional kindling of reality which is the true province of poetry.

Astronomers tell us that meteors are cold rock, cold as the frozen emptiness of space, molten by contact with our earthly atmosphere, and thence glowing like the stars. Thus do I conceive of poetry. The graceless, rigid,

dark facts of science, of philosophy, pass through the atmosphere of personality, of the hopes and fears of a human soul,
and issue illumined and to illuminate. Without the basis of
fact, of fact verifiable by science, our light is a will-o'-the-
wisp, a wandering flame generated in the stagnant marshes
of sentiment. In a word, there must be the possibility of
science and philosophy to criticise, to verify. Poets are indeed seers and makers; but if what they make has matter,
has weight, if what they see is more than shadow, the poets
must reveal, they must round out to high completeness, the
meaning of the life that is about them. Poets cannot be freed
from the conditions which attach to the intelligence of man
everywhere. The poet and the ploughman gaze at the same
scene, only the eyes of one are holden. If the life which the
poet presents to us as throbbing, as pregnant, ever new from
God, is other than the genuine revelation of the ordinary
day-by-day life of man, it is but dainty foolery or clumsy
masquerading. If life is, indeed, dull and blank and unap-
pealing, poetry will be depressing, mechanical, merely deco-
rative. If life is abundant, promising, endless, poetry will be
spontaneous, buoyant, passionate; it will have enjoyment. If
life carries meaning with it, fulfills purpose, makes exac-
tions which are opportunities, poetry will be high-minded, a
power to stay and to console.

Nor is this all. What life is found to be depends in
large measure upon the prevailing theory of life, upon the
interpretation of it which commends itself to the intelligence. Life is not a raw, unworked material to which the
poet may directly apply himself. As it comes to the poet, life
is already a universe of meanings, of interpretations, which
indeed the poet may fill out, but not dispense with. For good
or for ill, centuries of reflective thought have been interpreting life, and their interpretations remain the basis and furnish the instrument for all the poet may do; he may simply
use the assimilated results of the labors of scientific men and
philosophers. Let the philosophy of a time be materialistic,
mechanical, and the poetry of that time is artificial and
unworthy. If the poet succeeds in rising above the thought
that has taken possession of contemporary life, it is because
by instinct or by desire he falls back on the larger and freer

ideas of an earlier day. If the ideas of a time breathe the
solemn atmosphere of a divine order, if they find reality
surcharged with meaning, we can imagine the poetry that
results. It is the poetry of Homer, of Dante, of Shakespeare.
If the philosophy of a time is agnostic, if it utters a scorn of
life as it seems to be, that philosophy will also sound its note
in the poetry of its day.

Thus are we brought again to our starting-point. If we
are correct in our judgment that a poet must draw his
sustenance from the intelligence of his time, the poetry of
to-day must feel the touch of what we call our agnosticism,
and the poets of to-day must be somewhat moved by this
trait of contemporary life.

Are they thus moved? What is their attitude toward the
agnosticism, the doubt, the pessimism, of the present day?

I wish now to speak in this relation of two poets who
have recently passed from us. One of them is Mr. Arnold
himself, poet as well as critic; the other is Mr. Robert
Browning. How do these, both serious and high-minded
poets, stand affected by the popular philosophy? How do
they affect us who go to them to learn of life?

Nothing in Arnold the poet strikes us more than the
teaching of Arnold the critic. Translated from the impersonal narrative of prose into the warmth of poetry, it is the
same lesson. Compare the passage standing as our text with
this: —

> *Wandering between two worlds, one dead*
> *The other powerless to be born,*
> *With nowhere yet to lay my head,*
> *Like them, on earth I wait forlorn.*

Or with this: —

> *The sea of faith*
> *Was once, too, at the full, and round earth's shore*
> *Lay like the folds of a bright girdle furled:*
> *But now I only hear*
> *Its melancholy long withdrawing roar.*

Indeed, Arnold's distinguishing sign among modern poets is
the melancholy beauty with which he has voiced the sense of

loss; his sad backward glance at the departure of old faiths and ideals; the brooding memories of joys whose spring has fallen away; the shapeless, hopeless hope for the dawn of a new joy, new faith.

I should say that the source of regret which expires from Arnold's lines is his consciousness of a twofold isolation of man—his isolation from nature, his isolation from fellow-man. No longer, he seems to say, may man believe in his oneness with the dear nature about him: the sense of a common spirit binding them together has vanished; the sense of a common purpose outworking in both has fled. Nature, in ceasing to be divine, has ceased to be human. The faith that one idea, one fulfillment, unites in cherished bonds man to nature, is no more; in its stead, the consciousness of isolation. There is still, indeed, grateful companionship with nature, but below this companionship is the knowledge of an impassable gulf: —

> *Thou hast been, shalt be, art alone:*
> *Or, if not quite alone, yet they*
> *Who touch thee are unmating things,—*
> *Ocean and clouds, and night and day,*
> *Lorn autumns and triumphant springs.*

The companionship is not at bottom real: it is only on man's side; Nature lacks the element of purpose which alone could give joyful response to man's needs. Man solaces and strengthens his spirit by recourse to Nature, but Nature goes her own way and man must return to his; strengthened and solaced, indeed, but only that he may live self-poised like Nature, careless, unheeding of all beyond self. Companionship no longer is rooted in the heart of things; it is no longer the outcome of a single life.

Man, repulsed from the intimacy of communion with Nature, may turn to man for fellowship; but here, too, is found isolation: —

> *Like drift-wood spars which meet and pass*
> *Upon the boundless ocean plain,*
> *So on the sea of life, alas!*
> *Man meets man, meets and parts again.*

No reader of Arnold can fail to notice how spontaneously he takes his most characteristic metaphor from the sea and the matters of the sea. The verses I am about to quote have the same inspiration and tell the same story. As the islands of the sea are separated by that sea which is common to them all, so men are separated by that very life in which all share. Between them is

> *The unplumbed, salt, estranging sea.*
>
> *Yes, on the sea of life enisled,*
> *With echoing straits between us thrown,*
> *We mortal millions live alone.*

I am aware, however, of no passage of Arnold's which comes to us so laden with the gospel of the isolation of life as that poem which gives us his reading of history, "Obermann Once More." The sad tone reaches its highest note in the description of the loss of Christian faith. From the land whence once came the words of humanity's life,—

> *Ah, from that silent, sacred land*
> *Of sun and arid stone,*
> *And crumbling wall and sultry sand,*
> *Comes now one word alone!*
> *From David's lips that word did roll,*
> *'Tis true and living yet:*
> *No man can save his brother's soul,*
> *Nor pay his brother's debt.*
> *Alone, self-poised, henceforward man*
> *Must labor.*

Not from him who identified himself with the woe and the joy of all men's lives, but from David, sounds the final word of Palestine. The life of common brotherhood, struggle and destiny of Christianity has given way to the old isolated struggle of the individual.

> *No man can save his brother's soul*
> *Nor pay his brother's debt.*

That is, I take it, the last word of Arnold's poetic message, his last interpretation of life. Perhaps I should rather say this is the keynote of it all. To say it is the last is to say his last message is one of weakness and despair. Contrary to this, the philosophy which Mr. Arnold leaves us is one of endeavor, of strenuous, almost buoyant, endeavor, in spite of the fact that this endeavor must spring from sadness. If man is isolated, in that isolation he may find himself, and, finding himself, living his own life, lose all his misery. Although man may not commune with Nature, he may yet follow and repeat her. If the works of Nature go on,

> *Bounded by themselves, and unregardful*
> *In what state God's other works may be,*

man should emulate this self-sufficient energy. Isolation is translated into self-dependence. Separation throws man farther into himself, deepens his consciousness of his own destiny and of his own law. The verses which close the poem called "Youth of Man," while far from the most poetical of his lines, sum up, I think, his interpretation of life: —

> *Sink, O youth, in thy soul!*
> *Yearn to the greatness of nature;*
> *Rally the good in the depths of thyself.*

This is the outcome of the loneliness of life. Regret and melancholy are not the final fruit. Obey nature, go thy way, heeding nothing less than the concerns of men. As a consolation for thy loneliness, yearn to the greatness of nature. Is man helpless to save another's soul? Then all the more let him rally the good in the depths of himself!

How does this message stand related to the dictum of Arnold that poetry is to take the place of philosophy, of theology? How does it stand related to our dictum that the interpretation of life which poetry gives us must be parallel to the demonstrations of philosophy? I do not know how any one can apprehend the message uttered by Arnold and not feel its heart and substance to be that reflective and philo-

sophic interpretation of life given by one school of the
world's great moralists,—by the Stoics. As surely as Arnold's style, his deftness, his delicacy, his simplicity testify
to the influence of Virgil, of Æschylus, of Homer, so surely
do his ideas and their substance testify to Marcus Aurelius
and to Epictetus and to Kant. I do not mean by this that
Arnold has put the *Meditations* or the *Critique of Practical
Reason* into verse. I do not even imagine that Arnold had
much acquaintance with Kant, or was attracted by such as
he had. Speaking broadly, however, the ideas of the Stoics,
of Kant, and of Matthew Arnold, grow out of the same soil.
There is in all three the conception of the individual as shut
off from real communion with nature and with fellow-man,
and yet as bearing in himself a universal principle.

> *And thou, thou lonely heart,*
> *Which never yet, without remorse,*
> *Even for a moment didst depart*
> *From thy remote and spheréd course*
> *To haunt the place where passions dwell,*
> *Back to thy solitude again.*

This is precisely in the sense of Epictetus, precisely in the
vein of Kant. I would not, however, insist upon detailed
likeness in special points. What is alike in all is the underlying spirit, the attitude towards life. The individual flung
back from the world and from society upon himself, and
within himself finding the secret of a new strength, the
source of a new consolation,—this is the interpretation of life
common to all. How can such an interpretation have use,
have enjoyment, be a consolation, be a stay in poetry, and
yet have no legitimacy in theory? What alembic does the
poet possess that he may apply ideas to life with the assurance that in poetry the ideas are the fact, while the same
ideas in the hands of the philosopher are unverifiable, dis-
credited dogmas, shaken creeds, or failing traditions? I cannot rid myself of the conviction that the weight and the
humanity of the message of the poet are proportionate to the
weighty and human ideas which he develops; that these
ideas must be capable of verification to the intelligence,—

must be true in that system of knowledge which is science, in that discussion of the meaning of experience which is philosophy.

But what if Mr. Arnold's interpretation of life be partial? What if a completer account of experience, a deeper and more adventurous love of wisdom, should find community below all isolation? Would not the philosophy of life which revealed this limitation of Mr. Arnold's interpretation, reveal also the limitation of his poetry? This is the question that comes to me when I put Mr. Arnold's poetry, with all its nobility, beside the poetry of Robert Browning.

What a change from a serene yet cold air of one to the genial, glowing atmosphere of the other, which envelops and embraces everything in this world of ours as if in fear that something might escape its loving touch. What a change from the pallid colors in which one paints life to the varied warmth of the other! What a change from the almost remote and academic sympathies of the one to the passionate human sympathies of the other! Where Arnold finds food for pensive regret, a rendering of triumphant hope is borne to us from Browning. When the world tells a story of softened melancholy to Arnold, Browning reads a tale of keen and delicious joy. If Arnold sings of calm, self-poised resignation and endeavor, the trumpet peal of an abounding life bursts from Browning. Arnold stands upon the sandy, barren shore of that vast ocean where is seen only "the turbid ebb and flow of human misery," whence comes only the melancholy sounds of a withdrawing faith. Browning takes his place on this homely, every-day earth of ours: —

> *Do I stoop? I pluck a posey.*
> *Do I stand and stare? All's blue.*

Strenuous, abounding, triumphant optimism, — that is the note of Browning: —

> *How good is man's life, the men living! how fit to employ*
> *All the heart and the soul and the senses forever in joy!*

Buoyant faith, that is the attitude of Browning: —

> *God's in his heaven!*
> *All's right with the world!*

What is the source of this note of Browning, what the authority for his attitude? It is only when we go to his ideas, the ideas which he applies to life, by which he criticises and interprets life, that we get the secret of his superior passion, of his superior joy, of his superior sympathy. An adequate rendering of Browning's conception of the meaning of life does not come within the scope of this article. The most inadequate rendering cannot fail to note that Browning knows and tells of no isolation of man from nature, of man from man. No account, however brief, can fail to record the abundance, the intensity, the vibrating fullness, the impassioned sanity of his verse, basing themselves upon Browning's realization that the world was made for man, and that man was made for man: —

> *This world's no blot for us,*
> *No blank. It means intensely and means good.*

This is the uniform utterance of Browning.

> *Such a soul,*
> *Such a body, and then such an earth,*
> *For ensphering the whole!*
>
> *The earth's first stuff*
> *Was neither more nor less, enough*
> *To house man's soul, man's need fulfill.*
>
> *How the world is made for each of us!*
> *All we perceive and know in it*
> *Tends to some moment's product thus*
> *When the soul declares itself.*

In these verses we have the epitome of Browning's interpretation of life: the subordination of earth to man, to a common self. Just that which was conspicuously absent in Arnold is conspicuously present in Browning, —the sense of a common idea, a common purpose, in nature and in man.

Thus it is man need not simply look to nature for encouragement in bearing the burden of the world, for strength to be like her, self-poised, self-dependent. Man may rejoice in her every pulse of life, having the conviction that in her life he, too, lives; knowing that her every event furthers some deed of his, knowing that her beauty is the response to some aspiration of his. Let one know, as Browning sings in "Rabbi Ben Ezra," that nature, that the earthly life, and all "this dance of plastic circumstance," are but the machinery to shape the soul, to form the spirit; are but the potter's wheel that moulds the clay to "heaven's consummate cup"; let him know that the meaning of life, the "uses of the cup," are

> *The festal board, lamp's flash, and trumpet's peal,*
> *The new wine's foaming flow,*
> *The master's lips aglow!—*

let him know all this, and he will understand why the song of Browning is one of joy and victory.

Add to this Browning's conception of the relation of man to man. Consider how he finds in the contacts of life, not isolation, but companionship, service, love,—the first and the last word.

To relate how he finds, in the minglings of life and life, the secret and the key to our experience, would be to summarize, one by one, his poems. Even a casual acquaintance with Browning suffices to show that love, as he conceives it, is no accident and no mere occurrence of the life-journey, but at once its path and its goal. Everything

> *Of power and beauty in the world*
> *The mightiness of love is curled*
> *Inextricably round about.*
> *Love lies within it and without.*

We are led again to our old question. The greater vigor and sensuousness of Browning, his wider range, his more human touch, all spring from the ideas through which he sees and interprets life. But are the ideas true? Are they verifiable? Are they sporadic outbursts of a fancy which has no root in the nature of things, or are they the revelations of an imagination which is but another name for insight? If the ideas which give both substance and shape to Browning's poetry are only artificial make-ups of his individual fancy, what claim have they even for serious attention, to say nothing of power to stay by and to uphold? If these ideas are not ideas of soberness and of truth, as well as of fancy and passion, they are no more to us (the harsh word must be said) than freaks of a madman's brain.

If Mr. Arnold's message has weight and penetration with us, it is because that message conveys something of the reality of things. If there are messages, in comparison with which Mr. Arnold's seems pallid and academic, it is only because these other messages bring us word from a more abiding, a more human world than Mr. Arnold has known. The great power of poetry to stay and to console—a power which neither Arnold nor any other critic can exaggerate one whit—is just because of the truth, the rendering of the reality of affairs, which poetry gives us. The importance and the endurance of poetry, as of all art, are in its hold upon reality. We hear much, on this side and that, of realism. Well, we may let realism go, but we cannot let go reality. Here, too, we may turn to Robert Browning himself: —

> *Truth, truth, that's the gold. And all the good*
> *I find in fancy is, it serves to set*
> *Gold's inmost glint free.*

It is because, amid the conventionalities and make-believes of our ordinary life, poetry flashes home to us some of the gold which is at the very heart and core of our every-day existence, that poetry has its power to sustain us, its sympathy to enhearten us. Now science and philosophy, I repeat, however technical and remote in form and method, are the workings of the one selfsame spirit in its communing with this same world. There are, indeed, diversities of operation. And if the advantage in directness and universality of appeal, in wealth and passionateness of garb, is upon the side of poetry, let us remember that, after all, the advantage upon the side of method and standard are with the side of science and philosophy.

Indeed, this present separation of science and art, this division of life into prose and poetry, is an unnatural divorce of the spirit. It exists and endures, not because of a glow to life which philosophy cannot catch, nor because of a verifiable truth which poetry cannot detect and convey. It exists because in the last few centuries the onward movement of life, of experience, has been so rapid, its diversification of regions and methods so wide, that it has outrun the slower step of reflective thought. Philosophy has not as yet caught the rhythmic swing of this onward movement, and written it down in a score of black and white which all may read. Or if in some degree philosophy has laid hold of the secret of this movement, it has not yet been able to tell it in straightforward, simple syllables to the common consciousness. In its own theory, this common consciousness tells by rote a doctrine of an earlier and outworn world. But this movement, which has so escaped the surer yet heavier tread of critical thought, has in manifold ways danced itself into the poetic measures of our century. The deeper and wider spiritual life which makes this movement has found an expression in Wordsworth and Shelley, in Browning and in Mr. Arnold himself, which has, as yet, been denied to it in English philosophy. That which seemed to Mr. Arnold a flight from philosophy into poetry was in reality but a flight from a hard and partial philosophy to a fuller and freer one. It is not because poetry is divorced from science that it gave Mr. Arnold's nature such satisfaction, but because his philosophic instinct was so deep and real that he revolted from the professional philosophy of the day as he found it in Great Britain, and sought refuge in the unnamed, unprofessed philosophy of the great poets of England and of all time.

Here, indeed, is just our problem. We must bridge this gap of poetry from science. We must heal this unnatural wound. We must, in the cold, reflective way of critical system, justify and organize the truth which poetry, with its quick, naïve contacts, has already felt and reported. The same movement of the spirit, bringing man and man, man and nature, into wider and closer unity, which has found expression by anticipation in poetry, must find expression by retrospection in philosophy. Thus will be hastened the day in which our sons and our daughters shall prophesy, our young men shall see visions, and our old men dream dreams.

# The Present Position of Logical Theory

The remarkable fact in the intellectual life of to-day is the contradiction in which it is entangled. On one hand, we have an enormous development of science, both in specialisation of method and accumulation of material; its extension and thorough-going application to all ranges of experience. What we should expect from such a movement would be confidence of intelligence in itself, and a corresponding organisation of knowledge giving some guide and support to life. The strange thing is that instead of this we have apparently the greatest disorganisation of authority as to intellectual matters that the world has ever seen; while the prevalent attitude and creed of scientific men is philosophic agnosticism, or disbelief in their own method when it comes to fundamental matters. Such a typical representative of modern science as Mr. Huxley virtually laughs to scorn the suggestion of Mr. Frederic Harrison that science should or could become so organised as to give any support, any authoritative stay, to life.

Now I do not intend to discuss this apparent contradiction. It seems to me obvious enough that the contradiction is due to the fact that science has got far enough along to make its negative attitude towards previous codes of life evident, while its own positive principle of reconstruction is not yet evident. But without urging this view upon the reader, I wish to ask how and where in the prevailing confusion logical theory, as a synopsis of the methods and typical forms of intelligence, stands. Logical theory at once reflects

[*First published in the* Monist, *II* (*Oct. 1891*), *1–17. Not previously reprinted.*]

and transforms the existing status of matters intellectual at any period. It reflects this, for logical theory is only the express, the overt consciousness on the part of intelligence of its own attitude and prevailing spirit. It transforms the status, because this express consciousness makes intelligence know where it stands, makes it aware of its strength and of its weakness, and by defining it to itself forces it to take up a new and more adequate place.

It is obvious, then, that as the prevailing influence in the intellectual world to-day is science, so the prevailing influence in logical theory must be the endeavor to account for, to justify, or at least to reckon with this scientific spirit. And yet if there is such confusion as we have indicated, there is also some chaos in logical theory as to the true nature and method of science. Were it otherwise, were there at present a logical theory adequate to the specific and detailed practical results of science, science and scientific men would be conscious of themselves, and would be confident in their work and attitude.

The especial problem of logic, as the theory of scientific method, is the relation of fact and thought to each other, of reality and ideas. The problem is, however, differentiated from the metaphysical theory of knowledge. Logic does not inquire into the ultimate *meaning* of fact and thought, nor into their *ultimate* relations to one another. It simply takes them from the attitude of science itself; its business being, not the justification nor refutation of this attitude, but its development into explicit doctrine. Fact means to logic no more, but certainly no less, than it means to the special sciences: it is the subject-matter under investigation, under consideration; it is that which we are trying to make out. Thought means to logic what it means to science: method. It is the attitude and form which intelligence takes in reference to fact—to its subject-matter, whether in inquiry, experiment, calculation, or statement.

Logic, then, has for its essential problem the consideration of the various typical methods and guiding principles which thought assumes in its effort to detect, master, and report fact. It is presupposed here that there is some sort of fruitful and intrinsic connection of fact and thought; that thinking, in short, is nothing but the fact in its process of translation from brute impression to lucent meaning.

But the moment such a presupposition is stated, ninety-nine persons out of a hundred think that we have plunged, *ex abrupto*, from the certainty of science into the cloudland of metaphysic. And yet just this conception of the relation of thought (method) to fact (subject-matter) is taken for granted in every scientific investigation and conclusion. Here, then, we have in outline the present position of logic. Any attempt to state, in general, or to work out, in detail, the principle of the intrinsic and fruitful relation of fact and thought which science, without conscious reflection, constantly employs in practice, seems "metaphysical" or even absurd. Why is this? The answer to this question will give the filling-up of the outline just presented.

The chief cause is that superstition which still holds enthralled so much of modern thought—I mean formal logic. And if this seems like applying a hard name to what, at best and at worst, is only an intellectual gymnastic, I can only say that formal logic seems to me to be, at present, *fons et origo malorum* in philosophy. It is true enough that nobody now takes the technical subject of formal logic very seriously—unless here and there some belated "professor." It is true that it is generally relegated to the position of a subject which, for some unclear reason, is regarded as "disciplinary" in a young man's education;—just as certain other branches are regarded as elegant accomplishments in a young woman's finishing. But while the subject itself as a doctrine or science hardly ranks very high, the conception of thought which is at the bottom of formal logic still dominates the *Zeitgeist*, and regulates the theory and the method of all those who draw their inspiration from the *Zeitgeist*. Any book of formal logic will tell us what this conception of thought is: thought is a faculty or an entity existing in the mind, apart from facts, having its own fixed forms, with which facts have nothing to do—except in so far as to pass under the yoke. Jevons puts it this way: "Just as we thus familiarly recognise the difference of form and substance in common tangible things, so we may observe in logic, that the form of an argument is one thing, quite distinct from the various subjects or matter which may be treated in that form."[1]

Professor Stock varies the good old tune in this way: "In every act of thought we may distinguish two things— (1) the object thought about, (2) the way in which the mind thinks of it. The first is called the Matter; the second the Form of Thought. Now formal . . . Logic is concerned only with the way in which the mind thinks, and has nothing to do with the particular objects thought about."[2]

It is assumed, in fine, that thought has a nature of its own independent of facts or subject-matter; that this thought, *per se*, has certain forms, and that these forms are not forms which the facts themselves take, varying with the facts, but are rigid frames, into which the facts are to be set.

Now all of this conception—the notion that the mind has a faculty of thought apart from things, the notion that this faculty is constructed, in and of itself with a fixed framework, the notion that thinking is the imposing of this fixed framework on some unyielding matter called particular objects, or facts—all of this conception appears to me highly scholastic: to be, indeed, the last struggle of mediævalism to hold thought in subjection to authority. Nothing is more surprising than the fact that while it is fashionable to reject, with great scorn, all the results and special methods of scholasticism, its foundation-stone should still be accepted as the corner-stone of the edifice of modern doctrine. It is still more surprising when we reflect that the foundation-stone is coherent only with the mediæval superstructure. The scholastics were at least consistent in holding the method of thought to be a faculty pursuing its own method apart from the course of things. They did not conceive that thought was free, that intelligence had rights, nor that there was possible science independent of data authoritatively laid down. Really believing what they professed,— that thought was something *in se*,—they held that it must be supplied with a fixed body of dogmatic fact, from tradition, from revelation—from external authority. They held that

1      Jevons, *Elementary Lessons in Logic*, p. 5.
2      Stock, *Deductive Logic*, pp. 3–4.

thought in its workings is confined to extracting from this dogmatic body of fact what is already contained in it, and to rearranging the material and its implications. To examine the *material*, to test its truth; to suppose that intelligence could cut loose from this body of authority and go straight to nature, to history itself, to find the truth; to build up a free and independent science—to this point of incoherency mediæval scholasticism never attained. To proclaim the freedom of thought, the rejection of all external authority, the right and the power of thought to get at truth for itself, and yet continue to define thought as a faculty apart from fact, is reserved for modern enlightenment! And were it not somewhat out of my present scope, I should like to show that modern culture is thus a prepared victim for the skilful dialectician of the reactionary army. If the modern *Zeitgeist* does not fall a prey to the cohorts of the army of external authority, it is not because it has any recognised methods or any recognised criterion by which it can justify its raising the "banner of the free spirit." It is simply the obstinate bulwark of outer fact, built up piecemeal by science, that protects it.

The two main forces, which have been at work against the formulæ of formal logic, are "inductive" or empirical logic on one side, and the so-called "transcendental" logic, on the other. Of these two, the influence of inductive logic in sapping in practical fashion and popular results the authority of syllogistic logic has undoubtedly been much the greater. I propose, briefly, to give certain reasons for holding, however, that the inductive logic does not furnish us with the needed theory of the relation of thought and fact. To show this adequately would demand the criticism of inductive logic in the detail of its methods, in order to bring out where it comes short. As this is impossible, I shall now confine myself to a couple of general considerations.

To begin with, the empirical logic virtually continues the conception of thought as in itself empty and formal which characterises scholastic logic. It thus has really no theory which differentiates it, as regards the nature of thought itself, from formal logic. I cannot see, for example, what quarrel the most stringent upholder of formal logic can have with Mill as to the latter's theory of the syllogism. Mill's theory is virtually simply a theory regarding the formation of the major premiss—regarding the process by which we formulate the statement that All *S* is *P*. Now, if we once accept the syllogistic position, this process lies outside the scope and problem of formal logic. It is not an affair of what Jevons calls the form of argument at all, but simply of the matter, the particular facts which make the filling of the argument. I do not see that it is any part of the business of formal logic to tell where the major premiss comes from, nor how it is got. And, on the other hand, when it comes to the manipulation of the data contained in the premiss, Mill must fall back upon the syllogistic logic. Mill's theory, so far as the thought-element is concerned, presupposes the syllogistic theory. And if this theory, on its side, does not presuppose something like Mill's inductive theory, it is simply because the logician, as a *philosopher*, may prefer "intuitionalism" to "empiricism." He may hold, that is, that the content of some major premisses is given by direct "intuition" rather than gathered from experience. But in either case, the consideration of the source of the content of the premiss belongs not to formal logic, but to the theory of knowledge.

If, then, the theory of the syllogism is incorrect in its assumptions as to the relation of fact and thought, the inductive logic must be similarly in error. Its great advantage over the old scholastic logic lies not in its logic as such, but in something back of the logic—in its account of the derivation of the material of judgment. Whatever the defects of Locke's or Mill's account of experience, any theory which somehow presupposes a first-hand contact of mind and fact (though it be only in isolated, atomic sensations) is surely preferable to a theory which falls back on tradition, or on the delivery of dogma irresponsible to any intellectual criticism. However, in its account of the derivation of the material of judgment, inductive logic is still hampered by the scholastic conception of thought. Thought since confined to the rigid framework in which the material is manipulated once obtained, is excluded from all share in the gathering of material. The result is that this material, having no intrinsic thought-side, shrinks into a more or less accidental association of more or less shifting and transitory mental states.

I shall not stop to argue that, on this ground, the "inductive" logic deprives science of its most distinctive scientific features—the permanence and objectivity of its truths. I think no one can deny that there is at least an *apparent* gap between the actual results of concrete science, and these results as they stand after the touch of the inductive logic—that the necessity and generality of science seem rather to have been explained away, than explained. I think most of the inductive logicians themselves (while endeavoring to account for this apparent necessity as generated through association) would admit that something of science *seems*, at least, to have been lost, and that the great reason for putting-up with this loss is that the inductive logic is the sole alternative to a dogmatic intuitionalism and to arbitrary spinning-out of *a priori* concepts.

Certainly as long as thought is conceived after the fashion of syllogistic logic, as a scheme furnished and fixed in itself apart from reality, so long scientific men must protest against allowing thought any part or lot in scientific procedure, and so long some such *modus operandi* as that given by Mill must be resorted to in order to explain scientific methods and results. But, on the other hand, if the scholastic idea of thought as something having its character apart from fact is once given up, the force which at present cramps the logic of science into the logic of sensationalism and empiricism is also given up.

And this brings us to the other point in general regarding the inductive or empirical logic. It is not strictly a logic at all but a metaphysic. It does not begin with the datum of science, the fruitful inquiry into fact by intelligence, at all. It does not, starting from this datum analyse the various methods and types which thought must take upon itself in order to maintain this fruitful inquiry. On the contrary, it begins with sensations, and endeavors by a theory of knowledge on the basis of sensationalism to build up the structure of cognition, ordinary and scientific. I am not concerned here with the truth of sensationalism as a metaphysical theory of knowledge, nor with the adequacy of the notion of sensation advanced by Mill. It is enough from the logical point of view to point out that such a theory is not logic — that logic does not deal with something *back* of the fact of science, but with the analysis of scientific method as such. And is it forcing matters to indicate that this retreat from logic to metaphysic is also caused by the syllogistic notion of thought? Formal thought, with its formulæ for simply unfolding a given material, is of no use in science. There is, therefore, the need of some other machinery to take the place of thought. And this is found in sensation and in "experience" according to the peculiar notion of experience current in the inductive logic.

In a word, then (without attempting to show the insufficiency of inductive logic as the theory of science by reference to its treatment of specific points) inductive logic does not meet our needs because it is not a free, unprejudiced inquiry into the special forms and methods of science, starting from the actual sciences themselves. It is founded and built up with constant reference to the scholastic notion of thought. Where it is not affected positively by it, it is still affected by its reaction from it. Instead of denying once for all validity or even sense to the notion of thinking as a special, apart process, and then beginning a free, unhampered examination with an eye single to the fact of science itself, it retains the conception of thought as valid in a certain department, and then sets out to find something in another department to supply the gap. And thus we have the usual division of inductive and deductive logic, inductive being interpreted as empirical and particular, deductive as syllogistic and formal. They are counterpart and correlative theories, the two sides of the notion of the separateness of fact and thought; they stand and fall together.

"Transcendental" logic, while usually conceived as utterly opposed in spirit and in results to inductive logic, has yet been one with it in endeavoring to abolish formal logic as the sufficient method and criterion of scientific truth. I say this although well aware that inductive logic is usually conceived as specifically "scientific," while the transcendental movement is regarded as the especial foe of science — as a belated attempt to restore an *a priori* scholasticism, by finding a scheme for evolving truth out of pure thought. This is because when the "transcendental" school talks of thought, of the synthetic and objective character of thought, of the possibility of attaining truth through thought, and of the ontological value of thought, it is understood to mean thought in the old, scholastic sense, a process apart and fixed in itself, and yet somehow evolving truth out of its own inner being, out of its own enclosed ruminations. But on the contrary, the very meaning of "transcendentalism" is not only that it is impossible to get valid truth from the evolution of thought in the scholastic sense, but that there is no such thought at all. Processes of intelligence which have their nature fixed in themselves, apart from fact and having to be externally applied to fact, are pure myths to this school. Types of thought are simply the various forms which reality progressively takes as it is progressively mastered as to its meaning,—that is, understood. Methods of thought are simply the various active attitudes into which intelligence puts itself in order to detect and grasp the fact. Instead of rigid moulds, they are flexible adaptations. Methods of thought fit fact more closely and responsively than a worn glove fits the hand. They are only the ideal evolution of the fact—and by "ideal" is here meant simply the evolution of fact into meaning.

If this is a fair description of what the "transcendental" school means by thought, it is evident that it is a co-worker with the spirit and intent of "inductive" logic. Its sole attempt is to get hold of and report the presupposition and rationale of science; its practical aim is to lay bare and exhibit the method of science so that the only seat of authority—that is, the authority, the *backing*, of truth—shall be forever manifest. It has simply gone a step further than "inductive" logic, and thrown overboard once for all the scholastic idea of thought. This has enabled it to start anew, and to form its theory of thought simply by following the principles of the actual processes by which man has, thus far in history, discovered and possessed fact.

I shall not attempt here any defence of the "transcendental" logic; I shall not even attempt to show that the interpretation of it which I have given above is correct. It

must go, for the present, simply as my individual understanding of the matter. Taking this view of "transcendental" logic for granted, I wish, in order to complete our
notion of the present position of logic, to consider the reasons which have thus far prevented, say, the Hegelian logic
from getting any popular hold—from getting recognition
from scientific men as, at least in principle, a fair statement
of their own basic position and method.

The first of these reasons is that the popular comprehension of the "transcendental" movement is arrested at
Kant and has never gone on to Hegel. Hegel, it is true,
overshadowed Kant entirely for a considerable period. But
the Hegelian régime was partly pyrotechnical rather than
scientific in character; and, partly, so far as it was scientific,
it exhausted itself in stimulating various detailed scientific
movements—as in the history of politics, religion, art, etc. In
these lines, if we trust even to those who have no faith in the
Hegelian method or principles, the movement found some
practical excuse for being. But the result of the case was—
and its present status is—that the principle of Hegel being,
for the time, lost either in display of dialectical fireworks, or
in application to specific subjects, the principle itself has
never met with any *general* investigation. The immense
amount of labor spent on Kant during the past twenty years
has made the Kantian method and principle familiar, if not
acceptable, to the body of men calling themselves educated.
And thus, so far as its outcome is concerned, the transcendental movement still halts with Kant.

Now, at the expense of seeming to plunge deeper in
absurdity, I must say that the Kantian principle is far more
"transcendental" in the usual interpretation of that term—
more *a priori*, more given to emphasising some special function of some special thought-power—than the Hegelian. As
against the usual opinion of the possibility of some compromise between science and Kant, while the scientific spirit
and Hegel are at antipodes, it appears to me it is Kant who
does violence to science, while Hegel (I speak of his essential method and not of any particular result) is the quintessence of the scientific spirit. Let me endeavor to give some
reasons for this belief. Kant starts from the accepted scho-

lastic conception of thought. Kant never dreams, for a moment, of questioning the existence of a special faculty of thought with its own peculiar and fixed forms. He states and restates that thought in itself exists apart from fact and occupies itself with fact given to it from without. Kant, it is true, gives the death-blow to scholasticism by pointing out that such a faculty of thought is purely analytic—that it simply unfolds the material given, whether that material be true or false, having no method of arriving at truth, and no test for determining truth. This fact once clearly recognised, dogmatic rationalism, or the attempt to get truth from the "logical" analysis of concepts was forever destroyed. The way was opened for an independent examination of the actual method of science.

But while Kant revealed once for all the impossibility of getting truth, of laying hold of reality, by the scholastic method, he still retained that conception of thought. He denied not its existence, but its worth as relates to truth. What was the result? Just this: when he came to his examination (criticism) of knowledge, it fell apart at once into two separate factors, an *a priori* and *a posteriori*. For if Kant finds, as against the dogmatic rationalist, that formal thought cannot give knowledge, he also finds, as against the sceptical empiricist, that unrelated sensation cannot give knowledge. Here, instead of denying, *in toto*, the existence of unrelated sensation, he contented himself with denying its functional value for knowledge. Unrelated sensation and formal thought are simply the complementary halves of each other. Admit the one, and the other is its necessary counterpart.

Kant must now piece together his two separated factors. Sensation, unrelated manifold of sensation, is *there*; thought, isolated, analytic thought, is *here*. Neither is knowledge in itself. What more natural than to put them together, and hold that knowledge is the union of a matter or stuff, of sensations, atomic in themselves, on one hand, and a form, or regulating principle of thought, empty in itself, on the other? We have two elements, both existing in isolation, and yet both useless for all purposes of knowledge. Combine them, and presto, there is science.

Such a "transcendentalism" as this may well stick in the crop of scientific men. For consider what is involved in it: an *a priori* factor, on one side, and an *a posteriori*, on the other. Kant, from one point of view, seems thus to have simply combined the weaknesses of empiricism and rationalism. He still continues to talk of experience itself as particular and contingent, and denies that it gives a basis for any universal laws. Aside from his effort in the *Kritik der Urtheilskraft* to overcome his original separation, special scientific laws are to him only more or less extensive "generalisations from experience"—as much so to him as to Locke, or Mill. Scientific men, indeed, have accustomed themselves to this derogation of their own methods and results, and, as "inductive" logicians, indulge in it quite freely themselves. But an *a priori* element, supplied by a thought fixed and separate, scientific men cannot do away with. Nor do I know any reason why they should.

It is coming short, in my opinion, of the full stature of science to treat it as a quantitative and varying generalisation of contingent particulars, but this, at least, leaves what science there is free and unhindered. But *a priori* elements supplied from outside the fact itself, *a priori* elements somehow entering into the fact from without and controlling it—this is to give up the very spirit of science. For if science means anything, it is that our ideas, our judgments may in some degree reflect and report the fact itself. Science means, on one hand, that thought is free to attack and get hold of its subject-matter, and, on the other, that fact is free to break through into thought; free to impress itself—or rather to express itself—in intelligence without vitiation or deflection. Scientific men are true to the instinct of the scientific spirit in fighting shy of a distinct *a priori* factor supplied to fact from the mind. Apriorism of this sort must seem like an effort to cramp the freedom both of intelligence and of fact, to bring them under the yoke of fixed, external forms.

Now in Hegel there is no such conception of thought and of *a priori*, as is found in Kant. Kant formulated the conception of thought as objective, but he interpreted this as meaning that thought subjective in itself *becomes* objective when synthetic of a given sense-manifold. When Hegel calls thought objective he means just what he says: that there is no special, apart faculty of thought belonging to and operated by a mind existing separate from the outer world. What Hegel means by objective thought is the meaning, the significance of the fact itself; and by methods of thought he understands simply the processes in which this meaning of fact is evolved.

There has been, of late, considerable discussion of the place and function of "relations" in knowledge. This discussion in English speculation, at least, tends to turn largely about Thomas Hill Green's reconstruction of Kantianism. I consider it unfortunate that this discussion has taken the form of a debate between empiricism and Kantianism. The question of knowledge has thus come to be whether or not certain relations are supplied by thought to sensations in order to make an orderly whole out of the latter, chaotic in themselves. Now when Hegel talks of relations of thought (not that he makes much use of just this term) he means no such separate forms. Relations of thought are, to Hegel, the typical forms of meaning which the subject-matter takes in its various progressive stages of being understood. And this is what *a priori* means from a Hegelian standpoint. It is not some element *in* knowledge; some addition of thought to experience. It is experience itself in its skeleton, in the main features of its framework.

"Refutations" of Hegel, then, which attempt to show that "thought" in itself is empty, that it waits for content from experience, that it cannot by any manipulation evolve truth out of itself are, if taken as having relevance to Hegel, simply meaningless. Hegel begins where these arguers leave off. Accepting all that they can say, he goes one step further and denies that there is any such "thought" at all anywhere in existence. The question of the relations or "categories of thought" is just the question of the broad and main aspects of fact as that fact comes to be understood.

For example, Kant would prove the *a priori* character and validity of the principle of causation by showing that without it science is impossible, that it helps "make experience." Now, in terms, Hegel's justification of this relation would be the same; he too would show that the fabric of experience implies and demands the causal relation. But in Kant's case, the justification of the principle of causality by reference to the possibility of experience means that thought must continually inject this principle *into* experience to keep experience from disappearing: that experience must be constantly braced and reinforced by the synthetic action of thought or it will collapse. In short, the need of experience for this principle of causation means its need for a certain support outside itself. But Hegel's demonstration of the validity of the causal principle is simply pointing out that the whole supports the part, while the part helps make the whole. That is to say, Hegel's reference is not to some outside action of thought in maintaining fact as an object of knowledge; it is to the entire structure of fact itself. His contention is simply that the structure of fact itself, of the subject-matter of knowledge, is such that in one of its phases it presents necessarily the aspect of causality. And if this word "necessarily" gives pause, it must be remembered what the source of necessity is. It does *not* lie in the principle of causation *per se*; it lies in the whole fact, the whole subject-matter of knowledge. It is the same sort of necessity as when we say that a complete man *must* have an eye; *i.e.*, it is the nature of the human organism to develop and sustain this organ, while the organ, in turn, contributes to and thus helps constitute the organism.

The question upon which the "refutation" of Hegel turns is not in showing that formal "thought" cannot give birth to truth except through the fructifying touch of "experience." The question is simply whether fact—the subject-matter of knowledge—is such as Hegel presents it. Is it, in general, the connected system he holds it to be? And, if a system, does it, in particular, present such phases (such relations, categories) as Hegel shows forth? These are objective questions pure and simple; questions identical, in kind, with the question whether the constitution of glucose is what some chemist claims to have found it.

This, then, is why I conceive Hegel—entirely apart from the value of any special results—to represent the quintessence of the scientific spirit. He denies not only the possibility of getting truth out of a formal, apart thought, but he denies the existence of any faculty of thought which is other than the expression of fact itself. His contention is not that "thought," in the scholastic sense, has ontological validity, but that fact, reality is significant. Even, then, were it shown that Hegel is pretty much all wrong as to the special meanings which he finds to make up the significance of reality, his main principle would be unimpeached until it is shown that fact has not a systematic, or interconnected, meaning, but is a mere hodgepodge of fragments. Whether the scientific spirit would have any interest in such a hodgepodge may, at least, be questioned.

Having dealt at such length with the first reason why as yet the "transcendental" movement has found no overt coalescence with the scientific, we may deal briefly with the remaining reason.[3] In the second place, then, the rationality of fact had not been sufficiently realised in detail in the early decades of the century to admit of the principle of the "transcendental" movement being other than misunderstood. That is to say, the development of science and, more particularly, its application to the specific facts of the world was comparatively rudimentary. On account of this lack of scientific discovery and application, the world presented itself to man's consciousness as a blank, or at least as only stuff *for* meaning, and not as itself significant. The result was that Hegel had to be interpreted subjectively. The difficulties in the way of conceiving a world upon which science had not yet expended its energies in detail, as an organism of significant relations and bearings were so great that Hegel's attempt to point out these significant types and functions as immanent in reality was inevitably misconstrued as an attempt, on Hegel's part, to prove that a system of purely "subjective" thoughts could somehow be manipulated to give objectively valid results.

---

[3]     It should be understood that in the previous discussion so far as it relates to Kant, I have taken him at his lowest terms—those of logical self-consistency. So far as Kant does not succeed in freeing himself from his original position—the existence of a formal, or apart, faculty of thought —so far his emphasis of the *a priori* in the sense already attributed to him is inevitable. But that the *tendency* of Kant is to make the thought-relations *a priori* simply in the sense of being fact's own physiognomy I should not deny.

Hegel, in other words, anticipated somewhat the actual outcome of the scientific movement. However significant fact may be, however true it may be that an apart faculty of thought is an absurdity, however certain it may be that there are no real types or methods of thought excepting those of the object-matter itself as it comes to be understood, yet to man this objective significance cannot be real till he has made it *out* in the details of scientific processes, and *made* it in applied science, in invention. Hegel's standpoint was, therefore, of necessity obscure. When the significant character of fact was not yet opened up in detail, a method working upon the basis that the only possible thought is the reflection of the significance of fact, had no chance of fair interpretation. And thus it was (and largely is) when Hegel speaks of objective thought and its relations, he is understood as having the ordinary conception of thought (that is, of thought as a purely separate, and subjective faculty), and yet as trying to prove that this apart faculty has some mysterious power of evolving truth.

The question which now confronts us as to the present place of logic is just this: Has the application of scientific thought to the world of fact gone far enough so that we can speak, without seeming strained, of the rationality of fact? When we speak of the rationality, of the intrinsic meaning of fact, can these terms be understood in their direct and obvious sense, and not in any remote, or *merely* metaphysical sense? Has the theoretical consideration of fact in its detailed study, has practical invention, as the manifestation of the rationality of fact, gone far enough so that this significance has become, or could become with some effort, as real and objective a material of study as are molecules and vibrations?

It seems to me that we are already at this stage, or are at the point of getting to it. Without arguing this question, however, (which, indeed, can be proved only by acting upon it, only *ambulando*), I would point out that the constant detailed work of science upon the world in theory and in invention, must in time give that world an evident meaning in human consciousness. What prevents scientific men from now realising this fact, is that they are still afraid of certain "transcendent" entities and forces; afraid that if they relax their hostility to metaphysic, some one will spring upon them the old scholastic scheme of external, supernatural Unrealities. To those who take the prevailing agnosticism not as a thing, but as a symptom, this agnosticism means just this: The whole set of external, or non-immanent entities, is now on the point of falling away, of dissolving. We have got just so far, popularly, as holding that they are unknowable. In other words, they are crowded to the extreme verge. One push more, and off they go. The popular consciousness will hold them not only to be unknowable, but not to be.

What then? Science freed from its fear of an external and dogmatic metaphysic, will lose its fear of metaphysic. Having unquestioned and free possession of its own domain, that of knowledge and of fact, it will also be free to build up the intrinsic metaphysic of this domain. It will be free to ask after that structure of meanings making up the skeleton of the world of knowledge. The moment this point is reached, the speculative critical logic worked out in the development of Kantian ideas, and the positive, specific work of the scientific spirit will be at one. It will be seen that logic is no revived, redecked scholasticism, but a complete abandonment of scholasticism; that it deals simply with the inner anatomy of the realm of scientific reality, and has simply endeavored, with however much of anticipation, to dissect and lay bare, at large and in general, the features of the subject-matter with which the positive sciences have been occupying themselves in particular and in detail.

That we are almost at the point of such conflux, a point where the general, and therefore somewhat abstract lines of critical logic will run into the particular, and therefore somewhat isolated, lines of positive science, is, in my opinion, the present position of logical theory.

# How Do Concepts Arise from Percepts?

Failure to make some fundamental distinction may be the source of a confusion which makes all subsequent discussion mere blind thrashing in the air. The discussion of the nature of the concept has often suffered from failure to discriminate between a mental *state* and the *function* of that state. It is as if, in physiology, writers were to discuss the heart without having first decided whether they were writing of the *thing*, or of the *work* done by that thing and its *value* for the organism. Were such the case, it would not be surprising if one school of physiologists held the heart to be a definite, isolated thing, of a certain shape and size, composed of certain fibres, while another school held the heart to be a factor or member in an inter-connected unity; not a thing but an activity; and its special structure a matter of indifference compared with the general purpose subserved by this structure.

Carrying out the needed discrimination in the case of the concept, it may be said that the concept is not a term denoting a mental state or existence, but an intellectual *function* or *value*. Every mental state is, as a bare existence (taken, that is, statically) an image. As such, it is a particular, numerically and qualitatively different from every other existence and enduring only for a limited time. The nominalist is, therefore, quite right when he asserts that there is no such thing as a general idea—provided he is speaking of mental existences. But so speaking, he does not touch the question at all. The concept is the *power* which a particular

[*First published in the* Public-School Journal, *XI* (*Nov. 1891*), 128–30. *Not reprinted during the author's lifetime.*]

image has of standing for or conveying a certain meaning or intellectual value. Let me borrow an illustration from, I think, Mr. Bosanquet. It is a matter of indifference what kind of a flag be used as a danger signal on the railway. It may be eight inches square, or ten, or not square at all. It may be new or old, fresh or dirty, tattered or whole. *Prior* to its adoption as a signal, it may be of any color whatever. In other words, the main thing is not what the flag *is* as an existence. The main thing is what the flag *does*. So, when we are considering the structure of a particular mental image, we have not entered the domain of concepts, or universals, at all. The concept is something which the image does; some meaning which it conveys.

What meaning? The raising of this question brings us specifically to the question of the origin of the concept from the percept. My answer to the question is: the concept arises from the percept *through realizing the full meaning im-*plied, but not *ex*-plicit in the percept. For example, take the percept of a triangle. So far as this is a mere percept, it is regarded wholly as a particular thing. Knowledge of it from this point of view would be exhausted in getting its exact shape, size, length of sides, degree of angles, stuff made of, color, etc. The mind would nowhere be led beyond the consideration of the bare thing present. Even if it were found that the sum of its three interior angles was equal to two right angles, this would be a trait of the particular triangle, a bare item of information, of no more general value than that the length of one side was $1\frac{2}{17}$ inches. But suppose the mind advances beyond the particular triangle to the thought that there is a principle involved in the triangle; that the triangle, like everything in the world, is made upon a certain principle which is embodied in it; that this princi-ple furnishes the plans and specifications according to which anything must exist in order to be a triangle at all; a principle which, if exceeded or come short of, there is no triangle at all. What shall we call this principle? Is it not evident that, since it is this principle which constitutes the particular thing a triangle, rather than a pumpkin or a stove-pipe, it is this principle we really mean by triangle, and are attempting to know? Well, it is this principle which forms the concept, "triangle." The concept, "triangle," in other words, is the *way in which three lines are put together*; it is a *mode* or form of construction. Except as we know this mode of formation our idea of a triangle is exceedingly imperfect.

Hence, the characteristics of a concept. It is (1) "ideal" not sensuous. That is, as a mode or *way of mental action*, it cannot be felt or seen or heard. *It can be grasped only in and through the activity which constitutes it.* The only way to know the concept triangle is to make it—to go through the act of putting together the lines in the way called for. (I may remark, incidentally, that this reveals the impossibility of external or mechanical instruction. If a concept is the true meaning of a thing, and this true meaning is a mode of mental action, a process of intellectual construction, how possibly can true information be externally conveyed from one to another?) The concept is (2) general, not particular. Its generality lies in the very fact that it is a mode of action, a way of putting things or elements together. A cotton loom is particular in all its parts; every yard of cloth produced is particular, yet the way in which the parts go together and work together, the function of the loom is not particular.

So any given triangle, actual or as a mental existence, is particular. But the way of constructing triangles is not particular. It has no more to do with one triangle than with another. It is a principle in accordance with which any number of triangles may be brought into existence. *Anything* constituted in this way is a triangle.

It should be reasonably evident from what I have said that the concept of triangle contains not less but more than the percept. It is got, not by dropping traits, but by finding out what the real traits are.

It is true that certain features are excluded. But this dropping out of certain features is not what gives rise to the concept. On the contrary, *it is on the basis of the concept*, the principle of construction, *that certain features are omitted*. Nay, they are more than omitted. They are positively eliminated. They are declared to be irrelevant, to have nothing to do with the *real* triangle whatever.

The concept, in short, is knowledge of what the real object is—the object taken with reference to its principle of construction; while the percept, so called, is knowledge of the object in a more or less accidental or limited way. As to their intellectual value, concept means complete knowledge of an object—knowledge of it in its mode of genesis, and in its relations and bearings; while percept means incomplete (that is, "abstract," in the true sense of abstract) knowledge of an object,—knowledge of the object in its qualitative, spatial, and temporal limitations.

It must, however, be added that the concept always returns into and enriches the percept, so that the distinction between them is not fixed but movable. Let me once get the concept triangle; let me, that is, once see into the process by which a triangle is made a triangle, and I carry the knowledge thus gained into every particular triangle I see. The concept becomes an enriching of the meaning of the percept.

In ideal, in completed development, the percept and concept would have the same content. It would exceed my limits here to show this to be the case; but let me suggest that complete knowledge of a particular object, say a given maple tree (the percept) would involve knowledge not merely of every detail of that tree, but of *how it came to be so*. On the other hand, complete knowledge of tree-life (the concept) would involve not merely highly general ideas, but also knowledge of the particular circumstances and conditions under which tree-life became deciduous or non-deciduous; of the conditions under which the deciduous differentiated into maple, oak, beech, etc.; of the still more particular circumstances under which maple-life differentiated into this particular form of life, *this* maple tree.

Such a systematic knowledge, whether starting from an individual (when we call it percept) or starting from the principle (when we call it concept), is the ideal of every science. Our knowledge of the individual is limited until we have got at the principle involved in it. Our knowledge of the principle is imperfect (abstract) until we see how this principle acts under the multitude of different circumstances. As either is completed, it tends to approach the other.

I do not know that I am called upon to point any pedagogical morals, but I cannot resist the temptation. If what has been said is true, it is evident that there is but one genuine way to lead the mind of the pupil on from percept to concept: to present, from the first, the percept in its genesis, in its origin and growth, in its proper relations. It is *not* necessary that the rationale of the process should be explicitly pointed out, or the child made to give reasons for everything. On the contrary, prematurely fixing conscious attention upon the relations may be the very means of preventing their being grasped. But let the object be, as it were, *done* over and over again; let the relations in it be used; let the mind act in accordance with the principle involved; and sure ground is laid for the conscious apprehension of the concept later. The teacher's work is here largely confined in getting the idea to be known to the child's mind in such purified form that the child's mind must go through that constructive process which is involved in the concept. Later this process itself will become an object of reflection. First the process *used* by the mind; then the process *consciously thought* is always the normal psychological method.

# *Lectures* vs. *Recitations:*
# *A Symposium*

As to the question regarding the best method of lecturing, I can only say that I have been wrestling with the problem for some years, and have been regretfully forced to the conclusion that the best way a man can, is the best way for him to lecture. As to your other question, I have no doubt that the introduction of the lecture system has more than justified itself. It has, wherever introduced, destroyed, once for all, the superstition that the text-book is the sum and end of learning; it has helped dispel those vicious methods of *rote* study which that superstition fostered; it has compelled the instructor himself to broaden and freshen his knowledge; and, I doubt not, has increased the use of the Library a thousandfold. That there ever will be a return from it to old-fashioned text-book work I do not believe. Where it has not displaced the text-book, it has changed the mode of handling it.

That, in its present form, it is itself the final method of instruction I am not convinced. I am inclined to think that finally its chief value will be found to have consisted in destroying the text-book fetich. With an increasing use of the printing press in preparing outlines, syllabuses, selections from authorities etc., it is possible that the set lecture will, upon the whole, be displaced by readings, reports, discussions, etc., the teacher guiding the study by questions, references, printed helps, etc. This would give us a cross between the seminary and the recitation methods. The personal equation, however, may enter largely into this forecast.

[*First published in the* Castalian, *Published by the Independents of the Senior Class, University of Michigan, VI* (1891), 65. *Not previously reprinted.*]

# The Scholastic and the Speculator

## 1. The Scholastic

Strange stories gain credence. 'Tis currently reported the
Scholastic departed this life along with the Middle Ages,
driven hence by the great glare of light suddenly shed into
his cobwebbed retreat. It is more likely there was no flight,
only transformation. The evolutionist tells us that nothing
disappears; that apparent passing away is only transition
into something else. So the Scholastic changed his outward
garb, the eternal traits by which he had been identified, but
not his inner habit and tendency.

The character of the old Scholastic stands forth in his
treatment of Aristotle. First he transferred Aristotle from
the pellucid atmosphere of living Greece to his own stuffy
cell. He subtracted Aristotle from life; from the circumstance of time, of place, of social and intellectual life which
gave him his meaning, and regarded him *in abstracto*; in the
air, that is to say. Instead of a figure in the onmoving of
human intelligence, he became a philosophical pope, abstracted from all conditions, and issuing deliverances at
large. He was changed from a co-efficient, from an energy
contributing to the progress of mankind, to an "authority."
Instead of an exponent, an indication of the place of Greek
thought in the thought of humanity, he was a formula.
Instead of mobility, life, in a word, there was rigidity. And
all because of the abstraction, the sequestration of Aristotle
from his place in the moving procession of human thought.
We talk a great deal in philosophy of abstraction. It is well
to remember that abstraction means in philosophy just what

[*First published in the* Inlander (*University of Michigan*), *II*
(*Dec.* 1891), 145–48; *II* (*Jan.* 1892), 186–88. *Not previously*
*reprinted.*]

it means anywhere else—carrying something off. Now a man may carry something off for two reasons. One reason is to get a good look at it, to isolate it from the crowd of things which hide and confuse it, so that its own nature may stand out. Abstraction, here, is simply raising a thing up, distinguishing it, placing it, that is to say, where it belongs. It is the normal process of the human mind in getting hold of any fact. But there is another abstraction. When a newspaper says that a cashier abstracted the contents of a safe and made his way to Canada—this is a metaphysical terminology understood of all men. This is the false abstraction philosophy talks about. It is taking a thing not out of its apparent relations in order to get it into its real relations, but taking a thing out of relations and keeping it out. Not to put too fine a point upon it, the Scholastic was an embezzler. He attempted to take Aristotle away from humanity, away from his position in the advancing column of human thought and action; he wanted to keep him for himself, for the use of his own private system, his own class-interest. The Scholastic was not commercial; he did not give and take, take in order to give, and give in order to take; he took all he could get, and gave only under compulsion—the compulsion being what we call the Renaissance. The Scholastic was "abstract"; he was the miser of philosophy; the man who wanted to save truth lest it should get away. The strong box in which he kept his riches was called "system."

Is the Scholastic dead? Has Aristotle, for example, got wholly back to earth, back, that is to say, to the concrete conditions of human life? Does he belong to the crowd, to the mass, or is he still owned, as the politicians say, by philosophers who have appropriated him to themselves? Or, to generalize the question, what are philosophy and science as conceived to-day: means of understanding and facilitating human action, or separate bodies of theories and facts supposed to have value on their own account? If the latter, then the abstraction from life is still going on. The human mind is still engaged in the process of saving and storing. *It is this saving process of mind*, and not any special act or particular portion of history, which constitutes Scholasticism.

But I have dwelt so long upon this phase of the Scholastic that I must hurry on to his other main trait. The Scholastic, when he had suffocated Aristotle by removing him from the conditions of life, proceeded to dismember the remains. Even the miser, I suppose, has to do something with his gold, or else he wouldn't know he had it . He must count it over, he must jingle it together, he must bury his fingers in it and roll the coin about. So the Scholastic had to use his learning in some way. He pulled it this way and pulled it that until he pulled it all to pieces. When anything is abstracted, when it is taken off by itself, having lost its connections, all that remains is to go over and over the same thing, dissecting, dividing, analyzing, and then sorting out and piling up the fragments. Distinction-making and collecting always accompany the scholastic habit. In every phase of life the Scholastic sees only another fly which irritates him with its restless movement; a fly to be caught and carried off—and then to be arranged and re-arranged without end, stuck in a cardboard case along with other such facts. For this same fly-sticking of the amateur scientist is an allegory. All science, all philosophy that abstracts facts and ideas from their place in the movement of life, from what it is fashionable to call evolution, is so much fly-sticking. Life departs when the thing is removed from its place in the movement, and with life goes unity. Only *disjecta membra* remain for the show-case of science.

The dawn of modern science, of experimental and historical methods, did not then destroy the Scholastic. It only compelled another alteration of outward form. Indeed by as pretty a stratagem as history records, the Scholastic in seeming to surrender to the scientific man took him captive. The Scholastic got a wider range of action. He was no longer confined to Aristotle and the Scriptures, but new fields for pillage were open. Nature and history presented vast stores from which he could abstract. The wealth to be saved up had increased indefinitely. Even the outward change is less than it often seems. The monastic cell has become a professional lecture hall; an endless mass of "authorities" have taken the place of Aristotle. *Jahresberichte*, monographs, journals without end occupy the void left by the commentators upon Aristotle. If the older Scholastic spent his laborious time in erasing the writing from old manuscripts in order to indite thereon something of his own, the new Scholastic has also his palimpsest. He criticises the criticisms with which some other Scholastic has criticised other criticisms, and the writing upon writings goes on till the substructure of reality is long obscured.

But, after all, let us be fair to the Scholastic. Abstraction is justified when it is done on a large enough scale. Man must have something to live by, and how shall he get it if he does not take it off by itself away from the maddening crowd? The crowding, the confusion in life is so great that if a man did not isolate the truth which he grasped, the truth would be at once pulled away from him. Saving is necessary. What shall a man have to work with unless he has already saved? The commerce of mind with the world requires its fund, its capitalized store, as surely as the commerce in material products. Only through the Scholastic who has continually embezzled the facts from pressure of outward things and then stored them away in safe-keeping has mankind been secured from barbarism, from mental bankruptcy, that is to say from inability on the part of intelligence to meet the demands made upon it by the necessities of action. And yet this abstraction, this saving cannot be all there is to the matter; these must have some end, some use. What is it?

## II.   The Speculator

The comparison of thinking with commerce is no forced analogy. There is but one commerce: The meeting of Mind and Reality. Sometimes the meeting is of one kind and we call it Thought; sometimes it is of another and we call it Language; sometimes another and we call it Art; sometimes another and we call it Justice, Rightness; sometimes another and we call it Trade. Only because we are such materialists, fixing our attention upon the rigid thing instead of upon the moving act, do we identify the last exchange especially as commerce. There is only one economy in the universe; and of this, logic, political economy, and the movements of molecules are equally phases. All contact involves two parties; all contact means exchange, and all exchange is governed by the law of reciprocity, is commercial, whether it be exchange of thought with fact, or of cotton with shoes. As in every true bargain each side gives and each gets in proportion to its giving, so in thinking. The mind must give meaning, ideas to the world that confronts it, and in return for its investment the world gives back truth and power. The due proportion of outgo and income is the problem of intelligence as of business life.

To think is to balance an idea against a fact, and every project of manufacture or of trade is a similar balancing. Nature keeps her books by the double entry system, and every venture completed must in time be referred for accounting to the original capital of truth. The law of gravitation when it emerged from the mind of Newton was the attempted equating of the credit of thought with the debit of experience. The Standard Oil Company is as much, an attempted balancing of intelligence with existing social conditions. The metaphysician says truth consists in relations; the political economist says there is no value save in exchange; the physicist that action and reaction are equal; the chemist talks of the law of equivalency; the great Teacher of Mankind says that a man finds his life only as he loses it: everywhere the same great transaction—the same cross-action.

As man saves in order to produce, so he spends in order to receive. Human intelligence has always been gathering in wealth from the wreckage of time and hugging the salvage to itself to set out its full meaning: the *scholastic*. But intelligence must throw its fund out again into the stress of life; it must venture its savings against the pressure of facts: the *speculator*.

The Yankee is the great speculator. Undisturbed by the Anglo-purist he continues his great "guess" upon life. If he ceases in any measure to say "I guess" it is only because he has gone a step farther and learned to say "I bet" so and so. If the grammar which represents old conceptions of life is against such phrases the logic of moving truth is with them. Every thought, every judgment involves a leap forward, a jump, a venture. The formal logician may attempt to derive conclusions from premises; every practical man knows that premises are only the spring-board, the point of vantage where to jump into the flood of moving fact. Some may think to dignify this phase of thought by calling it hypothesis, or tentative induction, or what-not, but the largest term that can be invented can do no more than express the jump into the unknown ocean off the spring-board of the known. No rules have ever been devised for informing one who has not "sense" or "good judgment," as the plain man calls it, how to make this jump. It always is, and always must remain the individual venture: the stake of self or some part of self against the ongoing stream of life. Every judgment a man passes on life is perforce, his "I bet," his speculation. So much of his saved capital of truth he invests in the judgment: "The state of things is thus and so." The current of fact sweeps in this judgment and returns it to him with interest. His guess, his venture has won: the logicians call it verification. Or the stream of fact carries away his investment and he never sees it again. His speculation was against the set of the market and he has lost.

Immanuel Kant wrote a treatise on the subject: "How are synthetic judgments *a priori* possible?" The question sounds technical, and yet at bottom it means only this: How does it happen that the mind can bet upon truth and win? What sort of a world must it be that welcomes the ventures of the mind and returns them with added riches? What sort of a mind can it be that dare speculate upon that vast current outside it, which can stake its pile of truth upon the moving game and receive its own with usury?

But there are scholastics and scholastics: men who save in order to get a new purchase in action, and men who save for very sake of saving. So there are speculators and speculators. The business man saves, but the ideal saving is not to have a reserve which is never touched, but to have all so used that there is no waste. There is a saving which means withdrawal, separation; there is a saving which means use parallel with the realities of the situation. The cotton merchant saves best when he invests all his funds in accordance with the movement of the cotton market. The

talent hid in a napkin wasn't saved after all; the other man
got it at last. There is a speculation which exists just for the
sake of the speculation. Wall street is, if you please, the
symbol of this speculation, just as every large business
represents the speculation which occurs for the sake of getting a larger action under way. One speculation is for the
profit, the pot, the other is for the game. So in the history of
human intelligence there have been two kinds of thought-
speculators. There have been those who have hazarded, so
far as in them lay, all the store of truth for the profit of their
own private venture, their system. They have laid hands on
all the riches of the human race and staked them upon their
theory, their personal bet. All the great philosophers have
had something of this ruthless adventure of thought, this
reckless throwing of the accumulated store of truth. Although the prodigal is always a more attractive figure than
the miser, there must still be some better way. Only because
thinking has been separated from action, the theorist from
the economist in life, has speculation assumed this private
form. The speculation of the merchant is business, and not
gambling, just in the degree that it is itself action and action
in the light. The speculation of the broker is gambling and
not business just in the degree that it is not action itself, but
the attempt to take advantage of the action of others, and in
the degree that it is in the dark and not in the light. Action
upon truth marks the merchant of thought, who, though he
both saves and spends, yet neither embezzles nor gambles.

# Green's Theory of the Moral Motive

A somewhat peculiar difficulty seems to attend the discussion of ethical theory, on account of its characteristic relation to action. This relation gives rise, on one side, to the belief that ethics is primarily an "art." Ethics is so much the theory of practice that it seems as if its main business were to aid in the direction of conduct. This being premised, the next step is to make out of ethics a collection of rules and precepts. A body of rigid rules is erected with the object of having always some precept which will tell just what to do. But, on the other side, it is seen to be impossible that any body of rules should be sufficiently extensive to cover the whole range of action; it is seen that to make such a body results inevitably in a casuistry which is so demoralizing as to defeat the very end desired; and that, at the best, the effect is to destroy the grace and play of life by making conduct mechanical. So the pendulum swings to the other extreme; it is denied that ethics has to deal primarily or directly with the guidance of action. Limited in this way, all there is left is a metaphysic of ethic: —an attempt to analyze the general conditions under which morality is possible; to determine, in other words, the nature of that universe or system of things which permits or requires moral action. The difficulty, then, is to find the place intermediate between a theory general to the point of abstractness, a theory which provides no help to action, and a theory which attempts to further action but does so at the expense of its spontaneity and breadth. I do not know of any theory, however, which is quite consistent to either point of view. The theory which makes the most of being practical generally shrinks, as matter of fact, from the attempt to carry out into detail its rules for living; and the most metaphysical

[*First published in the* Philosophical Review, *I* (*Nov. 1892*), 593–612. *Not previously reprinted.*]

doctrine commonly tries to show that at least the main rules
for morality follow from it. The difficulty is imbedded in the
very nature of the science; so much so that it is far easier for
the school which prides itself upon its practicality (generally the utilitarian) to accuse the other (generally the "transcendental") of vagueness than to work out any definitely
concrete guidance itself; and easier for the metaphysical
school to show the impossibility of deducing any detailed
scheme of action from a notion like that of seeking the
greatest quantity of pleasures than for it to show how its
own general ideal is to be translated out of the region of the
general into the specific; and, of course, all action is specific.

The difficulty is intrinsic, I say, and not the result of
any mere accident of statement. Ethics is the theory of
action and all action is concrete, individualized to the last
ell. Ethical theory must have, then, a similar concreteness
and particularity. And yet no body of rules and precepts,
however extensive and however developed its casuistic, can
reach out to take in the wealth of concrete action. No theory,
it is safe to say, can begin to cover the action of a single
individual for a single day. Is not, then, the very conception
of ethical theory a misconception, a striving for something
impossible? Is there not an antinomy in its very definition?

The difficulty, it may be noticed, is no other and therefore no more impossible to solve than that involved in all
application of theory to practice. When, for example, a man
is to build a tunnel, he has to do something quite specific,
having its own concrete conditions. It is not a tunnel in
general which he has to make, but a tunnel having its own
special end and called for by its own set of circumstances—a
set of circumstances not capable of being precisely duplicated anywhere else in the world. The work has to be done
under conditions imposed by the given environment, character of soil, facility of access to machinery, and so on. It is
true that so many tunnels have now been built for similar
ends and under *substantially* like circumstances, that the
example errs on the side of excessive mechanicalness; but we
have only to imagine the tunnel building under untried
special conditions, as, say, the recent engineering below the
St. Clair River, to get a fair case. Now in such a case it is

requisite that science, that theory, be available at every step
of the undertaking, and this in the most detailed way. Every
stage of the proceeding must, indeed, be absolutely controlled by scientific method. There is here the same apparent
contradiction as in the moral case; and yet the solution in the
case of the engineering feat is obvious. Theory is used, not
as a set of fixed rules to lay down certain things to be done,
but as a tool of analysis to help determine what the nature of
the special case is; it is used to uncover the reality, the
conditions of the matter, and thus to lay bare the circumstances which action has to meet, to synthesize. The mathematical, the mechanical, the geological theories do not say
"Do this or that"; but in effect they do say, use me and you
will reduce the complex conditions of which you have only
some slight idea to an ordered group of relations to which
action may easily adjust itself in the desired fashion. Now
these conceptions of mechanics, of geology, which aid in
determining the special facts at hand, are themselves, it is to
be noticed, simply the *generic* statement of these same facts;
the mathematics are the most general statement of any
group of circumstances to be met anywhere in experience;
the geology is a general statement of the conditions to be
met with wherever it is an affair of the soil and so on. The
theory, in other words, is not a something or other belonging to an entirely different realm from the special facts to be
mastered. It is an outline statement of these same facts
wrought out from previous like experiences and existing
ready at hand to anticipate, and thus help solve, any particular experience. What we have then in this application of
theory to the special case, with all its wealth of concrete
detail, is the attack and reduction of a specific reality
through the use of a general precedent idea of this same
reality. Or what we have, putting it from the side of the
theory, is a general conception which is so true to reality
that it lends itself easily and almost inevitably to more
specific and concrete statement, the moment circumstances
demand such particularization. So far as the theory is
"false," so far, that is, as it is not a statement, however
general, of the facts of the case, so far, instead of lending
itself to more specific statement, instead of fertilizing itself

whenever occasion requires, it resists such specification and stands aloof as a bare generality. It neither renders individual experiences luminous, nor is fructified by them, gathering something from them which makes its own statement of reality somewhat more definite and thus more ready for use another time.

Now let us return to our moral case. The same law holds here. Ethical theory must be a general statement of the reality involved in every moral situation. It must be action stated in its more generic terms, terms so generic that every individual action will fall within the outlines it sets forth. If the theory agrees with these requirements, then we have for use in any special case a tool for analyzing that case; a method for attacking and reducing it, for laying it open so that the action called for in order to meet, to satisfy it, may readily appear. The theory must not, on one hand, stand aloof from the special thing to be done, saying, "What have I to do with thee? Thou art empirical and I am the metaphysics of conduct," nor must it, on the other hand, attempt to lay down fixed rules in advance exhausting all possible cases. It must wait upon the instruction that every new case, because of its individuality, its uniqueness, carries with it; but it must also bring to this special case such knowledge of the reality of all action, such knowledge of the end and process involved in all deeds, that it translates naturally into the concrete terms of this special case. If, for example, I object to the categorical imperative of Kant, or the pleasure of the Hedonist, that it does not assist practice, I do not mean that it does not prescribe a rigid body of fixed rules telling just what to do in every contingency of action; I mean that the theory so far comes short as a statement of the character of all moral action that it does not lend itself to uncovering, to getting at the reality of specific cases as they arise; and that, on the other hand, these special cases, not being the detailed exhibition of the same reality that is stated generally in the theory, do not react upon the theory and fructify it for further use.[1]

[1]    In the *International Journal of Ethics*, for January, 1891, I have developed this thought at greater length in an article upon "Moral Theory and Practice." [*Early Works*, III, 93–101.]

These remarks are introductory to a critical considera-tion of the theory of Thomas Hill Green regarding the moral motive or ideal. His theory would, I think, be com-monly regarded as the best of the modern attempts to form a metaphysic of ethic. I wish, using this as type, to point out the inadequacy of such metaphysical theories, on the ground that they fail to meet the demand just made of truly ethical theory, that it lend itself to translation into concrete terms, and thereby to the guidance, the direction of actual conduct. I shall endeavor to show that Green's theory is not meta-physical in the only possible sense of metaphysic, such general statement of the nature of the facts to be dealt with as enables us to anticipate the actual happening, and thereby deal with it intelligently and freely, but metaphysical in the false sense, that of a general idea which remains remote from contact with actual experience. Green himself is better than his theory, and engages us in much fruitful analysis of specific moral experience, but, as I shall attempt to show, his theory, taken in logical strictness, admits of no reduction into terms of individual deeds.

Kant's separation of the self as reason from the self as want or desire, is so well known as not to require detailed statement. That this separation compels the moral motive to be purely formal, having no content except regard for law just as law needs no exposition. So far as I know it has not been pointed out that Green, while arguing against such separation of sense and reason, on the ground that we can-not know sense or desire at all except as determined by reason, yet practically repeats the dualism of Kant in slightly altered form. For the conception of action deter-mined by the pure form of self, Green simply substitutes action determined by the self in its unity; for conduct deter-mined by mere appetite, he substitutes conduct determined by the self in some particular aspect. The dualism between reason and sense is given up, indeed, but only to be replaced by a dualism between the end which would satisfy the self as a unity or whole, and that which satisfies it in the particu-lar circumstances of actual conduct. The end which would satisfy the self as unity is just as far from the end which satisfies the self in any special instance of action, as, in

Kant's system, the satisfaction of pure reason is remote from the satisfaction of mere appetite. Indeed, we may go a step further, and say that the opposition is even more decided and intrinsic in Green than in Kant. It is at least conceivable, according to Kant, that in some happy moment action should take place from the motive of reason shorn of all sensuous content and thus be truly moral. But in no possible circumstance, according to Green, can action satisfy the whole self and thus be truly moral. In Kant the discrepancy between the force which appetite exercises, and the controlling force at the command of pure reason, is so great as to make very extraordinary the occurrence of a purely moral action; but at least there is no intrinsic impossibility in the conception, however heavy the odds against its actual happening. In Green, however, the thing is impossible by the very definition of morality. No thorough-going theory of total depravity ever made righteousness more impossible to the natural man than Green makes it to a human being by the very constitution of his being, and, needless to say, Green does not allow the supernatural recourse available to the Calvinist in the struggle for justification.

Let me now justify, by reference to Green, this statement that according to him the very conditions under which moral action is carried on make it impossible for a satisfactory moral action to occur. Green's analysis of the moral procedure is as follows: The difference between animal and moral action is that the animal deed simply expresses a want which impels the animal blindly forward to its own satisfaction. The want is not elevated into consciousness; that is, there is no conception of the end sought. The impulse which makes good the want is not brought into the focus of consciousness; that is, there is no conception of the nature of the means to be used in satisfying the want. Moral action arises, not through the intervention of any new kind of "nature" or want, but through the intervention of a self which reflects upon the existing wants, and through the reflection transforms them into ends or ideals conceived as satisfying the self. The self in seeing the want, in becoming conscious of it, objectifies the want, making out of it an ideal condition of itself in which it expects to find satisfaction. It is an animal thing to be simply moved by the appetite for food; it is a moral thing to become conscious of this appetite, and thereby transform the bare appetite into the conception of some end or object in which the self thinks to find its own satisfaction.[2]

The process of moral experience involves, therefore, a process in which the self, in becoming conscious of its want, objectifies that want by setting it over against itself; distinguishing the want from self and self from want. As thus distinguished, it becomes an end or ideal of the self. Now this theory so far might be developed in either of two directions. The self-distinguishing process may mean the method by which the self specifies or defines its own activity, its own satisfaction; all particular desires and their respective ends would be, in this case, simply the systematic content into which the self differentiated itself in its progressive expression. The particular desires and ends would be the modes in which the self relieved itself of its abstractness, its undeveloped character, and assumed concrete existence. The ends would not be *merely* particular, because each would be one member in the self's activity, and, as such member, universalized. The unity of the self would stand in no opposition to the particularity of the special desire; on the contrary, the unity of the self and the manifold of definite desires would be the synthetic and analytic aspects of one and the same reality, neither having any advantage metaphysical or ethical over the other. Such is *not* the interpretation Green gives. The self does not, according to him, define itself *in* the special desire; but the self distinguishes itself *from* the desire. The objectification is not of the self *in* the special end; but the self remains behind setting the special object over against itself as not adequate to itself. The self-distinction gives rise, not to a progressive realization of the self in a system of definite members or organs, but to an irreconcilable antithesis. The self as unity, as whole, falls over on one side; as unity, it is something not to be realized in any special end or activity, and therefore not in any

[2]    See, for example, Green, *Prolegomena to Ethics*, pp. 92, 118, 126, 134, and 160.

possible series of ends, not even a *progressus ad infinitum*. The special desire with its individual end falls over on the other side; by its contrast with the unity of the self it is condemned as a forever inadequate mode of satisfaction. The unity of the self sets up an ideal of satisfaction for itself as it withdraws from the special want, and *this* ideal set up through negation of the particular desire and its satisfaction constitutes the moral ideal. It is forever unrealizable, because it forever negates the special activities through which alone it might, after all, realize itself. The moral life is, by constitution, a self-contradiction. Says Green: "As the reflecting subject traverses the series of wants, which it distinguishes from itself while it presents their filling as its object, there arises the idea of a satisfaction on the whole—an idea never realizable, but forever striving to realize itself in the attainment of a greater command over means to the satisfaction of particular wants."[3] Green shows that the process of our active experience demands that the self, in becoming conscious of a want, set that want before itself as an object, thus distinguishing itself from the want; but he shows us no road back from the want thus objectified to the self. The unity of self has efficiency only in a negative way, to set itself up as an ideal condemning to insufficiency every concrete step towards reaching the ideal. The self becomes, not a systematic reality which is (or which may be) realizing itself in every special deed, but a far-away ideal which can be realized only through an absolute exhaustion of all its capacities. "Of a life of complete development, of activity with the end attained, we can only speak or think in negatives, and thus only can we speak or think of that state of being in which, according to our theory, the ultimate moral good must consist."[4]

Consider, then, how much worse off we are than the animals; they can get at least the satisfaction of their particular wants, while the supervention of the self in us makes us conscious of an ideal which sets itself negatively over against every attempt to realize itself, thus condemning us

3    *Prolegomena*, p. 91; see also p. 233.
4    *Prolegomena*, p. 180; and see also pp. 189, 204, 244.

to continued dissatisfaction. Speaking more accurately, the self supervenes, not completely or as an adequately compelling reality, but only as the thought of an ideal. It supervenes, not as a power active in its own satisfaction, but to make us realize the unsatisfactoriness of such seeming satisfactions as we may happen to get, and to keep us striving for something which we can never get! Surely, if Green is correct, he has revealed the illusion which has kept men striving for something which they cannot get, and, the illusion detected, men will give up the strife which leads only to dissatisfaction. Whatever may be said for an ascetic ethics, naked and professed, surely there is something at fault in the analysis which sets up satisfaction as the end, and *then* relapses into a thorough-going asceticism.

I have dwelt upon this contradiction at length, not for its own sake, but in order to emphasize the helplessness of such a theory with regard to action. It is not, I repeat, that a fixed body of precepts cannot be deduced from this conception of the moral ideal; it is that the idea cannot be *used*. Instead of being a tool which can be brought into fruitful relations to special circumstances so as to help determine what should be done, it remains the bare thought of an ideal of perfection, having nothing in common with the special set of conditions or with the special desire of the moment. Indeed, instead of helping determine the right, the satisfactory, it stands off one side and says, "No matter what you do, you will be dissatisfied. I am complete; you are partial. I am a unity; you are a fragment, and a fragment of such a kind that no amount of you and such as you can ever afford satisfaction." In a word, the ideal not only does not lend itself to specification, but it negates specification in such way that its necessary outcome, were it ever seriously adopted as a controlling theory of morals, would be to paralyze action.

The ideal of Green is thus the bare form of unity in conduct; the form devoid of all content, and essentially excluding all proposed content as inadequate to the form. The only positive significance which it has is: whatever the moral ideal, it must at least have the form of unity. Now it seems mere tautology to urge that the mere idea of unity, no matter how much you bring it in juxtaposition with concrete circumstances, does not tell *what* the unity of the situation is, or give any aid in determining that unity; at most it but sets the problem, saying, "Whatever the situation, seek for its unity." But Green's ideal cannot be made to go as far as this in the direction of concreteness; his unity is so thoroughly abstract that, instead of urging us to seek for the deed that would unify the situation, it rather says that *no* unity can be found in the situation because the situation is particular, and therefore set over against the unity.

But while it seems certain to me that any attempt to make the ideal definite must, by the very nature of the case, be at the expense of logical consistency, it will be fairer to describe briefly the various ways in which Green indicates an approach to concreteness of action. These ways may be reduced to three. In the first place, the setting of the self as ideal unity with its own unrealized satisfaction over against the particular desire with its particular satisfaction, gives rise to the notion of an unconditional good,—a good absolutely, to which, therefore, every special and relative good must conform. Hence the idea of obligation, the unquestioned ought or categorical imperative. Secondly, this same contrast keeps alive in the mind, in the face of every seeming good, the conception of a better, thus preventing the mind from sinking into any ignoble acquiescence with the present and keeping it alert for improvement. Hence the idea of moral progress. And, thirdly, this absolute good with its unqualified demands for regard upon humanity has secured in the past some degree of observance, however defective; it has compelled man to give it some shape and body. Hence the existence of permanent institutions which hold forth the eternal good not in its abstract shape but in some concrete embodiment.

The first of these modes for giving definiteness to the ideal, and thus making it available for actual conduct, may be soon dismissed. It is, over again, only the thought of *an* ideal, except it now takes the form of a law instead of that of a good or satisfaction. It is at most the consciousness *that* there is something to do and that this something has unconditioned claims upon us. We are as far as ever from any method of translating this something in general into the special thing which has to be done in a given case. And here, as before, this unconditioned law not simply fails to carry with itself any way of getting concrete, but it stands in negative relation to any transfer into particular action. It declares: "Whatever you do, you will come short of the law which demands a complete realization; and you can give only inadequate obedience, since your action is limited through your want at the moment of action." Given the general acceptance of the theory, the result would be, on account of the impossibility of conforming to the demands of the law, either a complete recklessness of conduct (since we cannot in any way satisfy this hard task-master, let us at least get what pleasure we can out of the passing moments) or a pessimism transcending anything of which Schopenhauer has dreamed.

I cannot see that the case stands any different with the idea of a Better. Granted that the thought of a better would arise from the opposition of a Good upon the whole to every special good, as depicted by Green, how are we to advance from this thought of *a* better to any notion of *what* that better is, either as to the prevailing tendency of life, the direction in which we are to look for improvement upon the whole, or in any special situation? The notion that there is a better, if a *mere* idea, that is, an idea not tending to define itself in this or that specific better, would be, it appears to me, hardly more than a mockery for all the guidance it would give conduct. How is the general consciousness of a better to be brought into such relation with the existing lines of action that it will serve as an organ of criticism, pointing out their defects and the direction in which advance is to be looked for? And I think it could be shown through a logical analysis that the conception of a good which cannot be realized "in any life that can be lived by man as we know him"[5] is so far from being a safe basis for a theory of moral progress, that it negates the very notion of progress. Progress would seem to imply a principle immanent in the process and securing continual revelation and expression there. I

5    *Prolegomena*, p. 189.

am aware of the logical difficulties bound up in the idea of progress, but these difficulties are increased rather than met by a theory which makes it consist in advance *towards* an end which is outside the process, especially when it is added that, so far as we can know, this end cannot be reached; that indeed the nature of the process towards it is such as to make the ideal always withdraw further. The only question on such a theory is whether the thought of advance *towards* the goal has any meaning, and whether we have any criterion at all by which to place ourselves; to tell where we are in the movement, and whither we are going—backward or forward.

We come, then, to the embodiment which the ideal has found for itself in the past as the sole reliance for getting self-definition into the empty form of unity of self. In their effort towards this full realization men have produced certain institutions, codes, and recognized forms of duty. In loyalty to these, taken not merely in themselves, but as expressions of the attempt to realize the ideal, man may find his primary concrete duties. Says Green: "However meagrely the perfection, the vocation, the law, may be conceived, the consciousness that there is such a thing, so far as it directs the will, must at least keep the man to the path in which human progress has so far been made. It must keep him loyal in the spirit to established morality, industrious in some work of recognized utility."[6] The criticism here may take several roads. We may point out that the question is not whether as matter of fact the ideal *has* embodied itself in institution and code with sufficient fulness so that loyalty to the institution and code is a means in which our duty and satisfaction comes specifically home to us: that the question is whether, *if* the ideal were the abstract unity—the unity negative to every special end—which Green makes it, any such embodiment would be possible. We may ask, in other words, whether Green, in order to help out the undefinable character of his ideal, its inability to assume concrete form, has not unconsciously availed himself of a fact incompatible with his theory, a fact whose very existence refutes his

6    *Prolegomena*, p. 184; see also p. 207.

theory. Or, we might approach the matter from the other side and inquire whether the relation of the absolute ideal to the special institutions in which it has found expression is of such a kind (according to the terms of Green's theory of moral experience) that loyalty to "established morality" is a safe ethical procedure. On the contrary, must not, according to the fundamental premise which Green has laid down, the relation of the ideal to *any* expression which it may have secured, be essentially—radically—negative? That is, does not the ideal in its remote and unrealizable nature stand off and condemn the past attempts to realize it as vain, as unworthy? Does not the ideal say, in substance, I am not in you; you are but nugatory attempts to shadow forth my unity? Such being the case, the path of morality would lie in turning *against* established morality rather than in following it. The moral command would be, "Be *not* loyal to existing institutions, if you would be loyal to me, the only true moral ideal." But this very negation, since it is a negation in general, since it negates not this or that feature of the established morality, but that morality *per se*, gives no aid in determining in what respect to act differently. It just says: "Do not do as you have been doing; act differently." And it is an old story in logic that an undetermined "infinite" negative conveys no intelligence. It may be true that a virtue is not an elephant, but this throws no light on the nature of either the virtue or the elephant. The negation must be with respect to an identity involved in both the compared terms before it assists judgment; that is, the ideal must be *in* the actual which it condemns, if it is to really criticise; an external standard, just because it is external, is no standard at all. There is no common ground, and hence no basis for comparison. And thus when Green goes on to say[7] that the same ideal which has embodied itself in institutions also embodies itself in the critical judgment of individuals, who are thereby enabled to look back upon the institutions and cross-examine them, thus raising up higher standards, he says something which it is highly desirable to have true, but which cannot be true, if his theory of the

7    *Prolegomena*, pp. 270 *et seq.*

purely negative relation of the unity of self-consciousness to every particular act is correct.

But we need not indulge, at length, in these various hypothetical criticisms. Green himself, with his usual candor in recognizing and stating all difficulties, no matter how hardly they bear upon his own doctrine, has clearly stated the fundamental opposition here; an opposition making it impossible that the ideal should concretely express itself in any institutional form in such way as to lend itself to the concrete determination of further conduct. The contradiction, as Green himself states it, is that while the absolute unity of self must, in order to translate into an ideal for man, find an embodiment in social forms, all such forms are, by their very nature and definition, so limited that no amount of loyalty to the institution can be regarded as an adequate satisfaction of the ideal. Or as Green puts it: "Only through society is any one enabled to give that effect to the idea of man as the object of his actions, to the idea of a possible better state of himself, without which the idea would remain like that of space to a man who had not the senses either of sight or of touch,"—that is, a merely ideal possibility, without actual meaning. And yet society necessarily puts such limits upon the individual that he cannot by his life in society give effect to the idea. "Any life which the individual can possibly live is at best so limited by the necessities of his position that it seems impossible, on supposition that a definite self-realizing principle is at work in it, that it should be an adequate expression of such a principle." "It is only so far as we are members of the society, by means of which we can conceive of the common good as our own, that the idea has any practical hold on us at all; and this very membership implies confinement in our individual realization of the idea. Each has primarily to perform the duties of his station; his capacity for action beyond the range of this duty is definitely bounded, and with it is definitely bounded also his sphere of personal interest, his character, his realized possibility."[8]

Here is the contradiction. If man were to withdraw

from his social environment, he would lose at once the idea of the moral end, the stimulus to its realization, and the concrete means for carrying it out. The social medium is to the moral ideal what language is to thought—and more. And yet if man stays in the social environment, he is by that very residence so limited in interest and power that he cannot realize the ideal. It is the old difficulty over again.

Just as the unity of the self, taken psychologically, sets itself, in a negative way, over against every special desire, so this same unity of self, taken socially, removes itself from every special institution in which it is sought to embody it—removes itself, be it noticed, not because the embodiment *succeeds* and through the very thoroughness of the embodiment creates a new situation, requiring *its* special unification, but because of the essential futility of the attempt at embodiment. The antithesis between form and content, ideal and actual, is an undoubted fact of our experience; the question, however, is as to the meaning, the interpretation, of this fact. Is it an antithesis which arises *within* the process of moral experience, this experience bearing in its own womb both ideal and actual, both form and content, and also the rhythmic separation and redintegration of the two sides? Or, is the antithesis between the process of moral experience, *as such*, and an ideal outside of this experience and negative to it, so that experience can never embody it? It is because Green interprets the fact in the latter sense that he shuts himself up to an abstract ideal which unqualifiedly resists all specification, and which is therefore useless as an organ for our moral activity.

I have now attempted to show that Green takes the bare fact that there is unity in moral experience, abstracts that unity from experience (although its sole function is to be the unity of experience) and then, setting this unity over against the experience robbed of its significance, makes of the unity an unrealized and unrealizable ideal and condemns the experience, shorn of its unity, to continual dissatisfaction. I have tried to show this, both in general, from the nature of Green's analysis, and, more in particular, from a consideration of the three special modes in which the ideal endeavors to get relatively concrete form. Since I have

treated the theory as reduced to its naked logical consistency, I may have appeared to some to have dealt with it
rather harshly, though not, I hope, unjustly. But aside from
the fact that the truest reverence we can render any of the
heroes of thought is to use his thinking to forward our own
struggle for truth, philosophy seems, at present, to be suffering from a refusal to subject certain ideas to unswerving
analysis because of sympathy with the moral atmosphere
which bathes those ideas, and because of the apparent service of those ideas in reclothing in philosophic form ideas
endeared to the human mind through centuries of practical
usefulness in forms traditional and symbolic.

In closing, I wish to point out that the abstract theories
of morals, of which we have just been considering the best
modern type, are not aberrations of an individual thinker;
that, on the contrary, they are the inevitable outcome of a
certain stage of social development, recurring at each of
those nodal points in progress when humanity, becoming
conscious of the principle which has hitherto unconsciously
underlain its activity, abstracts that principle from the institutions through which it has previously acted preparatory to
securing better organs for it—institutions, that is, through
which it shall flow more freely and more fully. The error
consists in transforming this purely historical opposition, an
opposition which has meaning only with reference to the
movement of a single process, into a rigid or absolute separation. That is to say, at the moment in which a given cycle
of history has so far succeeded that it can express its principle free from the mass of incident with which it had been
bound up (and so hidden from consciousness) at that moment this principle appears in purely negative form. It is the
negation of the preceding movement because in it that movement has succeeded—has summed itself up. Success always
negates the process which leads up to it, because it renders
that process unnecessary; it takes away from it all function
and thus all excuse for being. Just so, for example, Hellenic
life transcended itself in Socrates; in him it became conscious of the principle (the universality of the self, to express it roughly) which had been striving to realize itself.
The movement having come to consciousness, having gener-

alized itself, its principle at once assumed a negative relation to the forms in which this principle had been only partially embodied. Just because Socrates was, in his consciousness, a complete Greek, he wrote the epitaph of Greece. So, to take another obvious example, Jesus, in fulfilling the law, transcended it, so that those who were "in Christ Jesus, were no longer under the law." Now just because the principle in its completion, its generalization is negative to its own partial realizations or embodiments, just because it negates its own immediate historic antecedents, it is easy to conceive of it as negative to *all* embodiment. At a certain stage of the movement, this transformation of a historic into an absolute negative is not only easy, but, as it would seem, inevitable. This stage is the moment when the principle which sums up one movement is seen to be the law for the next movement and has not as yet got organized into further outward or institutional forms. For the moment (the moment may last a century) the principle having transcended one institutional expression, and not having succeeded in getting another, seems to be wholly in the air—essentially negative to all possible realization. The very completeness with which the principle sums up and states the reality of life seems, by the one great paradox, to put it in opposition to that reality—to make of it something essentially transcending experience. The great example of this is the fortune of the Christian idea. As it was originally stated, it was not put forth as a specially religious truth; religious, that is, in a sense which marked off religion as a sphere by itself; it was propounded as the realization of the meaning of experience, as the working truth which all experience bases itself upon and carries with itself. This truth was that man is an expression or an organ of the Reality of the universe. That, as such organ, he participates in truth and, through the completeness of his access to ultimate truth, is free, there being no essential barriers to his action either in his relation to the world or in his relations to his fellow-men. Stated more in the language of the time, man was an incarnation of God and in virtue of this incarnation redeemed from evil. Now this principle, if we regard it as having historical relations and not something intruded into the world from outside, without continuity with previous experience, this principle, I say, must have been the generalization of previous life; such a generalization as plucking its principle from that experience negated it. And yet this principle, at the outset, only quickened men's consciousness of their slaveries—this idea of participation in the Absolute only made men feel more deeply the limitations of their activity and hence their "finitude." Thus the principle seemed negative not only to preceding institutions but to all contemporaneous institutions; indeed, these contemporaneous institutions were, of course, only the survivals of the preceding institutions. Until such time, then, as the new principle should succeed in getting itself organized into forms more adequate to itself (the development of science, the conquest of nature through the application of this science in invention and industry, and its application to the activities of men in determining their relations to one another and the resulting forms of social organization) this principle must have seemed remote from, negative to, all possible normal life. Thus, in being forced apart from actual life, the principle was conceived, not any longer as a working method of life, but as something wholly supernatural. So absolutely was a negation which was only historic in its meaning frozen into an absolute negative.

Now the ethical theory which Green represents appears under similar historic conditions. Physical science in its advance has got to the thought of a continuous unity embodied in all natural process. In the theory of evolution this unity of process has ceased to be either a supernatural datum or a merely philosophic speculation. It has assumed the proportions of fact. So social organization has gone far enough in the direction of democracy that the principle of movement towards unity comes to consciousness in that direction. In every direction there is coming to consciousness the power of an organizing activity underlying and rendering tributary to itself the apparently rigid dualisms holding over from the mediæval structure. This unity, just because it is the manifestation of the reality realizing itself in the institutions characteristic of the past, is negative to those institutions; it is the reality of which they are the phenomena. That is, these institutions have their meaning as pointing to or indicating the organizing unity; they are the *attempts* to express it. Succeeding in their attempt at expression, they are superseded. They have realized their purpose, their function. The principle in which they have summed themselves up, in which they have executed themselves, has the floor; it has command of the scene of action. When that which is whole is come, that which is in part shall be done away. Now this principle of a single, comprehensive, and organizing unity being historically negative to its concrete conditions, to former institutions, is easily conceived as negative to all embodiment. While, in reality, we are conscious of this organizing principle only because it *is* getting concrete manifestation, only because, indeed, it *has* secured such embodiment as to appear as the directing principle or method of life, the first realization of the principle is negative; we become conscious, in the light of this organizing unity, of its *non-being*, of its still partial embodiment, of the resistances which it still has to overcome—this is, of its divided character. Translate this negation, which is a phase in every individualized movement, into a hard and fast thing, and you get an ideal set over against the actual (and the possible) experience as such. So it was with Green: only because the single organizing unity had got expression for itself could he conceive it at all; only because it had emerged so thoroughly as the reality of all experience could he contrast it, as he did, with the particular experiences of which it was the meaning. Only because the institutions of life had through centuries of conception finally given birth to this idea as their own idea and reality, could Green use this idea to condemn those institutions. Such is the irony of all history; it so thoroughly realizes and embodies ideas that these very ideas are turned against it as its own condemnation. But the life which is going on in history, instead of accusing its children of their ungratefulness, makes use of the very ideas by which it is condemned to secure still wider revelation of its own meaning.

# Two Phases of Renan's Life: The Faith of 1850 and the Doubt of 1890

I have been much interested in the recent articles upon Renan in the *Open Court*, and hope that the discussion may not end at once. Particularly do I hope that the discussion of his *Future of Science* may continue, as I think that book is far from having received the attention, or exercised the influence, it deserves. Many things in it tend to arouse interest. The way in which the great philosophic formulations of Germany, just then losing currency as official doctrine, were continued by passing over into the attitude and atmosphere of science, especially of historic science, is a point fastening attention. That which in Hegel had been an attempt at a comprehensive philosophising of the universe has become, in Renan, the conception and method of the science of philology. The conception of philology is a science of the human intellect as a single whole developing throughout all history, and having its record in language, in a sense which understands by language all records which the human race has left of itself, whether in the *form* of language, or in its substance—in literature. The method (and this is 1848) is fixed by the idea of evolution. "The science of man will only then be placed in its true light when students realise that consciousness is evolved—that it only attains its plenitude after having gone through diverse phases. . . . The great progress of modern thought has been the substitution of the category of *evolution* for that of

[*First published in the* Open Court, *VI* (*29 Dec.* 1892), 3505–6. *Reprinted in* Characters and Events, *I,* 18–23, *under the title* "*Ernest Renan.*"]

*being*; . . . formerly everything was conceived as 'being,' as an accomplished fact; people spoke of law, of religion, of politics, of poetry in an absolute fashion. At present everything is conceived as in process of *formation*" (p. 169. I refer to the American translation). And when we go on to consider the law of evolution: from the undifferentiated homogeneous, the syncrete, through the multiplicity which results from analysis, to a synthesis which comprehends, while it never destroys, the multiplicity: when we consider this, the transference of the Hegelian doctrine becomes even more marked. It is the same law, only considered now as the law of historic growth, not as the dialectic unfolding of the absolute.

Remembering the date, Renan's protest against the psychology of the time and his sketch of its true course attain importance. His protest is directed against the static and purely individual character of the current psychology. Psychology has confined itself to a study of the human intellect in its mature state. The necessity for the future is a form of psychology which Renan, significantly enough, terms an *embryogeny* of the human soul, a psychology which shall study the first appearance and gradual development of those powers which we now have ready-made. Not less striking, in its prevision, is the idea that this genetic science is to deal equally with the race and with the individual in their growth from infancy. Surely there is something more than a chance anticipation of the modern conception of the relation of ontogeny and phylogeny when Renan says, "Each individual travels in his turn along the line which the whole of mankind has followed, and the series of the development of human reason is parallel to the progress of individual reason." Aside, then, from the study of childhood, Renan suggests as a method of reproducing the mind of the past, the products, the monuments in which the mind has recorded itself. Chief of these records is language. "The deep study of its mechanism and history will always prove the most efficacious means of mastering primeval psychology." Through this study we should get, Renan goes on to say, "the facts which interested the mind at its first awakening, the influences that affected it, the laws that governed it." Beyond this, psychology is to give less emphasis, less absoluteness, to the manifestations of psychical life in the individual and more to those of humanity. History itself, in final definition is to be conceived as the psychology of humanity (pp. 152–68).

Of interest again is Renan's grasp of the conflict which is always going on between specialisation and generalisation in science, and his idea of the way to direct the conflict, so as to sustain the minimum of loss. The discussion is of special interest in connection with the present reaction against Renan's work as too viewy, too given to broad generalisation, lacking in the detailed element of technical research. The balance is difficult to keep, but certainly Renan's theory cannot be charged with erring in this direction, and if his practice errs the next generation may count the error no more heinous than that of a devotion to detail which carefully ignores all larger meaning. On one side, Renan demands an ever increasing amount of specialistic work, of monographs, of technical research, on every point however minute. Although the "grand" histories have already been attempted, yet without more numerous and extensive monographs, their real history cannot be written short of a century. He even goes to the point of saying that the "true heroes of science are they, who, capable of the loftiest views have been able to resign themselves to the rôle of humble monographers." And again, "the specialist-savant, instead of deserting the true arena of humanity, is the one who labors most efficaciously to the progress of the intellect, seeing that he alone can provide us with the materials for constructions." But all this is no excuse for the isolation and dispersion which exists at present. "The great present obstacle is the dispersion of work, the self-isolation among special studies which renders the labors of the philologist available only to himself and a small number engaged in the same subject." The defect is not in the multiplicity or minuteness of investigations, but in the fact that there is no machinery for distributing them, no apparatus for condensing and concentrating the results of the special research of one so as to put them at the disposal of all others. It is a form of egotism which insists that one's monograph shall always remain in just the state in which one wrote it; which resists all reduction of it to its gist so as to make it available, in its net outcome, for any and all investigators. The real need is for organisation, for control not of the liberty of individual specialisation, but of the results so reached. Our ideal must be to reproduce on a large scale the ideal attained, in small, in certain monastic orders—a grand scientific workshop (pp. 212–40).

Suggestive as are all these and many other special discussions of Renan, the most important thing to my mind is, after all, the conception which Renan had, in 1850, of the universal—the social, the religious significance of science and his partial retraction of this faith in 1890. The book in question, *The Future of Science*, was written, it may be of interest to recall, in 1848 and 1849. It was the outcome of the conflux of two movements—the growth of the scientific spirit in Renan in his progress out of Catholicism and of the political movement which found its expression in the various revolutions of '48. The volume breathes a constant and bracing tone of optimism: the *Future of Science* is not the future of erudition nor yet of knowledge as such. It is a social future, a development of humanity, which Renan has in mind. This was the origin of the book—"the need I felt of summing up in a volume the new [*i.e.*, social] faith which had replaced the shattered Catholicism." But just as he was ready to publish he went to Italy in connection with certain researches in the literary history of France and in Averroism. The artistic side of life, till then, as he says, closed to him, opened; it unbent him. Nearly all his ideals of 1848 vanished as impossible of realisation. He became, as he puts it, reconciled to reality—a world in which "a great deal of evil is the necessary condition to any good, in which an imperceptible amount of aroma requires for its extraction an enormous *caput mortuum* of dead matter." Was he reconciled to reality? or was it that the æsthetic spell passed over him, that he went to Italy a democrat—a believer in the universal function of science—and returned an aristocrat— sceptical of the intellectual and artistic life as one capable of being shared in by any beyond the select few? However it was, when he came back to his volume it no longer satisfied him, either in substance or in style. The *coup d'état*, happening soon after, added the finishing touch. The result was the Renan with whom we are most familiar: the man quite disillusioned, quite conscious of the impossibility of deciding among the multitude of ends which life presents, something of a dilettante, but always sympathetic and always conscientiously bent on the faithful culture of that spot of ground which belonged to him to till. The contrast between the enthusiast of 1848, apparently most interested in science because of the social mission of science, and the Renan of 1890, purposely ignoring its social function, is one of the most interesting things that I know of in literary history. I cannot do better than to close these remarks with a quotation from the *Moderne Geister* of Brandes. After quoting the later creed of Renan as summed up in the saying, "The scholar is a spectator in the universe; he knows the universe belongs to him only as an object of study," he goes on: "it is difficult to measure the demoralising effect upon French scholars exercised by the Second Empire; how their life became accommodated to the *fait accompli*. Everywhere under Napoleon III the higher French culture is characterised by an inclination to quietism and fatalism. Traces of this influence are to be seen everywhere. Complete freedom from enthusiasm was quite synonymous with culture and ripeness of judgment." Brandes quotes what Renan said to him in disparagement of universal education: in contrast read the enthusiastic plea for universal culture in the *Future of Science* and the transition is before you.

The Renan of 1848 wrote: "The most sublime works are those which humanity has made collectively and to which no name can be attached. . . . What do I care for the man that stands between humanity and me? What do I care for the insignificant syllables of his name? That name itself is a lie; it is not he; it is the nation; it is humanity toiling at a point of space and time that is the real author." In 1871, in his *Intellectual and Moral Reform* Renan writes: "At its outset, civilisation was an aristocratic accomplishment: it was the work of a very few—nobles and priests—who made it obtain through what the democrats call the imposition of force. The continued preservation of civilisation is also the work of the aristocratic class." In 1848 he wrote: "Only one course remains and that is to broaden the basis of the family and to find room for all at the banqueting table of light. . . . The aristocracy constitutes an odious monopoly if it does not set before it for its aim the tutelage of the masses — their gradual elevation." In 1871, his tone is: "The people properly so-called and the peasantry, to-day the absolute masters of the house, are in reality only intruders, wasps who have usurped possession of a hive they did not build."

# Book Reviews

*The Critical Philosophy of Immanuel Kant*, by Edward
Caird, LL.D., Professor of Moral Philosophy in the
University of Glasgow. Two volumes. Glasgow:
James Maclehose and Sons (Macmillan and Co.,
N. Y.), 1889.

Dr. Caird's former book on Kant has been out of print
for some years, and it was understood that its author was
preparing a more extended work. The first treatise, it will
be recalled, covered only the *Critique of Pure Reason*. The
implied promise has been most amply redeemed. We have
now a report upon all of Kant's work, the minor writings as
well as the three main *Critiques*, even the former exposition
being entirely rewritten. The reviewer who would under-
take to give anything approaching a fair account of these
thirteen hundred compact although clear octavo pages must
be either wiser than the present reviewer is, or more ignorant than he would be willing to confess himself. Yet there
are some things which at least may be said *about* these
volumes, — some things upon which there would be no difference of opinion among those competent to judge. All would
admit that Professor Caird has written *the* book upon Kant
in the English language, — most would add, in any language.
About the thoroughness, the accuracy, the clearness of the
exposition, there could hardly be two opinions. Concerning
the maturity, the lucidity, the deftness, the firm-handling of
the critical portion, I do not see how judgments could vary.
That Dr. Caird has made what is, as to substance, a contribution to the history of thought of the very first order, and
that in form his volumes have a unity, a massiveness, and a
simplicity of treatment which marks them as a work of art,
must be the verdict. All this, whatever philosophic stand-

[*First published in the* Andover Review, *XIII* (*Mar.* 1890), *325–
27. Not previously reprinted.*]

point the critic may himself occupy. The opinion of the absolute philosophic value of the work will of course depend upon the extent to which the critic shares the view of philosophic method and results embodied in it. To pretend in a short notice upon such a point to do more than express one's own conviction is sheer dogmatism. I can only say, then, that for myself I believe these volumes to be the richest and wisest outcome yet published of the philosophic Renascence now in progress in Great Britain. And I do not know who will transcend them until Professor Caird himself shall do it. Were I asked not only for the best English account of the Kantian philosophy, but for the best account of philosophy itself in the English language, I should point without hesitation to Caird's *Critical Philosophy of Kant*. But this judgment depends, as I said before, upon the critic's own philosophic position. That the work marks an epoch in the English treatment of the history of philosophy depends upon no position.

Only a few words may be said, to give the reader an idea of the method of Professor Caird in these volumes. After an extremely suggestive chapter upon "The Idea of Criticism," we have almost two hundred pages given to an account of Kant's life and relation to his times; his connection with his precursors from Descartes (this part is not quite so full as in Professor Caird's former book); and then what the Germans call an *Entwicklungsgeschichte* of Kant up to the point of his undertaking of the *Kritik der reinen Vernunft*. In this portion, the author has not only utilized the very numerous and detailed researches of German writers, but has materially added to them. Then follows an exposition of all Kant's critical writings, following approximately a chronological order. The account of the *Critique of Pure Reason* opens with a condensed and clear outline of the whole,—of its problem and the solution. From this point on, Dr. Caird's method is uniform. He first sets forth, in a way at once so accurate and so clear as to be the despair of the average reader who has struggled with Kant's tortuosities, Kant's own doctrine. Kant becomes fairly transparent in the lucidity of Caird's treatment, not, however, at the expense of any minimizing of difficulties.

Then follows the criticism. If the exposition is so admirable, what words remain with which to characterize the criticism? It is wholly an immanent criticism. We are shown whence Kant started; we are shown the nature and requirements of Kant's own method in dealing with the subject-matter; we are shown how far Kant goes in the reconstruction of the views from which he sets out; and we are shown how much further he should have gone in order to be true to his own principle. The great, the permanent value of Caird's work is to me the fact that he sets up no external standard by which to try Kant, but that he so develops Kant as to make him pass judgment upon himself. Here we have the Kant held back and hampered by prepossessions inherited from previous dualisms, set over against the Kant freed from his bonds and developed into consistency and integrity. In this way the book becomes, in effect, a summary of the entire Kanto-Hegelian movement, and, in addition, a statement of constructive philosophic results.

To summarize this re-creation of Kant is an impossibility,—the summary is the book itself. Professor Caird's philosophic position may, perhaps, be indicated, if I say that he has absorbed all the results of such criticism as that of Thomas Hill Green, but that he has a positive, constructive touch which in final seems to have been denied Green. The great Oxford thinker seems never to have quite freed himself from the negative element in Kant,—the idea that the regress from the world to self is an abstracting process, resulting in the notion of a spirit, *for* which indeed reality exists, but of which in itself nothing may be said. It may be roughly laid down as the purpose of Caird's work to show that, according to Kant's own principles, the movement from the world to mind, and from both to God, is a movement from the partial to the complete, from the abstract to the concrete, in which the lower becomes a factor in the spiritual process of the higher. The carrying-out of the purpose, not merely as a general principle, but in the treatment of all specific philosophic questions, is the heart of these two volumes. Dr. Caird shows that Kant reconstructed the previous dualism, that of mind set over against the world, so far as to show that all existence is existence *for* a self, for mind, but that, still in the toils of the very dualism which he was overthrowing, he denied that anything could be known of this self as such. Since, too, the known world is known only in relation to a self which is only logical, not real, that world was to Kant only phenomenal. The world of reality is shut off from intelligence. But Caird shows that the inevitable outcome of Kant is that existence is not only a phenomenon *for* self, but a phenomenon *of* self,—an element in the spiritual process of God. The result on the side of knowledge is to show that, since nature is only a factor in the self-determination of spirit, a solution of the most pressing of contemporary problems is possible. The categories of physical science can be reconciled with the principles of the moral and religious life by being taken up into them. Nature must, in Caird's words, take a new aspect, if it be conceived as standing in a necessary relation to spirit; "not only must we deny that the explanation which seems to be sufficient for matter is sufficient for life and mind, but, since matter is necessarily related to mind, we must deny that the explanation in question is sufficient even for matter. We must 'level up' and not 'level down'; we must not only deny that matter can explain spirit, but we must say that even matter itself cannot be fully understood except as an element in a spiritual world."

The same imperfect overcoming of the dualism between mind and the world, which is at the basis of Kant's unsatisfactory position as regards knowledge, affects also Kant's æsthetic, ethical, and religious position. In respect to the latter question, Caird shows clearly how the separation of the self from reality leads to Kant's conception of the moral law and of freedom as merely formal; to his conception of the moral ideal as something which merely *ought* to be, but is not; to his separation, in the name of freedom, of one individual from another; to his conception of society as essentially only an external collection of individuals; and to his denial of the possibility of any objective moral mediation. As a summary of Caird's idea of the relation of the moral will to nature, to humanity, and to God, the following quotation must serve: "Nature can be a means to the realization of our life, only in so far as in spirit nature comes to *a* self and to *its* self; that is, in so far as spirit reveals what nature implicitly contained. And other spiritual beings can be a means to the realization of our individual life, only in so far as our individual life itself becomes a means to the realization of a principle which is identical in them and in us. We cannot live except as we die to live; and the culmination of the effort after the realization of our own Will and our own Good must be the consciousness that *Deo parere libertas est*, and that all things 'can be ours' only as 'we are God's.'" So far, then, is freedom from being, as Kant conceives it, an assertion of the individual's will in his isolation, that "the *truth* of freedom lies in the unity of the self with the principle that is realizing itself in all nature and history. Behind the freedom that breaks the bonds of nature and necessity, we find a divine necessity in union with which alone man can be truly free. But, just because it is a divine necessity, it cannot really be an external necessity." With the impression derived from these words, we may fairly leave these volumes, hoping that we may have said enough of them to induce every philosophic-minded reader to turn to them himself.

*Kant's Critical Philosophy for English Readers*, by Mahaffy and Bernard. Vol. i, *The Kritik of the Pure Reason* explained and defended; Vol. ii, *The Prolegomena*, translated with Notes and Appendices. London and New York: Macmillan and Co., 1889.

In connection with Caird's book, it is worth while to direct attention to Mahaffy and Bernard's edition of the *Critique of Pure Reason* and of the *Prolegomena*. Mahaffy's books, almost a score of years ago, were practically the first to direct the attention of the English-speaking public to Kant as he really was. Mansel and Hamilton had indeed presented a Kant of whom the less said the better. Mahaffy, however, left his work in an incomplete form; with the aid

[*First published in the* Andover Review, *XIII* (*Mar. 1890*), *328. Not previously reprinted.*]

of Mr. Bernard it has now been happily completed, and reprinted in a more convenient and accessible form. The *Prolegomena* does not appear to have been much changed from the first edition; the *Critique*, with its omissions and additions, is practically a new work. The *Prolegomena* is a translation; the *Critique* a paraphrase and condensation, with occasional explanatory and critical remarks, which are, however, carefully distinguished from the exposition. The plan of the work is such and its carrying-out so careful and accurate that it fills a position not occupied by any other of the numerous Kant expositions. The writer speaks from personal experience in saying that it is a most admirable book with which to introduce advanced under-graduates in our colleges to Kant. The exposition of the "Transcendental Deduction" is hardly up to the level of the rest of the book. And one feels occasionally as if the authors, in their condensations, had omitted the nub of the matter; but, on the whole, the book is a judicious and accurate rendering of Kant's thought into a form more valuable for the ordinary student than that supplied by a translation. One who has been through this book will be admirably prepared to take up his Caird.

*A History of Philosophy*, by J. E. Erdmann, Professor of Philosophy in the University of Halle. English translation, edited by W. S. Hough, of the University of Minnesota. In three volumes. New York: Macmillan and Co., 1890.

The philosophic public has had of late its interest aroused by the prospectus of a "Library of Philosophy," promising to cover the field of philosophy in a wholly adequate way. The promise is large and taking. It includes three series of volumes, one containing works upon the development of particular schools; the second, the history of theory in particular departments; the third, original and independent contributions. The names of the writers are an

[*First published in the* Andover Review, *XIII* (*Apr. 1890*), *453–54. Not previously reprinted.*]

assurance that the execution will be as thorough and critical as the plan is comprehensive. They comprise, in the first series, such well-known authors as Professors Wallace, Seth, Sorley, and Watson; in the second, Adamson, Bosanquet, and Pfleiderer, of Berlin; in the third, Edward Caird, and Ward (the author of the article upon "Psychology" in the *Encyclopædia Britannica*). When the series is completed, the English reader of philosophy will not cast such longing and envious eyes upon Germany as at present.

The introductory and "inaugural" volume of the series is the one before us. It was, we think, a happy thought to open the series with a general history of philosophy, one giving in a summary and yet comprehensive and reasoned way an outlook over the entire field. Some writer of English might perhaps have been found who would have produced an original treatise as good as the one of Erdmann's. But to have attempted it would have involved taking a great risk. Authors who are competent for such work are apt to fly at higher game. The combination of qualities necessary to produce a work of the scope and grade of Erdmann's is rare. Industry, accuracy, and a fair degree of philosophic understanding may give us a work like Ueberweg's, but Erdmann's history, while in no way superseding Ueberweg's as a handbook for general use, yet occupies a different position. Erdmann wrote his book, not as a reference-book, to give in brief compass a digest of the writings of various authors, but as a genuine history of philosophy, tracing, in a genetic way, the development of thought in its treatment of philosophic problems. Its purpose is to develop a philosophic intelligence rather than to furnish information. When we add that, to the successful execution of this intention, Erdmann unites a minute and exhaustive knowledge of philosophic sources at first hand, equaled over the entire field of philosophy probably by no other one man (Teller, Benno, Erdmann, and others may excel in periods), we are in a condition to form some idea of the value of the book. To the student who wishes, not simply a general idea of the course of philosophy, nor a summary of what this and that man has said, but a somewhat detailed knowledge of the evolution of thought and of what this and the other writer have contributed to it, Erdmann is indispensable; there is no substitute. Were it not that the book has hitherto been shut up within the confines of a German style, often crabbed and almost always complex, I should feel myself guilty of impertinent condescension in even appearing to commend the book. To those who know the history, it stands for itself in no more need of a word of praise than Ueberweg in his line, Kuno Fischer in his, or Teller in his. Comparisons with the original German of portions of the text selected at random reveal, with one exception, a successful outcome of what must have been a difficult and often tedious task. The editor is to be congratulated that he has reduced to such uniformity of style and rendering the work of the six different hands (two of them, by the way, besides the editor, Americans) from whom the translation proceeded. The exception to the successful result is to be found in the work of the translator of the portion "Since Hegel." This is probably, from a translator's standpoint, the most difficult part of the whole history. It is the more to be regretted that it was not executed by a hand as competent as the other portions of the text found. It is a pity that Professor Hough did not exercise his editorial prerogatives more vigorously upon this part. Examination of pages 72–77 of Volume III shows nine renderings either incorrect or decidedly unhappy. It is only fair to add that other selections showed nothing like this proportion of error. The editor's own translations are, upon the whole, the most spirited and idiomatic of any. It is to be hoped that the book will find its way rapidly, and that a second edition will soon be called for.

*Studies in Hegel's Philosophy of Religion*, by J. Mac-Bride Sterrett, D.D., Professor of Ethics and Apologetics in the Seabury Divinity School. New York: D. Appleton and Co., 1890.

There is a prevailing impression that Hegel is synonymous with the "mystical," that is, misty, and that his very

[*First published in the* Andover Review, *XIII* (*June 1890*), *684–85. Not previously reprinted.*]

touch upon a commentator leaves confusion of thought and speech behind it. Dr. Sterrett has not so suffered. A more vigorous and straightforward piece of writing as well as of thinking it has not often been my fortune to meet with. The book before us is fairly buoyant in its vigor; fairly aggressive in its straightforwardness. The purpose of the book is, as Dr. Sterrett frankly informs us, in his Preface, apologetic. But he has a worthy conception of Apologetics. To show forth religion as a necessary and genuine factor in the conscious life of man, to show forth Christianity as the fruition of religion—this is what Dr. Sterrett understands by Apologetics. Early in the book he tells us that his "own interest in the study began and continues as a purely theological one—the intellectual search for God as the self-conscious Reason of all that really is" (p. 14). More particularly Dr. Sterrett considers Hegel's Philosophy of Religion in the assistance which it may give in the *present* needs of Apologetics—in the attempt to conceive God and religion under the conditions imposed by the changed state of modern science and culture. This is not, Dr. Sterrett remarks, the highest vindication that thought can make of religion; the highest is to show the authority of the absolute *idea* of Religion. Both in this higher work and in the translating of the ever-valid religious ideas out of outworn and inadequate forms and language into more adequate and convincing modern forms theology has much to learn from Hegel. This is the spirit in which Dr. Sterrett has undertaken his task.

His basis is, therefore, a broad one. It is nothing more nor less than that a Philosophy of Religion is the only final Apologetics for Christianity. "Either this Philosophy of Religion must be attained, or we must rest on the external evidences of miracle and councils. The only other alternative is to refuse to examine, to ask for no evidences, to keep the simple faith of childhood in mature years by arbitrary repression of thought" (p. 96). "The Bible, Reason, and the Church, one after another, are made the standing ground of Apologetics, and yet not one of them is infallible. Each one needs a larger apologetic to vindicate its authority. They are all relatively sufficient grounds when *themselves* grounded upon the authority of the absolute idea of Religion" (p. 97).

I emphasize this conception of the Philosophy of Religion as the basis of any Apologetics, because it seems to me the key-note of Dr. Sterrett's whole book. Discussion of this position is out of the question within the limits of my space, but I find myself in heartiest sympathy with it. A few words regarding the method of the book may be useful. The first two chapters are a running sketch, wholly informal and yet as accurate as their purpose requires, of Hegelianism and of the development of the philosophic treatment of religions. The third, fourth, seventh, and eighth chapters follow Hegel in the main, giving expositions of his "Introduction," of his chapters on the "Vital Idea of Religion," the "Classification of the Pre-Christian Religions," and "Christianity as the Absolute Religion." Chapters Five and Six do not claim any direct relation to Hegel, but are expositions from an independent, yet sympathetic, standpoint of the matters treated in the other chapters. As Dr. Sterrett, even when expounding Hegel, keeps in view not students desirous of making themselves specialists in the Hegelian technique, but those interested in the broader movement of the Hegelian ideas, it should be evident that he has produced a work of great value to all interested in the fundamental questions of modern theology. I cannot but think it a happy omen in the present juncture of our theology, when the attempt to find God immanent in the world and in history is becoming so manifest, that Dr. Sterrett should give us a book whose whole trend is so forcibly and consciously in that direction.

I cannot close without briefly calling attention to three further features of the book—and first, the notable appendix upon Church Union. For one, I am thoroughly convinced that when the happy day of church union comes, it will come not upon the lines laid down by Dr. Sterrett, for he refuses to lay down hard lines, but in the spirit which breathes through all his words. Another is the spirit of honesty, of fairness, of love for straightforward intellectual dealing which animates what Dr. Sterrett writes. It is sometimes reported that our Theological Seminaries are not favorable to intellectual light and honesty. There will hardly be a question about the Seminary from which issues this book and the one of Dr. Kedney's recently noticed in this *Review*. The third feature is that rare thing in philosophical writing—the happy and really illustrative use of the dangerous metaphor. I had a number of passages marked for quotation, but one or two must suffice. Speaking of agnosticism and mysticism, Dr. Sterrett says: "The one utterly saps the vitality of thought, the other only floods it with more sap than it has channels prepared to receive." And speaking of the way in which spirit finds itself in that which seems at first to limit it, he says: "Thus it was that old Rome realized herself. Her god *Terminus* was elastic enough to include and transform all *hostes* into *cives sui*, and she became the imperial mistress of the world."

*Elementary Psychology*, with Practical Applications to Education and Conduct of Life, including an Outline of Logic, by J. H. Baker, A.M. New York: Effingham Maynard and Co., 1890. 232 pp.

Mr. Baker has written a succinct and, as far as possible, clear condensation of the current Scotch psychology, enriching it, upon occasion, with material from the empiricist writers, especially Bain. The book shows no trace of the influence of German thought, whether from the schools of Kant, of Herbart, or of the modern experimentalists like Fechner and Wundt.

We are informed in the Preface that "the importance of physiological psychology is duly regarded," and near the beginning of the book there are six or eight pages devoted to a highly technical description of the nervous system, going into such points as a nerve-fiber "consists of three parts, an extremely thin outer membrane, a white, semi-liquid sheath, and a translucent axis cylinder." The description, however, is not always quite accurate; the account, *e.g.*, of the sympathetic system belongs to the realm of "popular" science rather than to science proper. We are told that the cerebrum is the seat of mind, and that lower centers constitute the

[*First published in the* Educational Review, *I* (*May 1891*), 495–96. *Not previously reprinted.*]

"reflex apparatus," by which, among other things, sensation is occasioned. Later on, sensation is taken out of this precarious position and restored to the mind. In spite of this account of nerve physiology, it cannot be said that the modern movement in physiological psychology has affected the standpoint or method of the book. Isolated items from the realm of cerebral physiology are scattered through the book, but are not assimilated in any organic way. They produce the effect of pieces of grit in a Scotch porridge.

When it is said that the book is not influenced in its inner spirit or practical outcome, either by German thought or modern experimental methods, but that it is a simple, well-condensed, and well-arranged exposition of the formulæ, which descend in the line of succession from Reid and Hamilton, vivified somewhat by Bain, the reader is in a fair position to judge the book. The term "faculty" is hardly used in the work, and we are told (p. 45) that the mind "is to be regarded as a unit." But as no attempt is made anywhere to find any fundamental mental function or process, and as perception, memory, phantasy, imagination, and thinking are all strung along one after the other, with no attempt to trace any unity, whether by way of underlying activity or by way of growth, the mind seems "to be regarded as a unit" for metaphysical rather than for psychological or practical purposes. We are informed, also, at large, that the mind is self-activity, but no attempt to connect the various details of physical life with this principle appears.

The educational applications are judicious and safe summaries of the usual "pedagogy" of teachers' institutes. Some are suggested more directly by the psychological theories themselves, and some have originated rather in the school-room, and then been attached to the psychology. Those who do not regard the Scotch psychology as very true, profound, or suggestive, will naturally prefer the latter to the former. Speaking from within the standpoint of the book itself, I see but one objection likely to arise—perhaps the attempt is made to cover too much ground within the compass of 232 pages. A summary of formal logic is introduced into the chapter on thinking, and there is the usual pocket of the Scotch school, labeled Intuitions, into which are stowed away, as self-evident, all the chief problems which have vexed the world's great reflective philosophers for two thousand years—problems like substance, personality, space, and time. Upon the whole, the book is, in form and in substance, an admirable reflection of the ideas and methods of the vast bulk of our teachers who are earnestly striving, along the lines of the ordinary pedagogy of our normal schools and teachers' institutes, to elevate education. To discuss, therefore, its substance would be to go beyond the limits of a review of this book into the question of the value, scientific and educational, of the current psychology.

## *What Is Reality?* by Francis Howe Johnson. Boston and New York: Houghton, Mifflin and Co.

The question, "What is Reality?" is a comprehensive question, and it is not to be expected that the answer should be a wholly conclusive one. It lies not much against Mr. Johnson, then, that he has been more successful in his inquiry than in his reply. In the course of his reflections he has at least gone over much of modern philosophy and presented it to the reader in a clear, straightforward style. As Mr. Johnson has obvious gifts of exposition, it is a pity his information is not always derived at first hand. His account of Hegel, for example, clearly comes not from Hegel himself but from Seth's refutation of him in his *Hegelianism and Personality*. This would not be of much account, if the "refutation" were other than a simple misunderstanding. As it is, the result is more than a mere misstatement of Hegel's position. It is a failure on the part of Mr. Johnson to grasp the meaning of the whole modern "idealistic" movement in thought, and the failure affects the constructive as well as the critical portion of the book before us. It rests on the assumption of the old dualism between the thought world and the thing world, and takes it for granted that the problem of philosophy is how to get the bridge that

[*First published in the* Inlander (*University of Michigan*), *II* (*Mar. 1892*), 282–83. *Not previously reprinted.*]

takes us across the chasm. Thus he divides modern methods into subjective and objective analyses, ranking the method of German philosophy as subjective, and the method of science as objective, and contrasts both with the appeal to life, his own position being that that proposition expresses reality whose affirmation it is necessary to *live*. Had Mr. Johnson seen that this was precisely the result which German philosophy from Kant to Hegel was driving at, had he seen, for example, that Hegel's logic is neither subjective nor objective analysis, but analysis of the life which underlies and overlies all division into objective and subjective, his own theory would have been more coherent than it is, especially as relates to the relation of revelation to knowledge. As it is, Mr. Johnson is left with a gap between the ordinary process of experience and the method of revelation. Mr. Johnson does his best to cover the gap by various connecting links, but the very fact that the links are required testifies to the gap.

Too much cannot be said in praise of the candor and honest purport of Mr. Johnson's work. It is a good omen for the future of American thought when a book having, in a sense an apologetic intent, is so fair (and so fair without effort) to opponents and so open to light as is the work of Mr. Johnson.

*The Story of the Odyssey*, by the Rev. A. J. Church. New York: Macmillan and Co.

If, as Mr. Howells says, the stories are all told, the *Odyssey* of Homer is more responsible for this result than any other one writing. As the *Iliad* is the heroic epic of humanity, the *Odyssey* is the story-book. The comparative philologist finds in it, by type or incident, the whole mythological repertory of the ancient world; the psychologist finds in it all the representative scenes and contacts of which the mind is possessed. That this story-book of the romantic childhood of the world should be retold for the childhood of

[*First published in the* Inlander (*University of Michigan*), *II* (*Mar. 1892*), *286–87. Not previously reprinted.*]

to-day is fitting. Professor Church has already demonstrated his capacity in this direction by his stories from the Bible, the *Iliad*, and from Lucian, and his telling of the *Odyssey* bears out his reputation. The educationalists of Germany use the *Odyssey* as one of the strongholds of children's training. It is a way as effective as charming for introducing the child into the inheritance of the race.

# The Angle of Reflection

## 1

The principle of universal suffrage has been making great strides of late. We have been accustomed, for some years, to its extension from the field of politics to those of social life and business. The determining of the most popular young lady in the Sandemenian parish by ballot at the church fair, or of the most gentlemanly clerk at Thread, Ribands and Co., by majority vote, are familiar enough. The principle was introduced into literature a number of years ago, by several so-called literary journals, in the matter of voting for the most popular or best novel, poem, etc., published within a given time. From this, it was an easy stage to voting for the "best" authors.

The *Critic* of New York—a journal which would probably object to the prefix of so-called to literary—took the last step. If we have a republic of letters, why not have universal suffrage there also? So several years ago the *Critic* opened the boxes to receive votes for an Academy—to consist of forty members like the institution of similar name in France. These immortals once banded together, what more natural than that the *Critic* should wish to weave a garland of immortelles? And a short time ago the *Critic* declared the polls open for receiving votes for an Academy of poetesses, fictionistes and authoresses in general. By what seems an ungallant discrimination, the number was limited to twenty. Not so the votes, however. Every one that voted seems to

[*First published in the* Inlander (*University of Michigan*), *I* (*Mar. 1891*), 35–37. *Not previously reprinted. Each of the six unsigned articles entitled "The Angle of Reflection" has been numbered in chronological order. See A Note on the Texts for details concerning Dewey's authorship of the articles.*]

have had a "lady friend," of a literary turn of mind; and the number of persons voted for must have surprised everybody except the increasing number of persons who hunt through the newspapers compiling selections of American literature. The particular incident ray, however, which has impinged so as to call out these reflections is the fact that no Michigan poetess or authoress seems to have received votes. Not even the whilom sweet singer of Michigan, whose refrain

> *That game they call croquet, croquet,*
> *That game they call croquet,*

must have haunted the head of many a distracted man, received any votes.

Many theories may, of course, be advanced to account for this state of things. It may be contended that Michigan people are not yet in favor of applying the principle of majority-rule to literature. Others may prefer to argue that Michiganders do not draw their literary sustenance from the *Critic*, and hence were not alive to the great campaign going on in the literary world. Something possibly might be made out for the assertion that the campaign was too languid to arouse a people habituated to warm political strife. We are too firm believers in the democratic principle to take interest in a vote taken without stump-speaking, torch-light processions, and inducements to "blocks of five." Where were the orators urging the claims of Blanche Willis Howard, and free trade with Germany, or the transparencies suggesting a vote for Gail Hamilton and the old flag?

But, after all, the dearth of candidates from this region may indicate that the star of literary empire does not westward take its way. It perhaps has transferred its central light from Boston to New York; but it does not seem to have the strength required to climb the Alleganies. The fixing of the Columbian Fair at Chicago rather than at New York marks a distinct shifting in matters industrial and social; signs are not wanting that the centre of political gravity is now in the Mississippi Valley. Western methods and styles of journalism have taken possession of Boston and New York. But where is the literature of the west? There has been, indeed, some western flora, but the plants are rather sporadic, local and tender. Mr. Howells—a westerner whose western spirit only in his last work has broken through its coat of Boston varnish—from his observatory in *Harper's Monthly* scours the prairies for literary comets, but reports with regret only an occasional flash-light.

Perhaps this failure of the west to produce as much literary crop to the acre as the territory about Boston and New York is more closely connected with the failure of the country to produce as yet a distinctively American literature than we think. We may flatter ourselves with the belief that the real life of America germinates in western soil, and its spirit broods over western plains. For the west then there can be no literature until this germinating life flowers, until this brooding spirit comes to consciousness of itself. The western literature must tarry until the American idea has come to know and to feel itself. The east with its more cramped position, more rigid traditions and more self-conscious attitude can do the partial thing, because it lacks the whole. It can follow English lines and take the British outlook, and thus bring forth what passes as literature until the vast, inchoate, turbid spirit of America shall find her own articulate voice. This view may express only the provincial pride of the woolly west—or there may be something in it.

At all events, to come from general speculation to actual business, if there is any of the *Ethos* of the west latent in or about this University, the *Inlander* is here for the purpose of helping it take form. By title and by position of the University, the *Inlander* stands in this middle western country which does not seem as yet to count (either by work or voting in the *Critic*) in the literary world. It desires both to express and to encourage the articulate voicing of that part of the vast dumb Inland to which it belongs. The reflector, who is occupying this angle at present, has a friend who says that the only literary sense is the ability to discriminate between hot and cold. And it is this literary sense which the *Inlander* would cultivate. That conception which regards literature as a sort of technical process or extra polish apart from the ordinary run of life it is not concerned with. But that literary sense which consists in the free perception and natural reporting of the currents of life which are actually in movement, it would desire to have expressed in its pages and to stimulate in its audience.


# 2


President Eliot, of Harvard, recently visited as is well known, the colleges of the West. It may not be as well known that on his return he gave in a public talk some account of the educational outlook in the West, with special reference to Harvard and its work. He found that the West is indebted to Harvard for three great educational gifts. The first is the elective system, which he finds to have been introduced more extensively throughout the West than in any New England college, save Harvard. Even the University of Minnesota, with comparatively small resources, offers a wider degree of election than Yale. The second gift of Harvard is the idea that increase of power is to be aimed at, rather than acquisition of knowledge. It is this idea that has led to modifications in the traditional curriculum, and to "the changes that were made here *first* (*sic*) in the conditions of entrance—the dropping of Greek and Latin from the requirements." The third contribution of Harvard to the West is individualization of instruction—the introduction of laboratory work, of conferences and seminaries, and other methods where the instructor must give personal attention to the student.

Without doubt, these principles will all pass as thoroughly sound in this locality, however it may be elsewhere. And we are all glad to join in President Eliot's congratulations at Cambridge that these principles, introduced by Harvard, have found such ready and ample welcome in the West. Nor is our pleasure to be marred by possible objections to President Eliot's facts, notably his assertions that seminary work and the dropping of Greek and Latin from

[*First published in the* Inlander (*University of Michigan*), I (*Apr. 1891*), 82–84. *Not previously reprinted.*]

entrance requirements are the original accomplishments of Harvard. We shall simply regret that with all the store of information that President Eliot gathered in his western trip, he could not have added the real facts in these directions. But the educational debt of the country to Harvard is, in all conscience, large enough when all corrections are made.

Give and take is the law of nature and of life; and it is not surprising to find that President Eliot, like a wise man, wishes to know what return Harvard is to have. His answer is that the West should send Harvard an increasing number of students. Here, too, we shall rejoice in the rejoicings of our sister University. But is it not possible that some exchange has already taken place? Is it not possible that the West has already made some educational gifts to Harvard and to the East, gifts greatly more important than any number of students would be? We of the University of Michigan, at least, are not accustomed to think of ourselves entirely as recipients, however tardy the colleges of the East may be in receiving our generous gifts.

Let us see whether we cannot parallel the three presents that we have received with three gifts that the West has made. First and foremost, there is the conception of the democratic idea in higher education. It is not too much to say that higher education in the East was built up and fostered upon the *class* idea. Even after the notion that the University was a training school for clergymen passed away, the idea lingered in the East that it was for special classes rather than for the people themselves. The conception that the University is only the culmination of the *common* school education belongs to the West;—may we not add, with proper modesty (since it was the doing of our forefathers and not of ourselves) to the University of Michigan? And the readjustment of the studies of the course, the readjustment of entrance requirements, the putting of all departments on the level of a free and generous competition belongs (*pace* President Eliot) to the working out of no pedagogical abstraction such as that power and not knowledge is the end of education. It is the easy and natural outcome of the democratic idea in education; the idea that higher education, as well as the three R's, is of and for the people, and not for some cultivated classes. Third, the earnest and systematic attempt to make an organic connection between the University and the preparatory schools is the affair of the West. Of course large preparatory schools with very intimate connections with the University are much older than the West; but the connection of the University with high schools, with the public schools as found in every village of any size, is the accomplishment of the West. To those who conceive of University education as a sort of sacred scholarship to be preserved, at all hazards, from the contaminating touch of the masses, all this must seem very grievous; but to those who believe in the democratic idea, it presents large and commanding features—features which need not fear to be set side by side with the contributions of any University. Meantime it is interesting to note the gradual shifting of the eastern colleges to this basis, and to hear the acclaim with which they greet as a new educational discovery every approach to what is now axiomatic in the West.

## 3

The Reflector in the last issue of the *Inlander*, made remark to the effect that one of the main functions of the typical Eastern educationalist is to raise a great noise, *pro* and *con*, about methods that have been quietly adopted for a greater or less period in the State Universities of the West. The remark has been twice underscored by events of the last month. One of these events was the rejection by the highest governing board of Harvard University of the plan of shortening the course formulated by the Faculty of Harvard. The other is the adoption (as reported in the newspapers) by Cornell of the so-called Columbia plan by which Law work may be combined with Senior Literary work so that a student may take both degrees in five years.

[*First published in the* Inlander (*University of Michigan*), *I* (*May* 1891), 119–20. *Not previously reprinted.*]

The Harvard plan was heralded through the newspapers as a sweeping reduction of the collegiate course to three years. Stated in this broad way, the plan is misreported. As matter of fact the plan looked towards the substitution of a certain number of courses or of hours for a certain number of years, making it possible for the better class of students to graduate in three or in three and a half years. This plan, it is hardly necessary to say to those acquainted with the University of Michigan, has been in operation here for a considerable number of years, without arousing one-fiftieth of the tempestuous agitation that the mere suggestion of it at Harvard awakened. And in the fashion of the East usual when discussing the matter of electives, co-education, the relation of the classics to the collegiate curriculum, etc., the proposal has been discussed wholly on *a priori* grounds, with no reference to experience. The bare fact that such a plan has been carried out, with relative, if not absolute, success in a western University, was too brutely empirical for the tender mental systems of our Eastern friends. Long may they be preserved from too close contact with the rude realities of experience! How could that refined discussion and argumentation which is so dear to every true Lover of Culture be carried on, if we were obliged to take heed of facts?

The Columbia plan, which so far has met a happier fate than the Harvard, has also been in practical, although not in nominal, operation in the University of Michigan for some time. The *modus operandi* is different, the actual outcome the same. In Cornell and Columbia, if I rightly understand it, the student is able to substitute the entire first year's work of the Law School for the fourth year's work of the Literary Department. Here a student who has only a certain number of hours to "get off" is able to carry part or all of the law work simultaneously with the literary work. Which of these two means of reaching the same end is the better remains to be decided by comparison of their actual workings. But taking such things as these into account, a Bureau for the Distribution of Western Collegiate Methods Among Eastern Universities might be a paying scheme.

The adoption of such methods in the West and their discussion in the East, are both, however, only symptoms of a larger movement—of the tendency to do what the politicians call "getting close to the hearts of the people." Pretty much all recent educational change falls into one or other of two lines, these two lines marking simply a growing division of labor. On one side, there is the tendency towards specialization, towards minute personal research, towards everything which the present educational predominance of Germany identifies with scholarship. The other tendency is towards the distribution of the resulting ideas. (I should call it the popularization of ideas were it not for the cold chill which runs down the spine of the aforesaid Lover of Culture whenever he hears the word "popular.") University extension, the forcing of technical instruction into institutions once priding themselves on being wholly literary, the tendency towards a closer union of academic and professional work, the shortening of the course, the broadening of the literary curriculum, are all only evidences of this movement. And democracy, popularization, as has been more than once remarked, is like the grave; it takes, but it never surrenders what it takes. We should cultivate the Lover of Culture carefully, for the time may be coming when he shall be a rare specimen—the prospect of his total extinction we veil our faces from.

# 4

A clever young Englishman—one of the literary Socialists who cluster about William Morris, who look upon Socialism as a religious rather than an economic movement, and who are bringing a distinctly new spirit into the critical treatment of literature through the press of Walter Scott—well, a clever young Englishman, to get back to my beginning, remarked to me that in many respects the social question

[*First published in the* Inlander (*University of Michigan*), *I* (*June 1891*), *153–56. Not previously reprinted.*]

seemed to him more promising in England than in America. As one evidence he noted that it was much easier to get together the working people and the men learned in economics in England than here. There the educated University men look upon it as almost a religious duty, certainly a privilege, to go to the workingmen's clubs and unions and to discuss social questions with them. The laboring class eagerly hang on the lips of these their teachers. It seemed to my friend that, while this country was nominally more democratic, there was no such willing commingling of classes here. The workingmen, here, think they know just as much as any college professor, and would be suspicious of the advances of the educated class. The University men, he thought, rather looked down, from their side, upon Knights of Labor and such like organizations, and hardly think it worth while to display their treasures before them.

As an American and a supposed democrat, I was led to think about this matter. As I thought, it occurred to me that my English socialistic friend was probably right in his facts but wrong in his inferences. The very fact in England, of which he was speaking, was based upon the idea of a separation of classes, and of a benevolent desire on the part of some of the "upper" class to aid the "lower." It implied that the democratic movement was not the life-blood flowing in the very veins of the social structure, but something to be passed about from hand to hand. The American laborer draws his sustenance from the same great currents of political and commercial life at which the professor or doctor of philosophy must drink. Often he feels that while he may not know as much of some abstract principles or as many statistical details as the University man, he is, in truth, nearer to the real sources of knowledge. In a word, if there is such a thing as democracy in the very life movements of the state, it is highly absurd to propose a "mingling of classes." This may mark a step *toward* democracy, but, democracy attained, it is not necessary to peddle it around from one individual to another.

The attempt to transfer the University Extension movement from England to America has led me to follow this line of thought somewhat further. There can be no doubt that in England this movement has assumed large social, and even, in the true sense, political proportions. It has not been merely a diffusion of learning, or a widening of information. It has not been simply an educational affair, in the limited sense of the term. It has marked the growth of common interests and actions between the educated young men of England and the laboring men. It has been a great step in the breaking down of class barriers. It has been one large phase and one large instrument in the democratic advance.

Is it reasonable to expect that University Extension will assume any such important social function in this country? Some of the managers of the Extension in this country seem to anticipate that it will. They are making a great stir, great claims, and are even proposing to raise a large sum of money, something like a hundred thousand dollars, as a permanent endowment fund. Now there need be no doubt of the *educational* importance of this movement. To extend learning, to diffuse the results of scholarly research, to give University men a closer contact with other phases of life than their own, is a useful thing. So regarded, the University Extension movement may be looked at as superimposing a higher layer and more advanced methods upon the Chautauqua substratum. Multitudes of literary clubs, clubs for study of social questions, now exist about the country in all stages of organization and disintegration. The University Extension movement affords these clubs and societies a centre. They may crystallize, so far as they have serious aims, about the Extension. Thus they will get better instruction, more definite and less floating ends, and some systematic supervision. But does this University Extension, after all, represent in principle anything more organic, more important socially, than these literary clubs, however much more effectively the University Extension may realize the principle?

Take the conditions, physical and social, under which the Extension must be carried on in this country. England is a compact country with dense population. All the University professors and fellows in Great Britain could be conveyed in carriages over the whole of England in a few days. Under such circumstances, University Extension is only a matter of extending professors; a matter of hiring a few carryalls or railway coaches, more or less, to deposit University men here and there. In other words, it becomes essentially an individual matter—a matter of getting certain men of one class face to face with men of another. The very increase of distance in the United States, those physical conditions which have compelled the development of the railway and the telegraph, and which have forced the substitution of large social tendencies for merely individual efforts, changed all this in our country. University Extension, in the ordinarily accepted sense, becomes a locality affair instead of an organized social affair as in England. The University of Michigan might, for example, lend its professors, and extend its courses to local audiences in Detroit, Grand Rapids, Saginaw, etc., but it is difficult to see how it, or any combination of American Universities, can do for this country, in any large sense, what the Universities of Oxford and Cambridge have done for England in this movement. This country is too big, its currents of life too organic.

On the other hand, what is University Extension? It must be the extension of the inner spirit of the University. Certainly no one would claim to-day that the lectures are the highest development of the University spirit. And yet the movement so far as already organized seems to propose nothing beyond an extension of lecturers and lectures, with assigned readings and examinations. Now this as an educational matter is well and good; as a social matter it is quite another affair. The vast mass of our population is already pretty well occupied; books, magazines and newspapers, to say nothing of theatres and lecture courses, fill up leisure moments. As a scheme for the diffusion of knowledge, in other words, the University Extension would seem to be somewhat anticipated by the wide-spread reading habits of the population. The Extension may direct and supplement somewhat this reading. How much more can it do? I cannot help thinking about this extension matter (on its social, as distinct from its merely educational, side) as I did about the remark of my Socialist friend. There can no large social importance attach to it, because democracy has already gone so much farther in this country than in England; it is so much in the atmosphere we breathe, in the currents in which we live that the merely individual phases of it are reduced to a minimum.

## *5*

It is striking that some of the most poetic features of our American life, centering in our politics, are just those which are popularly esteemed, not only non-poetic, but highly objectionable—even as blots upon our character and repute. The "intelligent foreigner," visiting our shores and seeing a certain easy expression of some large good nature of democracy which is to him inexplicable, "finds much to admire in the American civilization, but notes with regret one feature, which if not taken earnestly in hand by the American people —must in time"—etc., etc. The native editorial writer does not wish to rank in culture and refinement below the aristocratic visitor from abroad, and so takes up the cry, assuring the distinguished visitor that the "better classes" of America share his sentiments, his regrets and his fears, and beg of him that they may not be held responsible for the doings of the "lower classes"—in a word, of the bhoys. The Ward Association, the band which runs "wid de machine," its captain, the local boss, his lieutenant the heeler—this band, in reality one of the most picturesque features of American life, is the recipient of the largest amount of this condescending abuse.

In truth, only a Homer could do justice to the free and vivid experiences of one of the modern clans, with its Agamemnon, the local king of men, its Odysseus, skilled in wiles, its Nestor who narrates to the boys tales of the bygone days when he too went to Albany. Who but Homer could describe the gathering of the Cohorts in "de fift" or "de ate" ward as they pour forth to a campaign picnic? The

[*First published in the* Inlander (*University of Michigan*), *II* (*Oct. 1891*), *50–52. Not previously reprinted.*]

generosity of the great-souled Boss, who bears the entire expense of transporting the whole ward to the picnic grounds of a neighboring island; the orderly disorder of the tribe as to the martial music of "Comrades" or the soothing strains of "Annie Rooney" it marches to the dock; the plenteous breakfast feast, with its varied libations, its abundant larder; then the manly games, the foot race, the boxing-match, the tug of war, with the great-souled Boss encouraging and giving forth medals? Is there any one so lost to a sense of the unity of human nature as not to know that the ever fresh and naïve scenes depicted by the Greek bard had the same spirit and motives? Suppose that a picnic does sometimes threaten to end in a row, as in a recent one near New York City, because the chicken is kept till the third course—a time when the hearts of brave men are already so satisfied that they cannot do justice to the daintiest viand of the feast. Does any one believe that in the assemblies celebrated by Homer there were no heartburnings, because of unequal distributions of the swing-paced, crook-horned oxen? Are games less ideal, less manly now because the prizes are won by O'Flahertys and Weissenbrodts instead of by Laodamases and Euryaluses? Do you really think that Ajax or Agamemnon was entirely unmindful of the necessity of strengthening his "holt on the boys" when he furnished a great gala day? The facts are the same. Only the idealizing eye of the poet now fails.

No, let us be ashamed of our attempt to load the faults of the whole people upon a given class, especially when these faults are by no means the meanest or the most sordid of our deficiencies, when indeed they have a certain large heartedness and good faith all their own. Nothing is more ill-considered, nothing in worse taste than the denunciations of the "machine" and of the "boys" now so freely dispensed from the self-styled "better class" of journals. How comes it that the "boys" are in such full possession of the machine? Are politics an exception to the law that no result is attained save by the expenditure of energy, and will the ideal politics of the superior editorial writer do themselves? Who is to attend to the practical management of the details of party manœuvering and government? If the business class which

in the *New York Times* and *Evening Post* arrogates to itself
the possession of sound sense as to the state needs, and the
scholarly class which through the mouth of the *Nation*
assumes a monopoly of high ideals, if these classes are so
busy making money and acquiring culture that they have no
time or thought to give to political details, the "boys" may
well put in the claim to be occupying an otherwise unowned
and unworked field. Let us, at least, have the good taste not
to complain too loudly of the unsavory way in which one
class does a necessary work to which we refuse to put our
hands. Let us at least have the grace to permit the boys to
continue their parades, their picnics and their local sover-
eignties untroubled by our unmeaning scoldings. In a word,
let us no longer, in the plentitude of our wealth and wisdom,
blame one class when the whole organism is responsible. If
it is true that "we" are so superior in culture and business
ability, it is possible there may come a day when this superi-
ority will be deemed a reason for holding us, the "better
classes," chiefly responsible.

# 6

The Volapük fad seems to have suffered the fate of all fads.
All faddists are cannibals, save that they reverse the order.
The Sandwich Islander killed his victim and then ate him.
The faddist devours his fad, and the devoured fad expires.
The fad lasts only while acquiring, and once acquired but
whets the appetite for a new one. However, the natural
history of fads is not my topic. What an absurdity—to create
a language without an atmosphere, without a setting in
human thought, without an abyss of human emotions! Only
Jonathan Swift could do justice to the massive stupidity, to
the imbecility, lacking all the poetry of the genuine lunatic,
which conceived of a language meant to express "things,"
instead of ideas and feelings.

[*First published in the* Inlander (*University of Michigan*), *II* (*Nov.
1891*), *96–97. Not previously reprinted.*]

For language is the unexpugnable home, the reservoir that cannot be drawn dry, of poetry. M. Jourdain talked prose without knowing it, but a greater miracle than that enacts itself daily. The stiffnecked Prosaist, who is incarnate Philistinism, becomes a poet when he uses language. The generous mother of us all, foreseeing the narrow straits, the heavy ruts into which life was to come, bore us into an atmosphere where we cannot enter save by enduring it with ourselves, save by poetizing it. And this is the medium into which we must enter whenever we approach our fellows' language. The Volapükist was an enemy of the entire human race: he sought to sterilize with his noxious vapors the one unescapable, ever pregnant medium of imagination; to get the mind out of itself into bare contact with "things."

Any one who has occasion to read much in other languages, and especially to go abruptly from one tongue to another, must always notice how the entire atmosphere, intellectual and emotional, changes also. To *read* a language is to drink in, to absorb the whole *Gemüth* of a nationality: to *translate*—what is it but another way of thinking your own already sufficiently wearisome thoughts?

I do not suppose that any two minds get just the same atmospheric effect, the same over-tones, the same "physical fringe," the same coloring of accompanying mental images from a language. But as for myself, the French language produces upon me the effect of out-of-doors—not indeed the exhilaration of the open air, the brisk and driving wind, but the simple out-of-doors effect. There is expansion, but a bounded expansion, the definite horizon, the clearest perspective; the rounded dome is over all, a common air washes all. It is a sunlit out of doors; there are clouds and shadows, but clouds and shadows which, after all, only serve to mark out the light, to give solidity to the perspective. One walks easily, securely in such a world; he knows where he started from, where he is going; east and west, north and south are as distinct as in the world of nature. The eye is the guiding sense.

What a change when I go to a German book!—the change from *joli* to *schön*. I find my eye upon which I had been relying, gradually growing dim and blear. Tone takes the place of light. How different the shadings! In French they were shadings of color, which, with all their graduations and continuities yet define, each having its own characteristic value. In German the shading blends, mixes, runs all into one. It is the modulation of music. I leave out of doors, or if I remain without, it is no longer the landscape, half in sun, half in shade which I see; it is the murmuring of leaves, the rustling in the trees I hear. Everywhere a vague mysterious stirring which with some secret tie makes all things one. But generally I find myself taken within doors—the concert chamber, the lecture hall, the domestic fire place, these are the loved abodes of sound. Closeness has taken the place of openness; sometimes the closeness of suffocation, of an unaired room, sometimes the closeness of concentrated depth and power; but closeness always. In French I look on and the meaning unfolds. It is there—*Voilà*. In German the general meaning oozes in and fills me, I know not how, but the details, the particulars I have to struggle to catch. I have to listen hard for them. I do not know if you, my reader, have the same experience. I know, however, this is no general theory concocted by me, but an attempt to convey the kind of actual sensuous images which surrounds and bathes what I read.

# Introduction to Philosophy: Syllabus of Course 5

## Philosophical Department

UNIVERSITY OF MICHIGAN

February, 1892

SECTION 1.—Philosophy (science) is the conscious inquiry into experience. It is the attempt of experience to attain to its own validity and fullness; the realization of the meaning of experience.

Science and philosophy can only report the actual condition of life, or experience. Their business is to reveal experience in its truth, its reality. They state what *is*.

The only distinction between science and philosophy is that the latter reports the more generic (the wider) features of life; the former the more detailed and specific.

SECTION 2.—The separation of science and philosophy has reference to the incompleteness of knowledge. Although our experience goes on within the whole, the whole is the last thing of which we become conscious *as* a whole of included factors. Thus the trouble with philosophy is the difficulty of getting the whole, the generic, before consciousness in such a way that it may be naturally reported. The partial thing may be broken off from the whole and then described with comparative ease. But this process of multiplying pieces seems to leave the generic, the whole beyond and out of sight. It makes the whole remote, and capable of description only in unnatural ("metaphysical," "transcendental") terms. Thus science, as relating to the part, and philosophy as referring to the whole, fall apart. Philosophy suffers by being made vague and unreal; science in becoming partial and thus rigid.

The search for philosophy is not a peculiar or technical

[*Preserved in the University of Michigan Historical Collections. Not previously reprinted.*]

search; it is objective and general; it is the search for the real whole. Just so far as this whole is really attained in experience, it becomes possible to treat it in a direct, natural way, *but only in so far*. In two directions, the whole is now more definitely realized than ever before, so that we get a language for reporting it. These two directions are the two phases of action. On one hand, science has revealed to us, in outline, at least, the type action of the individual organism, the process involved in every complete act. On the other hand, as life has become freer, social action has revealed the principle involved in it. The action of the psycho-physical and of the political body, in other words, give us such perception of the whole that we may report the latter, thus translating philosophical truth into common terms.

## *Chapter First—the Psycho-Physical Act*

SECTION 3.—The unit of nervous action is called the reflex-arc. (See Spencer, *Psychology*, Vol. I, first three chapters, especially pp. 27 ff.; James, *Psychology*, Vol. I, p. 12, pp. 20–21; Von Hartmann, *Philosophy of Unconscious*, Vol. I, pp. 127 ff.) This term covers not simply the narrower "reflex" of physiology (the winking of an eye, for example) but every unified action, or completed portion of conduct. *Illustrations*: the movement of an amœba, the impulse of a child for food, the perception of color, a word like "civilization," with its whole meaning, a virtuous act, a philosophic theory. Each is a unified action; and in this unity of action various conditions are brought to a head or focussed. Each is a co-ordination of certain experiences; each is an *expression*, more or less direct, more or less explicit, of the whole of life; it is the manifold circumstance of the Universe attaining a unity in action.

Such an activity as finds expression then in an entire reflex-arc is a whole, a concrete, an individual. It is the *Self* in more or less developed form.

SECTION 4.—There are, evidently, two sides in the reflex-arc. These sides have no separation in fact, but may be distinguished by us. One side is the *diversity of conditions* involved; the other side is the *unity of action*.

To the unity corresponds the Self as *Will*; to the diversity, the Self as *Intelligence*. *Illustrations*: instinctive taking of food; hearing an enemy's footstep; hearing a bell; the scientific analysis of sound, and so on. *Problem.*—If Intelligence and Will are so closely connected, how do you account for their apparent disconnection in such an example as the last?

SECTION 5.—Taking up the reflex-arc on the side of its diversity, we may further distinguish two phases: There is the simple *diversity as such*; the multiple conditions involved in an act. This is the *sensory* side of knowledge. Any one of the diverse conditions taken *per se* constitutes *a* sensation or *stimulus*. Each of these in itself may be itself an act containing its conditions or factors. For example, within the action of taking food there is contained hunger as a condition. This hunger is itself, in turn, an activity, involving various factors of muscular change, and conditions of respiration, circulation, etc. The visual perception of the food is another element contained in the act. This, in turn, is itself an act unifying its conditions, etc. Either of these acts considered *per se* is a *stimulus* to the act of eating. In reality, it is simply one phase of, one process *within*, the act. *The sensory elements in experience are simply the various more or less distinct minor activities contained within an act of larger range.*

SECTION 6.—The diverse conditions, or minor acts, involved within a unified action, have also their adjustments to each other. Each holds in check the others, and in turn is held by them. No one of them discharges *by itself* but only in the whole of which it is one member. This mutual checking and re-inforcing of the various contained minor actions is the *co-ordination* of the sensory elements.

This co-ordination, co-operation, mutual adjustment, etc., is the *relation* of the sensory element. *It is thus the ideal side of knowledge.* For example, in an act, whether of taking food or of looking at a picture, what gives the activity of the optical apparatus—the sensation of color—its ideal value (its meaning) is the other similar minor activities or reflexes going on together with it, all within the larger reflex.

*Illustrations* may be found in cases of psychical blindness, deafness, aphasia, etc. See James' *Psychology*, Vol. I, pp. 48–52 and references there.

SECTION 7.—The sensation, the stimulus (the contained minor reflex) is evidently an abstraction taken *per se*. It acts only in its adjustment or co-ordination with other reflexes. This co-ordination or mutual re-inforcement and limitation, is equally an abstraction taken *per se*.

*Problem*:   Consider how the old question of sensationalism *vs.* rationalism stands when each element is considered from the standpoint of the whole action, or reflex-arc; when, that is, sensation is considered as itself an act, and the ideal element, or relation, as the active adjustment of that act.

SECTION 8.—The reflex-arc, in its unity, is thus a co-ordination of distinct but adjusted minor reflexes, or acts. It is a moving equilibrium of actions.

In other words, *will*, the action or whole self, is the ordered unity of action; this unity being constituted by the relationships of subordinate activities.

Will is evidently the more developed according (1) as there is a wider number of distinct activities (minor reflexes) contained within an act, and (2) as these minor activities are more thoroughly adjusted to one another—unified.

The stages and process of development will be described later. So far we have been dealing simply with the *accomplished* (objective) action.

## Chapter Second—the Philosophical Reading: the Objective Categories

SECTION 9.—In the type-action, we have the universe expressed, and from its structure, therefore, we may read the main philosophic ideas. Every such action is representative of the whole because it *is* the whole in concentrated form, *not* because it is part of the whole.

THE UNIT OR REPRESENTATIVE WHOLE IN EXPERI-
ENCE IS A CENTRALIZED, AND THEREFORE, ORDERED
MOVEMENT. (1) It is a movement in its every phase and
moment and (2) this movement is centred; it comes to a
head or unity in a certain doing.

SECTION 10.—Looking at any human experience, it is evident (1) that whatever occurs outside the body is motion;
(2) that what goes on within, say the eye, is motion; (3)
that this motion is continued along what we call the sensory
nerve; (4) that it is further propagated in the brain, entering there into the existing moving tensions and discharges;
(5) that this movement continues out through what we call
the motor nerve; (6) and effects some further movement in
muscle or gland—what we call an "outward act."

All this is one continuous movement without breach, or
insertion of any extraneous element. Viewed from the standpoint of the actual fact, the distinctions into external stimulus, receiving, conveying, registering, executing, organs are
wholly subordinate. They exist within the one movement
and are phases of its development. They are distinctions
referring to the *specific office* performed in each phase of
movement.

SECTION 11.—The centralized movement is *what is*. It is
the reality, the concrete fact, the individual (*i.e.*, the undi-
vided, the total).

Every such unity, no matter how apparently limited in
scope, *is*, and that absolutely or without qualification. It is
an end in itself; *i.e.*, an object. This is none the less true,
although, as we shall see, in reference to other similar
individuals or unified acts, it may be a contribution or
function.

SECTION 12.—Within the unity, or centred movement, certain distinctions occur. The first main distinction is that of
function and material. That is, the movement may be looked
at on either of two sides; as *proceeds*, the net outcome, and
as *process*. We have *what* is done or effected, and also *how*
it is done. The what, the proceeds, is the function side; the
how, the process, is the material side of a movement.

ı. The *function* is the office performed in a unified act, the service rendered; the contribution made.

The idea of function evidently comes in when we consider the reference of a given centred movement to other similar unities, or to a wider movement into which all enter. While the hearing of a bell is itself an end, or object, it may also be a factor in a larger movement—the operation of a factory. So considered, it is functional. *a*] The inclusive whole is the *standard* which measures the included unity. *b*] The contribution of the included movement, as measured by the larger whole, is the *value*. Function, value, standard are correlative categories.

*Note:* "Category" is a term used to denote any typical aspect or distinction of reality.

ıı. We may drop out of attention, for a time, the unity (the end or proceeds) of a given movement, and consider the elements entering into the movement as such. These elements are the material of the unity. The material is the *diverse* or *manifold* side of action, as the function is the *unity* side.

We may carry the abstraction further. (1) A given unity of action, as the movement of the eye, may in time largely lose its independent character, and become almost entirely a factor of a more inclusive end or object. This end or object may vary from time to time, and yet the special action (the eye movement) remains *pretty much* identical with what it was before. Thus we get to thinking of the movement, apart from any special function, simply as material at large for *some* function or other. Thus reduced in meaning, the material constitutes what we call *possibility* or *potentiality*. (2) We may now restore the function by thinking of the potential in some concrete movement, and then we get the category of *actuality—force*. The actual is thus, the material taken in specific operation; the possible is the material taken without reference to its specific operation.

SECTION 13.—The categories of "*condition*," and "*end*" refer to the same distinctions as material and function. The end is the movement taken *as centred—i.e.*, as to its unity. The conditions are the actions constituent of or included in the unity. Just as by abstraction—leaving out of account certain integral phases—we reduce the category of material to potential, so we reduce conditions to *means*. Then we think of the "means" as somehow leading up to an end outside of, or beyond, themselves, although, in reality, the means are simply the diverse phases or conditions *of* the end. The ideas of means and end fall apart because of the delay which may intervene between a given minor action and its operation in a further function.

SECTION 14.—The categories of *cause* and *effect* have the same reference; the effect is the proceeds; the cause, the process. We do not have first causes, and then an effect. The effect *is* always, and is the existing unity of movement—the aspect, again, of centralization. The "causes" are the diverse activities entering into, constituting the effect.

The mental separation of cause and effect has the same origin as the separation of potential and actual; conditions and end. A given action may be remote from a *specific* function upon which attention is concentrated, and may then through intermediate movements finally pass into a movement having the function under consideration. Here, that is as remote from one another, cause and effect do not refer directly to the same object.

SECTION 15.—A given movement considered as a centralization of diverse conditions, or included movements, is relatively *organic*. Each of the manifold included activities is relatively *mechanical*; that is, when taken out of the whole of which it is a constituent factor. The term *organism* refers equally to the whole and to the constituent factors. Each of these factors or conditions may be considered either as *member* or *organ*. It is organ when looked at as expressing the whole; it is member when regarded as contributing to the whole. The eye, for example, as active function, helps constitute the integral movement of the organism; it is a member, it *serves*. But the activity of the eye is, in reality, nothing but one differentiation of the action of the entire organism. The organism resides (dynamically) in the eye. So considered, the eye is organ.

SECTION 16.—Taken as material, or conditions, the various included movements are *static*. Taken in their operation (that is, their co-operation in constituting the unity) they are *dynamic*.

Static does not mean dead or at rest. It is movement taken as *position*. The static phase of an individual is the *distribution* of force involved in its operation. The dynamic is the individual considered not as distribution of force but as co-ordinated force. They are related as the divisions of labor and the working together of these divisions. Compare energy of position and kinetic energy.

SECTION 17.—The *particulars* are the differentiated or minor activities, the divisions of labor, involved in an individual, or unified movement. The *universals* are the *ways* in which these various subordinate activities *work*. They are the lines or modes of activity of the individual. The various minor activities (particulars) co-ordinate or unify, thus constituting, maintaining, the individual. The ways in which they link *together* are the universals. We may sum up as follows:

Individual; System; Organic; Standard; Unified Movement = The Real.

| Particular, | Universal, |
|---|---|
| Static, | Dynamic, |
| Mechanical, | Organic $\left\{\begin{array}{l}\text{Member,}\\\text{Organ,}\end{array}\right.$ |
| Causes, | Effect, |
| Conditions, | End, |
| Material, | Function, |
| [Possibility], | [Actuality], |
| Manifold, | Unity, |
| Sensory, | Ideal. |

SECTION 18.—The objective categories are the categories of the unified movement; *i.e.*, of the integral, complete or ordered action. The *object* is this unified action; anything is objective as far as it is such ordered action or a part of it.

What is called in psychology the percept (the individual or concrete object) is, in other words, a unified movement or expression of conditions. It is an action, a unity of construction, a doing, or performing. Perceiving an orange is experiencing and the complete percept is the full experience.

The *subjective* is this unified action in process of development. It is the unity in process of forming. It is the process of *working out* the action, of working out the proper divisions and co-operations of labor. Take the movement at any stage short of its attained unity and it is, relatively, subjective. The objective is the end at which the subjective is aiming. The subjective is complete in the objective. The categories of development (the subjective categories) will be taken up later.

## *Chapter Third—Social Action*

We have now to see how the universe is expressed in social action, and how the examination of any complete social action reveals the same processes and categories as the psycho-physical act.

SECTION 19.—Any social organization is a concrete unity, or true individual, for example, a family, a school or class, a business corporation, a political district. It is a unity; its unity is co-ordinated movement. In the co-ordinated movement we have, on one side, the divisions of labor; the various services or functions performed by the various members of the family. These are the *specific* directions of movement. On the other hand, we have the working together, the co-operation of these divisions. Each member of the family is (simply as member of the family) *what he does in constituting the family.* His *individuality* is found in his specific membership and organship. His *universality* is found in the fact that this individuality does not exist in isolation, but in action, that is in connection, in co-operation.

SECTION 20.—The particular member evidently has, then, two sides. He is an expression, or unification, of certain forces, forces of heredity manifested in bodily make up, and of environment, climate, occupation, etc. So taken, (leaving out of account, for the moment, the function which he performs in constituting a whole) the individual is a *natural* being. (Compare the sensory side of an object, or experience.) This is, relatively, the given, the material side. It is natural capacity. But so taken, the individual is pure abstraction. He is not simply an outcome of various currents, but, since a centralization, he performs, he *acts*. In this action, he becomes a factor in constituting the larger movement, the family, the business corporation, the class in college, etc. He *functions*. The natural individual by entering as member into the larger individual and sharing its action is *spiritualized*. His function, (*i.e.*, his natural capacities in *action*) is his spirit. (Compare the ideal side of an object.)

*Problem 1.* Consider from this point of view, a member of a nomadic tribe; a member of a village community; the citizen of Athens in the time of Pericles; a citizen of the U. S. to-day.

*Problem 2.* Work out here the categories of standard, value, static, organic, universal and particular.

SECTION 21.—The ways in which the social unity (movement) maintains itself are *laws*. The laws are not something imposed from without: they are not forces which "govern" something different submitted to these laws: they are the typical forms in which the one movement displays itself. (Compare with category.) The whole society, taken as movement, and not in cross-section or in arrest, is the standard; it is the system. To understand a given fact is to place it with reference to this system—just as to understand an astronomical fact is to place it with reference to the solar system. The possibility of a science of society consists in getting hold of the whole in its movement and then using that as standard to decide particular facts by.

*Problems*: Discover and state the meaning of government, of rights, in the light of the one co-ordinating movement. What is the meaning of the railroad, of the telephone? What is the meaning of hieroglyphics, of a book?

## *Chapter Fourth—the Subjective Categories*

We have been dealing with movement as centred or co-ordinated action. This is the *objective* (the end). We may leave out of account, however, the unity as attained and consider simply the process as working towards, as developing a unity. This is the *subjective*. In its *completeness*, the subjective is thus one with the objective; the subjective attains its meaning, its point, in its unity and is then objective. But taking it *short* of its attained unity, the process is subjective in a sense which *relatively* distinguishes it from the objective.

SECTION 22.—There are three types of objective categories, as we have seen; the Whole or System; the Particular as Specific mode or operation of the system; the Universal as co-operation of the particulars of the system. There are three stages which may be distinguished in the process *towards* the centre, and thus three types of subjective categories. The first of these is the starting point, the *undeveloped* or *implicit* material. This, *in itself*, is a unity of co-ordinated movements; but considered with reference to what is to come after, to come out of it, it is an undeveloped unity; its content is all bound up in it, and has yet to be freed (expressed or revealed), made explicit or brought to consciousness. Thus the amœba, with reference to itself, is an expression of the universe, being a co-ordination of its movement. But this unity taken as a starting point, is highly implicit; the universal is somehow *bound up* in the amœba, but it is not brought out. This stage may also be called the *syncrete*. It is the unity with the differences unrealized; they are somehow suppressed, covered up. (Man at first, for example, did not *consciously* distinguish himself from his environment. A child does not break up the world into a multiplicity of objects consciously distinct from one another. Knowledge begins with the "sensation continuum." A people's religion is in the beginning of history one with their art, science, politics. The historian of the universe begins with it as a nebulous gas, etc. In each case, we have at the outset, a unity in which differences are so fused as to be confused.)

SECTION 23.—This unity is, so far as differences are unexpressed, a passive or natural unity. As the differences emerge (through the continued movement) the unity seems to be lost, and we have instead a multitude of separate units. Thus the homogeneous nebulous gas is divided into an indefinite multitude of centres of force; the "sensation continuum" breaks up into a large number of apparently separate feelings, etc. This is the analytic (in the sense of divided, segregated) stage. The differences become explicit at the expense of unity. It may also be called *discrete*.

SECTION 24.—Third, is the period in which these various diverse units come together and are adjusted to one another. There is a putting together of the isolated units. This process has two sides, according as we look at either what we are emerging from or what we are going towards, the negative and the positive sides. As respects the old isolated units their first coming together appears as opposition and friction, and even as disintegration. The positive side is the new and wider unity emerging, which comprehends within itself all the old units, no longer isolated but so adjusted to one another that each now serves as a member of the new unity. This third phase of the subjective categories, in other words, is the working out of units hitherto isolated into distinct factors of a co-ordinated or centralized unity of movement. Compare, historically, the disintegration of old local centres when another community is coming into existence. Looked at from the standpoint of the old narrower unities, this is a process of disintegration. So the old Greek cities in the Macedonian supremacy; the house and guild industries through factory industry, etc. That is, the first of the categories of development is syncrete, or *internally* one, without divisions of labor. The second is discrete or *externally* separate. When these move into relations to one another, the first effect is to break up the syncrete internally, introducing diversities into it, and it is only at a later period that the co-ordination of the discrete effecting a new organization, is brought about.

SECTION 25.—It is obvious that there is a certain parallelism between the subjective and the objective categories. We may sum them up as follows:

1. Syncrete—internal unity.
2. Discrete—external diversity.
3. Process of Adjusting—negative, or disintegrating, as regards old unities; positive or integrating as regards new unity.
4. The Particular—an adjusted division of labor, or distribution of force—Static, etc.
5. The Universal—the correlation or active co-operation of the particulars—Dynamic, etc.
6. The Adjusted Individual—the organism, having, on one side, its distributions of force, on the other, its co-operations. Standard, etc.

In this catalogue, four is the same as one, but having become adjusted, so that it is no longer homogeneous or characterless in itself, but having become a definite member, with a definite function in a larger system. Five is the polar to two; while in two we have simply *external* relation between the particular unities, in five we have this relationship internal and organic. It is the *way* the particulars operate together. So six is the same as three; only in three the whole is simply in *process* of adjustment, the struggle is going on. In six, the adjustment is effected; the process of re-organization has completed itself in the new organization. These relations may be expressed as follows:

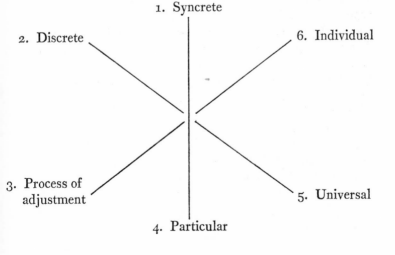

1. Syncrete
2. Discrete
6. Individual
3. Process of adjustment
5. Universal
4. Particular

Number six or the completed (organized) action may be simply the beginning of another activity—*i.e.*, it may be number one with reference to a further organization of action.[1]

## *Chapter Fifth—the Historical Development*

SECTION 26.—The general course of the development of thought has been from an *immediate* objective through a subjective back to an objective mediated by the subjective. That is from action without conscious principle through separation of the principle back to action controlled by it. The Greeks began by setting up some purely objective principle, as water, air, fire, number, reason (reason, *nous*, to the Greek was a principle of objective order or proportion, not a process of reasoning), and by attempting to refer all things *directly* to this principle. The difficulties, the contradictions arising made men conscious that the principle itself must be examined and criticised before it could be *used*. The process of explaining the universe by reference to the principle was checked, and the principle was turned back upon itself in reflection. In other words, it was recognized that principles of explanation are ideas, not bare things; that they are *tools* and, as tools, need perfecting if they are to be used properly. Thus there followed the *subjective* period, in which attention was seemingly withdrawn from the "objective" world, and riveted upon concepts or ideas. The development and systematizing of these was made an end in itself. But only *seemingly* withdrawn. These concepts were themselves abstractions, or reductions, of the original "objective"; and they were, in turn, only tools for getting at and handling a freer and fuller objective. While attention was concentrated on the concepts they seemed to be not tools but ends in themselves; this very concentration, however, served to bring the tools to a working point. Hence the transfer to the third period was made. In this period, attention is again directed to the objective, but the necessity of obtaining the objective through a certain *method*, in a certain *way*, instead of immediately, is recog-

---

[1]    This method of showing the relations of the categories is borrowed from Mr. Lloyd.

nized. The subjective, the concepts, of the second period become instruments for inquiring into fact and thus become modes of action.

SECTION 27.—The first period, which was at its height before the time of the Sophists and Socrates may be called the exclusively "scientific." That is, it assumed that reality surrendered its meaning directly; that method (an idea) was not required to get at the significance of reality. The second period, which was at its height in the Scholastic period of the Middle Ages, was the exclusively "philosophic." That is, it neglected the domain of particular fact, and devoted itself almost entirely to the consideration of generalities or concepts, without attempting to use these ideas. The third period, which has not yet reached its height, is the philosophic-scientific period. That is to say, it is recognized, on one hand, that fact does not give up its meaning of itself or directly, but only as apprehended through the medium of method or general ideas. On the other hand, it is recognized that general ideas are not ends in themselves, that they have no value by themselves, but only as the instruments with which to approach and test apparent fact and secure its real meaning. This reciprocal attitude sums up in the word *experiment*. Experiment is not a matter of physical manipulation, but of the method of applying "ideas" to "fact" (the isolated subjective to the isolated objective) in such way that they unite into a fact having meaning, or idea having body, that is, a concrete action. The whole process may be otherwise stated as the progress from *a*] the percept, as the universal concealed in the individual, through *b*] the concept, or universal abstracted from the individual back to *c*] a conceptualized percept, or intuition, that is, an individual transparent with genuine meaning, or relationships.

SECTION 28.—In more detail, the process has been as follows: Science began when men first conceived a distinction between appearance and reality; saw that the given experience, just as it happened, was not real of itself, but that there was some principle to which it must be referred. Then began the search for the principle, air, fire, water, logos, as the case might be. Thus there arose the primary distinctions of thought, as these were worked out in early Greek science.

1. The principle was the whole or unity—the "one," while the given events were the "many."

2. It was the "universal," while the special events were the "particulars."

3. It was the eternal and full ("Being"), while the events were the transitory and seeming ("Non-Being").

These two sides, however, were not separated; the universal and eternal was the unity of the particular and the many—not something existing side by side with them. As science proceeded, these objective distinctions came to be identified more and more with distinctions of knowledge. The universal and one was identified with "reason"; the changing and many was identified with the senses or "opinion." The source of truth—reality was placed in reason. Socrates logically declared that to "know self" was the root of all wisdom, and the universals were concepts—Platonic "Ideas"—as modes of operation of the self. Thus reality came to be conceived as an "Idea" or spiritual world abstracted from and even remote from the actual. Two worlds are now in process of development, each having its own sphere and character. This is well illustrated in Plato; the key to Plato being that, in his *intention*, the "Ideas" or universals are simply the reality of the sensible and phenomenal world, while in *practice*, he cannot succeed in thus interconnecting them.

SECTION 29.—The introduction of Christianity emphasized: the tendency commenced by Socrates to find reality in self, holding that the self is incarnate God, and hence, an absolute end superior to all its surroundings and merely particular experiences. It made the theoretical truth of Greek philosophy a practical or moral truth—one to be worked out in life. The same two opposed tendencies were now transferred over into Christianity. On one hand, the tendency was to regard the self as the reality, the embodied truth of the world, the free spirit for which all particular experience exists. Such was the doctrine at its beginning. But *practically* this conception seemed to be contradicted on all sides;

the self was not practically free, was not practically one with its surroundings. The institutions of life (industrial and political) did not lend themselves to the freedom of the self, but hemmed it in; they were not spiritual, but "evil," needing to be overcome and transformed. Thus the outcome was a translation of the dualistic tendency of Greek thought into a fixed and rigid separation. This as typified in the mediæval church involved:

*1.* A separation of the spiritual from the natural, the former being regarded as wholly supernatural—separation of God from the world.

*2.* A separation of theory from practice, of the subjective from the objective,—*i.e.*, separation of the *church* from the *state*. Man's relation to God having been abstracted from his relation to the world, two institutions grew up, each dealing with its own sphere. The former (church) was realized especially in the contemplative life—in consciousness as such; the state standing for practice has only finite or limited ends. (Hence the ease with which mediæval theology formulated itself in the philosophical ideas of Aristotle.)

*3.* A separation of the organ of knowledge by which man knew the "spiritual," or God, from that by which he knew the natural or secular—the separation of philosophy (theology) and science.

The contradiction here in every case is that the "natural" side, the state, the senses, the ordinary course of experience is no longer regarded as mere appearance, or nonbeing; but as *a* reality, side by side with the higher reality—two parallel realities, each real in its own sphere.

SECTION 30.—As the spiritual kept realizing itself more and more *in* the natural (that is, as the self instead of finding itself set over against a hostile nature and institutions, succeeded in subjugating nature and transforming institutions) the latter got additional meaning until each of the two sides come to have *equal* value. Thus modern times begin with the assertion of:

*1.* Mind *and* matter—as correlate realities.

*2.* Infinite *and* finite.

*3.* Reason *and* sense.

Nor, indeed, was it long before the tendency arose to give the latter of the two correlates superior practical value, and while still allowing the former superior theoretical value, to treat it virtually as an empty and powerless abstraction. (Compare the course of the old discussion of primary and secondary causes.) This complete dualism, however, was only a starting point for a movement towards a reconciliation towards making the spiritual the unity and law *of* the natural, and the natural simply the *embodied* or *expressed* spiritual.

SECTION 31.—The tendency toward integration grew up from each side separately. Each of the two phases separated in the mediæval period, the physical and the ideal, claimed to be the whole and strove to absorb the other. Modern times present not a passive parallelism, but an opposition of materialism and idealism. With the growth of physical science the whole world was conceived capable of adequate explanation in terms of matter and motion. The existence of the spiritual or ideal realm was denied; or, it was said, if there is any such world it cannot be known. But, upon the other side, analysis of the conditions of knowing seemed to reveal that "matter" or the "world" could not be known *per se* at all, but only in relation to the knower. Parallel with the development of physical science was a development of psychological science. While physical science went to make the "external" primary and the "internal" a derivative from it, psychological science reversed the process. The history of philosophy for the last four centuries is a record of this conflict within science itself. Upon the whole, philosophy, technically so-called, has tended to identify itself with the psychological side, but the tendency in this direction has been met and checked in the other direction by the rapid popular acceptance of the results of physical science.

SECTION 32.—It will be noticed that both of these tendencies, however opposed in conclusion, agree in their fundamental premise. *Both start from the standpoint of knowledge*, and attempt to read the world in terms of knowledge, that is, of contemplation or intellectual formulation. Just because both sides occupy the same fundamental standpoint the quarrel between them cannot be reconciled. The key to the reconciliation consists in shifting the point of view. *Reality is not to be read in terms of knowledge as such, but in terms of action.* So read, the opposition between the internal and the external, the physical and the psychical, ceases to be ultimate and becomes instrumental. We have in this distinction a *means* to the end of action. The physical and the psychical are recognized as the primary distributions of power requisite to the highest (freest) action. All action whatever is carried on through divisions of labor (distributions of power), and in order to get the most efficient action this division must go to the point of extreme tension or antagonism; the distribution of force must be polar. So in this case; the physical and the psychical represent the tension necessary to the exercise of force. Distinguished from each other as much as possible, the maximum of utilizable energy is developed.

SECTION 33.—Upon both sides (the physical and psychical) the tendency, at present, is (1) to pass over from the standpoint of knowledge to that of action, and (2) as passing over to demand the other side as the complementary division of labor, instead of standing over against it in irreconcilable opposition.

The development of industry and commerce in the modern world has gone to show that the "physical" as such is not an end in itself, but is material for human action. Iron, coal, cotton and water are seen not to have their reality by themselves, but in the developed action of man up to which they lead and of which they become factors. They are seen to be real not when isolated, *and thus fixed*, but only in their unification (their co-ordination) *and thus in movement.* Iron, coal and water, for example, get their fuller reality (unity of relations) in the locomotive when that functions as a part of man's action. Furthermore, taken as material *of action* they demand the other side, the psychical. The *relationship* into which coal, iron and water enter, *the way they move together*, is worked out through "mind"; the "mind" in discovering the relationships of the iron gives it its full reality, its free and complete movement. (I quote the word "mind" because mind is not some *thing which* does this relating; it *is* the unifying or relating as abstracted from that unified or related. The "mind," in other words, is simply the universal, the co-ordinating of the particulars in a given case.) On the other side, the more knowledge, understanding of things, we get, the less that knowledge is an end in itself, and the more it is simply a *way to act*, a tool or method of construction. Just as the physical turns out to be the *material or content of action* and not a something *per se*, so the psychical turns out to be the *form or method of action*. Each side involves the other; they are only the primary distinctions of action itself. Thus what the present period of science points to is a return to the earliest category of man, that of action, except that the earlier action was unconscious of itself, and therefore uncontrolled; while the later is thoroughly conscious (through science) of its two phases, (1) the *material* involved in action, the real possibilities of action, and (2) the *way* in which to handle this material in order to get out of it all there is in it.

## Chapter Sixth—the Divisions of Philosophy

SECTION 34.—There are three philosophic sciences, corresponding to three ways in which the individual, or organized action may be regarded. These are Logic, Æsthetic and Ethic. Logic is the general theory of science; the theory, that is, of the standard and method of knowledge. It deals with action on its mental side, setting forth the road by which action is reduced to its reality; set in order or subjected. It deals with truth as *method*. Æsthetic deals with truth as *expressed* or *embodied—i.e.*, with reference to its expression, the manner of uttering it so as to realize it in its fullness. It deals primarily with the outward side of action. Ethic treats action as action, analyzing it into its factors and relationships—it deals with the constitution of action. Internal and external are both alike to it—simply constituting elements.

## Chapter Seventh—Logic

SECTION 35.—Knowledge is *statement* of action. This statement is judgment. Action is stated through being arrested or checked, that is, viewed as if arrested. The checking breaks the action into two phases; the "what has been done" and the "what is to do." That is, the checking arrests action and makes a cross-section of it—this cross-section stands for the *factum* or thing done. But on the other hand, this very checking only makes the *direction* of action more prominent; it separates or abstracts the general direction or principle of action from the special thing done or doing. In becoming abstracted, the principle appears as that which is to be done with the fact; the way of handling it. It is an idea. In the technical terms of logic, the "fact" is the subject of the judgment; the "idea" is the predicate. That is, the action in arrest, the thing done, becomes the subject-matter or material. The subject of the judgment is thus always "sensuous," the predicate "ideal"—*i.e.*, what we call sense is the activity taken as arrested or "past," what we call ideal is the projection of the activity. So, also, a judgment read from the side of its subject is extensive, from the side of its predicate intensive. The subject-matter is the manifold particular conditions; the predicate is the meaning which unifies. Again, the subject is percept, the predicate concept. The point in each case is to see that we do not have two independent sides, but the differentiation, the main division of labor, of action. That is, it is again (see Sec. 29), a case of producing a tension or opposition of forces in order to realize the maximum energy. The connection of the two, the actual bringing of the method upon the material constitutes the *copula*. The reality or force of the judgment is the value effected; it is neither subject nor predicate nor a union of the two, but the action resulting from the handling of the "fact" by "idea"; the action resulting from reflecting a given mode of operating back into a given material. Every complete judgment, in other words, transcends itself, passing, when complete, over into action, and this action is the reality of the judgment.

SECTION 36.—A judgment thus involves differentiation and identification; the differences being the statement of the factors of the action, the identity being the uniting or coming together of these factors in the act itself; *i.e.*, the unity of a judgment is always the act which connects the various conditions stated in a judgment. Hence, also, the analytic and synthetic factors of every judgment. The analysis states the conditions of an action; the synthesis is the function which, on one side, is constituted by these conditions, and which, on the other side, realizes them.

SECTION 37.—Judgments are classified according to the extent to which they state (make explicit) the action involved. In the naïve or dogmatic judgment (the assertion of common sense), the action is almost all implicit or unrealized; *i.e.*, the judgment is an impression. Examples: "How hot it is!" "it rains"; "my tooth aches," etc. Such judgments are sometimes called sense judgments. These uncritical judgments develop in two directions, the categorical, and the hypothetical. *The categorical proceeds to develop the subject-matter of the judgment*; to tell *what* it is that is hot; to give all the particulars of the tooth ache, etc. That is, the categorical judgment isolates or abstracts the particular conditions, defining them just as far as possible. The judgment regarding the heat, for example, would tell the exact temperature in degrees; the exact latitude and longitude of the place; the exact humidity, state of the wind and sky and so on; it would attempt to register all the particular conditions involved in the state of the temperature. The result is to transform the vague subject-matter into a definite one. The categorical judgment is thus *descriptive*; and the descriptive side of every science (astronomy, geology, botany, etc.) is the categorical development of some subject-matter. At the same time, the hypothetical judgment takes up the connection or unity of the particulars. *It develops the predicate* of the judgment. The hypothetical judgment is thus at the other pole from the categorical. While the latter states only particulars, describing the "actual fact" as it is called, the hypothetical states only the universal, the *connection* of conditions. It does not pretend to state any existing thing, or historical event, but simply a relation or law; *if* or *where* one condition or circumstance is found there some other circumstance will also be found, leaving it an open question whether the conditions actually occur or not. While the categorical judgment by itself would only give us a mass or aggregate of brute facts, the hypothetical by itself would give us only an abstract idea. One is all on the ground without general meaning; the other is all in the air without specific existence. But neither the categorical nor the hypothetical judgment has any such separate existence; they are not so much *two* judgments, as they are developments of the two phases, subject and predicate, "fact" and "idea," of judgment.

SECTION 38.—This very separation creates the tension which compels the two phases back into their unity. The original action which was being stated has now been stretched to its utmost point (Analysis) and now must re-unite in further (freer) action (Synthesis). The process of uniting is experiment, or "verification." The "idea" (the predicate or hypothetical judgment) has to be tested, by being carried over into the particular conditions or "facts"; while these have to be connected together or given meaning, instead of remaining so many blank, separate particulars. The "idea" is tested, or verified; the "facts" are harmonized, explained, rationalized. The result is a new judgment, in which the idea is wholly embodied in facts, or in which the facts are self-luminous; the fact, the reality, in which there is no segregation whatever of the two factors. This is, in other words, a concrete action. The action which has had its various phases distinguished and then re-united is the *disjunctive* judgment—the statement of the individual or organic system. It should be noted here that what we call the "facts" (as distinct from the idea—the particular conditions into which an action is disintegrated when it is arrested) are not the test or standard by which the idea or hypothesis is measured. Both "facts" and "idea" are measured by the action in which they unite; *it* only is the test or standard, the truth. The standard of truth is not something arrested or fixed; it is the ongoing movement, the continued doing.

## Chapter Eighth—Art

SECTION 39.—Logic deals with the statement of action; the resolution of action into its constituent factors. Science deals with the manner or mode of action,—its *Law*. Even in experiment, where the idea or universal is, through action, carried out into the particulars, the look of logic is backward; how does the experiment affect the idea, what new light does it throw upon the facts? Art looks forward; how shall the action be brought into being and maintained? It is the expression or manifestation side it is concerned with; not the resolution or statement side.

SECTION 40.—The aim of art is to discover the method of expression which shall secure the best organization of action; the fullest or freest movement. It aims at seeing to it that the ideal side gets a complete embodiment in the fact side; or, what is the same thing, that the facts become completely permeated with their idea so as to move harmoniously and thus freely.

SECTION 41.—The historical classification of the arts depends upon the degree to which this complete interpenetration is attained. Certain special or limited regions of material will, *in their limitation*, first secure the desired end. Thus we have the "fine arts," technically so-called; *i.e.*, freedom of action is reached as to coloring or form or sound, and we have the special fine art of painting, sculpture, music, etc. Then the other and wider regions which have not as yet realized their unity (*i.e.*, been freed through attaining their idea or purpose) are regarded as "material," or "sensuous." The separation is even carried so far that people come to regard this distinction which is purely historical (showing how far at a given time action has realized itself or become free) as indicating two kinds of action in life, two spheres of existence, one beautiful, ideal, artistic, etc., the other merely useful and material. On the contrary, however, the distinction has only a *negative* value, showing the limit to free action at a given time. That is, if a statue at a given date is regarded as essentially artistic, and a locomotive as merely useful, it is because owing to the narrow relations of the former the whole has attained expression in it, while the whole (the function in the service of the organized action of man) has only partially subdued the latter. The limitation in the artistic character of the locomotive, in other words, is the extent to which it functions in the interest of a part or class, instead of in the interest of the whole, so that its full meaning and energy are not freed or realized in consciousness. The development of the arts is thus a political phenomenon, since the whole which is seeking to embody itself in every particular is nothing less than the organized action of man. So far as the whole moves freely through any part, that part is artistic.

## *Chapter Ninth — Ethic*

SECTION 42.—Ethic unites the two sides distinguished in logic and æsthetic. It deals with the practical situation; the organized action.

# OUTLINES

OF A

## Critical Theory of Ethics

BY
### JOHN DEWEY
PROFESSOR OF PHILOSOPHY IN THE UNIVERSITY OF MICHIGAN

---

ANN ARBOR, MICHIGAN
REGISTER PUBLISHING COMPANY
The Inland Press
1891

# Preface

Although the following pages have taken shape in connection with class-room work, they are intended as an independent contribution to ethical science. It is commonly demanded of such a work that its readers shall have some prefatory hint of its sources and deviations. In accordance with this custom, I may state that for the backbone of the theory here presented—the conception of the will as the expression of ideas, and of social ideas; the notion of an objective ethical world realized in institutions which afford moral ideals, theatre and impetus to the individual; the notion of the moral life as growth in freedom, as the individual finds and conforms to the law of his social placing—for this backbone I am especially indebted to Green's *Prolegomena to Ethics*, to Mr. Bradley's *Ethical Studies*, to Professor Caird's *Social Philosophy of Comte* and *Critical Philosophy of Kant* (to this latter book in particular my indebtedness is fundamental), and to Alexander's *Moral Order and Progress*. Although I have not been able to adopt the standpoint or the method of Mr. Spencer, or of Mr. Leslie Stephen, my obligation to the *Data of Ethics* and to the *Science of Ethics* (especially to the latter) is large.

As to the specific forms which give a flesh and blood of its own to this backbone, I may call attention to the idea of desire as the ideal activity in contrast with actual possession; to the analysis of individuality into function including capacity and environment; to the treatment of the social bearings of science and art (a point concerning which I am indebted to my friend, Mr. Franklin Ford); to the statement of an ethical postulate; to the accounts of obligation, of moral rules, and of moral badness.

While the book is an analysis, in outline, of the main elements of the theory of ethics rather than a discussion of all possible detailed questions, it will not be found the less fitted, I hope, to give a student an idea of the main methods and problems of contemporary ethics. Other teachers, indeed, may agree that a general outline is better than a blanket-mortgage spread over and forestalling all the activity of the student's mind.

I have not been unmindful of the advisability of avoiding in presentation both undue polemic, and undue dogmatism without sufficient reference to the statements of others. I hope the method hit upon, of comparing opposite one-sided views with the aim of discovering a theory apparently more adequate, will help keep the balance. I have quoted freely from the chief modern authorities, hoping that the tastes here given will tempt the reader to the banquet waiting in the authors themselves. The occasional references introduced are not bibliographical, nor intended as exhaustive statements of authorities consulted; they are meant as aids to an intelligent reading on the part of the general student. For this reason they are confined mainly to modern English writings.

# Introduction

## I.   Definition of Ethics

The term ethics is derived from a Greek word meaning
manners, customs, habits, just as the term morals is derived
from a Latin word with a similar meaning. This suggests
the character of the science as an account of human action.
Anthropology, ethnology, psychology, are also, in their way,
accounts of human action. But these latter branches of
knowledge simply *describe*, while the business of ethics is to
*judge*.

This does not mean that it belongs to ethics to prescribe what man ought to do; but that its business is to
detect the element of obligation in conduct, to examine
conduct to see what gives it its *worth*. Anthropology, etc.,
do not take into account the *whole* of action, but simply
some of its aspects—either external or internal. Ethics deals
with conduct in its entirety, with reference, that is, to what
makes it conduct, its *end*, its real meaning. Ethics is the
science of conduct, understanding by conduct man's activity
in its whole reach.

Three of the branches of philosophy may be called *normative*,
implying that they deal with some *norm*, *standard* or *end*, estimating
the value of their respective subject-matters as tested by this end.
These are Logic, dealing with the end Truth, and the value of intellectual processes with respect to it; Æsthetics, dealing with Beauty
and the value of emotional conditions as referred to it; and Ethics,
as defined above. But this norm in no case comes from outside the
subject-matter; it is the subject-matter considered in its totality.

## II.   Meaning of Moral

In its widest sense, the term moral or ethical means
nothing more than relating to conduct; having to do with

practice, when we look at conduct or practice from the point of view not of its occurrence, but of its value. Action is something which takes place, and as such it may be described like any objective fact. But action has also relation to an end, and so considered it is *moral*. The first step in ethics is to fix firmly in mind the idea that the term moral does not mean any special or peculiar kind of conduct, but simply means practice and action, conduct viewed not partially, but in connection with the end which it realizes.

It should be noted that the term moral has a wider and a narrower sense. In the wider sense it means action in the moral sphere, as opposed to *non*-moral, and thus includes both good and bad conduct. In the narrower sense it means moral, as opposed to *im*-moral. See Bradley, *Ethical Studies*, p. 53 n., for a further meaning.

## III.   Meaning of Conduct

Ethics then has to do with conduct or action viewed completely, or in relation to its end. But what is conduct? It must be distinguished from action in general; for any process of change, the working of a pump, the growth of a plant, the barking of a dog, may be called action. Conduct implies more than something taking place; it implies purpose, motive, intention; that the agent knows what he is about, that he has something which he is aiming at. All action accomplishes something or brings about results, but conduct has the result *in view*. It occurs for the sake of producing this result. Conduct does not simply, like action in general, have a cause, but also a reason, and the reason is present to the mind of the agent. There can be conduct only when there is a being who can propose to himself, as an end to be reached by himself, something which he regards as worth while. Such a being is a moral agent, and his action, when conscious, is conduct.

## IV.   Division of Ethics

The main ethical problem is just this: What is the conduct that really deserves the name of conduct, the conduct of which all other kinds of action can be only a perverted or deflected form? Or, since it is the end which gives action its moral value, what is the true end, *summum bonum* of man? Knowing this, we have a standard by which we judge particular acts. Those which embody this end are *right*, others wrong. The question of the rightness of conduct is simply a special form of the question concerning the nature of the end or good. But the end bears another relation to specific acts. They are not only marked off by it as right or wrong, but they have to fulfill it. The end or good decides what should be or *ought* to be. Any act necessary to fulfill the end is a *duty*. Our second inquiry will be as to the nature of obligation or duty. Then we have to discuss the nature of a being who is capable of action, of manifesting and realizing the end; capable of right (or wrong), of obligatory and good action. This will lead us to discuss the question of *Freedom*, or *Moral Capacity and its Realization*. The discussion of these three abstract questions will constitute Part One of our theory; Part Two will take up the various forms and institutions in which the good is objectively realized, the family, state, etc.; while Part Three will be devoted to an account of the moral experience of the individual.

## v. The Motive in Conduct

Before taking up the first problem presented, the nature of the good or the end of conduct, it is necessary to analyze somewhat further the various sides and factors of conduct in order to see where the distinctly ethical element is to be found. The elements particularly deserving consideration are (1) the Motive; (2) the Feelings or Sentiments; (3) Consequences of the Act; (4) Character of Agent. We shall begin with

### 1. *The Motive.*

The motive of the act is the end aimed at by the agent in performing the act. Thus the motive of Julius Cæsar in crossing the Rubicon was the whole series of results which he intended to reach by that act of his. The motive of a person in coming to college is to gain knowledge, to prepare himself for a certain profession. The motive is thus identical with the ideal element of the action, the purpose in view.

## 2. *The Feelings or Disposition.*

Some writers speak of the feelings under which the agent acts as his motive. Thus we may suppose Julius Cæsar "moved" by the feelings of ambition, of revenge, etc., in crossing the Rubicon. The student may be "moved" by curiosity, by vainglory, by emulation, by conscience, in coming to college. It is better, however, to regard the motive as the reason for which the act is performed, and to use the term moving or impelling cause for the feelings in their relation to action. Thus we may imagine a parent asking a child why he struck a playmate, meaning what was the motive of the action. If the child should reply that he struck his playmate because he was angry, this answer would give the moving cause or impelling force of the action, but not its motive. The motive would be the idea of punishing this playmate, of getting even with him, of taking something away from him. The motive is the end which he desired to reach by striking and on account of which he struck. This is implied by the fact that the parent would ask, "What *made* you *angry*?"

## VI. Moral Bearing of These Distinctions

It is the feelings which supply the impelling force to action. They may be termed, collectively, the *natural disposition*. The natural disposition in itself has no *moral* value. This has been well illustrated by Bentham.

> *Works*, I, *Principles of Morals and Legislation*, pp. 49–55. Bentham here uses the term "motive" to designate what we have called the moving cause.

We may select of the many examples which he gives that of curiosity. We may imagine a boy spinning a top, reading a useful book and letting a wild ox loose in a road. Now curiosity may be the "motive" of each of these acts, yet the first act would generally be called morally indifferent, the second good, the third abominable.

What we mean by the "natural" feelings, then, is the feelings considered in abstraction from activity. Benevolence, as a *mere* feeling, has no higher moral value than malevolence. But if it is directed upon action it gets a value at once; let the end, the act, be right, and benevolence becomes a name for a *moral* disposition—a tendency to *act* in the due way. Nothing is more important than to distinguish between mere sentiments, and feeling as an element in conduct.

## VII.  Relation of Consequences and Conduct

Do the consequences of an act have anything to do with its morality? We may say no, pointing to the fact that a man who does his best we call good, although the consequences of his act may be far from good. We say his purpose in acting was right, and using as he did all the knowledge that he had, he is not to be blamed for its bad consequences. On the other hand, it is evident that we do take into account consequences in estimating the moral value of an act. Suppose, to use one of Bentham's examples, a person were about to shoot an animal but foresaw that in doing so there was a strong probability that he would also wound some bystander. If he shot and the spectator were wounded, should we not hold the agent morally responsible? Are there not multitudes of intended acts of which we say that we cannot tell whether they are good or bad until we know how they are likely to turn out?

The solution of the difficulty is in recognizing the ambiguity of the term "consequences." It may mean the whole outcome of the act. When I speak, I set in motion the air, and its vibrations have, in turn, long chains of effects. Whatever I do must have an endless succession of "consequences" of which I can know but very little; just so far as, in any act, I am ignorant of the conditions under which it is performed, so far I am ignorant of its consequences. *Such* consequences are wholly irrelevant morally. They have no more to do with the morality of the act than has the fact that the earth is revolving while the act is taking place.

But we may mean by consequences the *foreseen* consequences of an act. Just in the degree that any consequence is considered likely to result from an act, just in that degree it gets moral value, for it becomes *part of the act* itself. The reason that in many cases we cannot judge of the morality of an intended act until we can judge its probable results, is that until we know of these results the action is a mere abstraction, having no content at all. *The conceived results constitute the content of the act to be performed.* They are not merely relevant to its morality, but *are* its moral quality. The question is whether any consequence is foreseen, conceived, or not. The foreseen, the *ideal* consequences are the end of the act, and as such form the *motive*.

See on Secs. VI and VII, Alexander, *Moral Order and Progress*, pp. 36–46; on Sec. VII, Green, *Prolegomena to Ethics*, pp. 317–23.

## VIII. Character and Conduct

We have seen that the moral sentiments, or the moral disposition (distinguished from the feelings as passing emotions), on one side, and the consequences as ideal or conceived (distinguished from the consequences that, *de facto*, result), on the other, both have moral value. If we take the moral feelings, not one by one, but as a whole, as an *attitude* of the agent toward conduct, as expressing the kind of motives which upon the whole moves him to action, we have *character*. And just so, if we take the consequences willed, not one by one, but as a whole, as the kind of end which the agent endeavors to realize, we have *conduct*. Character and conduct are, morally, the same thing, looked at first inwardly and then outwardly. Character, except as manifest in conduct, is a barren ideality. Our moral judgments are always severe upon a man who has nothing to show but "good intentions" never executed. This is what character comes to, apart from conduct. Our only way of telling the nature of character is the conduct that issues from it. But, on the other hand, conduct is mere outward formalism, excepting as it manifests character. To say that a man's conduct is good, unless it is the manifestation of a good character, is to pass a judgment which is self-contradictory.

See Alexander, *Moral Order*, pp. 48–50 and p. 39.

From this point of view we are enabled to identify the two senses of motive already discussed—the ideal of action and the moving feelings. Apart from each other they are abstractions. Cæsar's motive in crossing the Rubicon may have been "ambition," but this was not some bare feeling. It was a feeling of ambition produced in view of the contemplation of a certain end which he wished to reach. So a boy's motive in striking a playmate may be anger, but this means (if the act is anything more than one of blind physical reaction) an anger having its conscious cause and aim, and not some abstract feeling of anger in general. The feeling which has its nature made what it is by the conceived end, and the end which has ceased to be a bare abstract conception and become an interest, are all one with each other.

Morality is then a matter pertaining to character—to the feelings and inclinations as transformed by ends of action; and to conduct—to conceived ends transformed into act under the influence of emotions. But what *kind* of character, of conduct, is right or realizes its true end? This brings us to our first problem.

# PART ONE

# FUNDAMENTAL ETHICAL NOTIONS

## 1
## *The Good*

### ix.  Subdivision of Theories

We may recognize three main types of theories regarding the good, of which the first two represent (we shall attempt to show) each respectively one side of the truth, while the third combines the one-sided truths of the other two. Of the first two theories one is abstract, because it tends to find the good in the mere consequences of conduct aside from character. This is the hedonistic theory, which finds the good to be pleasure. This is either individualistic or universalistic according as it takes individual or general pleasure to be the good. The second type of theories attempts to find the good in the motive of conduct apart from consequences even as willed; it reduces the good to conformity to abstract moral law. The best type of this theory is the Kantian. We shall criticise these theories with a view to developing the factors necessary to a true moral theory.

### x.  Hedonism

According to the strict hedonistic position, the pleasure resulting to the agent from his act is the end of conduct and is therefore the criterion of its morality. The position as usually taken involves, first, that pleasure is psychologically the sole motive to action; and, secondly, that the results of an act in the way of the pain or pleasure it produces are the only tests we have of the rightness of the act.

It is said above that these two points are involved in the hedonistic position as *usually* taken. They are not *necessarily* involved.

Sidgwick (*Methods of Ethics*, Bk. I, Ch. 4 and Bk. IV, Ch. 1) holds that pleasure is not the object of desire or motive of action, but that happiness is the moral end and criterion. On the other hand Hodgson (*Theory of Practice*, Vol. II, Ch. 2) holds that pleasure may be the motive (in the sense of impelling force) but it is never the criterion of conduct. Kant adopts the psychology of hedonism regarding pleasure as the object of desire, but holds that on that very account no object of desire can be the standard of moral conduct.

A good statement of strict individualistic hedonism is the following from Barratt, *Physical Ethics*, p. 71: "If man aims at pleasure merely by the physical law of action, that pleasure must evidently be ultimately his own, and whether it be or not preceded by phenomena which he calls the pain and pleasure of others, is a question not of principle but of detail, just as the force of a pound weight is unaltered whether it be composed of lead or of feathers, or whether it act directly or through pulleys."

## XI.   The Hedonistic Position Supported

Hedonism holds that pleasure is both the natural end and the proper criterion of action:

The following quotation from Bentham (*Principles of Morals*, p. 1) gives a statement of both these elements. "Nature has placed man under the governance of two sovereign masters, pain and pleasure. It is for them alone to point out what we ought to do, [*i.e.*, they are criteria] as well as to determine what we shall do [motives]. On the one hand, the standard of right or wrong [criterion]; on the other the chain of causes and effects [motives], are fastened to their throne."

### 1. *Pleasure as Criterion*

That the tendency of an action to produce pleasure is the standard for judging its moral value is generally held by the hedonists to be so axiomatic as to be beyond argument.

See Bain, *Moral Science*, p. 27. "The ultimate data must be accepted as self-evident: they have no higher authority than that mankind generally are disposed to accept them. . . . Now there can

be no proof offered for the position that happiness is the proper end
of all human pursuits, the criterion of all right conduct. It is an
ultimate or final assumption to be tested by reference to the individual judgment of mankind." So Bentham, *Principles of Morals*, p. 2,
"The principle is not susceptible of direct proofs for that which is
used to prove everything else can not itself be proved; a chain of
proofs must have their commencement somewhere." Mill, *Utilitarianism* (*Dissertations and Discussions*, Vol. iii), pp. 348–49. "The only
proof capable of being given that an object is visible is that people
actually see it. In like manner the sole evidence it is possible to
produce that anything is desirable is that people do actually desire
it." See Stephen, *Science of Ethics*, p. 42; Spencer, *Data of Ethics*,
pp. 30–32 and p. 46; Lotze, *Practical Philosophy*, pp. 18–19; Sidgwick, *Methods of Ethics*, pp. 368–69.

Hedonism, then, represents the good or the desirable
and pleasure to be two names for the same fact. What
indeed can be worth while unless it be either enjoyable in
itself or at least a means to enjoyment? Would theft be
considered bad if it resulted in pleasure or truth itself good
if its universal effect were pain?

## 2. *Pleasure as Object of Desire*

It is also urged that psychological analysis shows that pleasure is not only the desirable, but also always the *desired*.
Desire for an object is only a short way of saying desire for
the pleasure which that object may bring. To want food is to
want the pleasure it brings; to want scientific ability is to
desire to find satisfaction, or attain happiness. Thus it is laid
down as a general principle that the invariable object of
desire, and motive of action is some pleasure to be attained;
the action itself and the direct end of action being simply
means to pleasure.

For a strong statement of this doctrine see Mill, *Utilitarianism*,
pp. 354–55. "Desiring a thing and finding it pleasant, aversion to it
and thinking of it as painful, are phenomena entirely inseparable, or
rather two parts of the same phenomenon,—in strictness of language,
two different modes of naming the same psychological fact; to think
of an object as desirable and to think of it as pleasant are one and
the same thing." See also, Bain, *Emotions and Will*, p. 436, *Senses
and Intellect*, pp. 338–44; Sully, *Outlines of Psychology*, p. 575,
"The inclination or tendency of the active mind towards what is

pleasurable and away from what is painful is the essential fact in willing." Also pp. 576–77.

## xii.  Criticism: Pleasure Not the End of Impulse

Taking up the points in reverse order, we shall endeavor to show first, that the motive of action, in the sense of end aimed at, is not pleasure. This point in itself, is, of course, rather psychological than ethical. Taking up then the psychology of pleasure in its connection with will, we shall discuss its relation to impulse, to desire and to motive.

It is generally agreed that the raw material of volition is found in some form or other of the impulsive or instinctive actions. Such tendencies (*e.g.*, the impulse for food, for drink, for unimpeded motion) clearly precede the reaching of an end, and hence the experience of any pleasure in the end. Our first actions, at least, are not for pleasure; on the contrary, there is an activity for some independent end, and this end being reached there is pleasure in an act which has succeeded. This suggests as a possible principle that pleasure is not so much the end of action, as an element in the activity which reaches an end. What Aristotle says of another matter is certainly true of instinctive action. "It is not true of every characteristic function that its action is attended with pleasure, *except indeed the pleasure of attaining its end.*"

See Martineau, *Types of Ethical Theory*, Vol. ii, pp. 299–300; Sidgwick, *Methods of Ethics*, pp. 38–45.

## xiii. Criticism: Pleasure Not the End of Desire

It may, however, be said that, while our instinctive actions have another end than pleasure, this is not true of conscious desires—that, indeed, just the difference between instinct and desire is that the former goes blindly to its end, while the latter superimposes the thought of the pleasure to be reached upon the mere instinct. So we have to analyze the nature of desire.

A child, led by impulse, has put a piece of sugar into his mouth, just as, under the same circumstances, he would put a piece of stone into his mouth. But his action results in a state of pleasure wholly unforeseen by him. Now the next time the child sees the sugar he will not merely have the impulse to put it in his mouth. There will also be the remembrance of the pleasure enjoyed from sugar previously. There is consciousness of sugar as satisfying impulse and hence desire for it.

1. This is a description of an instance of desire. Does it bear us out in the doctrine that pleasure is the object of desire? It is possible that, in an irrational animal, the experience of eating food reinforces the original instinct for it with associated images of pleasure. But even this is very different from a desire for pleasure. It is simply the primordial instinct intensified and rendered more acute by new sensational factors joined to it. In the strict sense, there is still no desire, but only *stronger* impulse. Wherever there is desire there is not only a feeling of pleasure associated with other feelings (*e.g.*, those of hunger, thirst), but there is the *consciousness of an object in which satisfaction is found*. The error of the hedonistic psychology is in omitting one's consciousness of an *object* which satisfies. The hedonists are quite right in holding that the end of desire is not any object external to consciousness, but a condition of consciousness itself. The error begins in eliminating all objective (that is, active) elements from consciousness, and declaring it to be a mere state of feeling or sensation. The practical consciousness, or will, cannot be reduced to mere feeling, any more than the theoretical consciousness, or knowledge, can be so reduced.

Even Mill, in his statement of the hedonistic psychology, does not succeed in making the object of desire mere pleasure as a state of feeling. It is the "pleasant *thing*" and not pleasure alone which he finds equivalent to the desire. It is true enough that sugar as an external fact does not awaken desire, but it is equally true that a child does not want a passive pleasure. What he wants is his own activity in which he makes the sugar his own. And it should be remembered that the case of sugar is at once a trivial and an exceptional one. Not even children want simply sweetmeats; and the larger the character which finds expression in wants, the more does the direct object of want, the bread, the meat, become a mere element in a larger system of activity. What a man wants is to live, and he wants sweetmeats, amusements, etc., just as he wants substantials—on account of their value in life.

Professor James compares the idea that pleasure is the end of desire to saying that "because no steamer can go to sea without incidentally consuming coal, . . . therefore no steamer can go to sea for any other motive than that of coal-consumption." *Psychology*, Vol. II, p. 558. See the entire passage, pp. 549–59.

2. But granting that an "object" and a "pleasure" are both necessary to desire, it may be argued that the "object" is ultimately a means to "pleasure." This expressly raises a question already incidentally touched upon: What is the controlling element in desire? Why is the object thought of as pleasant? Simply because it is thought of as satisfying want. The hedonists, says Green (*Prolegomena to Ethics*, p. 168), make the "mistake of supposing that a desire can be excited by the anticipation of its own satisfaction." This is to say, of course, that it exists before it exists, and thus brings itself into being.

Green, *Prolegomena*, p. 167, states the matter thus: "Ordinary motives are interests in the attainment of objects, without which it seems to the man that he cannot satisfy himself, and in the attainment of which, *because he has desired them*, he will find a certain pleasure, but only because he has previously desired them, not because pleasures are the objects desired." Bradley says on this same point (*Ethical Studies*, p. 230): "The difference is between my finding my pleasure in an end, and my finding means for the end of my pleasure, and the difference is enormous." Consult the entire passage, pp. 226–35. See also Caird, *Critical Philosophy of Kant*, Vol. II, p. 229.

It is the object, then, which controls, and the pleasure is on account of the attaining of the desired object. But even this statement makes more division in desire than actually exists; for

3. The real object of desire is activity itself. The will takes its rise, as we have seen, in impulse; in the reaching for something to satisfy some felt lack. Now, in reality,

desire adds nothing to impulse excepting *consciousness* of the impulse. Volitional action does not differ from impulsive or instinctive, *except in bringing to consciousness the nature of the want and of the activity necessary to satisfy it.* But this makes just the difference between "natural" or animal activity, and "moral" or human activity. To be conscious of the impulse is to elevate it from a blind impelling force to an intended or proposed end; and thus, by bringing it *before* consciousness, both to extend its range and to idealize it, spiritualize it. To be conscious of an impulse for food means to give up the unreasoned and momentary seizing of it; to consider the relation of things to this want, what will satisfy it best, most easily, etc. The *object* of desire is not something outside the action; it is an element in the enlarged action. And as we become more and more conscious of impulse for food, we analyze our action into more and more "objects" of desire, but these objects never become anything apart from the action itself. They are simply its analyzed and defined content. Man wants activity still, but he knows better what activity means and includes.

Thus, when we learn what the activity means, it changes its character. To the animal the activity wanted is simply that of eating the food, of realizing the momentary impulse. To man the activity becomes enlarged to include the satisfaction of a whole life, and not of one life singly, but of the family, etc., connected with the single life. The material well-being of the family becomes one of the objects of desire into which the original impulse has grown. But we misinterpret, when we conceive of this well-being as an external object lying outside the action. It means simply one aspect of the fuller action. By like growing consciousness of the meaning of the impulse, production and exchange of commodities are organized. The impulse for food is extended to include a whole range of commercial activities.

It is evident that this growing consciousness of the nature of an impulse, whereby we resolve it into manifold and comprehensive activities, also takes the impulse out of its isolation and brings it into connection with other impulses. We come to have not a series of disconnected impulses, but one all-inclusive activity in which various subordinate activities (or conscious impulses) are included. Thus, in the previous example, the impulse for food is united with the family impulse, and with the impulse for communication and intercourse with society generally. It is this growing unity with the whole range of man's action that is the "spiritualizing" of the impulse—the natural and brutal impulse being just that which insists upon itself irrespective of all other wants. The spiritualizing of the impulse is organizing it so that it becomes one factor in action. Thus we literally come to "eat to live," meaning by life not mere physical existence, but the whole possible sphere of active human relations.

4. Relation of activity to pleasure. We have seen that the "object" of desire in itself is a mere abstraction; that the real object is full activity itself. We are always after larger scope of movement, fuller income in order to get larger outgo. The "thing" is always for the sake of doing; is a part of the doing. The idea that anything less or other than life (movement, action, and doing), can satisfy man is as ridiculous when compared with the actual course of things in history, as it is false psychologically. Freedom is what we want, and freedom means full unimpeded play of interests, that is, of conscious impulses (see Secs. xxxiv and li). If the object is a mere abstraction apart from activity, much more is pleasure. Mere pleasure as an object is simply the extreme of passivity, of mere having, as against action or doing. It is *possible* to make pleasure to some degree the object of desire; this is just what the voluptuary does. But it is a commonplace that the voluptuary always defeats himself. He never gets satisfaction who identifies satisfaction with having pleasures. The reason is evident enough. Activity is what we want, and since pleasure comes from getting what we want, pleasure comes only with activity. To give up the activity, and attempt to get the pleasure is a contradiction in effect. Hence also the "hedonistic paradox" —that in order to get pleasure we must aim at something else.

There is an interesting recognition of this in Mill himself, (see his *Autobiography*, p. 142). And in his *Utilitarianism*, in discussing the feasibility of getting happiness, he shows (pp. 318–19) that the sources of happiness are an intelligent interest in surrounding things —objects of nature, achievements of art, incidents of history—and especially an unselfish devotion to others. Which is to say that man does not find satisfaction in pleasure as such at all, but only in objective affairs—that is, in complete interpretation, in activity with a wide and full content. Further consideration of the end of desire and its relation to pleasure may be found in Green, *Prolegomena*, pp. 123–32, 163–67; Bradley, *Mind*, Vol. XIII, p. 1; and Dewey, *Psychology*, pp. 360–65 [*Early Works*, II, 310–14].

## XIV. Criticism: Character and Pleasure

It now being admitted that the end of desire is activity itself in which the "object" and "pleasure" are simply factors, what is the moving spring to action? What is it that arouses the mind to the larger activity? Most of the hedonists have confounded the two senses of motive already spoken of, and have held that *because* pleasure is the end of desire, therefore it is the moving spring of conduct (or more often that because it is the moving spring of conduct it *therefore* is the end of desire).

Mr. Stephen (*Science of Ethics*, pp. 46–58), although classing himself as a hedonist, has brought out this confusion very clearly. Ordinary hedonism confounds, as he shows, the judgment of what is pleasant—the supposed end —with the pleasant judgment—the moving spring. (See also Bradley, *Ethical Studies*, pp. 232–36.) It may be admitted that it is feeling which moves to action, but it is the *present* feeling which moves. If the feeling aimed at moves, it is only as through anticipation it becomes the present feeling. Now is this present feeling which moves (1) mere pleasure and (2) mere feeling at all? This introduces us to the question of the relation of pleasure (and of feeling in general) to character.

*1.* If the existing state of consciousness—that which moves—were pure pleasure, why should there be any movement, any act at all? The feeling which moves must be in so far complex: over against the pleasure felt in the anticipation of an end as satisfying, there must be pain felt in the contrasting unsatisfactory present condition. There must be tension between the anticipated or ideal action, and the actual or present (relative) non-action. And it is this tension, in which pain is just as normal an element as pleasure, which moves. Desire is just this tension of an action which satisfies, and yet is only ideal, against an actual possession which, in contrast with the ideal action, is felt as incomplete action, or lack, and hence as unsatisfactory.

2. The question now comes as to the nature of this tension. We may call it "feeling," if we will, and say that feeling is the sole motive power to action. But there is no such thing as feeling at large, and the important thing, morally, is what *kind* of feeling moves. To take a mere abstraction like "feeling" for the source of action is, at root, the fallacy of hedonism. To raise the question, What is it that makes the feeling what it is, is to recognize that the feeling, taken concretely, is *character* in a certain attitude.

Stephen, who has insisted with great force that feeling is the sole "motive" to action, has yet shown with equal cogency the moral uselessness of such a doctrine, when feeling is left undefined (*Science of Ethics*, p. 44). "The love of happiness must express the sole possible motive of Judas Iscariot and his master; it must explain the conduct of Stylites on his column, of Tiberius at Capreæ, of A Kempis in his cell, and of Nelson in the cockpit of the Victory. It must be equally good for saints, martyrs, heroes, cowards, debauchees, ascetics, mystics, cynics, misers, prodigals, men, women, and babes in arms." Surely, this is only to say, in effect, that "love of happiness" is a pure bit of scholasticism, an undefined entity.

In a hedonistic argument (by Stanton Coit, *Mind*, Vol. XI, p. 349), the fallacy is seen in the following discussion. The story is told of Abraham Lincoln that he once passed an animal in distress by the side of the road, and that, after going by, he finally went back and got him out of the ditch. On being praised for his act, he replied that he did it on his own account, since he kept getting more uncomfortable as he thought of the animal in distress. From this, it cannot be inferred that love of pleasure is at the basis of moral acts. The mere lumping off of feeling as the spring of conduct overlooks the only important thing morally—the fact that Lincoln felt pain at the thought of the animal unrelieved, and pleasure at the idea of its relief, just because he was a man of compassionate *character*. It was not the feeling, but the character revealed in, and creative of, the feeling that was the real source of the act.

To connect this with our previous account of desire (p. 257): the important thing morally is that the nature of the tension between fact and idea—the actual state and the ideal activity—is an expression of character. What kind of activity does it take to satisfy a man? Does riding in a comfortable carriage, and following the course of his own reflections exhaust his need of action? or does his full activity require that note be taken of a suffering animal? It is the kind of character one is (that is, the kind of activity which satisfies and expresses one) which decides what pleasure shall be taken in an anticipated end, what feeling of lack or hindrance (what pain) there shall be in the given state, and hence what the resulting tension, or desire, shall be. It is, therefore, character which moves to conduct.

Mere wishing, the mere floating fancy of this or that thing as desirable, is not desire. To *want* is an active projection of character; really and deeply to want is no surface and passing feeling; it is the stirring of character to its depths. There may be repressed activity; that is not, of itself, desire. There may be an image of larger activity; that is not, of itself, desire. But given the *consciousness* of a repressed activity in view of the perception of a possible larger action, and a man strives within himself to break his bonds and reach the new satisfaction. This striving within one's self, before the activity becomes overt, is the emotional antecedent of action. But this inward striving or tension, which constitutes desire, is so far from being *mere* emotion that it is character itself—character as it turns an inward or ideal advance into an outward, or real progress, into action.

We may fall back on Aristotle's statement (p. 38, of Peters' translation of his *Ethics*): "The pleasure or pain that accompanies an act must be regarded as a *test* of *character*. He who abstains from the pleasures of the body and rejoices in his abstinence is temperate, while he who is vexed at having to abstain is still profligate. As Plato tells us, man needs to be so trained from youth up as to take pleasure and pain *in the right objects*."

## xv. Summary

The truth in hedonism is its conviction that the good, the end of man, is not to be found in any outward object, but only in what comes home to man in his own conscious experience. The error is in reducing this experience to mere having, to bare feelings or affections, eliminating the element of doing. It is this doing which satisfies man, and it is this which involves as its content (as knowledge of impulse, instead of blind impulse) objective and permanent ends. When Mill speaks of the end of desire as a "satisfied life," (p. 317 of *Utilitarianism*) he carries our assent; but to reduce this satisfied life to feelings of pleasure, and absence of pains, is to destroy the life and hence the satisfaction. As Mill recognizes, a life bounded by the agent's own feelings would be, as of course, a life "centred in his own miserable individuality" (Mill, *Utilitarianism*, p. 319). Such words have meaning only because they suggest the contrast with activity in which are comprehended, as "ends" or "objects" (that is, as part of its defined content) things—art, science and industry—and persons (see Secs. xxxiv and xxxv).

Here too we must "back to Aristotle." According to him the end of conduct is *eudaimonia*, success, welfare, satisfied life. But *eudaimonia* is found not in pleasure, but in the fulfillment of human powers and functions, in which fulfillment, since it is fulfillment, pleasure is had (*Ethics*, Bk. i, Chs. 4–8).

We now take up the question whether pleasure is a standard of right action, having finished the discussion concerning it as an end of desire.

## xvi. Pleasure as the Standard of Conduct

The line of criticism on this point may be stated as follows: Pleasure fails as a standard for the very reason that it fails as a motive. Pleasure, *as conceived by the hedonist*, is passive, merely agreeable sensations, without any objective and qualitative (active) character. This being so, there is no permanent, fixed basis to which we may refer *acts* and by which we may judge them. A standard implies a single comprehensive end which unifies all acts and through connection with which each gets its moral value fixed. Only action can be a standard for acts. To reduce all acts to means to getting a mere state of feeling is the inevitable consequence of hedonism. So reducing them is to deprive them of any standard of value.

An end to serve as standard must be (1) a comprehensive end for all the acts of an individual, and (2) an end comprehending the activities of various individuals—a common good.

*1.* The moral end must be that for the sake of which all conduct occurs—the *organizing principle* of conduct—a totality, a system. If pleasure is the end it is because each detail of conduct gets its placing, its moral value through relation to pleasure, through the contribution it makes to pleasure.

*2.* The moral end must also include the ends of the various agents who make up society. It must be capable of constituting a social system out of the acts of various agents, as well as an individual system out of the various acts of one agent; or, more simply, the moral end must be not only the good for all the particular acts of an individual, but must be a *common good*—a good which in satisfying one, satisfies others.

All ethical theories would claim that the end proposed by them served these two purposes. We shall endeavor to show that the hedonistic theory, the doctrine that the pleasure is the good, is not capable of serving either of them.

## XVII. Pleasure Not a Standard

*1.* It does not unify character. In the first place, the hedonistic theory makes an unreal and impossible separation between conduct and character. The psychology of hedonism comes into conflict with its ethics. According to the former the motive of all action is to secure pleasure or avoid pain. So far as the motive is concerned, on this theory there can be no immoral action at all. That the agent should not be moved by pleasure, and by what, at the time of acting, is the greatest pleasure possible, would be a psychological impossibility. Every motive would be good, or rather there would be no distinction of good or bad pertaining to the motive. The character of the agent, as measured by his motives, could never, under such circumstances, have any moral quality.

To the consequences of action, or the conduct proper, however, the terms good and bad might be applied. Although the agent is moved by pleasurable feelings, the result of his action may be painful and thus bad. In a word, on the hedonistic theory, it is only the external consequences of conduct, or conduct divorced from character, to which moral adjectives have any application. Such a separation not only contradicts our experience (see Sec. VIII), but inverts the true order of moral judgment. Consequences do not enter into the moral estimate at all, except so far as, being foreseen, they are the act in idea. That is, it is only as the consequences are taken up into the motive, and thus related to character, that they are subject to moral judgment. Indeed, except so far as action expresses character, it is not conduct, but mere physical sequence, as irrelevant to morality as the change in blood distribution, which also is the "result" of an action. Hedonism has to rule out at the start the only thing that gives totality to action—the character of the agent, or conduct as the outcome of motives. Furthermore, the ordinary judgment of men, instead of saying that the sole moral motive is to get pleasure, would say that to reduce everything to means for getting pleasure is the very essence of immorality.

On the point above, compare Bentham, *Principles of Morals*, p. 48. "A motive is substantially nothing more than pleasure or pain operating in a certain manner. Now pleasure is in itself a good: nay, even, setting aside immunity from pain, the only good; pain is in itself an evil, and, indeed, without exception, the only evil; or else the words good and evil have no meaning. And this is alike true of every sort of pain and of every sort of pleasure. It follows, therefore, immediately and incontestably, that there is no such thing as any sort of motive that is in itself a bad one. If motives are good or bad, it is only on account of their effects; good on account of their tendency to produce pleasure or avert pain; bad on account of their tendency to produce pain or avert pleasure. Now the case is, that from one and the same motive, and from every kind of motive, may proceed actions that are good, others that are bad and others that are indifferent." Further, on p. 60, Bentham asks: "Is there nothing, then, about a man that can properly be termed good or bad, when on such or such an occasion he suffers himself to be governed by such or such a motive? Yes, certainly, his *disposition*. Now disposition is a kind of fictitious entity, feigned for the convenience of discourse, in order to express what there is supposed to be *permanent* in a man's frame of mind. It is with disposition as with everything else; it will be good or bad according to its effects." The first quotation, it will be noticed, simply states that the motive is in itself always good, while conduct (*i.e.*, consequences) may be good, bad or indifferent. The second quotation seems, however, to pass moral judgment upon character under the name of disposition. But disposition is judged according to the tendency of a person's actions. A good or bad disposition, here, can mean nothing intrinsic to the person, but only that the person has been observed to act in ways that usually produce pain or pleasure, as the case may be. The term is a "fiction," and is a backhanded way of expressing a somewhat habitual *result* of a given person's conduct his motive remaining good (or for pleasure) all the time. The agent would never pronounce any such judgment upon his own disposition, unless as a sort of surprise that, his motive being "good," his actions turn out so "bad" all the time. At most, the judgment regarding disposition is a sort of label put upon a man by others, a label of "Look out for him, he is dangerous," or, "Behold, a helpful man."

The moral standard of hedonism does not, then, bear any relation to the character of the agent, does not enable us to judge it, either as a whole or in any specific manifestation.

## xviii. It Does Not Give a Criterion for Concrete Acts

Pleasure, as the end, fails also to throw light on the moral value of any specific acts. Its failure in this respect is, indeed, only the other side of that just spoken of. There is no organizing principle, no "universal" on the basis of which various acts fall into a system or order. The moral life is left a series of shreds and patches, where each act is torn off, as to its moral value, from every other. Each act is right or wrong, according as *it* gives pleasure or pain, and independently of any whole of life. There is, indeed, no whole of moral life at all, but only a series of isolated, disconnected acts. Possession, passivity, *mere* feeling, by its very nature cannot unite—each feeling is itself and that is the end of it. It is action which reduces multiplicity to unity. We cannot say, in the hedonistic theory, that pleasure is the end, but *pleasures*.

Each act stands by itself—the only question is: What pleasure will *it* give? The settling of this question is the "hedonistic calculus." We must discover the intensity, duration, certainty, degree of nearness of the pleasure likely to arise from the given act, and also its purity, or likelihood of being accompanied by secondary pains and pleasures. Then we are to strike the balance between the respective sums on the pleasure and pain sides, and, according as this balance is one of pleasure or pain, the act is good or evil.

Bentham, *Principles of Morals*, p. 16, was the first to go into detail as to this method. He has also given certain memoriter verses stating "the points on which the whole fabric of morals and legislation may be seen to rest.

> *Intense, long, certain, speedy, fruitful, pure*
> *Such marks in pleasures and in pains endure,*
> *Such pleasures seek, if private be thy end.*
> *If it be public, wide let them extend.*
> *Such pains avoid whichever be thy view,*
> *If pains must come, let them extend to few.*"

This, however, in its reference to others, states the utilitarian as well as the hedonistic view.

Now, it must be remembered that, if pleasure is the end, there is no intrinsic connection between the motive of the act, and its result. It is not claimed that there is anything belonging intrinsically to the motive of the act which makes it result in pleasure or pain. To make such a claim would be to declare the moral quality of the act the criterion of the pleasure, instead of pleasure the criterion of the act. The pleasures are external to the act; they are irrelevant and accidental to its quality. There is no "universal," no intrinsic bond of connection between the act and its consequences. The consequence is a mere particular state of feeling, which, in this instance, the act has happened to bring about.

More concretely, this act of truth-telling has in this instance, brought about pleasure. Shall we call it right? Right in *this* instance, of course; but is it right generally? Is truth-telling, as such, right, or is it merely that this instance of it happens to be right? Evidently, on the hedonistic basis, we cannot get beyond the latter judgment. *Prior* to any act, there will be plenty of difficulties in telling whether it, as *particular*, is right or wrong. The consequences depend not merely on the result intended, but upon a multitude of circumstances outside of the foresight and control of the agent. And there can be only a precarious calculation of possibilities and probabilities—a method which would always favor laxity of conduct in all but the most conscientious of men, and which would throw the conscientious into uncertainty and perplexity in the degree of their conscientiousness.

"If once the pleas of instinct are to be abolished and replaced by a hedonistic arithmetic, the whole realm of animated nature has to be reckoned with in weaving the tissue of moral relations, and the problem becomes infinite and insoluble."—Martineau, *Types of Ethical Theory*, Vol. ii, p. 334.

But waive this; let the particular case be settled. There is still no law, no principle, indeed no presumption as to future conduct. The act is not right *because* it is *truth-telling*, but because, in this instance, circumstances were such as to throw a balance of pleasure in its favor. This establishes no certainty, no probability as to its next outcome. The result *then* will depend wholly upon circumstances existing *then*—circumstances which have no intrinsic relation to the act and which must change from time to time.

The hedonist would escape this abolition of all principle, or even rule, by falling back upon a number of cases—"past experience" it is called. We have found in a number of cases that a certain procedure has resulted in pleasure, and this result is sufficient to guide us in a vast number of cases which come up.

Says Mill (*Utilitarianism*, pp. 332–34): "During the whole past duration of the species, mankind have been learning by experience the tendencies of actions, on which experience all the prudence as well as all the morality of life are dependent. . . . Mankind must by this time have acquired positive belief as to the effects of some actions on their happiness; and the beliefs which have thus come down are the rules of morality for the multitude, and for the

philosopher, until he has succeeded in finding better. . . . Nobody
argues that the art of navigation is not founded on astronomy, because sailors cannot wait to calculate the 'Nautical Almanac.' Being
rational creatures, they go to sea with it ready calculated; and all
rational creatures go out upon the sea of life with their minds made
up on the common questions of right and wrong, as well as on many
of the far more difficult questions of wise and foolish."

That we do learn from experience the moral nature of
actions is undoubted. The only question is: *if* hedonism
were true, *could* we so learn? Suppose that I were convinced
that the results of murder in the past had been generally, or
even without exception (though this could not be proved),
painful; as long as the act and the result in the way of
feeling (pain or pleasure) are conceived as having no intrinsic connection, this would not prove that in the present
instance murder will give a surplus of pain. I am not thinking of committing murder in general, but of murder under
certain specific present circumstances. These circumstances
may, and, to some extent, *must* vary from all previous
instances of murder. How then can I reason from them to it?
Or, rather, let me use the previous cases as much as I may,
the moral quality of the act I am now to perform must still
be judged not from them, but from the circumstances of the
present case. To judge otherwise, is, on hedonistic principles, to be careless, perhaps criminally careless as to one's
conduct. The more convinced a man is of the truth of
hedonism and the more conscientious he is, the more he is
bound *not* to be guided by previous circumstances, but to
form his judgment anew concerning the new case. This
result flows out of the very nature of the hedonistic ideal.
Pleasure is not an activity, but simply a particular feeling,
enduring only while it is felt. Moreover, there is in it no
principle which connects it intrinsically with any *kind* of
action. To suppose then that, because ninety-nine cases of
murder have resulted in pain, the hundredth will, is on a par
with reasoning that because ninety-nine days have been
frosty, the hundreth will be. Each case, taken as particular,
must be decided wholly by itself. There is no continuous
moral life, and no system of conduct. There is only a succession of unlike acts.

Mill, in his examination of Whewell, (*Dissertations*, Vol. III, pp. 158–59), tries to establish a general principle, if not a universal law, by arguing that, even in exceptional cases, the agent is bound to respect the rule, because to act otherwise would weaken the rule, and thus lead to its being disregarded in other cases, in which its observance results in pleasure. There are, he says, persons so wicked that their removal from the earth would undoubtedly increase the sum total of happiness. But if persons were to violate the general rule in these cases, it would tend to destroy the rule. "If it were thought allowable for any one to put to death at pleasure any human being whom he believes that the world would be well rid of,—nobody's life would be safe." That is to say, if every one were really to act upon and carry out the hedonistic principle, no rule of life would exist. This does very well as a *reductio ad absurdum* of hedonism, or as an argument against adopting hedonism, but it is difficult to see how Mill thought that it established a "rule" on a hedonistic basis. Mill's argument comes to saying that if hedonism were uniformly acted upon, it would defeat itself—that is, pleasure would not result. Therefore, in order to get pleasure, we must not act upon the principle of hedonism at all, but follow a general rule. Otherwise put: hedonism gives no general rule, but we must have a general rule to make hedonism work and therefore there is a general rule! This begging of the question comes out even more plainly as Mill goes on: "If one person may break through the rule on his own judgment, the same liberty cannot be refused to others; and, since no one could rely on the rule's being observed, the rule would cease to exist." All of this is obviously true, but it amounts to saying: "We *must* have a rule, and this we would not have if we carried out the hedonistic principle in each case; therefore, we must not carry it out." A principle, that carried out destroys all rules which pretend to rest upon it, lays itself open to suspicion. Mill assumes the entire question in assuming that there is a rule. Grant this, and the necessity of not "making exceptions," that is, of not applying the hedonistic standard to each case, on its own merits, follows. But the argument which Mill needs to meet is that hedonism *requires* us to apply the standard to each case in itself, and that, therefore, there *is* no rule. Mill simply says—*assume* the rule, and it follows, etc.

See Bradley, *Ethical Studies*, pp. 96–101; Green, *Prolegomena*, Bk. IV, Ch. 3; Martineau, *Types of Ethical Theory*, Vol. II, pp. 329–34.

# XIX. The Sum and Quality of Pleasure as the Standard

We have been dealing with hedonism in its strict form —that which makes *a* pleasure, considered as to its intensity, certainty, etc., the end of an act. Hedonism in this form fails to unify life, and fails, therefore, to supply any standard. But the end of conduct is often stated to be the greatest possible sum of pleasures, thus introducing a certain element of generality. Mill goes further and brings in the idea of quality of pleasure.

Regarding the sum of pleasures the following from Sidgwick (*Methods of Ethics*, p. 382; see also p. 114) gives the hedonistic statement. "The assumption is involved that all pleasures are capable of being compared qualitatively with one another and with all pains; that every feeling has a certain intensive quality, positive or negative (or perhaps zero) in respect to its desirableness and that the quantity may be known, so that each may be weighed in ethical scales against any other. This assumption is involved in the very notion of maximum happiness," as the attempt to make "as great as possible a sum of elements not quantitatively commensurable would be a mathematical absurdity."

## 1. *Sum of Pleasures as the Moral End*

This first, taken as criterion, comes into conflict with the hedonistic psychology of pleasure as the motive of acts; and, secondly, it requires some objective standard by means of which pleasure is to be summed, and is, in so far, a surrender of the whole hedonistic position.

*a*] If the object of desire is pleasure or a state of feeling which exists only as it is felt, it is impossible that we should desire a greatest sum of pleasures. We can desire a pleasure and that only. It is not even possible that we should ever desire a continuous series of pleasures. We can desire one pleasure and when that is gone, another, but we cannot unify our desires enough to aim at even a sum of pleasures.

This is well put by Green (*Prolegomena*, p. 236). "For the feeling of a pleased person, or in relation to his sense of enjoyment, pleasure cannot form a sum. However numerous the sources of a state of pleasant feeling, it is one and is over before another can be enjoyed. It and its successors can be added together in thought, but not in enjoyment or in imagination of an enjoyment. If the desire is only for pleasure, *i.e.*, for an enjoyment or feeling of pleasure, we are simply victims of words when we talk of desire for a sum of pleasures, much more when we take the greatest imaginable sum to be the most desirable." See the whole passage, pp. 235–46.

*b*] But the phrase "sum of pleasures" undoubtedly has a meaning—though the fact that it has a meaning shows the untruth of the hedonistic psychology. Surrendering this psychology, what shall we say of the maximum possibility of pleasure as the criterion of the morality of acts? It must be conceded that this conception does afford some basis—although a rather slippery one—for the unification of conduct. Each act is considered now not in its isolation merely, but in its connection with other acts, according as its relation to them may increase or decrease the possible sum of future happiness. But this very fact that some universal, or element of relation, albeit a quantitative one, has been introduced, arouses this inquiry: Whence do we derive it? How do we get the thought of a sum of pleasure, and of a maximum sum? *Only by taking into account the objective conditions upon which pleasures depend, and by judging the pleasures from the standpoint of these objective conditions.* When we imagine we are thinking of a sum of pleasures, we are really thinking of that totality of conditions which will come nearest affording us self-satisfaction—we are thinking of a comprehensive and continuous activity whose various parts are adjusted to one another. Because it is complete activity, it is necessarily conceived as giving the greatest possible pleasure, but apart from reference to complete activity and apart from the objects in which this is realized, the phrase "greatest sum of happiness" is a mere phrase. Pleasures must be measured by a standard, by a yard stick, before they can be summed in thought, and the yard stick we use is the activity in which the pleasure comes. We do not measure conduct by pleasure, but we compare and sum up pleasures on the basis of the objects which occasion them. To add feelings, mere transitory consequences, without first reducing those feelings to a common denominator by their relation to one objective standard, is an impossibility. Pleasure is a sort of sign or symbol of the object which satisfies, and we may carry on our judgment, if we will, in terms of the sign, without reference to the standard, but to argue as if the sign were the thing, as if the sum of pleasure were the activity, is suicidal.

Thus Green says (*Prolegomena*, p. 244): "In truth a man's reference to his own true happiness is a reference to the objects which chiefly interest him, and has its controlling power on that account. More strictly, it is a reference to an ideal state of well-being, a state in which he shall be satisfied; *but the objects of the man's chief interests supply the filling of that ideal state.*" See the argument as put by Alexander (*Moral Order and Progress*, pp. 199–200). Alexander has also brought out (*Moral Order*, pp. 207–10) that even if we are going to use a quantitative standard, the idea of a sum is not a very happy one. It is not so much a sum of pleasures we want, as a certain proportionate distribution and combination of pleasures. "To regard the greatest sum of pleasures as the test of conduct, supposing that we could express it in units of pleasure, would be like declaring that when you had an atomic weight of 98 you had sulphuric acid. The numerical test would be useless unless we knew what elements were to be combined, and in what proportion. Similarly till we know what kinds of activities (and therefore what kinds of pleasures) go with one another to form the end, the greatest sum of pleasures will give us only the equivalent of the end, but will not tell us what the composition of the end is, still less how to get at it; or, to put the matter more simply, when we know what the characters of persons are, and how they are combined in morality, we then estimate the corresponding sum of pleasures" (p. 209).

## 2. *A Certain Quality of Pleasure the End*

Some moralists, notably John Stuart Mill, introduce considerations regarding the quality of pleasure into the conception of the end. "It is quite compatible," says Mill, "with the principle of utility to recognize the fact that some kinds of pleasure are more desirable and more valuable than others" (*Utilitarianism*, p. 310). Is it compatible? Is kind of pleasure the same thing as pleasure? Does not strict hedonism demand that all kinds of pleasure equally present as to intensity in consciousness shall be of the same value? To say otherwise is to give up pleasure as such as the standard and to hold that we have means for discriminating the respective values of pleasures which simply, *as feelings*, are the same. It is to hold, that is to say, that there is some standard of value external to the pleasures as such, by means of which their moral quality may be judged. In this case, this independent standard is the real moral criterion which we are employing. Hedonism is surrendered.

Kant's position on this point seems impregnable. "It is surprising," he says, "that men otherwise astute can think it possible to distinguish between higher and lower desires, according as the ideas which are connected with the feeling of pleasure have their origin in the senses or in the understanding; for when we inquire what are the determining grounds of desire, and place them in some expected pleasantness, it is of no consequence whence the *idea* of this pleasing object is derived, but only how much it *pleases.* . . . The only thing that concerns one, in order to decide choice, is how great, how long continued, how easily obtained and how often repeated, this agreeableness is. For as to the man who wants money to spend, it is all the same whether the gold was dug out of the mountain or washed out of the sand, provided it is everywhere accepted at the same value; so the man who cares only for the enjoyment of life does not ask whether the ideas are of the understanding or the senses, but only *how much* and *how great pleasure* they will give for the longest time."

See also Bradley, *Ethical Studies*, pp. 105–10.

When we ask how the differences in quality are established and how we translate this qualitative difference into moral difference, the surrender of pleasure as the standard becomes even more evident. We must know not only the fact of different qualities, but how to decide which is "higher" than any other. We must bring the qualities before a tribunal of judgment which applies to them some standard of measurement. In themselves qualities may be different, but they are not higher and lower. What is the tribunal and what is the law of judgment? According to Mill the tribunal is the preference of those who are acquainted with both kinds of pleasure.

"Of two pleasures, if there be one to which all, or almost all who have experience of both, give a decided preference, irrespective of any feeling of moral obligation to prefer it, that is the more desirable pleasure." It is an unquestionable fact that such differences exist. "Few human creatures would consent to be changed into any of the lower animals for a promise of the fullest allowance of a beast's pleasures. No intelligent person would consent to be a fool; no instructed person would be an ignoramus; no person of feeling and conscience would be selfish and base, even though they should be persuaded that the fool, the dunce or the rascal is better satisfied with his lot than they are with theirs. . . . It is better to be a human being dissatisfied, than a pig satisfied; better to be a Socrates dissatisfied, than a fool satisfied. And if the fool or the pig are of a different opinion, it is because they only know their own side of the question. The other party to the comparison knows both sides."— Mill, *Utilitarianism*, pp. 311–13. And in an omitted portion Mill says the reason that one of the higher faculty would prefer a suffering which goes along with that higher capacity, to more pleasure on a lower plane, is something of which "the most appropriate appellation is a sense of dignity, which all human beings possess in one form or another."

A question immediately arises regarding this standard of preferability. Is it the mere historical fact that some man, who has experienced both, prefers A to B that makes A more desirable? Surely I might say that if that person prefers A, A is more desirable to him, but that I for my part prefer B, and that I do not intend to give up my preference. And why should I, even though thousands of other men happened to prefer A? B is the greater pleasure, none the less, to me, and as a hedonist I must cling to the only standard that I have. The hedonists, in a word, have appealed to feeling, and to feeling they must go for judgment. And feeling exists only as it is felt and only to him who feels it.

On the other hand, perhaps it is not the bare fact that some men prefer one pleasure to another that makes it more desirable, but something in the character of the men who prefer. And this is what Mill implies. It is a "sense of dignity" belonging to man which makes his judgment of pleasure better than that of animals; it is the human being against the pig, Socrates against the fool, the good man against the rascal. This is the complete surrender of hedonism, and the all but explicit assertion that human character, goodness, wisdom, are the criteria of pleasure, instead of pleasure the criterion of character and goodness. Mill's "sense of dignity," which is to be considered in all estimates of pleasures, is just the sense of a moral (or active) capacity and destiny belonging to man. To refer pleasures to *this* is to make it the standard, and with this standard the anti-hedonist may well be content, while asking, however, for its further analysis.

To sum up our long discussion of pleasure as a criterion of conduct in respect of its unity, we may say: Pleasure, *as it actually exists in man*, may be taken as *a* criterion, although not the really primary one, of action. But this is not hedonism; for pleasure as it *exists* is something more than pleasurable feeling; it is qualified through and through by the kind of action which it accompanies, by the kind of objects which the activity comprehends. And thus it is always a secondary criterion. The moment we begin to analyze we must ask what *kind of activity*, what kind of object it is which the pleasure accompanies and of which it is a symbol. We may, if we will, calculate a man's wealth in terms of dollars and cents; but this is only because we can translate the money, the symbol, into goods, the reality. To desire pleasure instead of an activity of self, is to substitute symbol for fact, and a symbol cut off from fact ceases to be a symbol. Pleasure, as the hedonist treats it, mere agreeable feeling without active and thus objective relationships, is wholly an abstraction. Since an abstraction, to make it the end of desire results in self-contradiction; while to make it the standard of conduct is to deprive life of all unity, all system, in a word—of all standard.

## xx. The Failure of Pleasure as a Standard to Unify Conduct Socially

Thus far our examination of the hedonistic criterion has been devoted to showing that it will not make a system out of individual conduct. We have now to recognize the fact that pleasure is not a common good, and therefore fails to give a social unity to conduct—that is, it does not offer an end for which men may co-operate, or a good which reached by one must be shared by another. No argument is needed to show, theoretically, that any proposed moral criterion must, in order to be valid, harmonize the interests and activities of different men, or to show, practically, that the whole tendency of the modern democratic and philanthropic movement has been to discover and realize a good in which men shall share on the basis of an equal principle. It is contended that hedonism fails to satisfy these needs. According to it, the end for each man is his own pleasure. Pleasure is nothing objective in which men may equally participate. It is purely individual in the most exclusive sense of that term. It is a state of feeling and can be enjoyed only while felt, and only by the one who feels it. To set it up for the ideal of conduct is to turn life into an exclusive and excluding struggle for possession of the means of personal enjoyment; it is to erect into a principle the idea of the war of all against all. No end more thoroughly disintegrating than individual agreeable sensation could well be imagined.

> Says Kant, (p. 116 of Abbott's trans., entitled *Kant's Theory of Ethics*), on the basis of the desire of happiness "there results a harmony like that which a certain satirical poem depicts as existing between a married couple bent on going to ruin: O, marvellous harmony, what he wishes, she wishes also; or like what is said of the pledge of Francis I to the emperor Charles V, what my brother Charles wishes that I wish also (viz., Milan)."

Almost all modern moralists who take pleasure as the end conceive it to be not individual pleasure, but the happiness of all men or even of all sentient creatures. Thus we are brought to the consideration of Utilitarianism.

> Says Mill, (*Utilitarianism*, p. 323), "The happiness which forms the Utilitarian standard of what is right in conduct is not the agent's own happiness, but that of all concerned; as between his own happiness and that of others, Utilitarianism requires him to be as strictly impartial as a disinterested and benevolent spectator." And (p. 315) the Utilitarian standard is "not the agent's own greatest happiness, but the greatest amount of happiness altogether." See also Sidgwick (*Methods of Ethics*, p. 379), "By Utilitarianism is here meant the ethical theory, first distinctly formulated by Bentham, that the conduct which, under any given circumstances is externally or objectively right is that which will produce the greatest amount of happiness *on the whole*; that is, taking into account all whose happiness is affected by the conduct. It would tend to clearness if we might call this principle, and the method based upon it, by some such name as Universalistic hedonism." As popularly put, the utilitarian standard is the "greatest happiness of the greatest number." While in its calculation "each is to count for one and only one" (Bentham). And finally Bain (*Emotions and Will*, p. 303), "Utility is opposed to the selfish theory, for, as propounded, it always implies the good of society generally, and the subordination of individual interests to the general good."

## XXI. Criticism of Utilitarianism

The utilitarian theory certainly does away entirely with one of the two main objections to hedonism—its failure to provide a general, as distinct from a private end. The question which we have to meet, however, is whether this extension of the end from the individual to society is consistent with the fundamental principles of hedonism. *How* do we get from individual pleasure to the happiness of all?

An intuitional utilitarian, like Sidgwick, has ready an answer which is not open to the empirical utilitarians, like Bentham, Mill and Bain. *Methods of Ethics*, Bk. III, Chs. 13–14, p. 355. "We may obtain the *self-evident principle* that the good of any one individual is of no more importance, as a part of universal good, than the good of any other. The abstract principle of the duty of benevolence, *so far as it is cognizable by direct intuition*" is, "that one is morally bound to regard the good of any other individual as much as one's own"—and p. 364, "*the principles, so far as they are immediately known by abstract intuition*, can only be stated as precepts to seek (1) one's own good on the whole, and (2) the good of any other no less than one's own, in so far as it is no less an element of universal good." Sidgwick, that is, differs in two important points from most utilitarians. He holds that pleasure is not the sole, or even the usual object of desire. And he holds that we have an immediate faculty of rational intuition which informs us that the good of others is as desirable an end of our conduct as is our own happiness. Our former arguments against pleasure as the *end*, bear, of course, equally against this theory, but not the following arguments. Criticisms of this position of Sidgwick's will be found in Green (*Prolegomena*, pp. 406–15); Bradley (*Ethical Studies*, pp. 114–17).

The popular answer to the question how we get from individual to general happiness, misses the entire point of the question. This answer simply says that happiness is "*intrinsically* desirable." Let it be so; but "happiness" in this general way is a mere abstraction. Happiness is always a particular condition of one particular person. Whose happiness is desirable and *to whom*? Because my happiness is intrinsically desirable to me, does it follow that your happiness is intrinsically desirable to me? Indeed, in the hedonistic psychology, is it not nonsense to say that a state of your feeling is desirable to me? Mill's amplified version of the popular answer brings out the ambiguity all the more plainly. He says (*Utilitarianism*, p. 349), "No reason can be given why the general happiness is desirable, except that each person, so far as he believes it to be obtainable, desires his own happiness. This, however, being a fact, we have not only all the proof which the case admits of, but all which it is possible to require, that happiness is a good; that each person's happiness is a good to that person; and the general happiness, therefore, a good to the aggregate of all persons." But does it follow that because the happiness of A is an end to A, the happiness of B an end to B, and the happiness of C an end to C, that, therefore, the happiness of B and C is an end to A? There is obviously no connection between the premises and the supposed conclusion. And there appears to be, as Mill puts it, only an account of the ambiguity of his last clause, "the general happiness a good to the aggregate of all persons." The good of A and B and C may be a good to the aggregate (A + B + C), but what universalistic hedonism requires is that the aggregate good of A + B + C, be a good to A and to B and to C taken separately—a very different proposition. Mill is guilty of the fallacy known logically as the fallacy of division—arguing from a collective whole to the distributed units. Because all men want to be happy, it hardly follows that every man wants all to be happy. There is, accordingly, no *direct* road from individualistic hedonism—private pleasure—to universalistic—general pleasure. Moreover, if we adopt the usual psychology of hedonism and say that pleasure is the motive of acting, it is absolutely absurd to say that general pleasure can be a motive. How can I be moved by the happiness which exists in some one else? I may feel a pleasure resembling his, and be moved by it, but that is quite a different matter.

## XXII. Indirect Means of Identifying Private and General Pleasure

Is there any *indirect* method of going from the pleasure of one to the pleasure of all? Upon the whole, the utilitarians do not claim that there is any natural and immediate connection between the desire for private and for general happiness, but suppose that there are certain means which are instrumental in bringing about an identity. Of these means the sympathetic emotions and the influence of law and of education are the chief. Each of these, moreover, co-operates with the other.

## 1. Sympathetic and Social Emotions

We are so constituted by nature that we take pleasure in the happiness of others and feel pain in their misery. A proper regard for our own welfare must lead us, therefore, to take an interest in the pleasure of others. Our own feelings, moreover, are largely influenced by the feelings of others toward us. If we act in a certain way we shall incur the disapprobation of others, and this, independently of any overt punishment it may lead them to inflict upon us, arouses feelings of shame, of inferiority, of being under the displeasure of others, feelings all of which are decidedly painful. The more enlightened our judgment, the more we see how our pleasures are bound up in those of others.

"The Dictates of Utility" (Bentham, *Principles of Morals*, p. 56), "are neither more nor less than the dictates of the most extensive and enlightened (that is, well advised) benevolence," and (p. 18), "The pleasures of benevolence are the pleasures resulting from the view of any pleasures supposed to be possessed by the beings who may be the objects of benevolence. . . . These may also be called the pleasures of good will, the pleasures of sympathy, or the pleasures of the benevolent or social affections"; and (pp. 143–44), "What motives (independent of such as legislation and religion may choose to furnish) can one man have to consult the happiness of another? . . . In answer to this, it cannot but be admitted that the only interests which a man at all times and upon all occasions is sure to find *adequate* motives for consulting, are his own. Notwithstanding this, there are no occasions in which a man has not some motives for consulting the happiness of other men. In the first place he has, on all occasions, the purely social motive of sympathy and benevolence; in the next place he has, on most occasions, the semi-social motives of love of amity and love of reputation." And so in the *Deontology*, which, however, was not published by Bentham himself, p. 203, "The more enlightened one is, the more one forms the habit of general benevolence, because it is seen that the interests of men combine with each other in more points than they conflict in."

## 2. Education and Law

Education, working directly and internally upon the feelings, and government, appealing to them from without through commands and penalties, are constantly effecting an increasing identity of self-interest and regard for others.

These means supplement the action of sympathy and the more instinctive emotions. They stimulate and even induce a proper interest in the pleasures of others. In governmental law, with its punishments, we have an express instrument for making the pleasures of one harmonize with (or at least not conflict with) the pleasures of others.

Thus Bentham, after stating that an enlightened mind perceives the identity of self-interest and that of others (or of *egoism* and *altruism*, as these interests are now commonly called), goes on (*Deontology*, p. 201): "The majority do not have sufficient enlightenment, nor enough moral feeling so that their character goes beyond the aid of laws, and so the legislator should supplement the frailty of this natural interest, in adding to it an artificial interest more appreciable and more continuous. Thus the government augments and extends the connexion which exists between prudence and benevolence." Mill says (*Utilitarianism*, p. 323): "To do as you would be done by, and to love your neighbor as yourself, constitute the ideal perfection of utilitarian morality. As the means of making the nearest approach to this ideal, utility would enjoin, first, that laws and social arrangements should place the happiness or the interest of every individual as nearly as possible in harmony with the interest of the whole; and, secondly, that education and opinion, which have so vast a power over human character, should so use that power as to establish in the mind of every individual an indissoluble association between his own happiness and the good of the whole."

## XXIII. Private Pleasures and General Welfare

In criticism of these indirect methods of establishing the identity of "egoism" and "altruism," it may be said:

*1.* That the supposed relation between the private and the general happiness is extrinsic, and hence always accidental and open to exception.

It is not contended that there is any order which *morally* demands that there be an identity of interests. It is simply argued that there are certain physical and psychological forces which operate, *as matter of fact*, to bring about such a result. Now we may admit, if we like, that such forces exist and that they are capable of accomplishing all that Bentham and Mill claim for them. But all that is established is, at most, a certain state of facts which is interesting as a state of facts, but which has no especial moral bearing. It is not pretended that there is in the very order of things any necessary and intrinsic connection between the happiness of one and of another. Such identity as exists, therefore, must be a mere external result of the action of certain forces. It is accidental. This being the case, how can it constitute the universal ideal of action? Why is it not open for an agent, under exceptional circumstances, to act for his own pleasure, to the exclusion of that of others? We may admit that, upon the whole (or that always, though this is wholly impossible to prove) in past experience, personal pleasure has been best attained by a certain regard for the pleasures of others; but the connection being wholly empirical (that is, of past instances and not of an intrinsic law), we may ask how it can be claimed that the same connection is *certain* to hold in this new case? Nor is it probable that any one would claim that the connection between individual pleasure and general pleasure had been so universal and invariable in past experience.

*Intrinsic moral considerations* (that is, those based on the very nature of human action) being put aside, a pretty strong case could be made out for the statement that individual happiness is best attained by ignoring the happiness of others. Probably the most that can be established on the other side is that a due prudence dictates that *some* attention be paid to the pleasures of others, in calculating one's own pleasures.

And this suggests:

2. That the end is still private pleasure, general pleasure being simply a means. Granting all that the hedonists urge, what their arguments prove is not that the general pleasure is the end of action, but that, private pleasure being the end, regard for the pleasures of others is one of the most efficient means of reaching it. If private pleasure is a selfish end, the end is not less selfish because the road to it happens to bring pleasure to others also.

See Royce, *Religious Aspect of Philosophy*, pp. 61–74.

3. The use of education and law to bring about this identity, presupposes that we already have the *ideal* of the

identity as something desirable to realize—it takes for
granted the very thing to be proved. Why should it occur to
men to use the private influence of opinion and education,
and the public influences of law and penalty to identify
private welfare with public, unless they were already convinced that general welfare was the end of conduct, the one
desirable thing? What the hedonist has to do is to show
how, from the end of private happiness, we may get to the
end of general happiness. What Bentham and Mill do show
is, that if we take general happiness as the end, we may and
do use education and law to bring about an identity of
personal and general pleasures. This may go undoubted, but
the question how we get the general happiness as the end,
the good, remains unanswered.

Nor is this all. The conception of general happiness,
taken by itself, has all the abstractness, vagueness and
uncertainty of that of personal happiness, multiplied indefinitely by the greater number of persons introduced. To
calculate the effects of actions upon the general happiness—
when happiness is interpreted as a state of feeling—is an
impossibility. And thus it is that when one is speaking of
pleasures one is really thinking of welfare, or well-being, or
satisfied and progressive human lives. Happiness is considered as it would be, if determined by certain active and well
defined interests, and thus the hedonistic theory, while con-
tradicting itself, gets apparently all the support of an opposed theory. Universalistic hedonism thus, more or less
expressly, takes for granted a social order, or community of
persons, of which the agent is simply one member like any
other. This is the ideal which it proposes to realize. In this
way—although at the cost of logical suicide—the ideal gets a
content and a definiteness upon which it is possible to base
judgments.

That this social organization of persons is the ideal which Mill
is actually thinking of, rather than any succession of states of
agreeable sensation, is evident by his treatment of the whole subject.
Mill is quite clear that education and opinion may produce *any* sort
of feeling, as well as truly benevolent motives to actions. For
example, in his critique of Whewell, he says, (*Dissertations*, Vol. III,
p. 154): "All experience shows that the moral feelings are preëmi-

nently artificial, and the products of culture; that even when reasonable, they are no more spontaneous than the growth of corn and wine (which are quite as natural), and that the most senseless and pernicious feeling can as easily be raised to the utmost intensity by inculcation, as hemlock and thistles could be reared to luxuriant growth by sowing them instead of wheat." It is certainly implied here that legislation, education and public opinion must have as a presupposed standard the identity of general and private interests or else they may produce anything whatever. That is to say, Mill instead of arriving at his result of general happiness simply takes it for granted.

This fact and the further fact that he virtually defines happiness through certain objective interests and ends (thus reversing the true hedonistic position) is obvious from the following, (Mill, *Utilitarianism*, pp. 343–47): After again stating that the moral feelings are capable of cultivation in almost any direction, and stating that moral associations that are of artificial construction dissolve through the force of intellectual analysis (*cf.* his *Autobiography*, p. 136), and that the association of pleasure with the feeling of duty would similarly dissolve unless it had a *natural* basis of sentiment, he goes on: "But there is this basis of powerful *natural* sentiment. This firm foundation is that of the social feelings of mankind; the desire to be in unity with our fellow-creatures. *The social state is at once so natural, so necessary, and so habitual to man that except in some unusual circumstances, or by an effort of voluntary abstraction he never conceives of himself otherwise than as a member of a body.* Any condition, therefore, which is essential to a state of society becomes more and more an inseparable part of every person's conception of the state of things which he is born into, and which is the destiny of a human being." Mill then goes on to describe some of the ways in which the social unity manifests itself and influences the individual's conduct. Then the latter "comes, as though instinctively, to be conscious of himself as a being who *of course* pays regard to others. The good of others becomes to him a thing naturally and necessarily to be attended to, like any of the physical conditions of our existence. *The deeply-rooted conception which every individual even now has of himself as a social being tends to make him feel it as one of his natural wants, that there should be harmony between his feelings and aims and those of his fellow-creatures.* This conviction is the ultimate sanction of the greatest happiness morality."

It is to be noticed that there are involved in this account three ideas, any one of which involves such a reconstruction of the pleasure theory as to be a surrender of hedonism.

*1.* There is, in one instance, a *natural* (or intrinsic) connection between the end of conduct and the feelings, and not simply an external or artificial bond. This is in the case

of the social feelings. In other words, in one case the ideal,
that is, happiness, is intrinsically, or necessarily connected
with a certain kind of conduct, that flowing from the social
impulses. This, of course, reverses hedonism for it makes
happiness dependent upon a certain kind of conduct, instead
of determining the nature of conduct according as it happens to result in pleasure or pain.

2. Man conceives of himself, of his end or of his
destiny as a member of a social body, and this conception
determines the nature of his wants and aims. That is to say,
it is not mere happiness that a man wants, but a certain *kind*
of happiness, that which would satisfy a man who conceived
of himself as social, or having ends and interests in common
with others.

3. Finally, it is not mere general "happiness" which is
the end, at all. It is social unity; "harmony of feelings and
aims," a beneficial condition for one's self in which the
benefits of all are included. Instead of the essentially vague
idea of states of pleasurable sensation we have the conception of a community of interests and ends, in securing
which alone is true happiness to be found. This conception
of the moral ideal we regard as essentially true, but it is not
hedonism. It gives up wholly the notion that pleasure is the
*desired*, and, since it sets up a standard by which it determines pleasure, it gives up equally the notion that pleasure
as such is the *desirable*.

In addition to the works already referred to, the following will
give fuller ideas of hedonism and utilitarianism: For historical
treatment see Sidgwick, *History of Ethics*; Jodl, *Geschichte der
Ethik*, Vol. II, pp. 432–68; Bain, *Moral Science*, [Historical Men-
tion]; Guyau, *La Morale Anglaise Contemporaine*; Wallace, *Epicu-
reanism*; Pater, *Marius, the Epicurean*; Paley, *Moral and Political
Philosophy*; Grote, *Examination of the Utilitarian Philosophy* (especially fair and valuable criticism); Lecky, *History of European
Morals*, Vol. I, Ch. 1; Birks, *Utilitarianism* (hostile); Blackie, *Four
Phases of Morals*, essay on "Utilitarianism" (hostile); Gizycki,
*Students' Manual of Ethical Philosophy* (Coit's trans., favorable);
Calderwood, *Handbook of Moral Philosophy* (opposed); Laurie,
*Ethica* (*e.g.*, p. 37). "The object of will is not pleasure, not yet
happiness, but reason-given law—the law of harmony; but this
necessarily ascertained through feeling, and, therefore, through hap-
piness."

Wilson and Fowler, *Principles of Morals*, Vol. i, pp. 98–112; Vol. ii, pp. 262–73; Paulsen, *System der Ethik*, pp. 195–210.

## xxiv. The Utilitarian Theory Combined With the Doctrine of Evolution

There has lately been an attempt to combine utilitarian morality with the theory of evolution. This position, chiefly as occupied by Herbert Spencer and Leslie Stephen, we shall now examine.

Alexander, also, *Moral Order and Progress*, makes large use of the theory of evolution, but does not attempt to unite it with any form of hedonism.

For the combination, at least three decided advantages are claimed over ordinary utilitarianism.

*1.* It transforms "empirical rules" into "rational laws." The evolutionary hedonists regard pleasure as the good, but hold that the theory of evolution enables them to judge *of the relation of acts to pleasure* much better than the ordinary theory. As Mr. Spencer puts it, the ordinary theory is not scientific, because it does not fully recognize the principle of causation as existing between certain acts as causes, and pleasures (or pains) as effects. It undoubtedly recognizes that some acts *do* result in pain or pleasure, but does not show *how* or *why* they so result. By the aid of the theory of evolution we can demonstrate that certain acts *must* be beneficial because furthering evolution, and others painful because retarding it.

Spencer, *Data of Ethics*, pp. 57–58. "Morality properly so-called—the science of right conduct—has for its object to determine *how* and *why* certain rules of conduct are detrimental, and certain other rules beneficial. Those good and bad results cannot be accidental, but must be necessary consequences of the constitution of things; and I conceive it to be the business of moral science to *deduce, from the laws of life and the conditions of existence,* what kinds of action *necessarily* tend to produce happiness, and what kinds to produce unhappiness. Having done this, its deductions are to be recognized as laws of conduct; and are to be conformed to irrespective of a direct estimation of happiness or misery. . . . The objection which I have to the current utilitarianism is, that it recognizes no more developed form of utility—does not see that it has reached but the initial stage of moral science. . . . It is supposed that in future, as now, utility is to be determined only by observation of results; and that there is no possibility of knowing by deduction from fundamental principles what conduct *must* be detrimental and what conduct *must* be beneficial." *Cf*. also Ch. 9, and Stephen, *Science of Ethics*, Ch. 9.

It is contended, then, that by the use of the evolutionary theory, we may substitute certain conditions, which in the very nature of things tend to produce happiness, for a calculation, based upon observation of more or less varying cases in the past, of the probable results of the specific action. Thus we get a fixed objective standard and do away with all the objections based upon the uncertainty, vagueness and liability to exceptions, of the ordinary utilitarian morality.

Spencer, *Data of Ethics*, p. 162: "When alleging that empirical utilitarianism is but introductory to rational utilitarianism I pointed out that the last does not take welfare for its *immediate* object of pursuit, but takes for its immediate object of pursuit conformity to certain principles which, in the nature of things, causally determine welfare."

2. It reconciles "intuitionalism" with "empiricism." The theory of evolution not only gives us an objective standard on which happiness necessarily depends, and from which we may derive our laws of conduct, instead of deriving them from observation of particular cases, but it enables us to recognize that there are certain moral ideas now innate or intuitive. The whole human race, the whole animal race, has for an indefinite time been undergoing experiences of what leads to pleasure and of what leads to pain, until finally the results of these experiences have become organized into our very physical and mental make-up. The first point was that we could substitute for consideration of results consideration of the causes which determine these results; the present point is that so far as we have to use results, we can use those of the race, instead of the short span of the individual's life.

Spencer, *Data of Ethics*, pp. 123–24. "The experiences of utility organized and consolidated through all past generations of the

human race have been producing corresponding nervous modifications, which, by continued transmission and accumulation, have
become in us certain faculties of moral intuition—certain emotions
corresponding to right and wrong conduct, which have no apparent
basis in the individual experiences of utility. . . . The evolution
hypothesis thus enables us to reconcile opposed moral theories. . . .
The doctrine of innate powers of moral perception become congruous
with the utilitarian doctrine, when it is seen that preferences and
aversions are rendered organic by inheritance of the effects of
pleasurable and painful experiences in progenitors."

3. It reconciles "egoism" with "altruism." As we
have seen, the relation of personal pleasure to general happiness presents very serious difficulties to hedonism. It is
claimed, however, that the very process of evolution necessitates a certain identity. The being which survives must be
the being which has properly adapted himself to his environment, which is largely social, and there is assurance that the
conduct will be adapted to the environment just in the
degree in which pleasure is taken in acts which concern the
welfare of others. If an agent has no pleasure in such acts he
will either not perform them, or perform them only occasionally, and thus will not meet the conditions of surviving.
If surrounding conditions demand constantly certain actions, those actions in time must come to be pleasurable.
The conditions of survival demand altruistic action, and
hence such action must become pleasurable to the agent
(and in that sense egotistic).

"From the laws of life (Spencer, *Data of Ethics*, p. 250) it
must be concluded that unceasing social discipline will so mould
human action, that eventually sympathetic pleasures will be pursued
to the fullest extent advantageous to each and all. . . . Though
pleasure may be gained by giving pleasure, yet the thought of the
sympathetic pleasure to be gained will not occupy consciousness, but
only the thought of the pleasure given."

## xxv. Criticism of Evolutionary Utilitarianism

Regarding the whole foregoing scheme, it may be said
so far as it is true, or suggestive of truth, it is not hedonistic.
It does not judge actions from their effects in the way of
pleasure or pain, but it judges pleasures from the basis of an
independent standard "in the nature of things." It is ex-

pressly declared that happiness is not to be so much the end, as the *test* of conduct, and it is not happiness in general, of every sort and kind, but a certain kind of happiness, happiness conditioned by certain modes of activity, that is the test. Spencer's hedonism in its final result hardly comes to more than saying that in the case of a perfect individual in a perfect society, every action whatever would be accompanied by pleasure, and that, therefore, *in such a society*, pleasure would be an infallible sign and test of the morality of action—a position which is not denied by any ethical writer whatever, unless a few extreme ascetics. Such a position simply determines the value of pleasure by an independent criterion, and then goes on to say *of pleasure so determined*, that it is the test of the morality of action. This may be true, but, true or not, it is not hedonistic.

Furthermore, this standard by which the nature of pleasure is determined is itself an ethical (that is, active) standard. We have already seen that Spencer conceives that the modes of producing happiness are to be deduced from the "laws of life and the conditions of existence." This might be, of course, a deduction from *physical* laws and conditions. But when we find that the laws and conditions which Spencer employs are mainly those of *social* life, it is difficult to see why he is not employing a strictly ethical standard. To deduce not right actions directly from happiness, but the kinds of actions which will produce happiness from a consideration of a certain ideal of social relationships seems like a reversal of hedonism; but this is what Mr. Spencer does.

## xxvi.  The Real Criterion of Evolutionary Ethics

Mr. Spencer expressly recognizes that there exists

1. An ideal code of conduct, formulating the conduct of the completely adapted man in the completely evolved society. Such a code is called absolute ethics as distinguished from relative ethics—a code the injunctions of which are alone to be considered "as absolutely right, in contrast with those that are relatively right or least wrong, and which, as a system of ideal conduct, is to serve as a

standard for our guidance in solving, as well as we can, the problems of real conduct" (p. 275 of the *Data of Ethics*). "The ideal code deals, it will be observed, with the behavior of the completely adapted man in a completely evolved society." This ideal as elsewhere stated, is "an ideal social being so constituted that his spontaneous activities are congruous with the conditions imposed by the social environment formed by other such beings. . . . The ultimate man is one in whom there is a correspondence between all the promptings of his nature and all the requirements of his life as carried on in society" (p. 275). Furthermore, "to make the ideal man serve as a standard, he has to be defined *in terms of the conditions which his nature fulfill*—in terms of the objective requisites which must be met before conduct can be right" (p. 279). "Hence it is manifest that we must consider the ideal man as existing in the ideal social state" (p. 280).

Here we have in the most express terms the recognition of a final and permanent standard with reference to which the nature of happiness is determined, and the standard is one of social relationships. To be sure it is claimed that the standard is one which results in greatest happiness, but every ethical theory has always claimed that the ideal moral condition would be accompanied by the maximum possible happiness.

2. The ideal state is defined with reference to the end of evolution. That is, Spencer defines pleasure from an independent standard instead of using pleasure as the standard. This standard is to be got at by considering that idea of "fully evolved conduct" given by the theory of evolution. This fully evolved conduct implies: (*i.*) Greatest possible quantity of life, both in length and breadth; (*ii.*) Similar maintenance of life in progeny; and (*iii.*) Life in which there is no interference of actions by one with those of another, and, indeed, life in which the "members of a society give material help in the achievement of ends," thus rendering the "lives of all more complete." (See Ch. 2 of *Data of Ethics*.) Furthermore, the "complete life here identified with the ideally moral life" may be otherwise defined as a life of perfect equilibrium (p. 74), or balance of func-

tions (p. 90), and this considered not simply with reference to the individual, but also with reference to the relation of the individual to society. "Complete life in a complete society is but another name for complete equilibrium between the co-ordinated activities of each social unit and those of the aggregate of units" (*Data of Ethics*, p. 74, and the whole of Ch. 5. See also pp. 169–70 for the position that the end is a society in which each individual has full functions freely exercised in due harmony, and is, p. 100, "the spontaneous exercise of duly proportioned faculties").

3. Not only is pleasure thus determined by an objective standard of "complete living in a complete society" but it is expressly recognized that *as things are now, pleasure is not a perfect guide to, or even test of action.* And this difficulty is thought to be removed by reference to the ideal state in which right action and happiness will fully coincide.

The failure of pleasure as a perfect test and guide of right conduct, comes out in at least three cases: —

1. There is the conflict of one set of pleasures with another, or of present happiness with future, one lot having to be surrendered for the sake of another. This is wrong, since pleasure as such is good, and, although a fact at present, exists only on account of the incomplete development of society. When there is "complete adjustment of humanity to the social state there will be recognition of the truth that actions are completely right only when, besides being conducive to future happiness, special and general, they are immediately pleasurable, and that painfulness, not only ultimate but proximate, is the concomitant of actions which are wrong" (*Data of Ethics*, p. 99. See for various cases in which "pleasures are not connected with actions which must be performed" and for the statement that this difficulty will be removed in an ideal state of society, p. 77; pp. 85–87; pp. 98–99).

2. There is also, at present, a conflict of individual happiness with social welfare. In the first place, as long as there exist antagonistic societies, the individual is called upon to sacrifice his own happiness to that of others, but "such moralities are, by their definition, shown to belong to incomplete conduct; not to conduct that is fully evolved"

(see *Data of Ethics*, pp. 133–37). Furthermore, there will be conflict of claims, and consequent compromises between one's own pleasure and that of others (p. 148), until there is a society in which there is "complete living through voluntary co-operation," this implying negatively that one shall not interfere with another and shall fulfill contracts, and positively that men shall spontaneously help to aid one another lives beyond any specified agreement (pp. 146–49).

3. There is, at present, a conflict of obligation with pleasure. Needed activities, in other words, have often to be performed under a pressure, which either lessens the pleasure of the action, or brings pain, the act being performed, however, to avoid a greater pain (so that this point really comes under the first head). But "the remoulding of human nature into fitness for the requirements of social life, must eventually make all needful activities pleasurable, while it makes displeasurable all activities at variance with these requirements" (*Data of Ethics*, p. 183). "The things now done with dislike, through sense of obligation, will be done then with immediate liking" (p. 184, and p. 186; and pp. 255–56). All the quotations on these various points are simply so many recognitions that pleasure and pain as such are not tests of morality, but that they become so when morality is independently realized. Pleasure is *not* now a test of conduct, but becomes such a test as fast as activity becomes full and complete! What is this but to admit (what was claimed in Sec. XIII) that activity itself is what man wants; not *mere* activity, but the activity which belongs to man as man, and which therefore has for its realized content all man's practical relationships.

Of Spencer's conception of the ideal as something not now realized, but to be some time or other realized once for all, we have said nothing. But see below, Sec. LXIV, and also Alexander, *Moral Order*, pp. 264–77, and also James, *Unitarian Review*, Vol. XXII, pp. 212–13.

We have attempted, above, to deal with evolutionary ethics only in the one point of its supposed connection with pleasure as a standard. Accounts and criticisms of a broader scope will be found in Darwin, *Descent of Man*; Martineau, *Types of Ethical Theory*, Vol. II, pp. 335–93; Schurman, *Ethical Import of Darwinism*; Sorley, *Ethics of Naturalism*, Chs. 5, and 6; Stephen, *Science of Ethics*, particularly pp. 31–34, 78–89, 359–79; Royce, *Religious Aspect of Philosophy*, pp. 74–85; Everett, *Poetry, Comedy and Duty*, essay on the "New Ethics"; Seth in *Mind*, Jan. 1889, on "Evolution of Morality"; Dewey, *Andover Review*, Vol. VII, p. 573 [*Early Works* I, 205]; Hyslop, *Andover Review*, Vol. IX, p. 348.

## XXVII.　Formal Ethics

We come now to the ethical theories which attempt to find the good not only in the will itself, but in the will irrespective of any end to be reached by the will. The typical instance of such theories is the Kantian, and we shall, therefore, make that the basis of our examination. Kant's theory, however, is primarily a theory not of the good, but of the nature of duty, and that makes a statement of his doctrine somewhat more difficult.

"The concept of good and evil must not be determined before the moral law (of which it seems as if it must be the foundation), but only after it and by means of it" (Kant's *Theory of Ethics*, Abbott's trans., p. 154).

Separating, as far as we can, his theory of the good from that of duty, we get the following results:

1. Goodness belongs to the will, and to that alone. "Nothing can possibly be conceived, in the world or out of it, which can be called good without qualification except a good will." The will is not good because of what it brings about, or what it is fitted to bring about; that is, it is not good on account of its adaptation to any end outside of itself. It is good in itself. "It is like a jewel which shines by its own light, having its whole value in itself."

2. The good, then, is not to be found in any *object* of will or of desire, nor in the will *so far as it is directed towards an end outside itself*. For the will to be moved by inclination or by desire is for it to be moved for the sake of some external end, which, moreover, is always pleasure (Kant, *i.e.*, agrees with the hedonists regarding the object of desire, but on that very ground denies that pleasure is the good or the desirable). If, then, no object of desire can be the motive of a good will, what is its motive? Evidently only some principle derived from the will itself. The good will is the will which acts from regard to its own law.

3. What is the nature of this law? All objects of desire (*i.e.*, all material) have been excluded from it. It must, therefore, be purely formal. The only content of the law of the good will is the *idea of law itself*. The good will acts from reverences for law *as law*. It not only acts *in conformity with law*, but has the conception of law as its directing spring.

4. There must, however, be some application of this motive of law in general to particular motives or acts. This is secured as follows: The idea of law carries with it the idea of universality or self-identity. To act from the idea of law is then so to act that the motive of action can be generalized—made a motive for all conduct. The good will is the *legislative* will; the will whose motive can be made a law for conduct universally. The question in a specific case is then: Can your motive here be made universal, *i.e.*, a law? If the action is bad, determined by an object of desire, it will be contingent and variable, since pleasures are different to different persons and to the same person from moment to moment. The will is good, then, when its motive (or maxim) is to be found solely in the *legislative form* of the action, or in its fitness to be generalized into a universal principle of conduct, and the law of the good will is: "Act so that the maxim of thy will can always at the same time hold good as a principle of universal legislation" (*Kant's Theory of Ethics*, Abbott's trans., p. 119; also p. 55).

5. The application may be illustrated by the following cases:

*a*] Some one, wearied by what he conceives to be the entire misery of life proposes to commit suicide, but he asks himself whether this maxim based on the principle of self-love could become a universal law of nature; and "we see at once that a system of nature in which the very feeling, whose office is to compel men to the preservation of life, should lead men by a universal law to death, cannot be conceived without contradiction." That is to say, the principle of the motive which would lead a man to suicide cannot be generalized without becoming contradictory—it cannot be made a law universal.

*b*] An individual wishes to borrow money which he

knows that he cannot repay. Can the maxim of this act be universalized? Evidently not: "a system of nature in which it should be a universal law to promise without performing, for the sake of private good, would contradict itself, for then no one would believe the promise—the promise itself would become impossible as well as the end it had in view."

*c*] A man finds that he has certain powers, but is disinclined to develop them. Can he make the maxim of such conduct a universal law? He cannot *will* that it should become universal. "As a rational being, he must will that his faculties be developed."

*d*] A prosperous individual is disinclined to relieve the misery of others. Can his maxim be generalized? "It is impossible to *will* that such a principle should have the universal validity of a law of nature. For a will which resolved this would contradict itself, in as much as many cases might occur in which one would have need of the love and sympathy of others, and in which, by such a law of nature, sprung from his own will, he would deprive himself of all hope of the aid he desires."

In conclusion, then, the good is the good will itself, and the will is good in virtue of the bare form of its action, independently of all special material willed.

See *Kant's Theory of Ethics*, Abbott's trans., pp. 9–46, 105–20. Caird's *Critical Philosophy of Kant*, Vol. ii, pp. 171–81, 209–12.

## XXVIII.   Relation of This Theory to Hedonism

The Kantian theory, as already noticed, agrees in its psychology with hedonism. It holds that pleasures are the objects of desire. But it reverses the conclusion which hedonism draws from this fact *as to the desirable*. Since pleasures are the object of desire, and pleasures can give no law, no universality to action, the end of action must be found wholly *outside* the pleasures, and wholly outside the desires. It can be found only in the bare law of the will itself.

1. Hedonism finds the end of conduct, or the desirable, wholly determined by the various particular desires which a

man happens to have; Kantianism holds that to discover the end of conduct, we must wholly exclude the desires.

2. Hedonism holds that the rightness of conduct is determined wholly by its consequences; Kantianism holds that the consequences have nothing to do with the rightness of an act, but that it is decided wholly by the motive of the act.

From this contrast, we may anticipate both our criticism of the Kantian theory and our conception of the true end of action. The fundamental error of hedonism and Kantianism is the same—the supposition that desires are for pleasure only. Let it be recognized that desires are for objects conceived as satisfying or developing the self, and that pleasure is incidental to this fulfillment of the capacities of self, and we have the means of escaping the one-sidedness of Kantianism as well as of hedonism. We can see that the end is neither the procuring of particular pleasures through the various desires, nor action from the mere idea of abstract law in general, but that it is the *satisfaction of desires according to law*. The desire in its particular character does not give the law; this, as we saw in our criticism of hedonism, is to take away all law from conduct and to leave us at the mercy of our chance desires as they come and go. On the other hand the law is not something wholly apart from the desires. This, as we shall see, is equally to deprive us of a law capable of governing conduct. The law is the law of the desires themselves—the harmony and adjustment of desires necessary to make them instruments in fulfilling the special destiny or business of the agent.

From the same point of view we can see that the criterion is found neither in the consequences of our acts as *pleasures*, nor *apart from consequences*. It is found indeed in the consequences of acts, *but in their complete consequences*: —those upon the agent and society, as helping or hindering them in fulfillment of their respective functions.

## xxix. Criticism of Kantian Criterion of Conduct

1. *With reference to the unification of the conduct of the individual.* Of pleasure as the object of desire, we need

now say nothing further, but may proceed at once to the criticism of the theory that the will, acting according to the mere idea of law in general, is the end of man and hence that it is the criterion of the rightness or wrongness of his acts. We shall attempt to show that such an end is wholly empty, and that it fails (as much as hedonism) to unify conduct or to place any specific act as to its morality.

The difficulty of the end proposed by Kant is that it is an abstraction; that it is remote. The hedonist leaves out one element from conduct, and takes into account the merely particular or individualistic side; the Kantian abstracts the opposite element—the merely universal. The formal universal, or universal stripped of all particular content, has, considered as an end of action, at least three defects.

*a*] It is an end which would make impossible that very conduct of which it is taken to be the end—that is, moral conduct. In denying that pleasure is the end of action, we took pains to show that it (or rather the feeling due to the tension between pleasure of a state considered better and the pain of the experienced worse state) is a necessary element in the force impelling to action. The mere conception of an end is purely intellectual; there is nothing in it to move to action. It must be *felt* as valuable, as worth having, and as more valuable than the present condition before it can induce to action. It must *interest*, in a word, and thus excite desire. But if feeling is, as Kant declares, to be excluded from the motive to action, because it is pathological or related to pleasure as the object of desire, how can there be any force moving to action? The mind seems to be set over against a purely theoretical idea of an end, with nothing to connect the mind with the end. Unless the end interests, unless it arouses emotion, why should the agent ever aim at it? And if the law does excite feeling or desire, must not this, on Kant's theory, be desire for pleasure and thus vitiate the morality of the act? We seem to be in a dilemma, one side of which makes moral action impossible by taking away all inducing force, while the other makes it impossible by introducing an immoral factor into the motive.

Kant attempts to escape from this difficulty by claiming that there is one feeling which is rational, and not sensuous in quality, being excited not by the conception of pleasure or pain, but by that of the moral law itself. This is the feeling of reverence, and through this feeling we can be moved to moral action. Waiving the question whether the mere idea of law in general would be capable of arousing any moral sentiment—or, putting the matter from the other side, whether Kant gives us a true account of the feeling of reverence—it is clear that this admission is fatal to Kant's theory. If desire or feeling as such is sensuous (or *pathological*, as Kant terms it), what right have we to make this one exception? And if we can make this one exception, why not others? If it is possible in the case of reverence, why not in the case, say, of patriotism, or of friendship, or of philanthropy, or of love—or even of curiosity, or of indignation, or of desire for approbation? Kant's separation of reverence, as the one moral sentiment from all others as pathological, is wholly arbitrary. The only distinction we can draw is of the feelings as they well up naturally in reaction upon stimuli, sentiments not conceived and thus neither moral nor immoral, and sentiments as transformed by ends of action, in which case all without exception may be moral or immoral, according to the character of the end. The Kantian separation is not only arbitrary psychologically, but is false historically. So far is it from true that the only moral sentiment is reverence for law, that men must have been moved toward action for centuries by motives of love and hate and social regard, before they became capable of such an abstract feeling as reverence. And it may be questioned whether this feeling, as Kant treats it, is even the highest or ultimate form of moral sentiment—whether it is not transitional to love, in which there is complete union of the individual interest on one hand, and the objective end on the other.

For these criticisms at greater length, see Caird, *Critical Philosophy of Kant*, Vol. ii, Bk. ii, Ch. 4.

*b*] The Kantian end would not bring about any system in conduct—on the contrary, it would tend to differences and collisions. What is required to give unity to the sphere of conduct is, as we have seen, a principle which shall comprehend all the motives to action, giving each its due place in contributing to the whole—a universal which shall organize the various particular acts into a harmonious system. Now Kant's conception of the good does not lead to such result. We may even say that it makes it impossible. According to Kant each act must be considered independently of every other, and must be capable of generalization on its own account. Each motive of action must be capable of being *itself* a universal law of nature. Each particular rule of action is thus made absolute, and we are left not with one universal which comprehends all particulars in their relations to one another, but literally with a lot of universals. These not only fail to have a unity, but each, as absolute, must contradict some other. If the principles always to tell the truth and always to preserve life are universal *in themselves*, and not universal simply *through their relation to some total and controlling principle of life*, it must be impossible to reconcile them when they come into conflict.

See Caird, *Critical Philosophy of Kant*, Vol. ii, pp. 187–90, and p. 215. *Cf.* "Treated as universal and without exception, even two such commands, as *e.g.*, 'Thou shalt not steal,' and 'Thou shalt not kill,' must ultimately come into conflict with each other; for, if all other interests are to be postponed to the maintenance of the rights of property, it is impossible that all other interests should also be postponed to the preservation of human life—and to make either property or life an absolute end is to raise a particular into a universal, to treat a part as if it were a whole. But the true moral vindication of each particular interest cannot be found in elevating it into something universal and absolute, but only in determining its place in relation to the others in a complete system of morality."

*c*] The principle is so empty of all content that it does not enable us to judge of any specific act.

A caution should be noticed here, which is equally applicable to the criticism of hedonism: When it is said that the end does not enable us to judge of specific acts, the objection is not that the *theory* (Kantianism or hedonism, as the case may be) does not give us rules for moral conduct. It is not the business of any theory, however correct as a theory, to lay down rules for conduct. The theory has simply to discover what the *end* is, and it is the end in view which determines specific acts. It is no more the business of ethics to tell what in particular a man ought to do, than it is of trigonometry to survey land. But trigonometry must state the principles by which land *is* surveyed, and so ethics must state the end by which conduct *is* governed. The objection to hedonism and Kantianism is that the end they give does not *itself* stand in any practical relation to conduct. We do not object to Kantianism because the *theory* does not help us as to specific acts, but because the *end*, formal law, does not help us, while the real moral end must determine the whole of conduct.

Suppose a man thrown into the complex surroundings of life with an intelligence fully developed, but with no previous knowledge of right or wrong, or of the prevailing moral code. He is to know, however, that goodness is to be found in the good will, and that the good will is the will moved by the mere idea of the universality of law. Can we imagine such an one deriving from his knowledge any idea of what concrete ends he ought to pursue and what to avoid? He is surrounded by special circumstances calling for special acts, and all he knows is that *whatever* he does is to be done from respect for its universal or legislative quality. What community is there between this principle and *what* he is to do? There is no bridge from the mere thought of universal law to any concrete end coming under the law. There is no common principle out of which grows the conception of law on one hand, and of the various special ends of action, on the other.

Suppose, however, that ends are independently suggested or proposed, will the Kantian conception serve to *test* their moral fitness? Will the conception that the end must be capable of being generalized tell us whether this or that end is one to be followed? The fact is, that there is no end whatever that *in* or *by itself*, cannot be considered as self-identical, or as universal. If we presuppose a certain rule, or if we presuppose a certain moral order, it may be true that a given motive cannot be universalized without coming into conflict with this presupposed rule or order. But aside from some moral system into connection with which a proposed end may be brought, for purposes of comparison, lying is just as capable as truth-telling of generalization. There is no more contradiction in the motive of universal stealing than there is in that of universal honesty—unless there is as standard some order or system of things into which the proposed action is to fit as a member. And this makes not the bare universality of the act, but the system, the real criterion for determining the morality of the act.

Thus Mill remarks, regarding Kant's four illustrations (*ante*, pp. 291–92), that Kant really has to employ utilitarian considerations to decide whether the act is moral or not.

For the foregoing criticisms, see Bradley, *Ethical Studies*, Essay IV; Caird, *Critical Philosophy of Kant*, Vol. II, pp. 185–86, and 212–14, and, indeed, the whole of Ch. 2 of Bk. II.

## XXX. Criticism of Kantian Criterion of Conduct

*2. With reference to the furnishing of a common good or end.* If the Kantian end is so formal and empty as not to enable us to bring into relation with one another the various acts of one individual, we may agree, without argument, that it does not provide us with an end which shall unify the acts of different men into a connected order of conduct. The moral end, the acting from regard for law as law, is presented to each individual by himself, entirely apart from his relations to others. That he has such relations may, indeed, furnish additional material to which the law must be applied, but is something to which the character of the law is wholly indifferent. The end is not in itself a social end, and it is a mere accident if in any case social considerations have to be taken into account. It is of the very quality of the end that it appeals to the individual as an isolated individual.

It is interesting to note the way in which Kant, without expressly giving up the purely formal character of the moral end, gives it more and more content, and that content social. The moral law is not imposed by any external authority, but by the rational will itself. To be conscious of a universal self-imposed law is to be conscious of one's self as having a universal aspect. The source of the law and its end are both in the will—in the rational self. Thus man is an end to himself, for the rational self is man. Such a being is a person—"Rational beings are *persons*, because their nature marks them out as ends in themselves, *i.e.*, as beings who should never be used merely as means. . . . Such beings are not ends simply *for us*, whose existence as brought about by our action has value, but *objective ends*, *i.e.*, beings whose existence is an end in itself, an end for which no other end can be substituted so as to reduce it to a mere means." Thus, we get a second formula. "Always treat humanity, both in your own person and in the person of others, as an end and never merely as a means" (*Kant's Theory of Ethics*, Abbott's trans., pp. 46–47; Caird, *Critical Philosophy of Kant*, Vol. II, p. 219). Here the criterion of action is no longer the bare self-consistency of its motive, but its consistency with the rational nature of the agent, that which constitutes him a person. And, too, "the will of every rational being is likewise a universally law-giving will" (*Kant's Theory of Ethics*, Abbott, p. 49). The conception of humanity embodied in others as well as in one's self is introduced, and thus our criterion is socialized. Even now, however, we have a lot of persons, each of whom has to be considered as an end in himself, rather than a social unity as to which every individual has an equal and common reference. Kant advances to this latter idea in his notion of a "Kingdom of ends." "We get the idea of a complete and systematically connected totality of all ends—a whole system of rational beings as ends in themselves as well as of the special ends which each of them may set up for himself—*i.e.*, a kingdom of ends. . . . Morality is the reference of all deeds to the legislation which alone can make such a kingdom possible." (See *Kant's Theory of Ethics*, Abbott's trans., pp. 51–52.) This transformation of a mere formal universal into a society or kingdom of persons—while not sufficiently analyzed as Kant states it (see Caird, *Critical Philosophy of Kant*, Vol. II, pp. 225–26)—gives us truly a social criterion, and we shall hereafter meet something resembling it as the true ideal. As finally stated, it does not differ in essential content from Mill's individual who "conceives of himself only as a member of a body," or from Spencer's free man in a free society.

# XXXI. Value of Kantian Theory

We must not leave the Kantian theory with the impression that it is simply the caprice of a philosopher's brain. In two respects, at least, it presents us, as we shall see, with elements that must be adopted; and even where false it is highly instructive.

Kant's fundamental error is in his conception that all desires or inclinations are for private pleasure, and are, therefore, to be excluded from the conception of the moral end. Kant's conclusion, accordingly, that the good will is purely formal follows inevitably if ever it is granted that there is any intrinsic opposition between inclination as such, and reason or moral law as such. If there is such an opposition, *all* desire must be excluded from relation to the end. We cannot make a compromise by distinguishing between higher and lower desires. On the contrary, if the end is to have content, it must include all desires, leaving out none as in itself base or unworthy. Kant's great negative service was showing that the ascetic principle logically results in pure formalism—meaning by ascetic principle that which discon-nects inclinations from moral action.

Kant's positive service was, first, his clear insight into the fact that the good is to be found only in activity; that the will itself, and nothing beyond itself, is the end; and that to adopt any other doctrine, is to adopt an immoral principle, since it is to subordinate the will (character, self and per-sonality), to some outside end. His second great service was in showing the necessity of putting in abeyance the immedi-ate satisfaction of each desire as it happens to arise, and of subordinating it to some law not to be found in the particu-lar desire. He showed that not the particular desire, but only the desire as controlled by the idea of law could be the motive of moral action. And if he fell into the error of holding that this meant that the desire must be excluded from the moral motive, this error does not make it less true that every particular desire must be controlled by a univer-sal law. The truth of asceticism is that the desire must be checked until subordinated to the activity of the whole man. See Caird, *Critical Philosophy of Kant*, Vol. ii, p. 200; pp. 203–7, 226–27.

## xxxii. The Problem and Its Solution

If we gather together the results of our observations of hedonism and of Kantianism we get something like the following problem and solution in outline. The end of ac-tion, or the good, is the realized will, the developed or satisfied self. This satisfied self is found neither in the getting of a lot of pleasures through the satisfaction of desires just as they happen to arise, nor in obedience to law simply because it is law. It is found in *satisfaction of desires according to law*. This law, however, is not something exter-nal to the desires, but is their own law. Each desire is only one striving of character for larger action, and the only way in which it can really find satisfaction (that is, pass from inward striving into outward action) is *as* a manifestation of character. A desire, taken as a desire for its own apparent or direct end *only*, is an abstraction. It is a desire for an entire and continuous activity, and its satisfaction requires that it be fitted into this entire and continuous activity; that it be made conformable to the conditions which will bring the whole man into action. It is this fitting-in which is the law of the desire—the "universal" controlling its particular nature. This "fitting-in" is no mechanical shearing off, nor stretching out, but a reconstruction of the natural desire till it becomes an expression of the whole man. The problem then is to find that special form of character, of self, which includes and transforms all special desires. This form of character is at once the Good and the Law of man.

We cannot be content with the notion that the end is the satisfaction of the self, a satisfaction at once including and subordinating the ends of the particular desire. This tells us nothing positive—however valuable it may be negatively in warning us against one-sided notions—until we know *what* that whole self is, and *in what* concretely its satisfaction consists. As the first step towards such a more concrete formula, we may say:

## XXXIII. The Moral End or the Good Is the Realization by a Person and as a Person of Individuality

In saying that this realization is *by a person* and *as a person* we are saying nothing new. We are simply repeating what we have already learned about moral conduct (Sec. III). Conduct is not that which simply reaches certain consequences—a bullet shot from a rifle does that; there is conduct only when the consequences are foreseen; made the reason of action. A person is a being capable of conduct—a being capable of proposing to himself ends and of attempting to realize them.

But what is the meaning of the rest of the formula? What do we mean by individuality? We may distinguish two factors—or better two aspects, two sides—in individuality. On one side, it means special disposition, temperament, gifts, bent, or inclination; on the other side, it means special station, situation, limitations, surroundings, opportunities, etc. Or, let us say, it means *specific capacity* and *specific environment*. Each of these elements, apart from the other, is a bare abstraction and without reality. Nor is it strictly correct to say that individuality is constituted by these two factors *together*. It is rather, as intimated above, that each is individuality looked at from a certain point of view, from within or from without.

If we are apt to identify individuality with the inner side alone, with capacity apart from its surroundings, a little reflection will show the error. Even the most devoted adherent of "self-culture" would not hold that a gift could be developed, or a disposition manifested, in isolation from all exterior circumstances. Let the disposition, the gift be what it may (amiable or irascible, a talent for music or for abstract science, or for engineering), its existence, to say nothing of its culture, apart from some surroundings is bare nonsense. If a person shuts himself up in a closet or goes out into the desert the better to cultivate his capacities, there is still the desert or the closet there; and it is as conditioned by them, and with reference to them that he must cultivate himself. For more is true than that, as a matter of fact, no man can wholly withdraw himself from surroundings; the important point is that the manner and the purpose of exercising his capacity is always *relative* to and *dependent* upon the surroundings. Apart from the environment the capacity is mere emptiness; the exercise of capacity is always establishing a relation to something exterior to itself. All we can say of capacity apart from environment is that *if* certain circumstances were supplied, there would be something there. We call a capacity *capability*, possibility, as if for the very purpose of emphasizing the necessity of external supplementing.

We get the same fact, on the other side, by calling to mind that circumstances, environment are not indifferent or irrelevant to individuality. The difference between one individual and another lies as much in the station in which each is placed as in the capacity of each. That is to say, environment enters into individuality as a constituent factor, helping make it what it is.

On the other hand, it is capacity which makes the environment really an environment *to* the individual.

The environment is not simply the facts which happen

objectively to lie about an agent; it is such part of the facts as may be *related* to the capacity and the disposition and gifts of the agent. Two members of the same family may have what, to the outward eye, are exactly the same surroundings, and yet each may draw from these surroundings wholly unlike stimulus, material and motives. Each has a different environment, made different by his own mode of selection; by the different way in which his interests and desires play upon the plastic material about him. It is not, then, the environment as physical of which we are speaking, but as it appeals to consciousness, as it is affected by the make-up of the agent. This is the *practical* or *moral* environment. The environment is not, then, what is then and there present in space. To the Christian martyr the sufferings of his master, and the rewards of faithfulness to come to himself were more real parts of his environment than the stake and fire. A Darwin or a Wallace may find his environment in South America or the Philippine Islands—or, indeed, in every fact of a certain sort wherever found upon the earth or in whatever geological era. A man of philanthropic instincts may find *his* environment among Indians or Congo negroes. Whatever, however near or remote in time and space, an individual's capacities and needs relate him to, is his environment. The moment we realize that only what one conceives as proper material for calling out and expressing some internal capacity is a part of his surroundings, we see not only that capacity depends upon environment, but that environment depends upon capacity. In other words, we see that each in itself is an abstraction, and that the real thing is the individual who is constituted by capacity and environment in their relation to one another.

*Function* is a term which we may use to express union of the two sides of individuality. The idea of function is that of an active relation established between power of doing, on one side, and something to be done on the other. To exercise a function as a student is not to cultivate tastes and possibilities internally; it is also to meet external demands, the demands of fact, of teachers, of others needing knowledge. The citizen exercises his function not simply in cultivating sentiments of patriotism within; one has to meet the needs of the city, the country in which one lives. The realization of an artistic function is not poring over emotions of beauty pumped up within one's self; it is the exercise of some calling. On the other hand, it hardly needs saying that the function of a student, a citizen, an artist, is not exercised in bare conformity to certain external requirements. Without the inner disposition and inclination, we call conduct dead, perfunctory, hypocritical. An activity is not functional, unless it is organic, expressing the life of the agent.

A function thus includes two sides—the external and the internal—and reduces them to elements in one activity. We get an analogy in any animal function. The digestive function includes the material appropriated, just as much as it does the organ appropriating. It is the service, the work which the organ does *in* appropriating material. So, morally, function is capacity *in action*; environment transformed into an element in personal service.

Thus we get another formula for the moral end:

The performance by a person of his specific function, this function consisting in an activity which realizes wants and powers with reference to their peculiar surroundings.

## xxxiv. Moral Functions as Interests

If morality consists in the exercise of one's *specific* functions, it follows that no *detailed* account of the content of the moral end can possibly be given. This content is thoroughly individual or infinite. It is concrete to the core, including every detail of conduct, and this not in a rigid formula, but in the movement of life. All we can do is, by abstraction, to select some of the main features of the end, such as the more common and the more permanent. While each individual has his own particular functions, which can no more be exhausted by definition or description than the qualities of any other individual object, it is also true that we can recognize certain typical functions to be found permanently and in all. These make, as it were, the skeleton of the moral end which each clothes with his own flesh and blood.

Functions are *interests*—objective interests were not

the term tautological. Interests have three traits worth special mention.

*1.* They are *active.* An interest is not an emotion produced from without. It is the reaction of the emotion to the object. Interest is identified, in ordinary speech, with attention; we *take* an interest, or, if we say simply "interested," that involves some excitation, some action just beginning. We talk of a man's interests, meaning his occupations or range of activities.

*2.* They are *objective.* The emotion aroused goes out to some object, and is fixed upon that; we are always interested *in something.* The active element of interest is precisely that which takes it out of the inner mood itself and gives it a terminus, an end in an object.

*3.* An interest is *satisfaction.* It is its own reward. It is not a striving for something unrealized, or a mere condition of tension. It is the satisfaction in some object which the mind already has. This object may be possessed in some greater or less degree, in full realization or in faint grasp, but interest attaches to it as possessed. This differentiates it from desire, even where otherwise the states are the same. Desire refers to the lack, to what is not present to the mind. One state of mind may be called both interest in, and desire for, knowledge, but desire emphasizes the unknown, while interest is on account of the finding of self, of intelligence, in the object. Interest is the union in feeling, through action, of self and an object. An interest in life is had when a man can practically identify himself with some object lying beyond his immediate or already acquired self and thus be led to further expression of himself.

To have an interest, then, is to be alert, to have an object, and to find satisfaction in an activity which brings this object home to self.

Not every interest carries with it *complete* satisfaction. But no interest can be wholly thwarted. The purer the interest, the more the interest is in the object for its own sake, and not for that of some ulterior consequence, the more the interest fulfills itself. "It is better to have loved and lost than never to have loved at all," and love is simply the highest power of interest—interest freed from all extrinsic stuff.

Of the interests, two abstract forms may be recognized, interest in persons and interest in things. And these may be subdivided: Interest in persons: interest in *self* and *others*. Interest in things—into their contemplation (*knowledge*) and into their production (*art*). And art again may be either productive of things to be contemplated (fine art), or useful—manufactures, industry, etc. The moral end, then, or the Good will consist in the exercise of these interests, varied as they may be in each individual by the special turn which his capacities and opportunities take.

## xxxv. The Exercise of Interests as the Moral End

Let us now, as a means of rendering our conception of the moral end more concrete, consider briefly each of the forms of interest.

### 1. *Interest in Self*

We must free ourselves from any notion that an interest in self is non-moral, if not actually immoral. The latter position is seldom consciously assumed, but it is not uncommon to have interest in self, under the name of prudence, marked off from the moral sphere. Interest in self, if the interest is pure, is just as much an interest in the moral end as interest in anything or anybody else. Interest in self may take the form of selfishness, or of sentimentalism; but this is only an *impure* interest, an interest not in self, but in some consequences to which the self may be directed. Interest in self may take many forms, according to the side of self which is the object of attention, and according to the range of the self taken into account. A *rudimentary* form is prudence, but even this, instead of being non-moral, is, in proper place and degree, moral, as moral as benevolence; and, if not in its proper place, immoral. From such an interest there are all stages up to the interest in self as it most deeply and broadly is, the sense of honor, moral dignity, self-respect, conscientiousness, that attempt to be and to make the most of one's self, which is at the very root of moral endeavor.

The ground that is usually given for making the distinction between Prudence, Self-Regard, Self-Love as non-moral, and Benevolence, Altruism, etc., as moral, is that in the former case a mere regard for one's own advantage dictates proper conduct, while in the latter case there must be a positive virtuous intent. We may, for example, be pointed to some cool calculating man who takes care of his health and his property, who indeed is generally "prudent," because he sees that it is for his advantage, and be told that while such an end is not immoral it is certainly not moral. But in return it must be asked what is meant here by advantage? If by it is meant private pleasure, or advantage over somebody else, then this conduct does not spring from interest in self at all, but from interest in some exterior consequence, and as springing from such an impure interest is not simply non-moral, but positively immoral. On the other hand, if "advantage" means regard for one's whole function, one's place in the moral order, then such interest in self is moral. Care for bodily health in the interest of efficiency in conduct is supremely moral beside reckless disregard of it in the interest of some supposed higher or more spiritual function.

If it is meant that conduct is immoral because it springs from some interest on the part of the agent, the reply is that all conduct must so arise, and that any other supposition leads us immediately into asceticism and into formalism.

## 2. *Interest in Others*

The generic form of interest in others is sympathy, this being specified by the various forms of social organization of which the individual is a member. A person is, we have seen, one who can conceive of ends and can act to realize these ends. Only a person, therefore, can conceive of others as ends, and so have true sympathy.

It is not meant, of course, that animals do not perform acts which, *de facto*, are altruistic or even self-sacrificing. What is meant is that the animal does not act from the *idea* of others of his kind as ends in themselves. If the animal does so act, it cannot be denied the name of person.

True interest in others is pure, or disinterested, in the sense of having no reference to some further and external consequence to one's self. Interest in others need not be moral (or pure) any more than interest in self is necessarily immoral (or impure). It is a mistake to distinguish interest in self as *egoistic* and interest in others as *altruistic*. Genuine interests, whatever their object, are both egoistic and altruistic. They are egoistic simply because they *are inter-*

*ests*—imply satisfaction in a realized end. If man is truly a social being, constituted by his relationships to others, then social action must inevitably realize himself, and be, in that sense, egoistic. And on the other hand, if the individual's interest in himself is in himself *as* a member of society, then such interest is thoroughly altruistic. In fact, the very idea of altruism is likely to carry a false impression when it is so much insisted upon, as it is nowadays in popular literature, as the essence of morality. The term as used seems to imply that the mere giving up of one's self to others, as others, is somehow moral. Just as there may be an immoral interest in self, so there may be an immoral "altruism." It is immoral in any case to sacrifice the actual relationships in the case, those which demand action, to some feeling outside themselves—as immoral when the feeling to which the sacrifice is offered up is labelled "benevolence," as when it is termed "greediness." It is no excuse when a man gives unwisely to a beggar that he feels benevolent. *Moral* benevolence is the feeling directed toward a certain end which is known to be the fit or right end, the end which expresses the situation. The question is as to the *aim* in giving. Apart from this aim, the act is simply relieving the agent's own feelings and has no moral quality. Rather it is immoral; for feelings do have a moral *capacity*, that is, a relation to ends of action, and hence to satisfy them on their account, to deprive them of their practical reference, is bad. Aside from what this illustrates, there is a tendency in the present emphasis of altruism to erect the principle of charity, in a sense which implies continued social inequality, and social slavery, or undue dependence of one upon another, into a fundamental moral principle. It is well to "do good" to others, but it is much better to do this by securing for them the freedom which makes it possible for them to get along in the future without such "altruism" from others. There is what has been well termed an "egotism of renunciation"; a desire to do for others which, at bottom, is simply an attempt to regulate their conduct. Much of altruism is an egoism of a larger radius, and its tendency is to "manufacture a gigantic self," as in the case where a father sacrifices everything for his children or a wife for her husband.

See Caird, *Critical Philosophy of Kant*, Vol. II, p. 402. See also Hinton, *The Law-Breaker*, pp. 287–88: "The real meaning of the difficulty about a word for 'regard for others' is that we do not want it. It would mislead us if we had it. It is not a regard for *others* that we need, but simply a *true* regard, a regard to the facts, to nature; it is only a truth to facts in our regard, and its nature is obscured by a reference to 'others,' as if that were the essential point. . . . It is not as being for others, but as being *true*, that the regard for others is demanded."

Some ethical writers have gone to the other extreme and held that all benevolence is a disguised or an enlightened selfishness, since having a necessary reference to self. The reference to self must be admitted; unless the action springs from an interest of the agent himself the act may be outwardly useful, but cannot be moral. But the argument alluded to inverts the true relation involved. If a man's interests are such that he can find satisfaction only in the satisfaction of others, what an absurdity to say that his acting from these interests is selfish! The very fact of such identity of self with others in his interest is the proof of his unselfishness.

See Leslie Stephen, *Science of Ethics*, p. 241, for an admirable discussion of this difficulty. When it is said that your pain is painful to me, he says, the inference is often "insinuated that I dislike your pain because it is painful to me in some special relation. I do not dislike it *as* your pain, but in virtue of some particular consequence, such, for example, as its making you less able to render me a service. In that case *I do not really object to your pain as your pain at all*, but only to some removable and accidental consequences." (And see his whole treatment of sympathy, pp. 230–45.) The whole question is shown to come to this: Is my interest in, my sympathy with, your joy and sorrow as such, or in your joy and sorrow as contributing to mine? If the latter, of course the interest is selfish, not being an interest in others at all. But if the former, then the fact that such sympathy involves one's own satisfaction is the best proof that man is not selfishly constructed. When Stephen goes on to say that such sympathy does not involve the existence of a real unity larger than the individual, he seems to me to misread his own facts, probably because he conceives of this unity as some abstract or external thing.

Discussion regarding self-love and benevolence, or, in modern phrase, egoism and altruism, has been rife in English ethics since the time of Hobbes, and especially of Shaftesbury and Butler. See, in particular, the *Sermons* of the latter, which gave the central point of discussion for almost a century. With reference to the special weakness of this point of view, with its co-ordination of two independent principles, see Green, *Philosophical Works*, Vol. III, pp. 99–104. The essential lack (the lack which we have tried to make good in the definition of individuality as the union of capacity and surroundings in function), was the failure to analyze the idea of the individual. Individuality being defined as an exclusive principle, the inevitable result was either (*i.*) the "disguised selfishness" theory; or (*ii.*) the assumption of two fundamentally different principles in man. The ordinary distinction between prudence and virtue is an echo of the latter theory. Then, finally, (*iii.*) a third principle, generally called conscience by Butler, was brought in as umpire in the conflict of prudence and virtue.

Suggestive modern treatment of the matter, from a variety of points of view, will be found in Spencer, *Data of Ethics*, Chs. 11–13; Stephen, *Science of Ethics*, Ch. 6; Sidgwick, *Methods of Ethics*, Bk. v, Ch. 7; Royce, *Religious Aspect of Philosophy*, Ch. 4; Sorley, *Ethics of Naturalism*, pp. 134–50; Alexander, *Moral Order*, pp. 172–80; Caird, *Critical Philosophy of Kant*, Vol. II, pp. 400–405; Paulsen, *System der Ethik*, pp. 295–311.

## *3. Interest in Science and Art*

Man is interested in the world about him; the knowledge of the nature and relations of this world become one of his most absorbing pursuits. Man identifies himself with the meaning of this world to the point that he can be satisfied only as he spells out and reads its meaning. (See, for example, Browning's "Grammarian's Funeral.") The scientific interest is no less a controlling motive of man than the personal interest. This knowledge is not a means for having agreeable sensations; it is not dilettanteism or "love of culture"; it is interest in the large and goodly frame of things. And so it is with art; man has interests which can be satisfied only in the reconstruction of nature in the way of the useful and the beautiful.

I have made no distinction between "fine" and "useful" art. The discussion of this question does not belong here, but the rigid separation of them in æsthetic theory seems to me to have no justification. Both are products of intelligence in the service of interests, and the only difference is in the range of intelligence and interests concerned. "Use" is a *limited* service and hence implies an external end; beauty is complete use or service, and hence not mere use at all, but self-expression. Historically, all art which has not been merely sentimental and "literary" has sprung from interest in good workmanship in the realizing of an idea.

It seems as if here interests violated their general law, and, in the case of use at least, were an interest in some ulterior end. But it may be questioned whether a carpenter whose aim was consciously beyond the work he was doing, would be a good workman—and this whether the further end is his own private advantage, or social benefit at large. The thought of the further benefit to self and of the utility to accrue to some one else, will, if it becomes a *part* of what he is doing, undoubtedly intensify his interest—it must do so, for it enlarges its content. But to *identify* one's own or another's well-being with work, and to make the work a mere *means* to this welfare, are two quite different things. The good artisan "has his heart in his work." His self-respect makes it necessary for him to respect this technical or artistic capacity, and to do the best by it that he can without scrimping or lowering. To a good business man business is not the mere means to money-making; and it is sentimentalism (and hence immoral) to demand that it be a mere means to the good of society. The business, if it is a moral one (and *any* business, *so far* as it is thus carried on, is moral), is carried on for the sake of the activity itself, as a realizing of capacity in a specific situation.

## xxxvi. The Moral Quality of Science

We seem, however, to meet here, in relation to science and art, a difficulty which threatens our whole theory. Can it be claimed, it may be asked, that devotion to science or art constitutes goodness in the same sense that devotion to the interests of one's family or state constitutes it? No one doubts that a good father or a good citizen is a good man, in so far forth. Are we ready to say that a good chemist or good carpenter, or good musician is, in so far, a good man? In a word, is there not a reference to the good of persons present in one case and absent in another, and does not its absence preclude the scientific and artistic activities from any share, *as such*, in the moral end?

It must be remembered that the moral end does not refer to some consequence which happens, *de facto*, to be reached. It refers to an end *willed*; *i.e.*, to an idea held to and realized as an idea. And this fact shows us the way to meet the query, in part at least. If, when we say good carpenter, or good merchant, we are speaking from the standpoint of results, independently of the idea conceived as end in the mind of the agent; if we mean simply, "we like what that man does," then the term good has no moral value. A man may paint "good" pictures and not be, in so far, a good man, but in this sense a man may *do* a great deal of "good," and yet not be a good man. It was agreed at the outset that moral goodness pertains to the kind of idea or end which a man clings to, and not to what he happens to effect visibly to others.

If a scientific man pursues truth as a mere means to reputation, to wealth, etc., we do not (or should not) hesitate to call him immoral.

> This does not mean that if he *thinks* of the reputation, or of wealth, he is immoral, for he may foresee wealth and the reputation as necessarily bound up in what he is doing; it may become a part of the end. It means that if knowledge of truth is a *mere means* to an end beyond it, the man is immoral.

What reason is there why we should not call him moral if he does his work for its own sake, from interest in this cause which takes him outside his "own miserable · individuality," in Mill's phrase? After all, the phrase a "good father" means but a character manifesting itself in certain relations, as is right according to these relations; the phrase has moral significance not in itself, but with reference to the end aimed at by character. And so it is with the phrase "a good carpenter." That also means devotion of character to certain outer relations for their own sake. These relations may not be so important, but that is not lack of moral meaning.

## XXXVII. Adjustment to Environment

So far we have been discussing the moral ideal in terms of its inner side—capacity, interest. We shall now discuss it on its outer or objective side—as "adjustment to environment" in the phrase made familiar by the evolutionists. Certain cautions, however, must be noted in the use of the phrase. We must keep clearly in mind the relativity of environment to inner capacity; that it exists only as one element of function. Even a plant must do something more than adjust itself *to* a fixed environment; it must assert itself *against* its surroundings, subordinating them and transforming them into material and nutriment; and, on the surface of things, it is evident that *transformation* of existing circumstances is moral duty rather than mere reproduction of them. The environment must be plastic to the ends of the agent.

But admitting that environment is made what it is by the powers and aims of the agent, what sense shall we attribute to the term adjustment? Not bare conformity to circumstances, nor bare external reproduction of them, even when circumstances are taken in their proper moral meaning. The child in the family who simply adjusts himself *to* his relationships in the family, may be living a moral life only in outward seeming. The citizen of the state may transgress no laws of the state, he may punctiliously fulfill every contract, and yet be a selfish man. True adjustment must consist in *willing* the maintenance and development of moral surroundings as *one's own end*. The child must take the spirit of the family into himself and live out this spirit according to his special membership in the family. So a soldier in the army, a friend in a mutual association, etc. Adjustment to intellectual environment is not mere conformity of ideas to facts. It is the living assimilation of these facts into one's own intellectual life, and maintaining and asserting them as *truth*.

There are environments existing prior to the activities of any individual agent; the family, for example, is prior to the moral activity of a child born into it, but the point is to see that "adjustment," to have a moral sense, means *making the environment a reality for one's self*. A true description of the case would say that the child takes for his own end, ends already existing for the wills of others. And, in making them his own, he creates and supports for himself an environment that already exists for others. In such cases there is no special transformation of the existing environment; there is simply the process of making it the environment for one's self. So in learning, the child simply appropriates to himself the intellectual environment already in existence for others. But in the activity of the man of science there is more than such personal reproduction and creation; there is increase, or even reconstruction of the prior environment. While the ordinary citizen hardly does more than make his own the environment of ends and interests already sustained in the wills of others, the moral reformer may remake the whole. But whether one case or the other, adjustment is not outer conformity; it is living realization of certain relations in and through the will of the agent.

## xxxviii.  The Moral End Is the Realization of a Community of Wills

Since the perfomance of function is, on the other side, the creation, perpetuation, and further development of an environment, of relations to the wills of others, its performance *is a common good*. It satisfies others who participate in the environment. The member of the family, of the state, etc., in exercising his function, contributes to the whole of which he is a member by realizing its spirit in himself. But the question discussed in Section xxxvi recurs under another aspect. Granting that the satisfying of personal interests realizes a common good, what shall we say of the impersonal interests—interests in science and art. Is the good carpenter or chemist not only in so far a good man, but also a good social member? In other words, does every form of moral activity realize a common good, or is the moral end partly social, partly non-social?

One objection sometimes brought to the doctrine that the moral end is entirely social, may be now briefly dismissed. This is the objection that a man has moral duties toward *himself*. Certainly, but what of *himself*? If he is essentially a social member, his duties toward himself have a social basis and bearing. The only relevant question is whether one is wholly a social member—whether scientific and artistic activities may not be non-social.

The ground here taken is that the moral end is wholly social. This does not mean that science and art are means to some social welfare beyond themselves. We have already stated that even the production of utilities must, as moral, be its own end. The position then is that intellectual and artistic interests *are themselves* social, when considered in the completeness of their relations—that interest in the development of intelligence is, in and of itself, interest in the well-being of society.

Unless this be true there is no moral end at all, but only moral ends. There is no comprehensive unity in life, but a number of ends which, being irreducible to a common principle, must be combined on the best principle of compromise available. We have no "The Good," but an aggregate of fragmentary ends.

It helps nothing to say that this necessary unity is found in the *self* to be realized, unless we are pointed to something in the self that unites the social and non-social functions. Our objection is that the separation of intellectual interests from social makes a chasm in the self.

For the same reason it follows that in the case of a collision of social with intellectual ends—say the conflict of a man's interests as a member of a family with his interests in new scientific discovery—no reconciliation is possible. If the interests are forms of social interest, there is a common end in both, on the basis of which the conflict can be resolved. While such considerations do not prove that there is but one end, and that social, they may well make us hesitate about carelessly taking a position of which they are the logical consequence.

Of course, every one recognizes that a certain amount of scientific and artistic interest is social in character. A certain amount of interest in truth, or in intelligence, a certain amount of susceptibility to beauty, a certain amount of devotion to utility, are universally recognized to be necessary to make judicious, agreeable and efficient social members. The whole system of modern education has meaning only on this supposition.

More than this: A certain amount of intelligence, and

a certain amount of susceptibility to embodied ideals, *must* exist to give moral conduct. A moral end is, as we have seen, always a *conception*, an idea. The very act of bringing conduct out of the impulsive into the moral sphere, depends upon the development of intelligence so as to transform a feeling into the perception of a situation. And, as we watch moral development from childhood to maturity, is it not evident that progress consists in power to conceive of larger and better defined ends? to analyze the situation which demands active response, the function which needs exercise, into specific relations, instead of taking it partially or even upon some one else's say so? Conduct, so far as not based upon an intelligent recognition and realization of the relationships involved, is either sentimental, or *merely* habitual —in the former case immoral, and in the latter failing of the complete morality possible.

If the necessary part played in conduct by artistic cultivation is not so plain, it is largely because "Art" has been made such an unreal Fetich—a sort of superfine and extraneous polish to be acquired only by specially cultivated people. In reality, living is itself the supreme art; it requires fineness of touch; skill and thoroughness of workmanship; susceptible response and delicate adjustment to a situation apart from reflective analysis; instinctive perception of the proper harmonies of act and act, of man and man. Active art is the embodiment of ideals; the clothing of ideas otherwise abstract in their peculiar and fit garb of concrete outward detail; passive art is the quick and accurate response to such embodiments as are already made. What were human conduct without the one and the other?

Granting the necessity of knowledge and of its artistic application in conduct, the question arises as to where the line is to be drawn. Evidently, if anywhere, at specialisms, remote philosophic or mathematical endeavors; life-times spent in inventive attempts without appreciable outcome. But to draw the line is not easy. The remote of one generation is the social tool of the next; the abstract mathematics and physics of the sixteenth and seventeenth centuries are the great social forces of the nineteenth—the locomotive, the telegraph, the telephone, etc. And how, in any case, can we tell a scientific investigator that up to a certain experiment or calculation his work may be social, beyond that, not? All that we can say is that beyond a certain point its social character is not obvious to sense and that the work must be carried on by faith.

Thus it is that we dispose of objections like Bradley's (*Ethical Studies*, p. 202): "Nothing is easier than to suppose a life of art or speculation which, as far as we can see, though true to itself, has, so far as others are concerned, been sheer waste or even loss, and which knew that it was so." That we cannot *see* any social *result* in such cases has nothing to do with the question whether or not the interests themselves are social. We may imagine a life of philanthropic activity, say of devotion to emancipation of slaves in a country wholly given over to slavery, or of a teacher in an unenlightened country, which, as far as we can see, (though, in this case, as in the one referred to by Mr. Bradley, everything depends upon how far we *can* see) has been sheer waste, so far as influence on others is concerned. The point is whether in such cases the life lived is not one of devotion to the interests of humanity as such.

We have been trying to show that every one admits that science and art, up to a certain point, are social, and that to draw a line where they cease to be so, is in reality to draw a line where we cease to *see* their social character. That we should cease to *see* it, is necessary in the case of almost every advance. Just because the new scientific movement is new, we can realize its social effects only afterwards. But it may be questioned whether the motive which actuates the man of science is not, when fully realized, a *faith* in the social bearing of what he is doing. If we were to go into a metaphysical analysis, the question would have to be raised whether a barely intellectual fact or theory be not a pure abstraction—an unreality if kept apart entirely from the activities of men in relation to one another.

## XXXIX.  Science and Art as Necessary Factors of Social Welfare

Let us consider the problem on its other side. What kind of an interest is our interest in persons, our distinctively social interest? Suppose we attempt to separate our interests in truth, beauty, and use from our interest in persons: *What remains in the persons to be interested in?* Is not a necessary part of our interest in persons, an interest in them as beings fulfilling their respective intellectual and artistic capacities; and if we cut this out of our social interest, have we not maimed and stunted our interest in persons? We wish the fullest life possible to ourselves and to others. And the fullest life means largely a complete and free development of capacities in knowledge and production — production of beauty and use. Our interest in others is not satisfied as long as their intelligence is cramped, their appreciation of truth feeble, their emotions hard and uncomprehensive, their powers of production compressed. To will their true good is to will the freeing of all such gifts to the highest degree. Shall we say that their true good requires that they shall go to the point of understanding algebra, but not quaternions, of understanding ordinary mechanics, but not to working out an electro-magnetic theory of light? to ability to appreciate ordinary chords and tunes, but not to the attempt to make further developments in music?

And this throws light upon the case referred to by Mr. Bradley. *Social* welfare demands that the individual be permitted to devote himself to the fulfilling of *any* scientific or artistic capacity that he finds within himself — provided, of course, it does not conflict with some more important capacity — irrespective of results. To say to a man: You may devote yourself to this gift, provided you demonstrate beforehand its social bearing, would be to talk nonsense. The new discovery is not yet made. It is absolutely required by the interests of a progressive society that it allow freedom to the individual to develop such functions as he finds in himself, irrespective of any *proved* social effect. Here, as elsewhere, morality works by faith, not by sight.

Indeed the ordinary conception of social interests, of benevolence, needs a large over-hauling. It is practically equivalent to doing something directly for others — to one form or another of charity. But this is only negative morality. A true social interest is that which wills for others freedom from dependence on our *direct* help, which wills to them the self-directed power of exercising, in and by themselves, their own functions. Any will short of this is not social but selfish, willing the dependence of others that we may continue benignly altruistic. The idea of "giving pleasure" to others, "making others happy," if it means anything else than securing conditions so that they may act freely in their own satisfaction, means slavery.

As society advances, social interest must consist more and more in free devotion to intelligence for its own sake, to science, art and industry, and in rejoicing in the exercise of such freedom by others. Meantime, it is truth which makes free.

See Spencer, *Data of Ethics*, pp. 249–57, where this doctrine is stated with great force.

Where, finally, does the social character of science and art come in? Just here: they are elements in the perfection of individuality, and they are elements whose very nature is to be moving, not rigid; distributed from one to another and not monopolistic possessions. If there are forms of science and art which, at present, are static, being merely owned collections of facts, as one may have a collection of butterflies in a frame, or of etchings in a closed portfolio, this is not because they are science and art, but imperfect science and art. To complete their scientific and artistic character is to set these facts in motion; to hurl them against the world of physical forces till new instruments of man's activity are formed, and to set them in circulation so that others may also participate in their truth and rejoice in their beauty. So far as scientific or artistic attainments are treasured as individual possessions, so far it *is* true that they are not social — but so far it is *also* true that they are immoral: indeed that they are not fully scientific or artistic, being subordinated to having certain sensations.

The intellectual movement of the last four or five centuries has resulted in an infinite specialization in methods, and in an immense accumulation of fact. It is quite true, since the diversity of fact and of method has not yet been brought to an organic unity, that their social bearing is not yet realized. But when the unity is attained (as attained it must be if there is unity in the object of knowledge), it will pass into a corresponding unity of practice. And then the question as to the social character of even the most specialized knowledge will seem absurd. It will be to ask whether men can co-operate better when they do not know than when they do know what they want. Meantime the intellectual confusion, and the resulting divorce of knowledge from practice, exists. But this constitutes a part of the environment of which action must take heed. It makes it one of the pressing duties that every man of intelligence should do his part in bringing out the public and common aspects of knowledge. *The* duty of the present is the socializing of intelligence—the realizing of its bearing upon social practice.

## XL. The Ethical Postulate

We have attempted to show that the various interests are social in their very nature. We have not attempted to show that this can be seen or proved in any given case. On the contrary, in most, if not all cases, the agent acts from a faith that, in realizing his own capacity, he will satisfy the needs of society. If he were asked to *prove* that his devotion to his function were right because certain to promote social good, he might well reply: "That is none of my affair. I have only to work myself out as strength and opportunity are given me, and let the results take care of themselves. I did not make the world, and if it turns out that devotion to the capacity which was given me, and loyalty to the surroundings in which I find myself do not result in good, I do not hold myself responsible. But, after all, I cannot believe that it will so turn out. What is really good for me *must* turn out good for all, or else there is no good in the world at all." The basis, in a word, of moral conduct, with respect to the exercise of function, is a faith that moral self-satisfaction (that is, satisfaction in accordance with the performance of function as already defined) means social satisfaction—or the faith that self and others make a true community. Now such faith or conviction is at the basis of all moral conduct —not simply of the scientific or artistic. Interest in self must mean belief in one's business, conviction of its legitimacy and worth, even prior to any sensible demonstration. Under any circumstances, such demonstration can extend only to past action; the social efficiency of any new end must be a matter of faith. Where such faith is wanting, action becomes halting and character weak. Forcible action fails, and its place is taken by a feeble idealism, of vague longing for that which is not, or by a pessimistic and fruitless discontent with things as they are—leading, in either case, to neglect of actual and pressing duty. The basis of moral strength is *limitation*, the resolve to be one's self only, and to be loyal to the actual powers and surroundings of that self. The saying of Carlyle's about doing the "duty that lies nearest," and of Goethe's that "America is here or nowhere," both imply that faith in the existing moral capacity and environment is the basis of conduct. All fruitful and sound human endeavor roots in the conviction that there is something absolutely worth while, something "divine" in the demands imposed by one's actual situation and powers. In the great moral heroes of the world the conviction of the worth of their destiny, and of what they were meant to do, has amounted to a kind of fatalism. They have done not simply what they *could* do, but what they *must* do.

On the other hand, effective social interest is based upon what is vaguely called "faith in humanity," or, more specifically, belief in the value of each man's individuality, belief in some particular function which he might exercise, given appropriate conditions and stimuli. Moral interest in others must be an interest in their possibilities, rather than in their accomplishments; or, better, in their accomplishments so far as these testify to a fulfilling of function—to a working out of capacity. Sympathy and work for men which do not grow out of faith in them are a perfunctory and unfertile sort of thing.

This faith is generally analyzed no further; it is left as faith in one's "calling" or in "humanity." But what is meant is just this: in the performing of such special service as each is capable of, there is to be found not only the satisfaction of self, but also the satisfaction of the entire moral order, the furthering of the community in which one lives. All moral conduct is based upon such a faith; and *moral theory must recognize this as the postulate upon which it rests.* In calling it a postulate, we do not mean that it is a postulate which our theory makes or must make in order to be a theory; but that, through analysis, theory *finds that moral practice makes this postulate*, and that with its reality the reality and value of conduct are bound up.

In calling it a postulate we do not mean to call it unprovable, much less unverifiable, for moral experience is itself, so far as it goes, its verification. But we mean that the further consideration of this postulate, its demonstration or (if the case so be) its refutation, do not belong to the realm of ethics as such. Each branch of human experience rests upon some presupposition which, *for that branch*, is ultimate. The further inquiry into such presuppositions belongs not to mathematics, or physics, or ethics, but to metaphysics.

Unless, then, we are to extend our ethical theory to inquire into the possibility and value of moral experience, unless, that is, we are to make an excursion into the metaphysics of ethics, we have here reached our foundation. The ethical postulate, the presupposition involved in conduct, is this:

IN THE REALIZATION OF INDIVIDUALITY THERE IS FOUND ALSO THE NEEDED REALIZATION OF SOME COMMUNITY OF PERSONS OF WHICH THE INDIVIDUAL IS A MEMBER; AND, CONVERSELY, THE AGENT WHO DULY SATISFIES THE COMMUNITY IN WHICH HE SHARES, BY THAT SAME CONDUCT SATISFIES HIMSELF.

Otherwise put, the postulate is that there is a community of persons; a good which realized by the will of one is made not private but public. It is this unity of individuals as respects the end of action, this existence of a practical common good, that makes what we call the moral order of the world.

Shakespeare has stated the postulate —

> *To thine own self be true;*
> *And it must follow, as the night the day,*
> *Thou can'st not then be false to any man.*

Its significance may be further developed by comparing it with the scientific postulate.

All science rests upon the conviction of the thoroughgoing and permanent unity of the world of objects known—a unity which is sometimes termed the "uniformity of nature" or the "reign of law"; without this conviction that objects are not mere isolated and transitory appearances, but are connected together in a system by laws or relations, science would be an impossibility. Moral experience *makes for the world of practice* an assumption analogous in kind to that which intellectual experience makes for the world of knowledge. And just as it is not the affair of science, as such, or even of logic (the theory of science) to justify this presupposition of science, or to do more than show its presence in intellectual experience, so it is not the business of conduct, or even of ethics (the theory of conduct) to justify what we have termed the "ethical postulate." In each case the further inquiry belongs to metaphysics.

## XLI. Does the End Proposed Serve as a Criterion of Conduct?

We have now concluded that an end which may be termed indifferently "The Realization of Individuality," "The Performance of Specific Functions," "The Satisfaction of Interests," "The Realization of a Community of Individuals" is the moral end. Will this end serve the two aims (see Sec. XVI) required of a criterion, or standard: (1) Will it unify individual conduct? (2) Will it afford a common good? We have just been endeavoring to show that it does both of these things; that as the realization of one's specific capacity, it unifies individual conduct, and that, as the performance of function, it serves to satisfy the entire community. To take up just these points, accordingly, would involve a repetition of what has been said, and we shall therefore take up instead some aspects of the individual and social unity of conduct, not already considered.

### 1. The System of Individual Conduct

We must be careful not to interpret the idea of specific function too rigidly or abstractly. It does not mean that each one has some supreme mission in life to which everything else must be sacrificed—that a man is to be an artist, or a soldier, or a student, or a day-laborer and nothing else. On the contrary, the idea of function is that which comprehends all the various sides of life, and it cannot be narrowed below the meaning we have already given: the due adjustment of capacity and surroundings. Whenever there is any capacity or any circumstance, no matter how trivial, there is something included in the exercise of function, and, therefore to be satisfied—according to its place, of course, in the whole of life. Amusements and all the minor details of life are included within the scope of morality. They are elements in the exercise of function, and their insignificance and triviality does not exclude them from the grasp of duty and of the good. It is a mistake to suppose that because it is optional or indifferent—as it constantly is—what acts among the minor details of life are to be done or left undone, or unimportant whether they are done or left undone at all, therefore such acts have no moral value. Morality consists in treating them just as they are—if they are slight or trivial they are to be performed as slight and trivial. Morality does not simply permit the performance of such acts, but demands it. To try to make, in the interests of duty, a serious matter out of every detail of life would be immoral—as much so, in kind, as to make light of momentous matters.

See Alexander, *Moral Order*, pp. 53–54; Bradley, *Ethical Studies*, pp. 194–97.

Consider, also, how this conception of the end stands in definite relation to concrete acts; how it explains the possibility of decision as to whether this or that proposed act is right. We do not have to trace the connection of the act with some end beyond, as pleasure, or abstract law. We have only to analyze the *act itself*. We have certain definite and wholly concrete facts; the given capacity of the person at the given moment, and his given surroundings. The judgment as to the nature of these facts is, in and of itself, a judgment as to the act to be done. The question is not: What is the probability that this act will result in the balance of maximum pleasure; it is not what general rule can we hunt up under which to bring this case. It is simply: *What is this case?* The moral act is not that which satisfies some far-away principle, hedonistic or transcendental. It is that which meets the present, actual situation. Difficulties indeed, arise, but they are simply the difficulty of resolving a complex case; they are intellectual, not moral. The case made out, the moral end stands forth. No extraneous manipulation, to bring the case under some foreign end, is required.

And this suggests the elasticity of the criterion. In fact moral conduct is entirely individualized. It is where, when, how and of whom. There has been much useless discussion as to the absolute or relative character of morals—useless because the terms absolute and relative are not defined. If absolute is taken to mean immobile and rigid, it is anything but desirable that morals should be absolute. If the physical world is a scene of movement, in which there is no rest, it is a poor compliment to pay the moral world to conceive of it as static and lifeless. A rigid criterion in a world of developing social relations would speedily prove no criterion at all. It would be an abstract rule, taking no account of the individualized character of each act; its individuality of capacity and of surroundings, of time, place and relationships involved. A truly absolute criterion is one which adjusts itself to each case according to the specific nature of the case; one which moves with the moving world. On the other hand, if relative means uncertain in application, changing in time and place without reason for change in the facts themselves, then certainly the criterion is not relative. If it means taking note of all concrete relations involved, it *is* relative. The absoluteness, in fine, of the standard of action consists not in some rigid statement, but in never-failing application. Universality here, as elsewhere, resides not in a thing, but in a way, a method of action. The absolute standard is the one applicable to all deeds, and the conception of the exercise of function is thus absolute, covering all conduct from the mainly impulsive action of the savage to the most complex reaches of modern life.

Aristotle's well known theory of the "mean" seems to have its bearing here. "It is possible," he says (Peters' trans. of *Ethics*, p.

46), "to feel fear, confidence, desire, anger, pity, and generally to be affected pleasantly and painfully, either too much or too little—in either case wrongfully; but to be affected thus at the right *times*, and on the right *occasions*, and toward the right *persons*, and with the right *object* and in the right *fashions*, is the mean course and the best course, and these are characteristics of virtue." The right time, occasion, person, purpose and fashion—what is it but the complete individualization of conduct in order to meet the whole demands of the whole situation, instead of some abstraction? And what else do we mean by fit, due, proper, right action, but that which just hits the mark, without falling short or deflecting, and, to mix the metaphor, without slopping over?

## 2. *The System of Social Conduct, or Common Good*

Moral conduct springs from the faith that all right action is social and its purpose is to justify this faith by working out the social values involved. The term "moral community" can mean only a unity of action, made what it is by the co-operating activities of diverse individuals. There is unity in the work of a factory, not in spite of, but *because of* the division of labor. Each workman forms the unity not by doing the same that everybody else does, or by trying to do the whole, but by doing his specific part. The unity is the one activity which their varied activities make. And so it is with the moral activity of society and the activities of individuals. The more individualized the functions, the more perfect the unity. (See Sec. LII.)

The exercise of function by an agent serves, then, both to define and to unite him. It makes him a *distinct* social member at the same time that it makes him a *member*. Possession of peculiar capacities, and special surroundings mark one person off from another and make him an individual; and the due adjustment of capacities to surroundings (in the exercise of function) effects, therefore, the realization of individuality—the realization of what we specifically are as distinct from others. At the same time, this distinction is not isolation; the exercise of function is the performing of a special *service* without which the social whole is defective. Individuality means not separation, but defined position in a whole; special aptitude in constituting the whole.

We are now in a position to take up the consideration

of the two other fundamental ethical conceptions—obligation and freedom. These ideas answer respectively to the two sides of the exercise of function. On the one hand, the performing of a function realizes the social whole. Man is thus "bound" by the relations necessary to constitute this whole. He is subject to the conditions which the existence and growth of the social unity impose. He is, in a word, under *obligation*; the performance of his function is duty owed to the community of which he is a member.

But on the other hand, activity in the way of function realizes the individual; it is what makes him an individual, or distinct person. In the performance of his own function the agent satisfies his own interests and gains power. In it is found his *freedom*.

Obligation thus corresponds to the *social* satisfaction, freedom to the *self*-satisfaction, involved in the exercise of function; and they can no more be separated from each other than the correlative satisfaction can be. One has to realize himself as a member of a community. In this fact are found both freedom and duty.

# 2

# *The Idea of Obligation*

## XLII. Theories Regarding Moral Authority

The idea of obligation or duty has two sides. There is
the idea of law, of something which controls conduct, and
there is the *consciousness* of the necessity of conforming to
this law. There is, of course, no separation between the two
sides, but the consideration of the latter side—the recognition of obligation—may be best dealt with in discussing
conscience. Here we shall deal simply with the fact that
there is such a thing in conduct as law controlling action,
and constituting obligation. Theories regarding obligation
may, for our purposes, be subdivided into those which make
its exercise restraint or coercion (and which therefore hold
that in perfect moral conduct, duty as such disappears); and
those which hold that obligation is a normal element in
conduct as such, and that it is not, essentially, but only
under certain circumstances, coercive. Of the former type,
some theories (mainly the hedonistic) regard the restraint
as originally imposed from without upon the desires of the
individual, while others (as the Kantian) regard it as imposed by man's reason upon his desires and inclinations.

## XLIII. Bain's Theory of Obligation

It is obvious that the question of obligation presents
considerable difficulty to the hedonistic school. If the end of
conduct is pleasure, as the satisfaction of desire, why should
not each desire be satisfied, if possible, as it arises, and thus
pleasure secured? What meaning is there in the term
"duty" or "obligation" if the moral end or good coincides
wholly with the natural end of the inclinations themselves?
It is evident, at all events, that the term can have signifi-

cance only if there is some cause preventing the desires as they arise from natural satisfaction. The problem of obligation in hedonism thus becomes the problem of discovering that outside force which restrains, or, at least, constrains, the desire from immediate gratification. According to Bain, this outside force is social disapprobation manifested through the form of punishment.

"I consider that the proper meaning, or import of the terms [duty, obligation] refers to that class of action which is enforced by the sanction of punishment. . . . The powers that impose the obligatory sanction are Law and Society, or the community acting through the Government by public judicial acts, and apart from the Government by the unofficial expressions of disapprobation and the exclusion from social good offices" *Emotions and Will*, p. 286. See also pp. 321–23 and p. 527.

Through this "actual and ideal avoidance of certain acts and dread of punishment" the individual learns to forego the gratification of some of his natural impulses, and learns also to cultivate and even to originate desires not at first spontaneous. "The child is open from the first to the blame and praise of others, and thus is led to do or avoid certain acts."

On the model, however, of the action of this external authority there grows up, in time an internal authority—"an ideal resemblance of public authority" (p. 287), or "a *fac simile* of the system of government around us" (p. 313).

"The sentiment, at first formed and cultivated by the relations of actual command and obedience, may come at last to stand upon an independent foundation. . . . When the young mind, accustomed at the outset to implicitly obeying any set of rules is sufficiently advanced to appreciate the motive—the utilities or the sentiment that led to their imposition—the character of the conscience is entirely changed. . . . Regard is now had to the intent and meaning of the law, and not to the mere fact of its being prescribed by some power" (*Emotions and Will*, p. 318).

But when the sense of obligation becomes entirely detached from the social sanction, "even then the notion, sentiment or form of duty is derived from what society imposes, although the particular matter is quite different. Social obligation develops in the mind originally the feeling and habit of obligation, and this remains although the particular articles are changed" (p. 319n.). *Cf.* also Bain, *Moral Science*, pp. 20–21 and 41–43.

## XLIV.  Spencer's Theory of Obligation

Spencer's theory is, in substance, an enlarged and better analyzed restatement of Bain's theory. Bain nowhere clearly states in what the essence of obligation consists, when it becomes independent, when the internal *fac simile* is formed. *Why* should I not gratify my desires as I please in case social pressure is absent or lets up? Spencer supplies the missing element. According to him, "the essential trait in the moral consciousness is the control of some feeling or feelings by some other feeling or feelings" (*Data of Ethics*, p. 113). The kind of feeling which controls is that which is more complex and which relates to more remote ends; or, we are "obliged" to give up more immediate, special and direct pleasures for the sake of securing more general, remote and indirect ones. Obligation, in its essence, is the surrender or subordination of present to future satisfaction. This control, restraint, or suppression may be "independent" or, self-imposed, but is not so at first, either in the man or in the child. Prior to self-restraint are the restraints imposed by the "visible ruler, the invisible ruler and society at large"—the policeman, the priest and public opinion. The man is induced to postpone immediate gratification through his fear of others, especially of the chief, of the dead and of social displeasure—"legal penalty, supernatural punishment and social reprobation." Thus there grows up the sense of obligation. This refers at first only to the above-mentioned extrinsic effects of action. But finally the mind learns to consider the intrinsic effect of the action itself—the evil inflicted by the evil deed, and then the sense of duty, or coercion, evolved through the aforesaid external agencies, becomes transferred to this new mode of controlling action. Desires are now controlled through considerations of what their *own* effects would be, were the desires acted upon.

It follows "that the sense of duty or moral obligation is transitory, and will diminish as fast as moralization increases" (*Data of Ethics*, p. 127). Even when compulsion is self-imposed, there is still compulsion, coercion, and this must be done away with. It *is* done away with as far as an act which is at first done only for the sake of its own remoter consequences comes to be done for its own sake. And this will ultimately occur, if the act is continued, since "persistence in performing a duty ends in making it a pleasure."

See Guyau, *La Morale Anglaise Contemporaine*, besides the works of Bain and Spencer. In addition to objections which will forthwith be made, we may here note a false abstraction of Spencer's. He makes the act and its consequences *two* things, while the act and its consequences (provided they are known as such) are the same thing, no matter whether consequences are near or remote. The only distinction is that consequences once not known as such at all are seen in time to be really consequences, and thus to be part of the content of the act. The transfer from the "external consequences" imposed by the ruler, priest and public-opinion to the intrinsic consequences of the act itself, is thus a transfer from an immoral to a moral basis. This is very different from a change of the form of obligation itself.

## XLV. Criticism of these Theories

Putting aside the consideration of the relation of desire to duty, (the question whether duty is essentially coercive), until after we have taken up the Kantian idea of obligation, we may note the following objections to the theories just stated. Their great defect is that they do not give us any method of differentiating moral coercion (or obligation) from the action of mere superior physical force. Taking it (first) upon the side of the individual: Is there any reason *why* the individual submits to the external authority of government except that he *has* to do so? He may argue that, since others possess superior force, he will avoid certain pains by conforming to their demands, but such yielding, whether temporary or permanent, to superior force is very far from being a recognition that one *ought* to act as the superior force dictates. The theories must logically commit us to the doctrine that "might makes right" in its baldest form. Every one knows that, when the individual surrenders the natural gratifications of his desires to the command of others, if his sole reason is the superior force of the commanding party, he does not forego in the surrender his right to such gratification the moment he has the chance to get it.

Actual slavery would be the model school of duties, if these theories were true.

The facts adduced by Bain and Spencer—the growth of the recognition of duties in the child through the authority of the parents, and in the savage through the use of authority by the chief—are real enough, but what they prove is that obligation may be brought home to one by force, not that force creates obligation. The child and the man yield to force in such a way that their sense of duty is developed only in case they recognize, implicitly, the force or the authority as already *right*. Let it be recognized that *rightful* force (as distinct from mere brute strength) resides in certain social authorities, and these social authorities may do much, beyond the shadow of doubt, to give effect to the special deeds and relations which are to be considered obligatory. These theories, in fine, take the fact of obligation for granted, and, at most, only show the historical process by which its fuller recognition is brought about. Force in the service of right is one thing; force as constituting and creating right is another.

And this is to say (secondly), considering the matter from the side of society, that the theories of Bain and Spencer do not explain why or how social authority should exercise coercive force over the individual. If it is implied that they do so in the moral interests of the individual or of the community, this takes it for granted that there already is in existence a moral ideal obligatory upon the individual. If it is implied that they exercise coercive force in the interests of their own private pleasure, this might establish a despotism, or lead to a political revolt, but it is difficult to see how it could create the fact of duty. When we consider any concrete case, we see that society, in its compelling of the individual, is possessed of moral ideals; and that it conceives itself not merely as having the *power* to make the individual conform to them, nor as having the *right* merely; but as under the bounden *duty* of bringing home to the individual *his* duties. The social authorities do not, perforce, create morality, but they embody and make effective the existing morality. It is only just because the actions which they impose are thought of as *good*, good for others as for themselves, that this imposition is taken out of the realm of tyranny into that of duty (see Sec. XXXVIII).

## XLVI. The Kantian Theory of Obligation

As we have seen, Kant takes the conception of duty as the primary ethical notion, superior to that of the good, and places it in the most abrupt opposition to desire. The relation of duty to desire is not control of some feelings by others, but rather suppression of all desire (not in itself, but as a *motive* of action) in favor of the consciousness of law universal. We have, on one side, according to Kant, the desire and inclination, which are sensuous and pathological. These constitute man's "lower nature." On the other side there is Reason, which is essentially universal, above all caprice and all prostitution to private pleasure. This Reason, or "higher nature," imposes a law upon the sentient being of man, a law which takes the form of a command (the "Categorical Imperative"). This relation of a higher rational nature issuing commands to a lower sensuous nature (both within man himself), is the very essence of duty. If man were wholly a sentient being, he would have only to follow his natural impulses, like the animals. If he were only a rational being, he would necessarily obey his reason, and there would still be no talk of obligation. But because of the dualism, because of the absolute opposition between Reason and Desire, man is a being subject to obligation. Reason says to the desires "Thou shalt" or "Thou shalt not." Yet this obligation is not externally imposed; the man as rational imposes it upon himself as sensuous. Thus Kant says that, in the realm of morality, man is both sovereign and subject.

The reflex influence of Rousseau's social theories upon Kant's moral doctrines in this respect is worthy of more attention than it usually receives. Kant's moral theory is hardly more than a translation of Rousseau's politics into ethical terms, through its union with Kant's previously established dualism of reason and sense.

## XLVII. Criticism of the Kantian Theory

*1.* No one can deny that a genuine opposition exists between the "natural" desires and moral activity. The being that satisfies each desire or appetite as it arises, without reference of it to, or control of it by, some principle, has not had the horizon of conduct lift before him. But Kant makes the satisfaction of desire *as such* (not of this or that desire) antagonistic to action from duty. Kant was forced into this position by his fundamental division of sense from reason, but it carries with it its own condemnation and thus that of the premises from which it is derived. It comes to saying that the actual desires and appetites are not what they ought to be. This, in itself, is true enough. But when Kant goes on to say, as he virtually does, that what ought to be *cannot* be, that the desires as such cannot be brought into harmony with principle, he has made the moral life not only a riddle, but a riddle with no answer. If mankind were once convinced that the moral ideal were something which ought to be but which could not be, we may easily imagine how much longer moral endeavor would continue. The first or immediate stimulus to moral effort is the conviction that the desires and appetites are not what they should be; the underlying and continuing stimulus is the conviction that the expression of desires in harmony with law is the sole abiding good of man. To reconcile the two is the very meaning of the moral struggle (see Sec. LXIV). Strictly, according to Kant, morality would either leave the appetites untouched or would abolish them—in either case destroying morality.

See Caird, *Critical Philosophy of Kant*, Vol. II, pp. 226–28.

2. Kant again seems to be on the right track in declaring that obligation is not anything externally imposed, but is the law of man's being, self-imposed. This principle of "autonomy" is the only escape from a theory of obligation which would make obligation external, and regard for it slavish fear, or servile hope of reward. To regard even a Divine Being as the author of obligation is to make it a form of external constraint, appealing only to hope or fear, unless this Divine Being is shown to be organically connected with self.

But this abstract universal reason which somehow dwells, without mediation or reason, in each individual, seems to be somewhat scholastic, a trifle mythological. There is undoubtedly in man's experience a function which corresponds to what Kant is aiming, thus mythologically, to describe. But it is one thing to recognize an opposition of a desire, in its isolation, to desire as organic to the function of the whole man; it is another to split man into a blank dualism of an abstract reason, on one side, having no antecedents or bearings, and of a mess of appetites, having only animal relationship, on the other. The truth that Kant is aiming to preserve seems to be fairly stated as two-fold: first, that duty is self-imposed, and thus the dutiful will autonomous or free; and, second, the presence of struggle in man between a "lower" and a "higher." The first point seems to be sufficiently met by the idea already advanced that self, or individuality, is essentially social, being constituted not by isolated capacity, but by capacity acting in response to the needs of an environment—an environment which, when taken in its fullness, is a community of persons. Any law imposed by such a self would be "universal," but this universality would not be an isolated possession of the individual; it would be another name for the concrete social relationships which make the individual what he is, as a social member or organ. Furthermore, such a universal law would not be formal, but would have a content—these same relationships.

The second point seems to be met by recognizing that in the realization of the law of social function, conflict must occur between the desire as an immediate and direct expression of the individual—the desire in its isolation—and desire as an expression of the whole man; desire, that is, as wholly conformable to the needs of the surroundings. Such a conflict is real enough, as every one's experience will testify, but it is a conflict which may be solved—which must be solved so far as morality is attained. And since it is a conflict within desire itself, its solution or morality, does not require any impossible obliteration of desire, nor any acting from an "ought" which has no relation to what "is." This, indeed, is *the* failure of the Kantian Ethics: in separating what should be from what is, it deprives the latter, the existing social world as well as the desires of the individual, of all moral value; while, by the same separation, it condemns that which should be to a barren abstraction. An "ought" which does not root in and flower from the "is," which is not the fuller realization of the actual state of social relationships, is a mere pious wish that things should be better. And morality, that is, right action, is not so feeble as this would come to.

## XLVIII.  The Source and Nature of Obligation

The basis of a correct theory of obligation lies, as already stated, in holding fast to its concrete relations to the moral end, or good. This end consists in an activity in which capacity is exercised in accordance with surroundings, with the social needs which affect the individual. It is implied in this very idea, that the end is not something which the individual may set up at his own arbitrary will. The social needs give control, law, authority. The individual may not manifest his capacity, satisfy his desires, apart from their specific relation to the environment in which they exist. The general fact of obligation which is constituted through this control of capacity by the wider function is, of course, differentiated into specific "laws" or duties by the various forms which the one function takes, as capacity and circumstances vary.

In other words, obligation or duty is simply the aspect which the good or the moral end assumes, as the individual conceives of it. From the very fact that the end is the good, and yet is not realized by the individual, it presents itself to him as that which *should be realized* — as the ideal of action. It requires no further argument to show that obligation is at once self-imposed, and social in its content. It is self-imposed because it flows from the good, from the idea of the full activity of the individual's own will. It is no law imposed from without; but is his own law, the law of his own function, of his individuality. Its social content flows from the fact that this individuality is not mere capacity, but is this capacity *acting*, and acting so as to comprehend social relationships.

Suppose that man's good and his conviction of duty were divorced from one another — that man's duty were other than to fulfill his own specific function. Such a thing would make duty purely formal; the moral law would have no intrinsic relation to daily conduct, to the expression of man's powers and wants. There have, indeed, been moralists who think they do the Lord service, who think they add to the dignity and sacredness of Duty by making it other than the idea of the activity of man, regulated indeed, but regulated only by its own principle of activity. But such moralists in their desire to consecrate the idea of duty remove from it all content, and leave it an empty abstraction. On the other hand, their eagerness to give absoluteness and imperativeness to duty by making it a law other than that of the normal expression of man, casts discredit upon the one moral reality—the full, free play of human life. In denying that duty is simply the *intrinsic* law, the *self*-manifestation of this life, they make this life immoral, or at least nonmoral. They degrade it to a bundle of appetites and powers having no moral value until the outside moral law is applied to them. In reality, the dignity and imperativeness of duty are simply the manifest dignity and unconditioned worth of human life as exhibited in its free activity. The whole idea of the separateness of duty from the concrete flow of human action is a virulent example of the fallacy mentioned in an early section—the fallacy that moral action means something more than action itself (see Sec. 11).

The attempt to act upon a theory of the divorce of satisfaction and duty, to carry it out in practice, means the maiming of desire through distrust of its moral significance, and thus, by withdrawing the impetus of action, the reduction of life to mere passivity. So far as this does not happen, it means the erection of the struggle itself, the erection of the opposition of law to desire, into the very principle of the moral life. The essential principle of the moral life, that good consists in the freeing of impulse, of appetite, of desire, of power, by enabling them to flow in the channel of a unified and full end is lost sight of, and the free service of the spirit is reduced to the slavish fear of a bond-man under a hard taskmaster.

The essential point in the analysis of moral law, or obligation, having been found, we may briefly discuss some subsidiary points.

## 1. *The Relation of Duty to a Given Desire*

As any desire arises, it will be, except so far as character has already been moralized, a demand for its own satisfaction; the desire, in a word, will be isolated. In so far, duty will be in a negative attitude towards the desire; it will insist first upon its limitation, and then upon its transformation. So far as it is merely limitative, it demands the denying of the desire, and so far assumes a coercive form. But this limitation is not for its own sake, but for that of the transformation of desire into a freer and more adequate form—into a form, that is, where it will carry with it, when it passes into action, *more of activity*, than the original desire would have done.

Does duty itself disappear when its constraint disappears? On the contrary, so far as an act is done unwillingly, under constraint, so far the act is impure, and *undutiful*. The very fact that there is need of constraint shows that the self is divided; that there is a two-fold interest and purpose —one in the law of the activity according to function, the other in the special end of the particular desire. Let the act be done *wholly as duty*, and it is done wholly for its own sake; love, passion take the place of constraint. This suggests:

## 2. *Duty for Duty's Sake*

It is clear that such an expression states a real moral fact; unless a duty is done *as* duty it is not done morally. An act may be outwardly just what morality demands, and yet if done for the sake of some private advantage it is not counted moral. As Kant expresses it, an act must be done not only in accordance with duty, but *from duty*. This truth, however, is misinterpreted when it is taken to mean that the act is to be done for the sake of duty, and duty is conceived as a third thing outside the act itself. Such a theory contradicts the true sense of the phrase "duty for duty's sake," for it makes the act done not for its own sake, but as a mere means to an abstract law beyond itself. "Do the right because it is the right" means do the right *thing* because it *is* the right thing; that is, do the act disinterestedly from interest in the act itself. A duty is always some act or line of action, not a third thing outside the act to which it is to conform. In short, duty means *the act which is to be done*, and "duty for duty's sake" means do the required act as it really is; do not degrade it into a means for some ulterior end. This is as true in practice as in theory. A man who does his duty not for the sake of the acts themselves, but for the sake of some abstract "ideal" which he christens duty in general, will have a morality at once hard and barren, and weak and sentimental.

## 3. The Agency of Moral Authority in Prescribing Moral Law and Stimulating to Moral Conduct

The facts, relied upon by Bain and Spencer, as to the part played by social influences in imposing duties, are undeniable. The facts, however, are unaccountable upon the theory of these writers, as that theory would, as we have seen, explain only the influence of society in producing acts done from fear or for hope of reward. But if the individual and others are equally members of one society, if the performance by each man of his own function constitutes a good common to all, it is inevitable that social authorities should be an influence in constituting and teaching duties. The community, in imposing its own needs and demands upon the individual, is simply arousing him to a knowledge of his relationships in life, to a knowledge of the moral environment in which he lives, and of the acts which he must perform if he is to realize his individuality. The community in awakening moral consciousness in the morally immature may appeal to motives of hope and fear. But even this fact does not mean that to the child, duty is necessarily constituted by fear of punishment or hope of reward. It means simply that his capacity and his surroundings are both so undeveloped that the exercise of his function takes mainly the form of pleasing others. He may still do his duty *as* his duty, but his duty now consists in pleasing others.

On Obligation see Green, *Prolegomena*, pp. 352–56; Alexander, *Moral Order*, pp. 142–47. For different views, Martineau, *Types of Ethical Theory*, Vol. ii, pp. 92–119; Calderwood, *Handbook of Moral Philosophy*, pp. 131–38; and see also, Grote, *Treatise on Moral Ideals*, Ch. 7.

# The Idea of Freedom

## XLIX. The Forms of Freedom

We may now deal, more briefly, with the problem of moral capacity. It is, in principle, the ability to conceive of an end and to be governed in action by this conceived end. We may consider this capacity in three aspects, as negative, as potential and as positive.

### 1. *Negative Aspect of Freedom*

The power to be governed in action by the thought of some end to be reached is freedom *from* the appetites and desires. An animal which does not have the power of proposing ends to itself is impelled to action by its wants and appetites just as they come into consciousness. It is *irritated* into acting. Each impulse demands its own satisfaction, and the animal is helpless to rise above the particular want. But a *person*, one who can direct his action by conscious ends, is emancipated from subjection to the particular appetites. He can consider their relation to the end which he has set before himself, and can reject, modify or use them as best agrees with the purposed end. This capacity to control and subjugate impulses by reflection upon their relationship to a rational end is the power of self-government, and the more distinct and the more comprehensive in scope the end is, the more real the self-government.

### 2. *Potential Freedom*

The power to conceive of ends involves the possibility of thinking of many and various ends, and even of ends which are contrary to one another. If an agent could conceive of but one end in some case, it would always seem to him afterwards that he had been necessitated to act in the direction of that end; but the power to put various ends before self constitutes "freedom of choice," or potential freedom. After action, the agent calls to mind that there was another end open to him, and that if he did not choose the other end, it was because of something in his character which made him prefer the one he actually chose.

## L.  Moral Responsibility

Here we have the basis of moral *responsibility* or *accountability*. There is no responsibility for any result which is not intended or foreseen. Such a consequence is only physical, not moral. (Sec. VII.) But when any result has been foreseen, and adopted as foreseen, such result is the outcome not of any external circumstances, nor of mere desires and impulses, but of the agent's conception of his own end. Now, because the result thus flows from the agent's own conception of an end, he feels himself responsible for it.

It must be remembered that the end adopted is that which is conceived *as satisfying self* — that, indeed, when we say end of action, we mean only some proposed form of self-satisfaction. The adopted end always indicates, therefore, that sort of condition which the agent considers to be good, or self-satisfactory. It is because a result flows from the agent's *ideal of himself*, the thought of himself which he considers desirable or worth realizing, that the agent feels himself responsible. The result is simply an expression of himself; a manifestation of what he would have himself be. Responsibility is thus one aspect of the identity of character and conduct. (Sec. VII.) We are responsible for our conduct because that conduct is ourselves objectified in actions.

The idea of responsibility is intensified whenever there have been two contrary lines of conduct conceived, of which one has been chosen. If the end adopted turns out not to be satisfactory, but, rather, unworthy and degrading, the agent feels that he *might* have chosen the other end, and that if he did not, it was because his character was such, his ideal of himself was such, that this other end did not appeal to him. The actual result is felt to be the outcome of an unworthy

character manifested in the adoption of a low form of satisfaction; and the evident contrast of this low form with a
higher form, present to consciousness but rejected, makes
the sense of responsibility more acute. As such, it is the
judgment of disapprobation passed upon conduct; the feeling of remorse and of the desert of punishment. Freedom as
the power of conceiving ends and of realizing the ideal end
in action, is thus the basis both of responsibility and of
approbation (or disapprobation).

*The Freedom of Indifference.* It is this potential freedom,
arising from the power of proposing various ends of action, which,
misinterpreted, gives rise to the theory of a liberty of indifferent
choice—the theory that the agent can choose this or that without any
ground or motive. The real experience is the knowledge, after the
choice of one end, that since another end was also present to
consciousness that other end might have been chosen, *if only the
character had been such as to find its satisfaction in that other end.*
The theory of indifference misconstrues this fact to mean that the
agent might just as well have chosen that other end, without any if
or qualification whatever. The theory of indifference, moreover,
defeats its own end. The point which it is anxious to save is
responsibility. It sees that if only one course of action were ever open
to an agent, without the possibility of any *conception* of another
course, an agent, so acting, could not be held responsible for not
having adopted that other course. And so it argues that there must
always be the possibility of indifferent or alternate choice; the
possibility of adopting this or that line of action without any motive.
But if such were the case responsibility would be destroyed. If the
end chosen is not an expression of character, if it does not manifest
the agent's ideal of himself, if its choice is a matter of indifference, it
does not signify morally, but is mere accident or caprice. It is
because choice is *not* a matter of indifference, but an outcome of
character that the agent feels responsibility, and approves or disap-
proves. He virtually says: "I am responsible for this outcome, not
because I could have chosen another end just as well *without any
reason*, but because I thought of another end and rejected it; because
my character was such that that end did not seem good, and was
such that this end did seem good. My character is myself, and in this
unworthy end I stand self-condemned."

## LI.   Moral Reformation

Freedom considered as potential, depending upon the
power of the agent to frame diverse ends, is the basis not

only of responsibility, but also of the possibility of reformation, or of change in character and conduct. All moral action is the expression of self, but the self is not something fixed or rigid. It includes as a necessary part of itself the possibility of framing conceptions of what it would be, and there is, therefore, at any time the possibility of acting upon some ideal hitherto unrealized. If conduct were the expression of character, in a sense which identified character wholly with past attainments, then reformation would be impossible. What a man once was he must always continue to be. But past attainments do not exhaust all the possibilities of character. Since conduct necessarily implies a continuous adjustment of developing capacity to new conditions, there is the ability to frame a changed ideal of self-satisfaction—that is, ability to lead a new life. That the new ideal is adopted from experience of the unworthy nature of former deeds is what we should expect. The chosen end having proved itself unsatisfactory, the alternative end, previously rejected, recurs to consciousness with added claims. To sum up: The doctrine that choice depends upon character is correct, but the doctrine is misused when taken to mean that a man's outward conduct will always be in the same direction that it has been. Character involves all the ideas of different and of better things which have been present to the agent, although he has never attempted to carry them out. And there is always the possibility that, if the proper influences are brought to bear, some one of these latent ideals may be made vital, and wholly change the bent of character and of conduct.

## LII.  Positive Freedom

The *capacity* of freedom lies in the power to form an ideal or conception of an end. *Actual* freedom lies in the realization of that end which actually satisfies. An end may be freely adopted, and yet its actual working-out may result not in freedom, but in slavery. It may result in rendering the agent more subject to his passions, less able to direct his own conduct, and more cramped and feeble in powers. Only that end which executed really effects greater energy and comprehensiveness of character makes for actual freedom. In a word, only the good man, the man who is truly realizing his individuality, is free, in the positive sense of that word.

Every action which is not in the line of performance of functions must necessarily result in self-enslavement. The end of desire is activity; and it is only in fullness and unity of activity that freedom is found. When desires are not unified—when, that is, the idea of the exercise of function does not control conduct—one desire must conflict with another. Action is directed now this way, now that, and there is friction, loss of power. On account of this same lack of control of desires by the comprehensive law of social activity, one member of society is brought into conflict with another, with waste of energy, and with impeded and divided activity and satisfaction of desire. Exercise of function, on the other hand, unifies the desires, giving each its relative, although subordinate, place. It fits each into the others, and, through the harmonious adjustment of one to another, effects that complete and unhindered action which is freedom. The performance of specific function falls also into free relations with the activities of other persons, co-operating with them, giving and receiving what is needed, and thus constituting full liberty. Other aspects of freedom, as the negative and the potential, are simply means instrumental to the realization of individuality, and when not employed toward this, their true end, they become methods of enslaving the agent.

On the subject of moral freedom, as, upon the whole, in agreement with the view presented here: See Green, *Prolegomena to Ethics*, pp. 90–117, 142–58; Bradley, *Ethical Studies*, Ch. 1; Caird, *Philosophy of Kant*, Vol. ii, Bk. ii, Ch. 3; Alexander, *Moral Order*, pp. 336–41.

And, for a view agreeing in part, Stephen, *Science of Ethics*, pp. 278–93.

For presentations of the freedom of indifference, see Lotze, *Practical Philosophy*, Ch. 3; Martineau, *Types of Ethical Theory*, Vol. ii, pp. 34–40; Calderwood, *Handbook of Moral Philosophy*.

# PART TWO

# THE ETHICAL WORLD

## LIII. The Reality of Moral Relations

The habit of conceiving moral action as a certain *kind* of action, instead of all action so far as it really is action, leads us to conceive of morality as a highly desirable something which somehow ought to be brought into our lives, but which upon the whole is not. It gives rise to the habit of conceiving morality as a vague ideal which it is praiseworthy for the individual to strive for, but which depends wholly for its existence upon the individual's wish in the matter. Morality, that is, is considered as a relation existing between something which merely *ought to be*, on one hand, and the individual's choice, or his conscience on the other. This point of view has found typical expression in Bishop Butler's saying: "If conscience had might as it has right, it would rule the world."

But right is not such a helpless creature. It exists not in word but in power. The moral world is, here and now; it is a reality apart from the wishes, or failures ιo wish, of any given individual. It bears the same relation to the individual's activity that the "physical world" does to his knowledge. Not till the individual has to spin the physical world out of his consciousness in order to know it, will it be necessary for him to create morality by his choice, before it can exist. As knowledge is mastery in one's self of the real world, the reproduction of it in self-consciousness, so moral action is the appropriation and vital self-expression of the values contained in the existing practical world.

The existence of this moral world is not anything vaguely mysterious. Imagine a well organized factory, in which there is some comprehensive industry carried on—say the production of cotton cloth. This is the end; it is a common end—that for which each individual labors. Not all individuals, however, are doing the same thing. The more perfect the activity, the better organized the work, the more differentiated their respective labors. This is the side of individual activity or freedom. To make the analogy with moral activity complete we have to suppose that each individual is doing the work because of itself, and not merely as drudgery for the sake of some further end, as pay. Now these various individuals are bound together by their various acts; some more nearly because doing closely allied things, all somewhat, because contributing to a common activity. This is the side of laws and duties.

This group of the differentiated and yet related activities is the analogue of the moral world. There are certain wants which have constantly to be fulfilled; certain ends which demand co-operating activities, and which establish fixed relations between men. There is a world of ends, a realm of definite activities in existence, as concrete as the ends and activities in our imagined factory. The child finds, then, ends and actions in existence when he is born. More than this: he is not born as a mere spectator of the world; he is born *into* it. He finds himself encompassed by such relations, and he finds his own being and activity intermeshed with them. If he takes away from himself, as an agent, what he has, as sharing in these ends and actions, nothing remains.

## LIV. Moral Institutions

This world of purposes and activities is differentiated into various institutions. The child is born as a member of a *family*; as he grows up he finds that others have possessions which he must respect, that is, he runs upon the institution of *property*. As he grows still older, he finds persons outside of the family of whose actions he must take account as respects his own: *society*, in the limited sense as meaning relations of special intimacy or acquaintanceship. Then he finds the political institutions; the city, state and nation. He finds an educational institution, the school, the college; religious institutions, the church, etc., etc. Everywhere he finds men having common wants and thus proposing common ends and using co-operative modes of action. To these organized modes of action, with their reference to common interests and purposes, he must adjust his activities; he must take his part therein, if he acts at all, though it be only negatively or hostilely, as in evil conduct. These institutions *are* morality real and objective; the individual becomes moral as he shares in this moral world, and takes his due place in it.

Institutions, then, are organized modes of action, on the basis of the wants and interests which unite men. They differ as the family from the town, the church from the state, according to the scope and character of the wants from which they spring. They are not bare *facts* like objects of knowledge; they are *practical*, existing for the sake of, and by means of the will—as execution of ideas which have interest. Because they are expressions of common purposes and ideas, they are not merely private will and intelligence, but, in the literal sense, *public* will and reason.

The moral endeavor of man thus takes the form not of isolated fancies about right and wrong, not of attempts to frame a morality for himself, not of efforts to bring into being some praiseworthy ideal never realized; but the form of sustaining and furthering the moral world of which he is a member. Since the world is one of action, and not of contemplation like the world of knowledge, it can be sustained and furthered only as he makes its ends his own, and identifies himself and his satisfaction with the activities in which other wills find their fulfillment.

This is simply a more concrete rendering of what has already been said about the moral environment (see Sec. XXXIII).

## LV. The Aspects of a Moral Institution

An institution is, as we have seen, the expression of unity of desires and ideas; it is general intelligence in action, or common will. As such common will, it is, as respects the merely private or exclusive wants and aims of its members, absolutely *sovereign*. It must aim to control them. It must set before them the common end or ideal and insist upon this as the only real end of individual conduct. The ends so imposed by the public reason are *laws*. But these laws are for the sake of realizing the *common* end, of securing that organized unity of action in which alone the individual can find freedom and fullness of action, or his own satisfaction. Thus the activity of the common will gives freedom, or *rights*, to the various members of the institution.

Every institution, then, has its sovereignty, or authority, and its laws and rights. It is only a false abstraction which makes us conceive of sovereignty, or authority, and of law and of rights as inhering only in some supreme organization, as the national state. The family, the school, the neighborhood group, has its authority as respects its members, imposes its ideals of action, or laws, and confers its respective satisfactions in way of enlarged freedom, or rights. It is true that no one of these institutions is isolated; that each stands in relation with other like and unlike institutions. Each minor institution is a member of some more comprehensive whole, to which it bears the same relation that the individual bears to it. That is to say, *its* sovereignty gives way to the authority of the more comprehensive organization; its laws must be in harmony with the laws which flow from the larger activity; its rights must become aspects of a fuller satisfaction. Only humanity or the organized activity of all the wants, powers and interests common to men, can have absolute sovereignty, law and rights.

But the narrower group has its relations, none the less, although, in ultimate analysis, they flow from and manifest the wider good, which, as wider, must be controlling. Without such minor local authorities, rights and laws, humanity would be a meaningless abstraction, and its activity wholly empty. There is an authority in the family, and the moral growth of the child consists in identifying the law of his own conduct with the ends aimed at by the institution, and in growing into maturity and freedom of manhood through the rights which are bestowed upon him as such a member. Within its own range this institution is ultimate. But its range is not ultimate; the family, valuable and sacred as it is, does not exist for itself. It is not a larger selfishness. It exists as one mode of realizing that comprehensive common good to which all institutions must contribute, if they are not to decay. It is the same with property, the school, the local church, and with the national state.

We can now translate into more concrete terms what was said, in Part One, regarding the good, obligation and freedom. That performance of function which is "the good," is now seen to consist in vital union with, and reproduction of, the practical institutions of which one is a member. The maintenance of such institutions by the free participation therein of individual wills, is, of itself, the common good. Freedom also gets concreteness; it is the assured rights, or powers of action which one gets as such a member: —powers which are not mere claims, nor simply claims recognized as valid by others, but claims reinforced by the will of the whole community. Freedom becomes real in the ethical world; it becomes force and efficiency of action, because it does not mean some private possession of the individual, but means the whole co-operating and organized action of an institution in securing to an individual some power of self-expression.

## LVI. Moral Law and the Ethical World

Without the idea of the ethical world, as the unified activity of diverse functions exercised by different individuals, the idea of the good, and of freedom, would be undefined. But probably no one has ever attempted to conceive of the good and of freedom in total abstraction from the normal activity of man. Such has not been the lot of duty, or of the element of law. Often by implication, sometimes in so many words, it is stated that while a physical law may be accounted for, since it is simply an abstract from observed facts, a moral law stands wholly above and apart from actual facts; it expresses solely what "ought to be" and not what is; that, indeed, whether anything in accordance with it ever has existed or not, is a matter of no essential moral importance theoretically, however it may be practically. Now it is evident that a law of something which has not existed, does not and perhaps never will exist, is essentially inexplicable and mysterious. It is as against such a notion of moral law that the idea of a real ethical world has perhaps its greatest service.

A moral law, *e.g.*, the law of justice, is no more *merely* a law of what ought to be than is the law of gravitation. As the latter states a certain relation of moving masses to one another, so the law of justice states a certain relation of active wills to one another. For a given individual, at a given time and circumstances, the law of justice may appear as the law of something which ought to be, but is not: —is not *for him in this respect*, that is to say. But the very fact that it ought to be for him implies that it already is for others. It *is* a law of the society of which he is a member. And it is because he *is* a member of a society having this law, that is a law of what *should* be for him.

Would then justice cease to be a law for him if it were not observed at all in the society of which he is a member? Such a question is as contradictory as asking what would happen to a planet if the solar system went out of existence. It is the law of justice (with other such laws) that *makes* society; that is, it is those active relations which find expression in these laws that unify individuals so that they have a common end, and thus mutual duties. To imagine the abolition of these laws is to imagine the abolition of society; and to ask for the law of individual conduct apart from all relationship, actual or ideal, to society, is to ask in what morality consists when moral conditions are destroyed. A society in which the social bond we call justice does not obtain to some degree in the relations of man to man, is *not* society; and, on the other hand, wherever some law of justice actually obtains, there the law *is* for every individual who is a member of the society.

This does not mean that the "is," the actual status of the moral world, is identical with the "ought," or the ideal relations of man to man. But it does mean that there is no obligation, either in general or as any specific duty, which does not *grow* out of the "is," the actual relations now obtaining.[1] The ethical world at any given time is undoubt-

[1]    See Secs. LIX, LX and LXIII for discussion of other aspects of this question.

edly imperfect, and, *therefore*, it demands a certain act to meet the situation. The very imperfection, the very badness in the present condition of things, is a part of the environment with reference to which we must act; it is, thus, an element in the *law* of future action that it shall not exactly repeat the existing condition. In other words, the "is" gives the law of the "ought," but it is a part of this law that the "ought" shall not be as the "is." It is because the relation of justice does hold in members of a stratum of society, having a certain position, power or wealth, but does not hold between this section and another class, that the law of what should be is equal justice for all. In holding that actual social relations afford the law of what should be, we must not forget that these actual relations have a negative as well as a positive side, and that the new law must be framed in view of the negatives, the deficiencies, the wrongs, the contradictions, as well as of the positive attainments. A moral law, to sum up, is the principle of action, which, acted upon, will meet the needs of the existing situation as respects the wants, powers, and circumstances of the individuals concerned. It is no far-away abstraction, but expresses the *movement* of the ethical world.

One example will help define the discussion. Take the case of a street railway conductor, whose union has ordered a strike. What determines the law of his conduct under the circumstances? Evidently the existing ethical institutions of which he is a member, so far as he is conscious of their needs. To determine what he should do, he does not hunt up some law of an "ought" apart from what is; if he should hunt for and should find such a law he would not know what to do with it. Just because it is apart from his concrete circumstances it is no guide, no law for his conduct at all. He has to act not in view of some abstract principle, but in view of a concrete situation. He considers his present wage, its relation to his needs and abilities; his capacity and taste for this and for that work; the reasons for the strike; the conditions of labor at present with reference to winning the strike, and as to the chance of getting other work. He considers his family, their needs and developing powers; the demand that they should live decently; that his children should be fairly educated and get a fair start in the world; he considers his relationships to his fellow members in the union, etc. These considerations, and such as these, give the law to his decision in so far as he acts morally and not instinctively. Where in this law-giving is there any separation from facts? On the contrary, the more right the act (the nearer it comes to its proper law), the more it will simply express and reflect the actual concrete facts. The law, in other words, of action, is the law of actual social forces in their onward movement, in so far as these demand some response in the way of conduct from the individual.

We may restate from this point of view, what we have already learned: A moral law is thoroughly individualized. It cannot be duplicated; it cannot be for one act just what it is for another. The ethical world is too rich in capacity and circumstance to permit of monotony; it is too swift in its movement to allow of bare repetition. It will not hold still; it moves on, and moral law is the law of action required from individuals by this movement.

The consideration of specific institutions, as the family, industrial society, civil society, the nation, etc., with their respective rights and laws, belongs rather to political philosophy than to the general theory of ethics.

# PART THREE

# THE MORAL LIFE OF THE INDIVIDUAL

## LVII. Division of Subject

We have now analyzed the fundamental moral notions—the good, duty and freedom; we have considered their objective realization, and seen that they are outwardly expressed in social relations, the more typical and abiding of which we call institutions; that abstract duties are realized in the laws created and imposed by such institutions, and that abstract freedom is realized in the rights possessed by members in them. We have now to consider the concrete moral life of an individual born into this existing ethical world and finding himself confronted with institutions in which he must execute his part, and in which he obtains his satisfaction and free activity. We have to consider how these institutions appeal to the individual, awakening in him a distinct *moral* consciousness, or the consciousness of active relations to persons, in antithesis to the theoretical consciousness of relations which exist in contemplation; how the individual behaves towards these institutions, realizing them by assuming his proper position in them, or attempting to thwart them by living in isolation from them; and how a moral character is thus called into being. More shortly, we have to deal (1) with the practical consciousness, or the formation and growth of ideals of conduct; (2) with the moral struggle, or the process of realizing ideals, and (3) with moral character, or the virtues.

# 1

# *The Formation and Growth of Ideals*

## LVIII. Analysis of Conscience

The practical consciousness, or the recognition of ends and relations of action, is what is usually termed *conscience*. The analysis of conscience shows that it involves three elements, which may be distinguished in theory, although they have no separate existence in the actual fact of conscience itself. These three elements are (1) the knowledge of certain specific forms of conduct, (2) the recognition of the authority or obligatoriness of the forms, and (3) the emotional factors which cluster about this recognition. That is to say, we often speak (1) of conscience telling or informing us of duties; we speak of an enlightened or unenlightened conscience; of savage, or mediæval, or modern conscience. Here we are evidently thinking of the kind and range of particular acts considered right or wrong. But we also speak (2) of the authority and majesty of conscience; of the commands of conscience, etc. Here we are thinking of the consciousness of *obligation in general*. The savage and the civilized man may vary greatly in their estimate of what particular acts are right or wrong, and yet agree in the recognition that such acts as are right are absolutely obligatory. Finally we speak of an approving or disapproving, or remorseful conscience, of a tender or a hardened conscience, of the pangs, the pricks of conscience, etc. Here (3) we are evidently dealing with the responsiveness of the disposition to moral distinctions, either in particular acts, or in the recognition of moral law in general.

## LIX. Conscience as the Recognition of Special Acts as Right or Wrong

Conscience in this sense is no peculiar, separate faculty of mind. It is simply intelligence dealing with a certain subject-matter. That is, conscience is distinguished not by the kind of mental activity at work, but by the kind of material the mind works upon. Intelligence deals with the nature and relations of things, and we call it understanding; intelligence deals with the relations of persons and deeds, and it is termed conscience.

We may, with advantage, recognize these stages in the development of intelligence as dealing with moral relationships:

### 1. The Customary or Conventional Conscience

The existing moral world, with the types and varieties of institutions peculiar to it, is constantly impressing itself upon the immature mind; it makes certain demands of moral agents and enforces them with all the means in its power — punishment, reward, blame, public-opinion, and the bestowal of social leadership. These demands and expectations naturally give rise to certain convictions in the individual as to what he should or should not do. Such convictions are not the outcome of independent reflection, but of the moulding influence of social institutions. Moreover the morality of a time becomes consolidated into proverbs, maxims and law-codes. It takes shape in certain habitual ways of looking at and judging matters. All these are instilled into the growing mind through language, literature, association and legal custom, until they leave in the mind a corresponding habit and attitude toward things to be done. This process may be compared to the process by which knowledge of the world of things is first attained. Certain of the more permanent features of this world, especially those whose observance is important in relation to continued physical existence and well-being, impress themselves upon the mind. Consciousness, with no reflective activity of its own, comes to mirror some of the main outlines of the world. The more

important distinctions are fixed in language, and they find
their way into the individual mind, giving it unconsciously
a certain bent and coloring.

## 2. *The Loyal Conscience*

But just as the mind, which seems at first to have the facts
and features of the world poured into itself as a passive
vessel, comes in time through its own experience to appreciate something of their meaning, and, to some extent, to
verify them for itself; so the mind in its moral relations.
Without forming any critical theory of the institutions and
codes which are forming character, without even considering whether they are what they should be, the individual yet
comes at least to a practical recognition that it is in these
institutions that he gets his satisfactions, and through these
codes that he is protected. He identifies himself, his own life,
with the social forms and ideals in which he lives, and repels
any attack upon them as he would an attack upon himself.
The demands which the existing institutions make upon him
are not felt as the coercions of a despot, but as expressions of
his own will, and requiring loyalty as such. The conventional conscience, if it does not grow into this, tends to
become slavish, while an intelligence which practically realizes, although without continual reflection, the *significance* of
conventional morality is *free* in its convictions and service.

## 3. *The Independent or Reflective Conscience*

The intelligence may not simply appropriate, as its own,
conventions embodied in current institutions and codes, but
may *reflect* upon them. It may ask: What is this institution
of family, property for? Does the institution in its present
form work as it should work, or is some modification required? Does this rule which is now current embody the true
needs of the situation, or is it an antiquated expression of
by-gone relations? What is the true spirit of existing institutions, and what sort of conduct does this spirit demand?

Here, in a word, we have the same relation to the
ethical world, that we have in physical science to the external world. Intelligence is not content, on its theoretical side,
with having facts impressed upon it by direct contact or

through language; it is not content with coming to feel for itself the value of the truths so impressed. It assumes an independent attitude, putting itself over against nature and cross-questioning her. It proposes its own ideas, its own theories and hypotheses, and manipulates facts to see if this rational meaning can be verified. It criticises what passes as truth, and pushes on to more adequate statement.

The correlative attempt, on the part of intelligence on its practical side, may have a larger or a smaller scope. In its wider course it aims to criticise and to re-form prevailing social ideals and institutions—even those apparently most fixed. This is the work of the great moral teachers of the world. But in order that conscience be critical, it is not necessary that its range be so wide. The average member of a civilized community is nowadays called upon to reflect upon his immediate relationships in life, to see if they are what they should be; to regulate his own conduct by rules which he follows not simply because they are customary, but the result of his own examination of the situation. There is no difference in kind between the grander and the minuter work. And it is only the constant exercise of reflective examination on the smaller scale which makes possible, and which gives efficiency to, the deeper criticism and transformation.

## LX. Reflective Conscience and the Ethical World

This conception of conscience as critical and reflective is one of the chief fruits of the Socratic ethics, fructified by the new meaning given life through the Christian spirit. It involves the "right of free conscience"—the right of the individual to know the good, to know the end of action, for himself, rather than to have some good, however imposing and however beneficent, enjoined from without. It is this principle of subjective freedom, says Hegel, which marks the turning-point in the distinction of modern from ancient times (Sec. 124, *Grundlinien der Philosophie des Rechts*, Vol. VIII of Hegel's *Works*).[2]

---

[2]    I hardly need say how largely I am indebted in the treatment of this topic, and indeed, in the whole matter of the "ethical world," to Hegel.

But this notion of conscience is misinterpreted when the content as well as the form of conscience is thought to be individual. There is no right of private judgment, in the sense that there is not a public source and standard of judgment. What is meant by this right is that the standard, the source, is not the opinion of some other person, or group of persons. It is a common, objective standard. It is that embodied in social relationships themselves.

The conception of conscience as a private possession, to be exercised by each one in independence of historical forms and contemporary ideals, is thoroughly misleading. The saying "I had to follow my own notion of what is right" has been made the excuse for all sorts of capricious, obstinate and sentimental performance. It is of such notions that Hegel further says: "The striving for a morality of one's own is futile, and by its very nature impossible of attainment; in respect of morality the saying of the wisest men of antiquity is the only true one: To be moral is to live in accordance with the moral tradition of one's country" (Hegel, *Works*, Vol. I, p. 389). And in discussing the same question, Bradley has said that the wish to have a morality of one's own better than that of the world is to be on the threshold of morality (*Ethical Studies*, p. 180).

Yet, on the other hand, conscience should not simply repeat the burden of existing usages and opinions. No one can claim that the existing morality embodies the highest possible conception of personal relations. A morality which does not recognize both the possibility and the necessity of advance is immorality. Where then is the way out from a capricious self-conceit, on one hand, and a dead conformity on the other? Reflective conscience must be *based* on the moral consciousness expressed in existing institutions, manners and beliefs. Otherwise it is empty and arbitrary. But the existing moral status is never wholly self-consistent. It realizes ideals in one relation which it does not in another; it gives rights to "aristocrats" which it denies to low-born; to men, which it refuses to women; it exempts the rich from obligations which it imposes upon the poor. Its institutions embody a common good which turns out to be good only to a privileged few, and thus existing in self-contradiction. They suggest ends which they execute only feebly or intermittently. Reflective intelligence cross-questions the existing morality; and extracts from it the ideal which it pretends to embody, and thus is able to criticise the existing morality in the light of its *own* ideal. It points out the inconsistencies, the incoherencies, the compromises, the failures, between the actual practice and the theory at the basis of this practice. And thus the new ideal proposed by the individual is not a product of his private opinions, but is the outcome of the ideal embodied in existing customs, ideas and institutions.

## LXI. The Sense of Obligation

There has been much discussion regarding the nature of the act of mind by which obligation is recognized. A not uncommon view has been that the sense of duty as such must be the work of a peculiar faculty of the mind. Admitting that the recognition of this or that particular thing as right or wrong, is the work of ordinary intelligence, it is held that the additional recognition of the absolute obligatoriness of the right cannot be the work of this intelligence. For our intellect is confined to judging what is or has been; the conception of obligation, of something which should be, wholly transcends its scope. There is, therefore, some special faculty called conscience which affixes to the ordinary judgments the stamp of the categorical imperative "You ought."

See for example Maurice on *The Conscience*. The view is traceable historically to Kant's conception of Practical Reason, but as the view is ordinarily advanced the function of Practical Reason in Kant's philosophy is overlooked. The Practical Reason is no special faculty of man's being; it is his consciousness of himself as an acting being; that is, as a being capable of acting from ideas. Kant never separates the consciousness of duty from the very nature of will as the realization of conceptions. In the average modern presentation, this intrinsic connection of duty with activity is absent. Conscience becomes a faculty whose function it is to clap the idea of duty upon the existent conception of an act; and this existent conception is regarded as morally indifferent.

It is true that Kant's Practical Reason has a certain separateness or isolation. But this is because of his general separation of the rational from the sensuous factor, and not because of any separation of the consciousness of action from the consciousness of duty. If Kant erred in his divorce of desire and duty, then even the relative apartness of the Practical Reason must be given up. The consciousness of obligation is involved in the recognition of *any* end of conduct, and not simply in the end of abstract law.

Such a conception of conscience, however, is open to serious objections. Aside from the fact that large numbers of men declare that no amount of introspection reveals any such machinery within themselves, this separate faculty seems quite superfluous. The real distinction is not between the consciousness of an action with, and without, the recognition of duty, but between a consciousness which is and one which is not capable of conduct. Any being who is capable of putting before himself ideas as motives of conduct, who is capable of forming a conception of something which he would realize, is, by that very fact, capable of a sense of obligation. The consciousness of an end to be realized, the idea of something to be done, is, in and of itself, the consciousness of duty.

Let us consider again the horse-car conductor (see Sec. LVI). After he has analyzed the situation which faces him and decided that a given course of conduct is the one which fits the situation, does he require some additional faculty to inform him that this course is the one which should be followed? The analysis of practical ideas, that is, of proposed ends of conduct, is from the first an analysis of what should be done. Such being the case, it is no marvel that the conclusion of the reflection is: "This should (ought to) be done."

Indeed, just as every judgment about existent fact naturally takes the form "s *is* P," so every judgment regarding an activity which executes an idea takes the form, "s ought (or ought not) to be P." It requires no additional faculty of mind, after intelligence has been studying the motions of the moon, to insert itself, and affirm some objective relation or truth—as that the moon's motions are explainable by the law of gravitation. It is the very essence of theoretical judgment, judgment regarding fact, to state truth—what is. And it is the very essence of practical judgment, judgment regarding deeds, to state that active relation which we call obligation, what *ought to be*.

The judgment as to what a practical situation *is*, is an untrue or abstract judgment.

The practical situation is itself an *activity*; the needs, powers, and circumstances which make it are moving on. At no instant in time is the scene quiescent. But the agent, in order to determine his course of action in view of this situation, has to *fix* it; he has to arrest its onward movement in order to tell what it is. So his abstracting intellect cuts a cross-section through its on-going, and says "This *is* the situation." Now the judgment "This ought to be the situation," or "in view of the situation, my conduct ought to be thus and so," is simply restoring the movement which the mind has temporarily put out of sight. By means of its cross-section, intelligence has detected the principle, or law of movement, of the situation, and it is on the basis of this movement that conscience declares what ought to be.

Just as the fact of moral law, or of authority, of the incumbency of duty, needs for its explanation no separation of the "is" from the "ought" (see Sec. LVI), but only recognition of the law of the "is" which is, perforce, a law of movement, and of change;—so the consciousness of law, "the sense of obligation" requires no special mental faculty which may declare what ought to be. The intelligence that is capable of declaring truth, or what is, is capable also of making known obligation. For obligation is only *practical* truth, the "is" of doing.

See upon this point, as well as upon the relation of laws and rules to action, my article in Vol. I, No. 2, of the *International Journal of Ethics*, entitled "Moral Theory and Practice." [*Early Works*, III, 93–109.]

## LXII.  Conscience as Emotional Disposition

Probably no judgment is entirely free from emotional coloring and accompaniments. It is doubtful whether the most indifferent judgment is not based upon, and does not appeal to, some interest. Certainly all the more important judgments awaken some response from the self, and excite its interests to their depths. Some of them may be excited by the intrinsic nature of the subject-matter under judgment, while others are the results of associations more or less accidental. The former will necessarily be aroused in every being, who has any emotional nature at all, whenever the judgment is made, while the latter will vary from time to time, and may entirely pass away. That moral judgments, judgments of what should be (or should have been) done, arouse emotional response, is therefore no cause for surprise. It may help clear up difficulties if we distinguish three kinds of such emotional accompaniment.

1. There are, first, the interests belonging to the sense of obligation as such. We have just seen that this sense of obligation is nothing separate from the consciousness of the particular act which is to be performed. Nevertheless the consciousness of obligation, of an authority and law, recurs with every act, while the special content of the act constantly varies. Thus an idea of law, or of duty in general, is formed, distinct from any special duty. Being formed, it arouses the special emotional excitation appropriate to it. The formation of this general idea of duty, and the growth of feeling of duty as such, is helped on through the fact that children (and adults so far as their moral life is immature) need to have their moral judgments constantly reinforced by recurrence to the thought of law. That is to say, a child, who is not capable of seeing the true moral bearings and claims of an act, is yet continually required to perform such an act on the ground that it *is* obligatory. The feeling, therefore, is natural and legitimate. It must, however, go hand in hand with the feelings aroused by the special moral relations under consideration. Disconnected from such union, it necessarily leads to slavish and arbitrary forms of conduct. A child, for example, who is constantly taught to perform acts simply because he *ought* to do so, without having at the same time his intelligence directed to the nature of the act which is obligatory (without, that is, being led to see how or why it is obligatory), may have a strongly developed sense of obligation. As he grows up, however, this sense of duty will be largely one of dread and apprehension; a feeling of constraint, rather than of free service.

Besides this, it will be largely a matter of accident to what act this feeling attaches itself. Anything that comes to the mind with the force of associations of past education, any ideal that forces itself persistently into consciousness from any source may awaken this sense of obligation, wholly irrespective of the true nature of the act. This is the explanation of strongly "conscientious" persons, whose morality is yet unintelligent and blundering. It is of such persons that it has been said that a thoroughly *good* man can do more harm than a number of bad men.

When, however, the feeling of obligation in general is developed along with particular moral judgments (that is, along with the habit of considering the special nature of acts performed), it is one of the strongest supports to morality. Acts constantly need to be performed which are recognized as right and as obligatory, and yet with reference to which there is no fixed habit of conduct. In these cases, the more direct, or spontaneous, stimulus to action is wanting.

If, however, there is a strong sense of obligation in general, this may attach itself to the particular act and thus afford the needed impetus. In unusual experiences, and in cases where the ordinary motive-forces are lacking, such a feeling of regard for law may be the only sure stay of right conduct.

2. There is the emotional accompaniment appropriate to the special content of the act. If, for example, the required act has to do with some person, there arise in consciousness the feelings of interest, of love and friendship, or of dislike, which belong to that person. If it relate to some piece of work to be done, the sweeping of a room, the taking of a journey, the painting of a picture, there are the interests natural to such subjects. These feelings when aroused necessarily form part of the emotional attitude as respects the act. It is the strength and normal welling-up of such specific interests which afford the best assurance of healthy and progressive moral conduct, as distinct from mere sentimental dwelling upon ideals. Only interests prevent the divorce of feelings and ideas from habits of action. Such interests are the union of the subjective element, the self, and the objective, the special relations to be realized (Sec. xxxiv),

and thus necessarily produce a right and healthy attitude towards moral ends. It is obvious that in a normal moral life, the law of obligation in general, and the specific interests in particular cases, should more and more fuse. The interests, at their strongest, take the form of *love*. And thus there is realized the ideal of an effective character; the union of law and inclination in its pure form—love for the action in and of itself.

3. Emotions due to accidental associations. It is matter of common notice that the moral feelings are rarely wholly pure; that all sorts of sentiments, due to associations of time and place and person not strictly belonging to the acts themselves, cluster about them. While this is true, we should not forget the great difficulty there is in marking off any associations as *wholly* external to the nature of the act. We may say that mere fear of punishment is such a wholly external feeling, having no place in moral emotion. Yet it may be doubted whether there is any feeling that may be called mere fear of punishment. It is, perhaps, fear of punishment by a parent, for whom one has love and respect, and thus the fear has partially a genuinely moral aspect. Some writers would call the æsthetic feelings, the feelings of beauty, of harmony, which gather about moral ends adventitious. Yet the fact that other moralists have made all moral feelings essentially æsthetic, as due to the perception of the fitness and proportion of the acts, should warn us from regarding æsthetic feelings as wholly external. About all that can be said is that feelings which do not spring from *some* aspect of the content of the act itself should be extruded, with growing maturity of character, from influence upon conduct.

## LXIII. Conscientiousness

Conscientiousness is primarily the virtue of intelligence in regard to conduct. That is to say, it is the formed habit of bringing intelligence to bear upon the analysis of moral relations—the habit of considering what ought to be done. It is based upon the recognition of the idea first distinctly formulated by Socrates—that "an unexamined life is not one that should be led by man." It is the outgrowth of the customary morality embodied in usages, codes and social institutions, but it is an advance upon custom, because it requires a meaning and a reason. It is the mark of a "character which will not be satisfied without understanding the law that it obeys; without knowing what the good is, for which the demand has hitherto been blindly at work" (Green, *Prolegomena*, p. 270). Conscientiousness, then, is reflective intelligence grown into character. It involves a greater and wider recognition of obligation in general, and a larger and more stable emotional response to everything that presents itself as duty; as well as the habit of deliberate consideration of the moral situation and of the acts demanded by it.

Conscientiousness is an analysis of the conditions under which conduct takes place, and of the action that will meet these conditions; it is a thoroughly *objective* analysis. What is sometimes termed conscientiousness is merely the habit of analyzing internal moods and sentiments; of prying into "motives" in that sense of motive which identifies it not with the end of action, but with some subjective state of emotion. Thus considered, conscientiousness is morbid. We are sometimes warned against *over*-conscientiousness. But such conscientiousness means simply over-regard of one's private self; keeping an eye upon the effect of conduct on one's internal state, rather than upon conduct itself. Over-conscientiousness is as impossible as over-intelligence, since it is simply the application of intelligence to conduct. It is as little morbid and introspective as is the analysis of any fact in nature. Another notion which is sometimes thought to be bound up with that of conscience, also has nothing to do with it; namely, the notion of a precision and coldness opposed to all large spontaneity and broad sympathy in conduct. The reflective man of narrow insight and cramped conduct is often called the conscientious man and opposed to the man of generous impulses. This comes from identifying conscience with a ready-made code of rules, and its action with the application of some such fixed code to all acts as they come up. It is evident, on the contrary, that such a habit is opposed to conscience. Conscience means the consideration of each case *in itself*; measuring it not by any outside code, but in the existing moral situation.

> On conscientiousness, see Green, *Prolegomena*, pp. 269–71 and 323–27; and Alexander, *Moral Order*, pp. 156–60. These writers, however, seem to identify it too much with internal scrutiny. Green, for example, expressly identifies conscientiousness with a man's "questioning about himself, whether he has been as good as he should have been, whether a better man would not have acted otherwise than he has done" (*Prolegomena*, p. 323). He again speaks of it as "comparison of our own practice, as we know it on the inner side in relation to the motives and character which it expresses, with an ideal of virtue." The first definition seems to be misleading. Questioning as to whether the end adopted was what it should have been, *i.e.*, whether the analysis of the situation was correctly performed, may be of great service in aiding future decisions, but questioning regarding the purity of one's own "motive" does not seem of much avail. In a man upon the whole good, such questioning is apt to be paralyzing. The energy that should go to conduct goes to anxiety about one's conduct. It is the view of goodness as directed mainly towards one's own private motives, which has led such writers as Henry James, Sr., and Mr. Hinton, to conceive of "morality," the struggle for goodness, to be in essence bad. They conceived of the struggle for "private goodness" as no different from the struggle for private pleasure, although likely, of course, to lead to better things. Nor in a bad man is such scrutiny of "motive," as apart from objective end, of much value. The bad man is generally aware of the badness of his motive without much close examination. The truth aimed at by Green is, I think, amply covered by recognizing that conscientiousness as a constant will to know what should be, and to re-adjust conduct to meet the new insight, is the spring of the moral life.

## LXIV.  Moral Commands, Rules and Systems

What is the part played by specific commands and by general rules in the examination of conduct by conscience? We should note, in the first place, that commands are not rules, and rules are not commands. A command, to be a command, must be specific and individual. It must refer to time, place and circumstance. "Thou shalt do no murder" is not strictly speaking a command, for it allows questioning as to what is murder. Is killing in war murder? Is the hanging of criminals murder? Is taking life in self-defense murder? Regarded simply as a command, this command would be "void for uncertainty." A true command is a specific injunction of one person to another to do or not to do a stated thing or things. Under what conditions do commands play a part in moral conduct? In cases where the intelligence of the agent is so undeveloped that he cannot realize for himself the situation and see the act required, and when a part of the agent's environment is constituted by others who have such required knowledge, there *is* a moral element in command and in obedience.

This explains the moral responsibility of parents to children and of children to parents. The soldier, too, in recognizing a general's command, is recognizing the situation as it exists for him. Were there simply superior force on one side, and fear on the other, the relation would be an immoral one. It is implied, of course, in such an instance as the parents' command, that it be so directed as to enable the child more and more to dispense with it—that is, that it be of such a character as to give the child insight into the situation for himself. Here is the transition from a command to a rule.

A rule does not tell what to do or what to leave undone. The Golden Rule, for example, does not tell me how to act in any specific case. *A rule is a tool of analysis*. The moral situation, or capacity in its relation to environment, is often an extremely complicated affair. How shall the individual resolve it? How shall he pick it to pieces, so as to see its real nature and the act demanded by it? It is evident that the analysis will be the more truly and speedily performed if the agent has a method by which to attack it, certain principles in the light of which he may view it, instruments for cross-questioning it and making it render up its meaning. Moral rules perform this service. While the Golden Rule does not of itself give one jot of information as to what I should do in a given case, it does, if accepted, immensely simplify the situation. Without it I should perhaps have to act blindly; with it the question comes to this: What should I, under the given circumstances, like to have done to me? This settled, the whole question of what should be done is settled.

It is obvious, then, that the value of a moral rule depends upon its potency in revealing the inner spirit and reality of individual deeds. Rules in the negative form, rules whose application is limited in scope because of an attempt to be specific, are midway between commands proper and rules. The Golden Rule, on the other hand, is positive, and not attempting to define any specific act, covers in its range all relations of man to man. It is indeed only a concrete and forcible statement of the ethical principle itself, the idea of a common good, or of a community of persons. This is also a convenient place for considering the practical value of ethical systems. We have already seen that no system can attempt to tell what in particular should be done. The principle of a system, however, may be of some aid in analyzing a specific case. In this way, a system may be regarded as a highly generalized rule. It attempts to state some fundamental principle which lies at the basis of moral conduct. So far as it succeeds in doing this, there is the possibility of its practical application in particular cases, although, of course, the mediate rules must continue to be the working tools of mankind—on account of their decided concrete character, and because they have themselves taken shape under the pressure of practice rather than of more theoretical needs.

## lxv.  Development of Moral Ideals

Thus far we have been speaking of conscience mainly as to its method of working. We have now to speak more definitely of its content, or of the development of ideals of action.

It is of the very nature of moral conduct to be progressive. Permanence of *specific* ideals means moral death. We say that truth-telling, charity, loyalty, temperance, have always been moral ends and while this is true, the statement as ordinarily made is apt to hide from us the fact that the content of the various ideals (what is *meant* by temperance, etc.) has been constantly changing, and this of necessity. The realization of moral ends must bring about a changed situation, so that the repetition of the same ends would no longer satisfy. This progress has two sides: the satisfaction of wants leads to a larger view of what satisfaction really is, *i.e.*, to the creation of new capacities and wants; while adjustment to the environment creates wider and more complex social relationships.

Let the act be one of intelligence. Some new fact or law is discovered. On one hand, this discovery may arouse a hitherto comparatively dormant mind; it may suggest the possession of capacities previously latent; it may stimulate mental activity and create a thirst for expanding knowledge. This readjustment of intellectual needs and powers may be comparatively slight, or it may amount, as it has with many a young person, to a revolution. On the other hand, the new fact changes the intellectual outlook, the mental horizon, and, by transforming somewhat the relations of things, demands new conduct. All this, even when the growth of knowledge concerns only the physical world. But development of insight into social needs and affairs has a larger and more direct progressive influence. The social world exists spiritually, as conceived, and a new conception of it, new perception of its scope and bearings, is, perforce, a change of that world. And thus it is with the satisfaction of the human want of knowledge, that patience, courage, self-respect, humility, benevolence, all change character. When, for example, psychology has given an increase of knowledge regarding men's motives, political economy an increase of knowledge regarding men's wants, when historical knowledge has added its testimony regarding the effects of indiscriminate giving, charity must change its content. While once, the mere supplying of food or money by one to another may have been right as meeting the recognized relations, charity now comes to mean large responsibility in knowledge of antecedents and circumstances, need of organization, careful tracing of consequences, and, above all, effort to remove the conditions which made the want possible. The activity involved has infinitely widened.

Let the act be in the region of industrial life—a new invention. The invention of the telephone does not simply satisfy an old want—it creates new. It brings about the possibility of closer social relations, extends the distribution of intelligence, facilitates commerce. It is a common saying that the luxury of one generation is the necessity of the next;

that is to say, what once satisfied a somewhat remote need becomes in time the basis upon which new needs grow up. Energy previously pent up is set free, new power and ideals are evoked. Consider again a person assuming a family relation. This seems, at first, to consist mainly in the satisfaction of certain common and obvious human wants. But this satisfaction, if moral, turns out rather to be the creation of new insight into life, of new relationships, and thus of new energies and ideals. We may generalize these instances. The secret of the moral life is not getting or having, it is doing and thus being. The getting and the possessing side of life has a moral value only when it is made the stimulus and nutriment of new and wider acting. To solve the equation between getting and doing is the moral problem of life. Let the possession be acquiesced in for its own sake, and not as the way to freer (and thus more moral) action, and the selfish life has set in (see Sec. LXVII). It is essential to moral activity that it feed itself into larger appetites and thus into larger life.

> This must not be taken to deny that there is a mechanical side even to the moral life. A merchant, for example, may do the same thing over and over again, like going to his business every morning at the same hour. This is a moral act and yet it does not seem to lead to a change in moral wants or surroundings. Yet even in such cases it should be noted that it is only outwardly that the act is the *same*. In itself, that is, in its relation to the will of the agent, it is simply one element in the whole of character; and as character opens up, the act must change somewhat also. It is performed somehow in a new spirit. If this is not to some extent true, if such acts become wholly mechanical, the moral life is hardening into the rigidity of death.

This progressive development consists on one side in a richer and subtler individual activity, in increased individualization, in wider and freer functions of life; on the other it consists in increase in number of those persons whose ideal is a "common good," or who have membership in the same moral community; and, further, it consists in more complex relations between them. It is both intensive and extensive.

History is one record of growth in the sense of specific powers. Its track is marked by the appearance of more and more internal and distinguishing traits; of new divisions of labor and corresponding freedom in functioning. It begins with groups in which everything is massed, and the good is common only in the sense of being undifferentiated for all. It progresses with the evolution of individuality, of the peculiar gifts entrusted to each, and hence of the specific service demanded of each.

The other side, the enlargement of the community of ends, has been termed growth in "comprehensiveness." History is again a record of the widening of the social consciousness—of the range of persons whose interests have to be taken into account in action. There has been a period in which the community was nothing more than a man's own immediate family group, this enlarging to the clan, the city, the social class, the nation; until now, in theory, the community of interests and ends is humanity itself.

This growth in comprehensiveness is not simply a growth in the number of persons having a common end. The quantitative growth reacts upon the *nature* of the ends themselves. For example, when the conceived community is small, bravery may consist mainly in willingness to fight for the recognized community against other hostile groups. As these groups become themselves included in the moral community, courage must change its form, and become resoluteness and integrity of purpose in defending manhood and humanity as such. That is to say, as long as the community is based largely upon physical facts, like oneness of blood, of territory, etc., the ideal of courage will have a somewhat external and physical manifestation. Let the community be truly spiritual, consisting in recognition of unity of destiny and function in co-operation toward an all-inclusive life, and the ideal of courage becomes more internal and spiritual, consisting in loyalty to the possibilities of humanity, whenever and wherever found.

On this development of moral ideals, and especially of the growth in "comprehensiveness" as reacting upon the intrinsic form which the ideal itself takes, see Green, *Prolegomena*, pp. 264–308, followed by Alexander, *Moral Order*, pp. 384–98. For the process of change of ideals in general, see Alexander, pp. 271–92, and 369–71.

## 2

# *The Moral Struggle or the Realizing of Ideals*

### LXVI. Goodness as a Struggle

We have already seen that the bare repetition of identically the same acts does not consist with morality. To aim at securing a satisfaction precisely like the one already experienced, is to fail to recognize the altered capacity and environment, and the altered duty. Moral satisfaction prior to an act is *ideal*; ideal not simply in the sense of being conceived, or present to thought, but ideal in the sense that it has not been already enjoyed. Some satisfaction has been enjoyed in a previous activity, but that very satisfaction has so enlarged and complicated the situation, that its mere repetition would not afford moral or active satisfaction, but only what Kant terms "pathological" satisfaction. Morality thus assumes the form of a struggle. The past satisfaction speaks for itself; it has been verified in experience, it has conveyed its worth to our very senses. We have tried and tasted it, and know that it is good. If morality lay in the repetition of similar satisfactions, it would not be a struggle. We should know experimentally beforehand that the chosen end would bring us satisfaction, and should be at rest in that knowledge. But when morality lies in striving for satisfactions which have not verified themselves to our sense, it always requires an effort. We have to surrender the enjoyed good, and stake ourselves upon that of which we cannot say: We *know* it is good. To surrender the actual experienced good for a possible ideal good is the struggle.

We arrive, in what is termed the opposition of desire and duty, at the heart of the moral struggle. Of course, taken strictly, there can be no opposition here. The duty which did not awaken *any* desire would not appeal to the mind even as a duty. But we may distinguish between a desire which is based on past satisfaction actually experienced, and desire based simply upon the idea that the end is *desirable*—that it ought to be desired. It may seem strange to speak of a desire based simply upon the recognition that an end *should* be desired, but the possibility of awakening such a desire and the degree of its strength are the test of a moral character. How far does this end awaken response in me because I see that it is the end which is fit and due? How far does it awaken this response although it does not fall into line with past satisfactions, or although it actually thwarts some habitual satisfaction? Here is the opposition of duty and desire. It lies in the contrast of a good which has demonstrated itself as such in experience, and a good whose claim to be good rests only on the fact that it is the act which meets the situation. It is the contrast between a good of possession, and one of action.

From this point of view morality is a life of *aspiration*, and of *faith*; there is required constant willingness to give up past goods as the good, and to press on to new ends; not because past achievements are bad, but because, being good, they have created a situation which demands larger and more intricately related achievements. This willingness is aspiration and it implies *faith*. Only the old good is of sight, has verified itself to sense. The new ideal, the end which meets the situation, is felt as good only in so far as the character has formed the conviction that to meet obligation is itself a good, whether bringing sensible satisfaction or not. You can prove to a man that he ought to act so and so (that is to say, that such an act is the one which fits the present occasion), but you cannot *prove* to him that the performance of that duty will be good. Only faith in the moral order, in the identity of duty and the good, can assert this. Every time an agent takes as his end (that is, chooses as good) an activity which he has not already tried, he asserts his belief in the goodness of right action as such. This faith is not a mere intellectual thing, but it is practical —the staking of self upon activity as against passive possession.

LXVII.  Moral Badness

Badness originates in the contrast which thus comes about between *having* the repetition of former action, and *doing*—pressing forward to the new right action. Goodness is the choice of doing; the refusal to be content with past good as exhausting the entire content of goodness. It is, says Green, "in the continued effort to be better that goodness consists." The man, however bad his past and however limited his range of intellectual, æsthetic and social activity, who is dissatisfied with his past, and whose dissatisfaction manifests itself in act, is accounted better than the man of a respectable past and higher plane of life who has lapsed into contented acquiescence with past deeds. For past deeds are not *deeds*, they are passive enjoyments. The bad man, on the other hand, is not the man who loves badness *in and for itself*. Such a man would be a mad man or a devil. All conduct, bad as well as good, is for the sake of *some* satisfaction, that is, some good. In the bad man, the satisfaction which is aimed at is *simply* the one congruent with existing inclinations, irrespective of the sufficiency of those inclinations in view of the changed capacity and environment: it is a good of *having*. The bad man, that is to say, does not recognize any *ideal* or *active* good; any good which has not already commended itself to him as such. This good may be good in *itself*; but, as distinguished from the good which requires action, that which would fulfill the present capacity or meet the present situation, it is bad.

Thus Alexander terms badness *a survival*, in part at least, of former goodness. Hinton says (*Philosophy and Religion*, p. 146), "That a thing is wrong does not mean that it ought never to have been done or thought, but that it ought to be left off." It will be noted that we are not dealing with the metaphysical or the religious problem of the nature and origin of evil, but simply with an account of bad action as it appears in individual conduct.

Badness has four traits, all derivable from this basal fact. They are: (1) Lawlessness, (2) Selfishness, (3) Baseness, (4) Demoralization.

## 1. *Lawlessness*

When desire and duty, that is, when desires based on past having and on future acting, conflict, the bad man lets duty go. He virtually denies that it is a good at all—it may be a good in the abstract but not a good for him. He denies that obligation as such has any value; that any end is to be consulted save his own state of mind. He denies that there is law for conduct—at least any law beyond the inclination which he happens to have at the time of action. Keeping himself within that which has verified itself to his feeling in the past, he abrogates all authority excepting that of his own immediate feelings.

## 2. *Selfishness*

It has already been shown that the self is not necessarily immoral, and hence that action for self is not necessarily bad —indeed, that the true self is social and interest in it right (see Sec. xxxv). But when a satisfaction based on past experience is set against one proceeding from an act as meeting obligation, there grows up a divorce in the self. The actual self, the self recognizing only past and sensible satisfaction, is set over against the self which recognizes the necessity of expansion and a wider environment. Since the former self confines its action to benefits demonstrably accruing to itself, while the latter, in meeting the demands of the situation, necessarily contributes to the satisfaction of others, one takes the form of a *private* self, a self whose good is set over against and exclusive of that of others, while the self recognizing obligation becomes a social self—the self which performs its due function in society. It is, again, the contrast between getting and doing.

All moral action is based upon the presupposition of the identity of good (Sec. xL), but it by no means follows that this identity of good can be demonstrated to the agent at the time of action. On the contrary, it is matter of the commonest experience that the sensible good, the demonstrable good (that is, the one visible on the line of past satisfaction) may be contradictory to the act which would satisfy the interests of others. The identity of interests can be proved *only by acting upon it*; to the agent, prior to action, it is a matter of faith. Choice presents itself then in these cases as a test: Do you believe that the Good is simply your private good, or is the true Good, is *your* good, one which includes the good of others? The condemnation passed upon the "selfish" man is that he virtually declares that good is essentially exclusive and private. He shuts himself up within himself, within, that is, his past achievements, and the inclinations based upon them. The good man goes out of himself in new action. Bad action is thus essentially narrowing, it confines the self; good action is expansive and vital, it moves on to a larger self.

In fine, all conduct, good and bad, satisfies the self; bad conduct, however, aims at a self which, keeping its eye upon its private and assured satisfaction, refuses to recognize the increasing function with its larger social range, — the "selfish" self.

Light is thrown upon this point by referring to what was said about interest (Sec. xxxiv). Interest is *active* feeling, feeling turned upon an object, and going out toward it so as to identify it with self. In this active and objective interest there is satisfaction, but the satisfaction is *in* the activity which has the object for its content. This is the satisfaction of the good self. In the bad self, interest is reduced to mere feeling; for the aim of life in such a self is simply to have certain feelings as its own possession; activity and its object are degraded into mere means for getting these sensations.

Activity has two sides; as activity, as projection or expression of one's powers, it satisfies self; as activity, also, it has some end, some object, for its content. The activity as such, therefore, the activity for its own sake, must involve the realization of this object for its own sake. But in having, in getting, there is no such creation or maintenance of an object for itself. Objects cease to be "ends in themselves" when they cease to be the content of action; and are degraded into means of private satisfaction, that is, of sensation.

## 3. *Baseness*

For, when we say that bad action takes account of ideals only on the basis of possession, we say, in effect, that it takes account only of *sensible* satisfaction. As it is in the progressive movement of morality that there arises the distinction of the law-abiding and the lawless self, of the social and the selfish self, so in the same aspect there comes into existence the distinction of the low, degraded, sensual self, as against the higher or spiritual self. In themselves, or naturally, there is no desire high, none low. But when an inclination for an end which consists in possession comes into conflict with one which includes an active satisfaction—one not previously enjoyed—the contrast arises. It is wrong to say, with Kant, that the bad act is simply for pleasure; for the bad act, the choice of a past satisfaction as against the aspiration for a wider good, may have a large content—it may be the good of one's family; it may be scientific or æsthetic culture. Yet the moment a man begins to live on the plane of past satisfaction as such, he has begun to live on the plane of "sense," or for pleasure. The refusal to recognize the ideal good, to acknowledge activity as good, throws the agent back into a life of dwelling upon his own sensible good, and thus he falls more and more into a life of dwelling upon mere sensations. What made the past good a good at all was the spirit, the activity, in it, and when it is no longer an activity, but a mere keeping, the life is gone out of it. The selfish life must degenerate into mere sensuality—although when sensuality is "refined" we call it sentimentality.

## 4. *Demoralization*

Morality is activity; exercise of function. To cease this activity is not to remain on the attained level, for that, *when attained*, was active. It is to relapse, to slip down into badness. The moral end is always an activity. To fail in this activity is, therefore, to involve character in disintegration. It can be kept together only by constant organizing activity; only by acting upon new wants and moving toward new situations. Let this activity cease, and disorganization ensues, as surely as the body decays when life goes, instead of simply remaining inert as it was. Bad conduct is thus *unprincipled*; it has no centre, no movement. The good man is "organic"; he uses his attainments to discover new needs, and to assimilate new material. He lives from within outwards, his character is compact, coherent; he has *integrity*. The bad man, having no controlling unity, has no consistent line of action; his motives of conduct contradict one another; he follows this maxim in relation to this person, that in relation to another; character is *demoralized*.

The bad man is unstable and double-minded. He is not one person, but a group of conflicting wills. So far as he is really bad he becomes as many persons as he has desires. His conduct cannot be made universal. He always makes exceptions in favor of himself. He does not want moral relations abolished, but relaxed or deflected in his own case, while they still hold for other men.

This is the truth at the basis of Kant's contention regarding goodness as conduct whose maxim is capable of generalization. See also Bradley, *Ethical Studies*, pp. 261–71. And Alexander, *Moral Order*, pp. 309–12.

## LXVIII. Goodness in its Relation to the Struggle

1. Two aspects of this we have already noted; one, that of conscientiousness, or habitual alertness and responsiveness of intelligence to the nature of obligation, both in general and as to the specific acts which are obligatory. The other is that goodness, in this relation, consists in *progressive* adjustment, involving aspiration as to future conduct, and correlative humility as to present achievements of character.

2. We may state what has already been suggested, that goodness as self-sacrifice or self-renunciation has also its place here. The moral attitude is one of renunciation, because, on account of the constantly growing wants and circumstances, the satisfactions which belong to the actually realized self must be given up for active goods. That the self-sacrifice takes largely the form of the surrender of private interests to the welfare of the whole, is explained by what has just been said regarding selfishness. Self-sacrifice is not in any way the moral end or the last word. Life is lost that it may be found. The smaller local life of the private self is given up in order that the richer and fuller life of the social or active self may be realized. But none the less the self-sacrifice at the time that it is made is genuine and real.

While it is involved in the very nature of morality that moral conduct shall bring greater activity, larger life, the motive of the agent in self-sacrifice is not to give up the lesser satisfaction for the sake of getting a greater. It is only so far as he is already moral that he is convinced that the new duty will bring satisfaction, and his conviction is not one of sense, but of faith. To the agent at the time of action, it is a real satisfaction which is given up for one that is only ideal, and given up because the ideal satisfaction is ethical, active—one congruent to duty, while the actual satisfaction is only pathological; that is, congruent to the actualized self —to the having, instead of the doing self.

3. Goodness is not remoteness from badness. In one sense, goodness is based upon badness; that is, good action is always based upon action good once, but bad if persisted in under changing circumstances. The moral struggle thus presents itself as the conflict between this "bad" and the good which would duly meet the existing situation. This good, of course, does not involve the annihilation of the previously attained good—the present bad—but its subordination; its use in the new function. This is the explanation of the apparently paradoxical statement that badness is the material of good action—a statement literally correct when badness is understood as it is here. Evil is simply that which goodness has to *overcome*—has to make an element of itself.

Badness, as just spoken of, is only potential—the end is bad as contrasted with the better. Badness may also, of course, be actual; the bad end may be chosen, and adopted into character. Even in this sense, goodness is not the absence of evil, or entire freedom from it. Badness even on this basis is the material of goodness; it is to be put under foot and made an element in good action. But how can actual evil be made a factor of right conduct? In this way; the good man learns from his own bad acts; he does not continue to repeat such acts, nor does he, while recognizing their badness, simply endeavor to do right without regard to the previous bad conduct. Perceiving the effect of his own wrong acts, the change produced in his own capacities, and his altered relations to other people, he acts so as to meet the situation which his own bad act has helped to create. Conduct is then right, although made what it is, to some degree, by previous wrong conduct.

In this connection, the introduction of Christianity made one of its largest ethical contributions. It showed how it was possible for a man to put his badness behind him and even make it an element in goodness. Teaching that the world of social relations was itself an ethical reality and a good (a redeemed world), it taught that the individual, by identifying himself with the spirit of this ethical world, might be freed from slavery to his past evil; that by recognizing and taking for his own the evil in the world, instead of engaging in an isolated struggle to become good by himself, he might make the evil a factor in his own right action.

Moreover, by placing morality in activity and not in some thing, or in conformity to an external law, Christianity changed the nature of the struggle. While the old struggle had been an effort to get away from evil to a good beyond, Christianity made the struggle itself a good. It, then, was no longer the effort to escape to some fixed, unchanging state; the constant onward movement was itself the goal. Virtue, as Hegel says, is the battle, the struggle, carried to its full.

4. The conception of merit. This is, essentially, the idea of social desert—the idea that an agent deserves well of others on account of his act or his character. An action evokes two kinds of judgments: first, that the act is right or virtuous, that it fulfills duty. This judgment may be passed by any one; as well by the agent as by any one else. It is simply the recognition of the moral character of the act. But a right act may also awaken a conviction of desert; that the act is one which furthers the needs of society, and thus is meritorious.

*This* is *not* a judgment which the agent can pass upon his own act. Virtue and duty are strictly coextensive; no act can be so virtuous, so right, as to go beyond meeting the demands of the situation. Everything is a duty which needs to be done in a given situation; the doing of what needs to be done is right or virtuous. While the agent may and must approve of right action in himself, he cannot claim desert or reward because of its virtuousness; he simply does what he should.

Others, however, may see that the act has been done in the face of great temptation; after a hard struggle; that it denotes some unusual qualification or executes some remarkable service. It is not only right, but obligatory, for others to take due notice of these qualities, of these deeds. Such notice is as requisite as it is to show gratitude for generosity, or forgiveness to a repentant man.

Two errors are to be avoided here; both arising from the identification of merit with virtue. One view holds that the virtue and merit consist in doing something over and above duty. There is a minimum of action which is obligatory; to perform this, since it is obligatory, is no virtue. Anything above this is virtuous. The other view reverses this and holds that since no man can do more than he ought, there is no such thing as merit. Great excellence or heroism in one man is no more meritorious than ordinary conduct in another; since the one man is naturally more gifted than the other. But while one act is no more right or virtuous than another, it may be more meritorious, because contributing more to moral welfare or progress. To depreciate the meritorious deed is a sign of a carping, a grudging or a mean spirit.

The respective relations of duty, virtue and merit have been variously discussed. Different views will be found in Sidgwick, *Methods of Ethics*, Bk. III, Ch. 4; Alexander, *Moral Order*, pp. 187–95 and 242–47; Stephen, *Science of Ethics*, pp. 293–303; Martineau, *Types of Ethical Theory*, Vol. II, pp. 78–81; Laurie, *Ethica*, pp. 145–48.

## 3

# *Realized Morality or the Virtues*

## LXIX. Goodness as Found in Character

We have treated of the forming of moral ideals, and of the attempt to realize them against the counter attractions of sensible desire. We have now to treat these ideals as actual ends of conduct and thus reacting upon the agent. The good character, considered in relation to the moral *struggle*, is the one which chooses the right end, which endeavors to be better. The good character *in itself* is that made by this choice. It is good for the self to choose a due end in an effort caused by contrary allurements. But the very fact of the struggle witnesses that morality is not yet the natural and spontaneous manifestation of character. A *wholly* good man would feel such satisfaction in the contemplation of the ideal good that contrary desires would not affect him. He would take pleasure only in the right. Every accomplished moral deed tends to bring this about. Moral realization brings satisfaction. The satisfaction becomes one with the right act. Duty and desire grow into harmony. Interest and virtue tend toward unity.

This is the truth aimed at, but not attained, by the hedonistic school. In complete moral action, happiness and rightness know no divorce. And this is true, even though the act, in some of its aspects, involves pain. The act, so far as its quality of rightness is concerned, calls forth unalloyed satisfaction, however bound up with pain to self and to others in some respects. The error of hedonism is not in insisting that right action is pleasurable, but in its failure to supply content to the idea of happiness, in its failure to define what happiness is. In the failure to show those active relations of man to nature and to man involved in human satisfaction, it reduces happiness to the abstraction of agreeable sensation.

A virtue then, in the full sense, that is as the expression of virtuous character, and not of the struggle of character to be virtuous against the allurements of passive goods, is an *interest*. The system of virtues includes the various forms which interest assumes. Truthfulness, for example, is interest in the media of human exchange; generosity is interest in sharing any form of superior endowment with others less rich by nature or training, etc. It is distinguished from natural generosity, which may be mere impulse, by its being an interest in the activity or social relation itself, instead of in some accidental accompaniment of the relation.

Another way of getting at the nature of the virtues is to consider them as forms of freedom. Positive freedom is the good, it is realized activity, the full and unhindered performance of function. A virtue is any one aspect which the free performance of function may take. Meekness is one form of the adjustment of capacity to surroundings; honesty another; indignation another; scientific excellence another, and so on. In each of these virtues, the agent realizes his freedom: Freedom from subjection to caprice and blind appetite, freedom in the full play of activity.

## LXX. Two Kinds of Virtues

We may recognize two types of virtuous action. These are:

### 1. *The Special Virtues*

These arise from special capacities or special opportunities. The Greek sense of virtue was almost that of "excellence," some special fitness or power of an agent. There is the virtue of a painter, of a scientific investigator, of a philanthropist, of a comedian, of a statesman, and so on. The special act may be manifested in view of some special occasion, some special demand of the environment—charity, thankfulness, patriotism, chastity, etc. Goodness, as the realization of the moral end, is a system, and the special virtues are the particular members of the system.

### 2. *Cardinal Virtues*

Besides these special members of a system, however, the whole system itself may present various aspects. That is to say, even in a special act the whole spirit of the man may be called out, and this expression of the whole character is a cardinal virtue. While the special virtues differ in content, as humility from bravery, earnestness from compassion, the cardinal virtues have the same content, showing only different sides of it. Conscientiousness, for example, is a cardinal virtue. It does not have to do with an act belonging to some particular capacity, or evoked by some special circumstance, but with the spirit of the whole self as manifested in the will to recognize duty—both its obligatoriness in general and the concrete forms which it takes. Truthfulness as a special virtue would be the desire to make word correspond to fact in some instance of speech. As a cardinal virtue, it is the constant will to clarify and render true to their ideal all human relations—those of man to man, and man to nature.

## LXXI. The Cardinal Virtues

The cardinal virtues are marked by

### 1. *Wholeness*

This or that virtue, not calling the whole character into play, but only some special power, is partial. But a cardinal virtue is not *a* virtue, but the spirit in which all acts are performed. It lies in the attitude which the agent takes towards duty; his obedience to recognized forms, his readiness to respond to new duties, his enthusiasm in moving forward to new relations. It is a common remark that moral codes change from "Do not" to "Do," and from this to "Be." A Mosaic code may attempt to regulate the specific acts of life. Christianity says, "Be ye perfect." The effort to exhaust the various special right acts is futile. They are not the same for any two men, and they change constantly with the same man. The very words which denote virtues come less and less to mean specific acts, and more the spirit in which conduct occurs. Purity, for example, does not mean freedom from certain limited outward forms of defilement; but comes to signify rightness of natures as a whole, their freedom from all self-seeking or exclusive desire for private pleasure, etc. Thus purity of heart comes to mean perfect goodness.

## 2. *Disinterestedness*

Any act, to be virtuous, must of course be disinterested, but we may now connect this disinterestedness with the integral nature of moral action just spoken of. Immoral action never takes account of the whole nature of an end; it deflects the end to some ulterior purpose; it bends it to the private satisfaction of the agent; it takes a part of it by making exceptions in favor of self. Bad action is never "objective." It is "abstract"; it takes into account only such portion of the act as satisfies some existing need of the private self. The immoral man shows his partial character again by being full of casuistries, devices by which he can get the act removed from its natural placing and considered in some other light: —this act, for example, *would* be dishonest, of course, if done under certain circumstances, but since I have certain praiseworthy feelings, certain remote intentions, it may now be considered otherwise. It is a large part of the badness of "good" people that instead of taking the whole act just as it is, they endeavor to make the natural feelings in their own mind—feelings of charity, or benevolence—do substitute duty for the end aimed at; they excuse wrong acts on the ground that their "intentions" were good, meaning by intentions the prevailing mood of their mind. It is in this sense that "hell is paved with good intentions."

Now it is against this deflection, perversion and mutilating of the act that disinterestedness takes its stand. Disinterested does not mean without interest, but without interest in anything except *the act itself*. The interest is not in the wonderful moods or sentiments with which we do the act; it is not in some ulterior end to be gained by it, or in some private advantage which it will bring, but in the act itself— in the real and concrete relations involved. There is a vague French saying that "morality is the nature of things." If this phrase has a meaning it is that moral conduct is not a manifestation of private feelings nor a search for some unattainable ideal, but observance and reproduction of actual relations. And this is the mark of a disinterested character.

# Conclusion

## LXXII. The Practical End of Morality

Virtues, then, are cardinal, and character is integral, just in the degree in which every want is a want of the whole man. So far as this occurs, the burden of the moral struggle is transformed into freedom of movement. There is no longer effort to bring the particular desire into conformity with a law, or a universal, outside itself. The fitting-in of each special desire, as it arises, to the organism of character takes place without friction; as a natural re-adjustment. There is not constraint, but growth. On the other side, the attained character does not tend to petrify into a fixed possession which resists the response to needs that grow out of the enlarged environment. It is plastic to new wants and demands; it does not require to be wrenched and wracked into agreement with the required act, but moves into it, of itself. The law is not an external ideal, but the principle of the movement. There is the identity of freedom and law in the good.

This union of inclination and duty in act is the practical end. All the world's great reformers have set as their goal this ideal, which may be termed either the freeing of wants, or the humanizing of the moral law. It will help summarize our whole discussion, if we see how the theories of hedonism and of Kant have endeavored to express this same goal. Hedonism, indeed, has this identity for its fundamental principle. It holds strongly to the idea of moral law immanent in human wants themselves. But its error lies in taking this identity of desire and the good, as a direct or immediate unity, while, in reality, it exists only in and through activity; it is a unity which can be attained only as the result of a process. It mistakes an ideal which is realized only in action for bare fact which exists of itself.

Hedonism, as represented by Spencer, recognizes, it is true, that the unity of desire and duty is not an immediate or natural one; but only to fall into the error of holding that the separation is due to some external causes, and that when these are removed we shall have a fixed millennium. As against this doctrine, we must recognize that the difference between want and duty is always removed so far as conduct is moral; that it is not an ideal in the sense of something to be attained at some remote period, but an ideal in the sense of being the very meaning of moral activity whenever and wherever it occurs. The realizing of this ideal is not something to be sometime reached once for all, but progress is itself the ideal. Wants are ever growing larger, and thus freedom ever comes to have a wider scope (Sec. lxv).

Kant recognizes that the identity of duty and inclination is not a natural fact, but is the ideal. However, he understands by ideal something which ought to be, but is not. Morality is ever a struggle to get desire into unity with law, but a struggle doomed, by its very conditions, not to succeed. The law is the straight line of duty, which the asymptotic curve of desire may approximate, but never touch. An earthly taint of pleasure-seeking always clings to our wants, and makes of morality a striving which defeats itself.

The theory that morality lies in the realization of individuality recognizes that there is no direct, or natural, identity of desire and law, but also recognizes that their identification is not an impossible task. The problem is solved in the exercise of function, where the desires, however, are not unclothed, but clothed upon. Flowing in the channel of response to the demands of the moral environment, they unite, at once, social service and individual freedom.

## lxxiii. The Means of Moralization

This practical end of the unification of desire and duty, in the play of moral interests, is reached, therefore, so far as the desires are socialized. A want is socialized when it is not a want for its own isolated and fixed satisfaction, but reflects the needs of the environment. This implies, of course, that it is bound by countless ties to the whole body of desires and capacities. The eye, in seeing for itself, sees for the whole body, because it is not isolated but, through its connections, an organ of a system. In this same way, the satisfaction of a want for food, or for commercial activity, may necessitate a satisfaction of the whole social system.

But how shall this socialization of wants be secured? It is in answering this question that we are brought again to a point already discussed at length: the moral bearings of intelligence. It is intelligence that is the sole sure means of taking a want out of the isolation of merely impulsive action. It is the passing of the desire through the alembic of ideas that, in rationalizing and spiritualizing it, makes it an expression of the want of the whole man, and thus of social needs.

To know one's self was declared by Socrates, who first brought to conscious birth the spirit of the moral life, to be the very core of moral endeavor. This knowledge of self has taken, indeed, a more circuitous and a more painful path, than Socrates anticipated. Man has had, during two thousand years of science, to go around through nature to find himself, and as yet he has not wholly come back to himself —he oftentimes seems still lost in the wilderness of an outer world. But when man does get back to himself it will be as a victor laden with the spoils of subdued nature. Having secured, in theory and invention, his unity with nature, his knowledge of himself will rest on a wide and certain basis.

This is the final justification of the moral value of science and art. It is because through them wants are interconnected, unified and socialized, that they are, when all is said and done, the preëminent moral means. And if we do not readily recognize them in this garb, it is because we have made of them such fixed things, that is, such abstractions, by placing them outside the movement of human life.

Checklist of references
Textual note for this reprinting

# Checklist of references

In Dewey's references, corrections and expansions in titles, authors' names, etc., have been made silently and conform to those in the original works. Corresponding corrections which became necessary in the texts appear in the List of Emendations in the Copy-Texts.

Following each Checklist entry are the symbol references to the work in which Dewey mentions or quotes from that entry in the present volume. When Dewey's reference included page numbers, it was possible to identify the edition he used. In other references, among the various editions possibly available to him, the one listed is the most likely source by reason of place or date of publication, or on the evidence from correspondence and other materials, and its general accessibility during the period.

Adler, Felix. "The Freedom of Ethical Fellowship," *International Journal of Ethics*, I (Oct. 1890), 16–30. (MT)

Alexander, Samuel. *Moral Order and Progress: An Analysis of Ethical Conceptions*. London: Trübner and Co., 1889. (OE)

Aristotle. *The Nicomachean Ethics of Aristotle*. 2d ed. Trans. F. H. Peters. London: Kegan Paul, Trench and Co., 1884. (OE)

Arnold, Matthew. *Poems*. II. London: Macmillan and Co., 1869. [The Dewey quotations appear in the following poems: "Switzerland," pp. 78–101; "Dover Beach," pp. 108–9; "Youth of Man," pp. 162–67; "Self-Dependence," pp. 198–99; "Stanzas From the Grand Chartreuse," pp. 215–25; and "Obermann Once More," pp. 239–56.] (P1)

———. "Introduction," in *The English Poets*, I, xvii–xlvii. Ed. Thomas Humphry Ward. London, New York: Macmillan and Co., 1881. (P1)

Bain, Alexander. *The Emotions and the Will*. London: John W. Parker and Son, 1859. (OE)

———. *Moral Science: A Compendium of Ethics*. New York: D. Appleton and Co., 1882. (OE)

Baker, James Hutchins. *Elementary Psychology, With Practical Applications to Education and Conduct of Life*. New York: Effingham Maynard and Co., 1890. (BP)

Barrett, Alfred. *Physical Ethics; or, the Science of Action.* London: Williams and Norgate, 1869. (OE)

Bentham, Jeremy. *Deontology; or the Science of Morality.* Ed. John Bowring. 2 vols. London: Longman, Rees, Orme, Browne, Green, and Longman, 1834. (OE)

———. *The Works of Jeremy Bentham.* Ed. John Bowring. 11 vols. Edinburgh: William Tait, 1838–43. (OE)

Bernard, John H., and Mahaffy, John P. *Kant's Critical Philosophy for English Readers.* 2 vols. London: Macmillan and Co., 1889. (MK)

Birks, Thomas Rawson. *Modern Utilitarianism; or, the Systems of Paley, Bentham, and Mill Examined and Compared.* London: Macmillan and Co., 1874. (OE)

Blackie, John Stuart. *Four Phases of Morals: Socrates, Aristotle, Christianity, Utilitarianism.* Edinburgh: Edmonston and Douglas, 1871; *ibid.*, New York: Scribner, Armstrong and Co., 1872. (OE)

Bosanquet, Bernard. "The Communication of Moral Ideas as a Function of an Ethical Society," *International Journal of Ethics,* I (Oct. 1890), 79–97. (MT)

Bourget, Paul. *Essais de psychologie contemporaine.* Paris: A. Lemerre, [1883]. (F)

———. *Nouveaux essais de psychologie contemporaine.* Paris: Alphonse Lemerre, 1886. (F)

Bradley, Francis Herbert. *Ethical Studies.* London: H. S. King and Co., 1876. (OE)

———. "On Pleasure, Pain, Desire and Volition," *Mind,* XIII (Jan. 1888), 1–36. (OE)

Brandes, Georg Morris Cohen. *Moderne Geister.* Frankfurt: Rütten and Loening, 1887. (R)

Browning, Robert. *The Poetical Works of Robert Browning.* III–VII, XIV–XV. London: Smith, Elder, and Co., 1888, 1889. [The poems Dewey quotes from or mentions are: "Pippa Passes," III, 5–79; "Fra Lippo Lippi," IV, 205–20; "A Grammarian's Funeral," V, 154–60; "Christmas Eve and Easter Day," V, 209–307; "Saul," VI, 98–124; "By the Fireside," VI, 126–41; "Rabbi Ben Ezra," VII, 109–19; "At the 'Mermaid,'" XIV, 31–38; "The Two Poets of Croisic," XIV, 205–79; "Martin Relph," XV, 3–16; and "Clive," XV, 88–107.] (MT, P1, OE)

Butler, Joseph. *Fifteen Sermons.* London: Longman, Brown, Green, and Longmans, 1856. (OE)

Caird, Edward. *The Critical Philosophy of Immanuel Kant.* 2 vols. Glasgow: James Maclehose and Sons, 1889. (PM, CK, OE)

———. *The Social Philosophy and Religion of Comte.* New York: Macmillan and Co., 1885. (OE)

————. "Preface," in *Essays in Philosophical Criticism*, eds. Andrew Seth and R. B. Haldane, pp. 1–7. London: Longmans, Green, and Co., 1883. (G)

Calderwood, Henry. *Handbook of Moral Philosophy*. London: Macmillan and Co., 1872. (OE)

Carlyle, Thomas. *Critical and Miscellaneous Essays*. IV. London: Chapman and Hall, 1872. (P1)

Church, Alfred John. *The Story of the Odyssey*. New York: Macmillan and Co., 1891. (CR)

Coit, Stanton. "The Final Aim of Moral Action," *Mind*, XI (July 1886), 324–52. (OE)

Darwin, Charles Robert. *The Descent of Man, and Selection in Relation to Sex*. 2 vols. London: J. Murray, 1871. (OE)

Dewey, John. *Early Essays and LEIBNIZ'S NEW ESSAYS CONCERNING THE HUMAN UNDERSTANDING (The Early Works of John Dewey, 1882–1898, I)*. Carbondale: Southern Illinois University Press, 1969.

————. *Psychology (The Early Works of John Dewey, 1882–1898, II)*. Carbondale: Southern Illinois University Press, 1967. (PM, OE)

————. "Ethics and Physical Science," in *Early Works*, I, 205–26. (OE)

————. "Is Logic a Dualistic Science?" in *Early Works*, III, 75–82. (LV)

————. "Moral Theory and Practice," in *Early Works*, III, 93–109. (GT, OE)

Erdmann, J. E. *A History of Philosophy*. English trans., ed. N. S. Hough. 3 vols. New York: Macmillan and Co., 1890. (EH)

Everett, Charles Carroll. *Poetry, Comedy, and Duty*. Boston, New York: Houghton, Mifflin and Co., 1888. (OE)

Fowler, Thomas. *The Elements of Inductive Logic*. 3d ed. cor. and rev. Oxford: Clarendon Press, 1876. (PM)

————, and Wilson, John Matthias. *The Principles of Morals*. 2 vols. Oxford: Clarendon Press, 1886–87. (OE)

Galton, Francis. *Natural Inheritance*. London, New York: Macmillan and Co., 1889. (GS)

Gizycki, Georg von. *A Students' Manual of Ethical Philosophy*. Trans. S. Coit. London: Sonnenschein and Co., 1889. (OE)

Green, Thomas Hill. *Prolegomena to Ethics*. Ed. A. C. Bradley. Oxford: Clarendon Press, 1883. (G, GT, OE)

————. *Works of Thomas Hill Green*. Ed. R. L. Nettleship. 3 vols. London, New York: Longmans, Green, and Co., 1885–88. [Vol. I contains the "Introductions" to *A Treatise of Human Nature* by David Hume; Green's *Lectures on the Principles of Political Obligation* are printed in Vol. II.] (G, OE)

————. "Mr. Herbert Spencer and Mr. G. H. Lewes," Pt. 1, *Contemporary Review*, XXXI (Dec.–Mar. 1878), 25–53; Pt. 2, *ibid.*, XXXI (Dec.–Mar. 1878), 745–69; Pt. 3, *ibid.*, XXXII (Apr.–July 1878), 751–72. (G)

————. "Mr. Hodgson's Article 'Professor Green as a Critic,'" *Contemporary Review*, XXXIX (Jan.–June 1881), 109–24. (G)

Grote, John. *An Examination of the Utilitarian Philosophy.* Cambridge, England: Deighton, Bell, and Co., 1870. (OE)

————. *A Treatise on the Moral Ideals.* Cambridge, England: Deighton, Bell and Co., 1876. (OE)

Guyau, Jean-Marie. *La morale anglaise contemporaine, morale de l'utilité et de l'évolution.* Paris: G. Baillière, 1879. (OE)

Hamilton, D. H. "The Kantian Philosophy," *New Englander*, XV (Feb. 1857), 16–101. (MK)

Hartmann, Eduard von. *Philosophy of the Unconscious.* Trans. William Chatterton Coupland. 3 vols. London: Trübner and Co., 1884. (PS)

Hegel, Georg Wilhelm Friedrich. *Die Logik.* Pt. 1 of *Encyclopædie der philosophischen Wissenschaften.* 2d ed. Heidelberg: A. Oswald, 1827. English translation by W. Wallace. Oxford: Clarendon Press, 1874. (CS, PM)

————. *Werke.* Eds. Philipp Marheineke *et al.* 19 vols. Berlin: Duncker and Humblot, 1832–45, 1887. (CS, OE)

Hinton, James. *The Law-Breaker and the Coming of the Law.* Ed. M. Hinton, with introd. by H. H. Ellis. London: Kegan Paul and Co., 1884. (OE)

————. *Philosophy and Religion.* 2d ed. Selections from the late J. H. Ed. Caroline Haddon. London: Kegan Paul, Trench and Co., 1884. (OE)

Hodgson, Shadworth Holloway. *The Theory of Practice, an Ethical Enquiry.* 2 vols. London: Longmans, Green, Reader and Dyer, 1870. (OE)

Homer. *Homer.* Trans. Alexander Pope. 3 vols. New York: Harper and Bros., 1848. (CR)

Hyslop, James Hervey. "Evolution and Ethical Problems," *Andover Review*, IX (Apr. 1888), 348–66. (OE)

James, William. *The Principles of Psychology.* 2 vols. New York: Henry Holt and Co., 1890. (PS, OE)

————. "The Dilemma of Determinism," *Unitarian Review*, XXII (Sept. 1884), 193–224. (OE)

Jevons, William Stanley. *Elementary Lessons in Logic: Deductive and Inductive.* New ed. London, New York: Macmillan and Co., 1881. (PM, LT)

————. *Studies in Deductive Logic: A Manual for Students.* New York: Macmillan and Co., 1880. (PM)

Jodl, Friedrich. *Geschichte der Ethik, in der neueren Philosophie.* 2 vols. Stuttgart: J. G. Cotta, 1882–89. (OE)

Johnson, Francis Howe. *What Is Reality? An Inquiry as to the Reasonableness of Natural Religion, and the Naturalness of Revealed Religion.* New York: Houghton, Mifflin and Co., 1891. (J)

Kant, Immanuel. *Immanuel Kants sämmtliche Werke.* Eds. Karl Rosenkranz and Friedrich Wilhelm Schubert. 14 vols. Leipzig: L. Voss, 1838–42. (MT, LT, SS)

————. *Kant's Critique of Practical Reason and Other Works on the Theory of Ethics.* 3rd ed. Trans. Thomas Kingsmill Abbott. London: Longmans, Green, and Co., 1883. (OE)

————. *Kritik der reinen Vernunft.* Riga: Johann Friedrich Hartknoch, 1781; 2d ed., *ibid.,* 1787. (CS, CK)

Laurie, Simon Somerville (Scotus Novanticus). *Ethica: or, the Ethics of Reason.* London: Williams and Norgate, 1885. (OE)

Lecky, William Edward Hartpole. *History of European Morals from Augustus to Charlemagne.* 3d ed. rev. 2 vols. New York: D. Appleton and Co., 1879. (OE)

Lotze, Hermann. *Outlines of Practical Philosophy.* Trans. George T. Ladd. Boston: Ginn and Co., 1885. (OE)

Mahaffy, John P., and Bernard, John H. *Kant's Critical Philosophy for English Readers.* 2 vols. London: Macmillan and Co., 1889. (MK)

Mansel, Henry Longueville. *A Lecture on the Philosophy of Kant.* Oxford: John Henry and James Parker, 1856. (MK)

Martineau, James. *Types of Ethical Theory.* 2 vols. Oxford: Clarendon Press, 1885. (OE)

Maurice, John Frederick Denison. *The Conscience.* London: Macmillan and Co., 1868. (OE)

Mill, John Stuart. *Autobiography.* London: Longmans, Green, Reader and Dyer, 1873. (OE)

————. *Dissertations and Discussions, Political, Philosophical and Historical.* 4 vols. New York: Henry Holt and Co., 1874. [*Utilitarianism* is printed in Vol. iii.] (OE)

Morris, George Sylvester. *British Thought and Thinkers: Introductory Studies, Critical, Biographical and Philosophical.* Chicago: S. C. Griggs and Co., 1880. (M)

————. *The Final Cause as Principle of Cognition and Principle in Nature.* London: Robert Hardwicke, 1875. (M)

————. *Hegel's Philosophy of the State and of History* (German Philosophical Classics for English Readers and Students, ed.

George S. Morris). Chicago: S. C. Griggs and Co., 1887. (M)

———. *Kant's Critique of Pure Reason* (German Philosophical Classics for English Readers and Students, ed. George S. Morris). Chicago: S. C. Griggs and Co., 1882. (M)

———. *Philosophy and Christianity.* New York: Robert Carter and Bros., 1883. (M)

———. *The Theory of Unconscious Intelligence as Opposed to Theism.* London: Hardwicke and Bogue, [n.d.]. (M)

———. *University Education* (University of Michigan Philosophical Papers, First Series, No. 1). Ann Arbor: Andrews and Witherby, 1886. (M)

———. "Friedrich Adolph Trendelenburg," *New Englander,* xxxiii (Apr. 1874), 287–336. (M)

———. "Philosophy and Its Specific Problems," *Princeton Review,* N.S. ix (Mar. 1882), 203–32. (M)

———. "The Philosophy of Art," *Journal of Speculative Philosophy,* x (Jan. 1876), 1–16. (M)

Newman, John Henry (Cardinal). *The Idea of a University Defined and Illustrated.* 4th ed. London: Basil Montagu Pickering, 1875. (C)

Paley, William. *Moral and Political Philosophy.* New York: S. King, 1824. (OE)

Pater, Walter Horatio. *Marius the Epicurean: His Sensations and Ideas.* 2d ed. London: Macmillan and Co., 1885. (OE)

Paulsen, Friedrich. *System der Ethik.* 2 Pts. Berlin: Besser, 1889. (OE)

Plato. *The Dialogues of Plato.* Trans. B. Jowett. I. New York: Charles Scribner and Co., 1871. (M, MT, OE)

Pringle-Pattison. [See Seth Pringle-Pattison, Andrew.]

Renan, Ernest. *The Future of Science.* Trans. [?]. Boston: Roberts Bros., 1891. (R)

———. *La réforme intellectuelle et morale.* Paris: Michel-Lévy frères, 1871. (R)

Royce, Josiah. *The Religious Aspect of Philosophy: A Critique of the Bases of Conduct and of Faith.* Boston, New York: Houghton, Mifflin and Co., 1885. (OE)

Salter, William M. "A Service of Ethics to Philosophy," *International Journal of Ethics,* I (Oct. 1890), 114–19. (MT)

Schurman, Jacob Gould. *The Ethical Import of Darwinism.* New York: C. Scribner's Sons, 1887. (OE)

Seth, James. "The Evolution of Morality," *Mind,* xiv (Jan. 1889), 27–49. (OE)

Seth Pringle-Pattison, Andrew. *Hegelianism and Personality.* Edinburgh, London: William Blackwood and Sons, 1887. (CS, J)

———. *Scottish Philosophy: A Comparison of the Scottish and German Answers to Hume.* Edinburgh, London: William Blackwood and Sons, 1885. (CS)

———. "Hegel and His Recent Critics," *Mind*, XIV (Jan. 1889), 116–19. [One of several essays in the section in *Mind* entitled "Discussions."] (CS)

Sidgwick, Henry. *The Methods of Ethics.* 2d ed. London: Macmillan and Co., 1877. (OE)

———. *Outlines of the History of Ethics, for English Readers.* London, Edinburgh: Macmillan and Co., 1886. (OE)

———. "The Morality of Strife," *International Journal of Ethics*, I (Oct. 1890), 1–15. (MT)

Sorley, William Richie. *On the Ethics of Naturalism.* London, Edinburgh: William Blackwood and Sons, 1885. (OE)

Spencer, Herbert. *The Data of Ethics.* 2d ed. New York: D. Appleton and Co., 1880. (OE)

———. *The Principles of Psychology.* New York: D. Appleton and Co., 1878. (PS)

Stephen, Leslie. *The Science of Ethics.* London: Smith, Elder, and Co., 1882. (OE)

Sterrett, James MacBride. *Studies in Hegel's Philosophy of Religion.* New York: D. Appleton and Co., 1890. (SH)

Stock, St. George. *Deductive Logic.* Oxford, London: Longmans, Green and Co., 1888. (LT)

Sully, James. *Outlines of Psychology, with Special Reference to the Theory of Education.* London: Longmans, Green, and Co., 1884. (OE)

Ueberweg, Friedrich. *A History of Philosophy from Thales to the Present Time.* Trans. George Sylvester Morris. 2 vols. New York: Charles Scribner and Co., 1871–73. (M, EH)

Venn, John. *The Principles of Empirical or Inductive Logic.* London, New York: Macmillan and Co., 1889. (L, LV)

Wallace, William. *Epicureanism.* New York: Pott, Young, and Co., 1880. (OE)

Ward, Mrs. Humphry. *Robert Elsmere.* London, New York: Macmillan and Co., 1888. (G)

Ward, James. "Psychology," *Encyclopædia Britannica* (9th ed.), xx, 37–85. (EH)

Wilson, John Matthias, and Fowler, Thomas. *The Principles of Morals.* 2 vols. Oxford: Clarendon Press, 1886–87. (OE)

# Textual note for this reprinting

Six corrections have been made in this printing.

| 9.11 | spiritual of | [spiritual. Of |
|---|---|---|
| 9.14 | any theory | [any other theory |
| 79.18 | snythesis | [synthesis |
| 93.25 | attribted | [attributed |
| 185.25 | N. S. Hough | [W. S. Hough |
| 229.21 | conplementary | [complementary |